Lies Between Us

What Unites Us, Divides Us and the Untruths We Spew

Also by Roger Ray Bird

Daddy, Why Were You A Drug Addict?
Winning the War Amid My Angel and Devil Within

Lies Between Us

My breath, I breathe, for you
My heart beats, first, for you

You, without equal
You, my entirety

You, my all that is
You, my beloveds

You, my better versions of me
You, my precious.

My brood, my loves, my precious...
Live your life your way
Dance your life your dance
Sing your life your song

Soar high your life my dear darling baby birds
Soar high, soar high...soar high.

Love you, love you more, love you most,
BigBirdy-BigBoyd.

A.I. cover art by Mister Damon Nawrozki, Mooresville North Carolina, USA, Planet Earth.

Launch idea and bird string pulled by Ms. SuperStarSarah Young, aka Coach Sarah.

Signature from thy heart and scattering crumbs for thy brood embolden to my pop BigBird.

All persons identified within are real, and their actions are depicted as they factually occurred, without enrichment, unless otherwise plainly explained. When preferring to not be full name identified, a slight number of parental-assigned monikers were either shortened to initials, called out by first name only, or covered up with altered smokescreen identifiers, awhile elsewise introduced by the phrase, "I'll call them…". Otherwise, all people and details as stated are nonfiction accurate.

This here bird hatched March 1964, Cleveland Ohio, USA, Earthmass, Earthbomb.

Punk ass bitch boy deep thinking started in the late 1970s.

Documentation of life lessons birthed in the late 1980s.

Engineering of life values, rules drools and tools kicked off in the 1990s.

Defining an unvarnished intentional life and experimentation to prove began in the early 2000s.

The first word crumb of these here book-book-sorta-bookers typed for you both February 1, 2020.

Delivered November 2024 with all-all the love-love I have-have to give-give, all the love I have left, every single drip-drip drop-drop to you my darlings, to you my brood, you my precious, you the only everlasting true loves of my life.

United our hands
Divided our downfall
Interminable our untruths.

Fell

~

Cold Hard Beginnings

The monster inside, charging after me
Lost and running, running, and running
Not pausing to think or feel
Just keep moving, just keep moving, just…keep…moving
For I am nothing other than, a wild and wandering creature.

Huminity

The way of the human spirit

The wonderous beauty of life

The treasureful together today

We plan our own way

Construct our own crafts

Adventure own paths

The living to be learned

The learnings along the way

Decided alone, our solo single oneself.

CHAPTERS

With disdain for disconnected introductory writings and confuzzled order, I instead use straight-up numbered chapters. Disregarding whatever writing format protocol exists out in the world, I do admire pre-words executed appropriately. Quite possibly maybe just a recreation of semantics, I deliver my why and supply some forewords, but do it my way.

1. Friendwords   Page 9
2. Pieces of Me   Page 31
3. I am Not Writing a Fucking Book   Page 61
4. Liar   Page 81
5. Kicking the Elephant Out of the Room   Page 147
6. Life With(out) Mother   Page 209
7. School's Out, Forever   Page 241

A Happening of Consciousness

Fortunate, seen much of everything
Traveled 'round the globe, lived out loud
Silver linings, truthful meanings

Thankful...schooled in pain all too well
Shook by hurt repeatedly, finally rocked awake
Lost within the storybook of great love, twice

Survivors, winners, some of us
Victims, losers, some of us
Choose wisely, yet still, we are both

Choice, endless possibilities to do life
Work, shop, date remotely...sheltered behind screens
Existing vividly, sans roof...our residence a van, a bike

These, my truths, here, my adventures, this, my life
I give it all to you, all I have, all I know, all I am
This, my life, take it, it is yours.

One

~

Friendwords

Some Thinkings From Foreword-Thinking Friends.
The treasureful covet of presence, love, and furtherance from others as integral to
our existence. The magic of community…known humans and strangers alike, we
are in this thing together so this chapter is about us.

Chapter One, Friendwords ~

Repeatedly I charged the large metal trashcan's rounded edge, after a barrage of self-inflicted lower ribcage blows failed to produce any positive outcome. Then knowing a more concerted effort was required I ran for the damn bathroom, toot suite. Hurling myself against the cornered expanse of white marble sink counter, shit, still no change, except oh shit, oh shit no, oh fuck, oh fuck yup, I grew dizzy as my oxygen-starved brain unnerved.

For fact if not leaving the bathroom immediately while still containing the energy to walk, I knew to not make it out of there alive. The fricking lodged bagel bit was not coming out, not by my own doing anyway…I could not clear my airway, and I knew my journey time to The Other Side was threateningly near.

Stumbling back into the secluded hotel hallway while gasping like a dying baby calf, I still could not see Kevin. No way was I going back to the breakfast nook full of total strangers, I just couldn't do it, it was too embarrassing. Standing over that same confounded unproductive trashcan, I attempted more Heimlich Maneuvers, punching myself upward into the top of my stomach just below my ribs.

As things went from horrible to absolute fricking hell in the hallway, I finally saw Kevin and gave him the international distress signal for choking, wrapping both hands around my throat. I could barely move another inch, and was a mere few seconds from falling straight to the ground. Kevin ran over to help but overwhelmed with confused desperation, he barely knew what to do. I guided his hands below my ribcage for the Heimlich. He tried to force the blockage but his movements were too soft. I pushed his hands violently two times into my own gut…*oh*, then he understood, my pal Kevin cleared my airway right then and there, the bagel chunk popping out into that same damn rounded trashcan.

Hero
By most measures, a person who either jumps into action or steps forward from outside their safe comfy little world to save another human life is called a hero. We do not encounter a life-saving moment regularly, the critical times few and far between. And with precious seconds ticking away while a beating heart is so close to extinction, rarely a dedicated discussion in our head occurs, rather an instinctual reaction gets us up off our keister rushing to help. We our lonesome on the fly chooses if willing to put ourselves at risk to help another. If and when we face the choice of helping, possibly saving another person's life, and even if decided, not everyone is willing to lay their hands on a stranger, or even put hands on a known someone, attempting to keep the person alive.

      Before 25 years young, five people stepped forward to save my life, not including the medical personnel tending to me during my many trips to the hospital, mostly after pitching myself into the dirt riding my mountainbike.

In the resulting 30 years afterward, an additional five people also stepped up to save me from certain death, so far. If not, your dad only then a mere long-ago distant memory.

Me, as Me

Many people along my journey influenced me, taught me, pushed me, comforted me, and helped show me the way. Recognizing the void of traditional academia, I honor my attained wisdom from dealings on the street, interactions with coworkers and the tit-for-tat shared love with other humans while rounding the rollercoaster puzzle game of life. I requested 600 words or less from two hands full of friends, partly because of their wicked smartness while also as a distraction, sprinkling some flavorful spice atop my otherwise relentless fatherly tone. Before we explore the chirp-chirp-chirpings of this here your poppa bird's magnum opus, soon to follow are the assembled Friendwords. Intentionally placing Friendwords within chapter one, I decisively put first things fucking first: I am nothing, I am no one without the loving hands of others. Because why precisely? Well, because I cannot do life alone. Much as we think capable to stand atop our own feet unsupported, and much as we try, we cannot endure without the aid of others. Besides, most of us are not so darn crafty or wilderness-survivable when getting right down to it. Before them there aforementioned upcoming Friendwords, three things worth bird-noting.

ONE of three: A scientific study published some years ago detailed secrets to a long life. For decades before the particular results were publicly shared, a barrage of constant announcements pelted us one after another, claiming all we should eat or not so as to live longer. How much we should exercise, what we should do or not with our sleep, how to better control stress, hydration guidelines, and even reports saying longer life comes if eating more dark chocolate and drinking more red wine. Hah, traditionally my eyes rolled, shunning claims of living a longer life. For one thing, I was not signing up for the extended-play package. Besides, I do not listen to reports certain about much of anything. No, I knew better…almost anything can happen and sometimes does. The newer study however, holding proper accreditation, said something quite different from all reports heard before.

The secret to a long life is the dedicated and continued connection with other humans.

Oh my, I liked where this is going, I am listening now. We should be sure to stay in touch, we should not retreat, not shut down, and not become desolate or recluse, even when shit in our lives gets worse and all we want to do is climb into bed and never join in any more human games. Staying in touch with others will help us live longer, compared to turning off connections with friends and family.

TWO of three: The deepest of deep root of tree type shit is a proven and successful childhood education development process called *Conscious Discipline*. Three principles exist at the core of Conscious Discipline, and I believe these core principles remain long after our little developmental kiddo years are over. First and foremost, before anything else can happen, we must sense we are safe. We must not feel we are lost in the proverbial woods, or in danger. We need first a solid foundation, a stable base before we can move.

Second we need connection, we need to feel love and really feel it, not just hear lip service of love-you-type words. These first two things, in order, are requirements before anything else like paying attention, following directions, regulation of emotions, learning, positive action, effectively-managed behavior, collaboration, or quality work can be expected.

Operating only from my bird brain opinion and street-enhanced education, I believe the void of security and lack of loving connection is much the reason so many kids go adrift or get kicked out of school. The reason being that the kids are not safe at home and safety does not just fucking magically appear when arriving at school. At school their fear is still with them, and might even become heightened while amongst their brutally vicious and monstrous peer students. So in school, the kid is losing their shit and no one steps forward from a position of questioning, learning, empathy or comfort. Too often as I perceive, punishment rains down because the kid is not following directions…just shut up sit down and learn. Said traumatized kid cannot do what they are told because of overwhelmingly fearsome conditions at home. So now in such perilous state, the scared and uncared-for or unprotected kid, aka troubled punk child, most times lacks a loving connection or even position of understanding with school authoritarians.

I am NOT slamming teachers or school administrators, no way, most seem to do their best, operating from less-than shoestring rusty-bucket-type of available resources. The tragedy of these lost young souls originates from a higher level of restricted respect for our teachers, not keeping first things first, and pathetic less than adequate allocation of school funding. How much is our future worth if not investing in those citizens who will one day run our world, well as create our problems and simultaneously solve our difficulties?

The castaway-troubled-expelled kid scenario is a true-true tragic shame and quite frankly a horrific loss to us all, because duh, like are you kidding me or what…our children are our fucking future.

Truthful Beginnings

The frightful disconnectedness began at four years old, such turmoil initiating before any memories did. By six my disrespect for all adults was in full bloom. My Roger Ray fearful voids snowballed for 12 years and at 16, I dropped out of school. Not one staff adult stepped forward to ask what was going on, but maybe such inquisitions were not at all their responsibilities at the time, IDK. I left school after straight up believing zip-zero nothing more existed for me there. Throughout my high school sophomore year and during my shorty-short junior year, all my educators asked of me, all they seemingly wanted, was for me to leave them alone…*You're not here much anyway, you don't seem to be interested, so why don't you just leave?,* such literal spewings tossed into my ears multiple times. Well hold up hum, uh and no…fuck that shit, let me be crystal-as-ice clear, I quit school my own damn self.

I harbor zero blame toward anyone else. No one is accountable for my actions except me, not a single no one.

Not my mother who was so sick she was locked up, not my father who gave up on me but did his best, not my grandparents who were horrendously cruel when I lived with them but also acted in ways they believed were helpful by their measure, and not my educators already stretched beyond their point of snapping. I did this, I did all of this. I exist here now because of everything I fucking did, or did not, no one else. I accept 100% responsibility for my own life, and I certainly own up to the act of dropping out.

We utilize the Conscious Discipline curriculum at my second non-profit, The Playing Field Madison, co-founded with executive director Abbi Kruse. The next Conscious Discipline principle is problem solving and such skills are learned after safety and love solidly exist. I erased my ideals of bad and penalty with you both, aka timeouts, once taught and learned the critical and proven Conscious Discipline concepts. Conscious Discipline drops the reward and punishment standard like a hot potato, favoring instead the aforementioned three principles helping children develop responsibly, and I believe develop correctly. Conscious Discipline offers valuable insight into the foundation of developmental human behavior for sure, and one I lived hand-first: Safety and connection before all, then the ability to figure shit out myself.

Certainly when up against poor mental health, struggling with hardship and wrestling with addiction, the value of loving and engaged humans around us is immeasurable. I make endless reference in this here your book to my lived learned and known core truths, well as the critical-to-me nature of foundational introspection. Often I journey deep into my head and far into my heart, attempting to unravel what holds me back and tries to stop me.

I go often, deep within, looking to understand and attain comprehension then ask…how do I best live the life I desire instead of just dreaming it?

My introspection do's and do not's:
A. I recognize my desired outcome requires my best darn try, meaning my best damn effort. My best effing effort demands the willingness to endure no matter the challenge, even to struggle, even to cry, even to bleed, even to break. Therefore fact one, I calibrate myself for the strain of the endeavor.
B. Aside, not mistaken to linger longer, not stay too long buried inside of my emotional brain, chanced to unwittingly get caught in the endless sticky web of thoughts and feelings.
C. Sorting shit out best I can, I get going in the best direction I can see, knowing the hardest part is getting up, aka just get started. Dead serious, getting up is the gosh-darn hardest component of doing anything. Elsewhere (in the Addict book) I address the getting up part and share my practice named *Get to the Curb.*
D. Once doing, I act with purposeful intention, not beating myself up when unexpected results follow. Soundly, I try to find peace in the fact that I fricking did *something*, that I got up and tried to try.

These some of my learned truths, by my own damn measure. I try, I try to live joyfully within the precious sunny moments, and within the presence of others.

Others who bring more harmony, beauty, and love to my life than I could plausibly do on my own. Oh yes-yes and for sure the complex life math puzzle game also includes the critical time of being alone in silence, thinking and letting go, and this too like our human connections is non-negotiable.

THREE of three: Finally, thirdly and lastly before Friendwords, some of my favorite music comes by way of a Duluth Minnesota progressive bluegrass band called *Trampled By Turtles*. Them Turtles have a song that speaks to me and I believe gives serious attention to the fact we are connected, whether we fricking like it or not. Their song is called *Alone*. The opening lyrics cut to the heart of the matter, "We come into this world alone and we go out of this world alone, and in between is you and me". What I hear in the song and the main point I take away is we do not have influence over when and from where we came, and certainly little to no power over when our organic time is done on earth.

During our between time though, life is ours to live in ways of our choosing, side by side and in the arms of others.

Chapters Organizational Overview
Within this here your lead-off opus book are seven chapters. The first five chapters are experienced topic chapters. Chapters six and seven are life period chapters, in chronological order. I attempt no leave behind word crumbs, you know, terms left unexplained or undefined, those perhaps creating confusion in your darling bird brains. Look to the glossary found in chapter two for your way back home to the sense and understandability of crumbs found along your path. If I fail to mark the trail with word-loop-back-arounds or miss fixing any narrative bridges, please ring me up sooner than later my precious.

This Here Chapter One, Friendwords
Here I accentuate the merited human connection to my life's balance or more accurately, my life's counterbalance. The following value add propositions are solely of the author's choosing, absent of prominence from me on what or how to write. I delivered my request for Friendwords along with vague instructions, allowing the paged written characters to exist void of influence. The submissions rolled in, printed here in order of receipt. While graced by the heartfelt writings, also I am humbled by the dedication of the friend time required to sit and do the work. I made notta solo single edit to the words, not a plain period nor common comma, none. I did not touch the words, the words are not mine, they have been gifted to you both my precious.

These here Friendwords possibly possess a thing or three you might not otherwise know, and most likely so. Not necessarily from my oldest or closest friendships do the morsels come, but from people I love, my friends, my family. These my sampled friend family lovelies, them possessing something to say along with the craft and time to say so. If nothing else, chapter one serves to disrupt the fucking monotonous tone of your otherwise well-intentioned but preachy-preachy-preachy poppa bird.

Only in the shelter of others do we truly live.

Friendship I measure none

My friends *are* my family

No gradient of computation exists for family

Family is family, no matter the years between, no matter the miles apart, no matter the struggle or disagreements in play

Family is love, forever love.

Most of us have a highly refined instinct to seek security, avoid suffering, and prioritize our own comforts. A lifetime lived without challenge is undefined; we can scarcely appreciate the highest highs unless we've lived through the lowest lows. As I've come to know Roger, first in a professional context and now as a personal friend, I can only admire his character and will to seek the good. He would have every right to be cynical, to dwell in indignation, and to distrust the universe. But he isn't and doesn't. The challenges, the low-points, the injustices have been markers along the journey where he has made the difficult decisions, committed to the work, and grown in his humanity.

In my family, we like to be 'show-up people'. Our time is perhaps the most valuable resource we have and when we choose to spend it with others, it demonstrates care, it creates connection, it makes an impression- the universe expands. Roger is also a 'show-up person' and I believe the energy he brings into the room is what is needed. It can be intense, it can be gentle; it can be serious, it can be silly; but ultimately his vulnerability is disarming, and it draws you near, and you are grateful to receive his care.

It is said that an unexamined life is not worth living and I see Roger Bird as doing more than most to examine his own life, to live with intention, to be better- he makes a difference.
~ **Noel Kegel**

Dear Travis and Lauren,

It was an afternoon in February when your dad realized what he was meant to do.

He was meant to write.

Not for others; for an audience somewhere, out there; for an editor or a publisher - but for you. Travis and Lauren. His kids. His biggest rocks. His most important priorities.

From the moment that this clarity struck, your dad began working furiously - feverishly at times - on the memoir. As we all know, he is not one to do things half-assed or lacking in gusto.

He wrote at home, in the quiet of the house, to the sounds of the wind chimes.

He wrote up north, at the cabin, in the quiet of the north woods.

He wrote at 3 am and 3 pm and at many moments in between.

He wrote this memoir for each of you - an expression of his greatest purpose, to his greatest loves.

Happy Reading.

With Love,

Roger's Good Friend and Business Coach,

Sarah ~ **Sarah Young**

Whether you're 18 or 27 or 44 or 61 or 80, you'll never stop thinking about making sure your life has some meaning. There isn't some age threshold after which people collectively say: "Now I have it all figured out."

Sure, lots of people are not particularly introspective, which is fine, and they'll go about their life, consciously or subconsciously weighing the good stuff with the bad stuff and, hopefully, trying to be a decent person along the way. They'll get a job or maybe a career, meet someone and start a family, buy a house, upgrade that house along the way, maybe take a few trips, retire and then spend their remaining years in the company of family and friends relaxing, perhaps in an RV.

But other people are more engaged than that and certainly your dad, Roger, is one of those folks. In a funny coincidence, my dad's name was also Roger. He passed-away at the end of 2015 unfortunately, so about five years ago as I write this. I wish he would have written something like your dad has written here. Even if there are only a few kernels buried in his words that you decide have value, you'll feel lucky to have them as you get older.

I've known your dad Roger since I was probably about 14 or 15 when I started working at the bike shop where he had been turning wrenches for a few years. These are the years when your dad was still struggling with addiction but regardless of that, he was the center of the universe at the bike shop. He was such a skilled rider and it was like we had LeBron James as a colleague and everyone knew Roger.

It was still the early days of mountain bike racing and we used to head to races in little podunk towns. There are a lot of stories from those days but I won't bore you with them. The main point is that there was this group of folks and your dad Roger was the glue. 35 years later a bunch of us are still friends and much of that is down to his efforts to keep people connected.

The amazing thing about your dad other than being this awesome connector of people, is the truly remarkable way that he managed to beat the odds. With a troubled mom, drug addictions and quitting school early the odds were stacked in a way where a good outcome was probably unlikely. But that's not what happened.

Your dad kicked those addictions, had an amazing run at Trek where he accumulated a huge amount of responsibility, and most importantly he's got two great kids who have their own bright futures. It's been perhaps a less conventional route than some take, but Roger has figured-out a life full of meaning. This book should prove to be priceless over the rest of your long years ahead. ~ **Anthony Brown**

"The Edge… There is no honest way to explain it because the only people who really know where it is are the ones who have gone over." ~ Hunter S. Thompson

I met Roger sometime around 2003. I knew him first, as a competitive athlete. He came to see me as a massage client. His body showed the ravages of a man that had pushed it to the edge, and maybe gone over a few times. He had broken his collar bones more times than I can count, and I could feel the plates and screws that held them together. His scars and broken bones told the story of his racing career. I recall one race where he broke his ankle so severely it was turned 180 degrees backwards. After making his way back to the previous checkpoint of the race, he was taken by Med Flight to the hospital for emergency surgery. Many people would think it crazy. Maybe even reckless. But nothing Roger did was without thought and calculated risk. He was fearless. He was driven. And above all, he was humble. I remember thinking how much respect I had for someone with so much passion and focus. Someone willing to ride that edge, and willing to suffer the consequences if they misjudged, knowing that the outcome was worth the risk. Someone that didn't live their life playing it safe. I would come to find that this pretty much defined who Roger was as a person, and how he lived every aspect of his life. With passion and focus. Head on. No letting life decide his fate for him. No sitting on the sidelines.

That was how I knew Roger first. The athlete. I would quickly find he was so much more than that. An intelligent and successful businessman, an amazing friend that always put others first, and a loyal father that loved his kids more than anything in the world. He has always been so proud of them. I remember over the years how much time and planning he put into their Christmas gifts. It was always about creating memories and experiences for Travis and Lauren. Spending meaningful time together. Whether it was a Packer game, skiing trip, or dogsledding adventure. I was always amazed.

I could go on and on about what an incredible person Roger is. The things he won't tell you, because he is always more focused on listening to what you have to say and hearing how you are doing. He almost seems superhuman. But, as he will tell you in his story, he has flaws and has made mistakes, just like the rest of us.

He will be the first to admit them. With those mistakes and failures comes an opportunity for tremendous growth. And Roger has never taken that for granted. Nor has he lost his ability to look at life through a lens of gratitude. It's part of what makes him so special.

Travis and Lauren, this book is an amazing gift. You may find meaning in it now. Or maybe you aren't in a place yet to get the most out of his story. It might mean more to you down the road. The biggest lesson that I learned from my relationship with my father, is that your perceptions and views change as you gain life experience.

My father and I had a challenging relationship. We often did not agree on things. At times he would tell me I was too young to understand. Even when I was an adult. What he meant was that I did not have the life experience to understand or pass judgment. And he was right. I couldn't fully understand until I had made my own mistakes and experienced successes and failures, love and heartbreak, wins, and losses. Looking back there were many times I had opinions and passed judgment on his life, unfairly. The more life experience I gained over time, the more I understood my father, and the more I was able to appreciate the life he lived and the person he was.

Travis and Lauren, I wish the same for you both. The opportunity to see your Dad through eyes unclouded by a lifetime of meaningful and extraordinary experiences of your own! ~ **Sonya Plavcan**

Thirty-some years ago I was a salesman who hated his job. Then I got an idea: I'll become a freelance writer. I'll write stories for newspapers and get paid.

I'll stop being a salesman.

Reality hit: Write about what? Well, there was this new East Coast phenomenon, mountain biking. I'll write about that. It's something I already do. It's fun. People will want to read about it.

I sold my first article to Spokes, about riding the trails at Loch Raven reservoir. I was on my way.

Writing about mountain biking in the Baltimore area, it didn't take long to cross paths with Roger Bird.

Thirty-some years later, I'm realizing how much Roger helped me in my new career. As I progressed from writing for local rags to becoming a stringer for VeloNews and other national magazines, so did my friendship and respect for Roger, professionally and personally.

Like what it means to be a pro level athlete- the commitment and training and the character that it takes. The parallels with writing are pretty stark.

With Roger, it was simple: See what needs to be done and do it. No fucking around.

Like training. When you get home, no matter how late and whether it's raining or you're tired or it's dark and you don't feel like it, you change your clothes and get on the bike.

I'd see Roger do that and think, that's how you get things done. That's how you change your life, make a new career happen. Roger was the role model I needed.

Like when Baltimore City banned mountain biking at Loch Raven.

Roger organized the resistance and led the fight. It felt like it took forever, but we not only won the battle, but we (Roger mostly) got mountain bikers engrained into the city's infrastructure.

As I reported on races in Maryland, West Virginia, Pennsylvania, Virginia and World Cup championships in Vermont, I got to hang out with the big dogs- Roger, David Duvall, Gunnar Shogren, Laird Knight, Chris Scott, and Floyd Landis, just to name a few.

Before long, Roger was recruiting me as a soigneur at 24-hour races. No more camping. Roger would rent a six-bedroom villa so the team could sleep on real beds close to the start line. It's what Roger did: Figure out what it takes to win and do it.

The culmination was the inaugural 24 Hours of Moab, an East Coast-to-Rocky Mountains expedition. Roger had the vision, rented a 40-foot Winnebago, signed me up on as a helper (among others), and we were off to Utah.

It was a huge undertaking and Roger orchestrated it to the last detail- recruiting the team, the mechanic, the helpers, massage therapists, raising money, laying out the plan, being team captain.

Other than finishing second (to a team led by a former world mountain bike champion), the trip went without a glitch. I filed a couple stories with the Baltimore Sun and VeloNews, got to know a future Tour de France winner, and got as close to world-class cycling as you can without actually racing.

Those are the highlights of a friendship that goes way beyond bike racing and reporting. It has a lot to do with character, knowing and trusting someone to do the right thing when it needs to be done.

I'm a lucky guy to have crossed paths with Roger Bird at just the right time. And just as lucky to call him one of my best friends. ~ **Joe Surkiewicz**

How did I meet your father Roger?

Was it Fate?

Was it luck?

I called it good fortune.

I was a couple of months in, on my solo motorcycle journey around the USA back in 2016. I'd made friends with a family living in Rapid City SD and while I was waiting for my trailer hitch to turn up.

My new friend Randy from Rapid City suggested I see Colorado before the weather rolled in, so on that note, I made a beeline for the Rockies. I was just making the route up as I went along and found myself in Leadville, the highest town in the Rockies.

I'd pitched my tent in the campsite and had dinner in town, arriving back after dark, so I didn't notice the other tents around me then.

A cool morning and I was up, planning to get an early head start to the four corners, when while fluffing around getting organised, one of the occupants from the tent next door approached me and asked if I'd like a coffee as he was making one.

He introduced himself as Roger and we got chatting. He was most curious about where I was from and what I was doing. I was taken by his warmth and friendliness, plus a hot cup of Joe on a cold morning was a welcome tonic.

As always, when you make great connections, it's always a shame to move on but the road was calling. Before leaving Roger said, 'Here is our address, look us up if you're heading to Wisconsin!' As I hit the road, I was struck about how kind and open everyone was who I'd met on the road so far. I hadn't planned to visit Wisconsin but being a fan of the 70s show and an offer of a bed, I decided to keep that in mind. I did indeed take Roger and Nora up on their kind offer and I had a great time at the H-D museum as well as being taken to their favourite eating places.

The only thing about being in another country is it's very difficult to meet up with great friends.

As we say in the UK and NZ, your dad is a 'Top Bloke' and his car is the 'Dogs Bollocks' (meaning awesome).

Kind Regards

Heath ~ **Heath Ling**

There is a certain romanticism in being young. Knowing your life is spread out ahead of you while scary is also exhilarating. The journey of self-discovery. I remember thinking now that I was free of my parents I would be able to find myself- separate myself from who they were enough to live my own experiences, make my own mistakes and find who I really am deep down as my own person- not as a daughter living their values, rules and expectations. An exciting prospect to be sure. At the time I felt that 'Who I Am' was a place that I would one day arrive at (funny now, but I imagined somewhere around my early 30s). I would know it when I got there- a soft and welcoming place that would feel like my own home that I built with my own two hands. A safety and comfort in my own skin that could only be had through my own experiences and thoughts- like a prize. I would certainly know it when I arrived.

Many years have passed since then, and I have come to see it quite differently. Partly through becoming a parent myself but it is more than that. What I have realized is that there is no final destination of finding who you are. Turns out it is an ever changing and evolving venture. There are times that you can coast and there are times you are moved to seek in a more active way, but it is certainly not a place that you one day find yourself in, put your feet up and congratulate yourself. It takes thought and consideration. It takes patience and grace and a willingness to reassess when needed. Sometimes it requires forgiveness for ourselves or others. It is a lifelong journey.

I also realized the separation of who we are and where we come from is not as simple as I once believed. Studies now indicate that trauma can be passed down generationally through DNA. That life experiences of our parents can be hurtful as well as healing at the *molecular level*. Our own experience has been authored, if unconsciously to carry our parent's experience into the future. If trauma is generational, it stands to reason that other things are as well- resiliency, courage, triumph, joy…it all plays a part on them and on us and eventually on our own kids. Whether we like it or not, we are a tapestry of the culture, traditions, and histories we inherit from our families. Understanding that gives new meaning to the essential questions of 'Who am I?' Who am I in reference to my family?' and of these ties, 'Which do I keep, and which do I reject?'.

Knowing ourselves requires an understanding of how we got this way and accepting our parents for who they are- not only as our parents but as individuals with real feelings, insecurities, and mistakes. This is intertwined with accepting ourselves.

I am not a beginning. I am not an end. I am a link in a chain ~ Keith Haring

The poet Mary Oliver asks us to consider what we plan to do with our one wild and precious life. As you go about that for yourself may the story you hold in your hand shed light on your path and help you find your way. May it serve as a beacon during the times you feel adrift and act as a compass when you are lost. May it provide you with the vast reservoirs of courage needed to find and speak and live your own truth. May it remind you to keep your heart soft when your protective instinct is to armor up. May it inspire you to view your own mistakes as precious opportunities and your vulnerabilities as strengths. One day your own story which is unfolding before you will do the same for the people you love. ~ **Tara LoBreglio**

Dear Lauren and Travis,

I met your Dad at a rollerski camp in Cable, WI in August of 2018. It also happened to be at the most challenging time of my life thus far for me. One of my daughters was struggling with severe OCD (Obsessive Compulsive Disorder) and possibly borderline personality or severe depression and was in a lockdown residential treatment center. She was unreachably angry with her mother and me, her sister, and anyone trying to help her. Seeing her struggle and failing to be able to connect with or rescue her was immensely painful and traumatic for our family.

Nordic skiing was a big part of how I was coping with the fear, sadness, anger, shame and confusion of the time. Exercise was a way to keep things in my life as normal as possible at a time when my world was upside down. I have always been physically active and it was something I could depend on to help keep me going. Nordic skiing was a relatively new physical outlet for me and I was at the rollerski camp to learn how to be a better skier. The act of having hope about something was helpful.

But the camp meant meeting new people and that was difficult. I found myself explaining our life situation many times. Everyone there was understanding and sympathetic to our situation as fellow skiers were parents themselves and had experienced their own challenges and pain with the lives of their children. Your Dad's reaction to and understanding of our situation was instantly recognizable as different than others.

Your Dad's interest, understanding and compassion for the experience we were living immediately struck me as deeper and more authentic than that of others at the camp. Even though I had just met Roger, he made me feel like he cared about me deeply. There wasn't a feeling of being sized up by him like there generally is in a competitive athletic setting like the camp we were in. Roger didn't seem to care if I was a good skier or a beginner, had money or not - he just seemed to recognize that there was a big part of me that was in pain and he wanted to do anything to help.

It seemed that your Dad could just listen to me and my problems as long as I felt like talking about them.

He held a place for my pain. He was patient. He let me fill the space. He let me set the agenda. He did not ask me too many questions. He respected my privacy while showing his interest in me, my pain and my way through this.

Importantly, your Dad did not suggest solutions. He seemed to understand that we were not short of solutions but rather had the need to find a way through the pain that we had not yet found. Suggesting solutions, that we already knew about, only intensified our anxiety and grief for where our daughter was at. Your Dad knew that more than anything what someone like myself needed was to be heard and supported.

My friendship with your Dad grew over the weekend camp and continues to grow. One of the qualities I like best about him is his ability to listen and make you feel heard and supported. My life, like most lives, is a twisted path with real enjoyment and real challenge while facing an unknown future. Having friends like your Dad helps make our twisted paths in life a little less hard, a little less challenging and a lot more fulfilling.

Lauren and Travis, I am grateful that I know your Dad. He has a lot of life experience to offer as guidance and yet he has the humility to listen to and value others life experiences. Your Dad speaks of both of you every time we see each other or talk on the phone. You are so precious to him. He loves you deeply and is immensely proud of both of you. I believe that you have a great partner in your Dad to navigate the ups and downs of your own lives. I know I do. ~ **Steve Gayner**

I was born in the Detroit suburb of Highland Park, Michigan in 1933 during the Great Depression. Later my parents moved to Dearborn, Michigan, where they spent most of their adult lives. My brother Ray was born there in 1937 and my sister Carol in 1940.

Ray was a nice little brother and a very good man. For many years he was a minister. During my years as commanding officer of a nuclear powered submarine and later as a Rear Admiral I called on Ray when a Navy chaplain would normally participate in ceremonies such as a change of command. He was always impressive and effective, and his audiences were always complimentary.

All except me are now dead. My parents and Carol are buried in the Bird family plot in Boyne City, Michigan.

My parents Thurman Bird and Gladys Stephenson Bird grew up in Boyne City, and graduated from Boyne City High School with the class of 1924. They were active in the Presbyterian Church. Thurman worked briefly in the two industries in the area, a sawmill and a leather tannery. He then attended business school, embarked on a career in banking in the Detroit area, and married Gladys. Soon after I was born, my parents became residents of Dearborn, Michigan, where they remained until after my mother's death in 1981. My father lived alone in Dearborn for several years and eventually returned to Boyne City where he and my sister Carol shared a house and assisted him. Thurman died in 1998 at the age of 91.

I will now provide some family history.

My mother's favorite aunt, Elsie Perkins, was an unmarried schoolteacher. She was a very attractive and elegant lady who made a strong positive impression on me. Aunt Elsie was interested in genealogy and spent many months of her summer vacations searching, largely in Britain and the U.S. She has documented our linkage to the Mayflower voyagers, and to participants in the U.S. Revolution.

On the Bird side, I have some oral history. My great-great-grandfather Bird immigrated from England and, I think, settled in southern Michigan.

My great grandfather, James Bird, took his family, including several children, by covered wagon from Michigan in the late nineteenth century and established a homestead near Aberdeen, South Dakota. After several years of crop failures, they returned to Michigan and settled on a small farm near Boyne City.

My grandparents, Elmer and Vera Bird lived in Boyne City and provided many wonderful summers for my brother Ray and me. My sister Carol also developed an attachment to Boyne City and shared a home there with our father Thurman during the last few years of his life.

When I was in high school in Dearborn, Michigan looking for a way to finance college, I obtained a navy ROTC scholarship. After attending the University of Michigan engineering school for one year, and with help from a friend of my father's, I received an appointment to the U.S. Naval Academy in Annapolis, Maryland. After graduating in the top 2 percent of my class I spent most of the next 28 years on sea duty in nuclear powered submarines which culminated in early promotions to Captain and Rear Admiral. Awards included several unit commendations, the Defense Superior Service Medal, and four awards of the Legion of Merit.

As a civilian I worked as an executive and as a consultant in the commercial nuclear power industry, in uranium mining and processing, and as a expert witness for law firms involved with uranium and with nuclear power plants. During those years I was also able to travel, often for hunting and fishing, to every continent except Antarctica. I also learned to fly helicopters and owned three of them over a twelve year period.

Since 1992 I have been a resident of Jackson Hole, Wyoming, where my home is bounded by Grand Teton National Park and has a direct view of the Grand Tetons. ~ **Ralph Gordon Bird**

We are not meant
to walk this life alone.

Fam-Fam

Knowing not these strange creatures we encounter along our journeyed path, our assumptions and judgments form quickly

Some folk we eyeball as odd random and insignificant walking and talking humanoids within the whole of our lives. The connection, the value, and the love shared may not impress upon us when first seeing their face, hearing their tone, or sensing their touch

Feelings form as perhaps attractive, familiar, interesting, or even unsettling when we meet these new-to-us peoples. We may draw close to learn more, or run away placing great distance between them and us, fast

Perhaps after too late to say, we realize others gave some of our best gifts ever received over a lifetime of feasted struggle...pieces of themselves, when otherwise not intending to do so or when frankly, having nothing at all left to give

I lovingly recognize others as influences on who I have and will become, my once-strangers, my now friends, hence holdup there is more. Friends do not reside outside and surface layer upon my heart yet rather, my friends are my family, resting soundly, deeply, and lovingly within my core oracle, aka my very being

I cherish what my friend family has done for me. True-truth and quite literally, I would not be of breath now without them, no doubt

Lacking additional words, my intent and attempt rests to honor and share the first truth of this here bird brain life...the treasure of you, me, us and we, all as one, all as family.

Two

~

Pieces of Me

A quick eyes-forward stare, peradventure preparing for oncoming conditions. A hard look back, prospecting for purpose and lessons learned below surface-level consciousness. Settling into this here life's reality and handing it all to you both, just so you know.

Chapter Two, Pieces of Me ~

Standing inside Princeton Sports the fancy downhill ski shop in Columbia Maryland, I could not decide which one of the many stylish ski suits to pick out, yet still, oh bloody hell, I had to fricking choose.

Some minutes earlier I popped by the shop to bid farewell before fleeing town. My ex-boss Alan offered no explanation except leave his office immediately, go down to the sales floor, pick out a suit of my liking and bring it back up to him, "Right now", as he instructed then pointed me away, "Go!".

Alan's comfortably sized swanky office was located in the upstairs loft area at one end of the spacious retail building, co-located against a slightly bigger upper-level inside space including the employee lunchroom and a few additional work desks. The remainder of the store possessed a vast open ceiling area. Alan's executive room was semi-throne-like, with a dark expansive wood desk, an appearing ridiculously expensive presidential chair, and the place was cluttered with a large array of the latest downhill skis. Alan was not storing spillover inventory and rather, his king's room was filled with a heavy quiver of hard-to-get boards: Special makeup skis which were production cores with custom one-off personalized graphics on top, well as special samples, and next year's test demo skis. Of course every pair of planks in Alan's command center were in his size because you know, gear is cool and more gear is cooler.

The second-story loft looked out across the main sales floor of the 12,000-square-foot ski and bike shop. This Columbia location was the newer offspring retail outlet of Princeton Sports, the first parental store operating about thirty miles north in Baltimore. The remaining Baltimore location was where I started my bicycle industry work career more than four years earlier.

These superfly overalls were the bulk of rage at the time and if sporting a one piece, you were cosmo ski fashionable. Looking through the sweet yet ungodly expensive alpine suits available, I grew more uncomfortable by the fucking second, wanting to just run out the door, or maybe puke into the bathroom sink but tried to stick, so to not be an idiotic weirdo.

I stopped in to say goodbye to Alan only a few days before escaping Maryland.

I did not know the deal...unsure if Alan was giving me a killer price on my awkwardly new jumper, or gifting it to me outright. If but a discount, I could honestly afford jack squat fricking nothing. Not wanting to engage in this queasy guessing gameshow, I tried to motion forward out of respect for my pal Alan, but it was hard AF.

Dismissing my natural inclination of stoner sourpuss hesitation, I jumped in and played onward. Assuming Alan was least silent offering me a deep discount, I thought to know which one I'd pick out. Honoring his long-standing support while attempting not to be a greedy lowlife asshole, I chose the bare bones cheapest suit I could fit into, and one cool enough for me to actually wear.

My selection was an era en-vogue teal green one-piece jumpsuit, featuring an outer layer made from water-repellent fabric, not constructed with the otherwise more expensive waterproof material of the many suits I passed up. The chosen jumper had a little fashionable white stripe of fabric sewn across one shoulder, with an additional black stripe of fabric the same size sewn into the suit directly adjacent next to the whitey one. The suit looked kind of cool, although it was still way too fricking fancy for me. I was a struggling bike and ski mechanic who spent every penny I made on drugs and bike parts, not fancy fucking ski suits. Besides, I did not fricking deserve it. I was a wannabe Punk Ass Bitch poser who taught myself to ski at the little hills around Baltimore, shortly to be outclassed in every way by real skiers in real mountains. My downhill ski technique honestly sucked ass at the time, but I hoped to grow moderately better, if perchance later chasing real shredders around on peaks out west.

Still, I collected the suit and walked it back upstairs. Alan took the long teal rag from me, remarked if I was sure, possibly disappointed I did not treat myself to one of the nicer suits, one of the real suits. He removed it from the hanger, dramatically and forcefully ripping the price tag off and with that big loving smirk of his, crammed it back into my hands along with a $100 bill and said, "Have fun out west". Uh, well, I was practically speechless, humbled, and almost cried, almost.

I loved working with Alan a few years earlier in Baltimore. Alan without exception showed me unwavering kindness, even under some heavy and difficult circumstances. I did not share the fact I was broke with anyone, not even my super cool friend boss Alan. Viewing my life comprehensively I had one intentional destination: Locating the meadow of continued breaths. The greatest challenge revealing itself to me on my journey will be the wavering of my willingness, I knew so. Factually, money was one of the least things I worried about, I had way bigger problems than the fill of my fucking pockets.

Standing weakened afront of Alan with my new suit and a fresh slightly green paper Benjamin, I was majorly breathless. Both my quivering chin and my stoner glare dropped toward the floor. I shook my head back and forth in humbled disbelief of his support and generosity, then peeked up through my PAB long hair, attempting to mumble some slight gratitude. My appreciation far exceeded my vocabulary, yet because it was Alan Davis and because of the special working relationship we shared, it was not necessary for me to say a single goddamn word. Alan knew what I was feeling, and knew what I would say if I were able to say it. That day, it seemed a sheepish and mumbled thank you sufficed.

Years previous, Alan's dad Sonny hired me for my first bike shop job, 40 minutes northeast of Alan's thrown-like office in Columbia. Sonny ran Princeton Sports in southern Baltimore County, after taking over from his lovable old mom Lucille. I worked with Sonny's mom Lucille, aka Alan's grandmother, back in Baltimore. In her 80's at the time and Lucille Davis was still sharp as a tack…a certified public accountant, she did the bookkeeping, well as building all of our bike wheels by hand. Lucille sat in her office performing financial paperwork while lacing up wheels from a pile of spokes, a rim, a hub, and completing her job in mere minutes. Lucille emerged to drop the laced-up wheels at our workbenches, for me and my two peer mechanics to tension and perform final wheel truing. Regularly I followed the same instructions: Take Sonny's fancy Volvo auto and go pick up his mom at the local Pikesville grocery store.

Lucille and I made slight chit chat as I drove her and her packages home, before rushing back to continue my busy schedule in the bike and ski service shop. Alan was the ski department manager and also, clearly number two in command overall of the Baltimore store. During the rare occasions Sonny was gone from the building, Alan was the big boss.

Kicking off my fulltime career, I worked a couple years for Sonny in Baltimore then left, me quitting in a huff and storming out of the entire scene.

Wildly derailed for a while, I discovered that malicious motherfucker the drug needle and danced around demonically, me partnered with His Heinousness the Prince of Darkness Himself.

However then eventually, fuck knows how, I went back to work in the bicycle business. After aggressively walking out on Sonny, I later joined the team at another shop only two miles down the road from Princeton Sports, sparsely junkie-existing on the clock at a joint called Mount Washington Bike Shop in northern Baltimore City. I lasted a couple more years at Mount Washington before facing the one and only open route available to me, I had to get the hell away from the east coast, toot suite.

While I was wrenching for Mount Washington, Sonny and Alan opened their new second store, partway to Washington DC. Sonny stayed to command the Baltimore store while Alan, the eldest of Sonny's three kids, moved to Columbia to assume the role of retail president in the new location. Alan The Awesome ran his southern store without any assistance from his dad Sonny.

Taking my suit and my hundred bucks, I said goodbye to Alan and went back downstairs. I visited the workshop, saying goodbye to the mechanics and gave Alan a one last time humble and appreciative head nod, as I walked under his second-floor office then out the front door to the parking lot. Although my eye sockets were flooded with tears the entire time, they withheld any flow onto my face. Day by day over the past nine years as a committed drug addict, I became more and more hardened, I had no choice. It had been a year or three since I shed a tear about any fricking thing.

A few days later my car was loaded and fucking finally, I was ready to get the hell out of town. But first I stopped in Mount Washington to give my most recent former work family members last goodbyes, then bumped into one of our best customers, Trina. Trina and her boyfriend Jeff were not only dedicated consumers, but Jeff would later become owner of Mount Washington Bike Shop. Trina was excited for me and my upcoming adventure, however the necessary journey that it was. Looking back, I see she was probably hoping I would begin a new and better life for myself elsewhere, yet I am assuming.

A proper punk and on the wrong path in Baltimore, I was a loser-loser junkie lowlife dropout loser and I presumed everyone knew it, most of all Trina.

Whenever Trina visited the bike shop, her and I spent hours chatting about life's general opportunity awhile the harsh detail of it all.

Unexpectedly, Trina also gave me $100 to help me on my way and I thought to myself wow, now I am rich. Guess I was broadcasting some sort of silent I am pathetically broke-please help-help signal unto the world unbeknownst to me. I graciously accepted the dough and because she did not clearly state it was a gift, I said to try and pay Trina back later, if I could. I never did pay her back but I assume Trina was ok with me keeping the hundred bucks. Not that I thought it odd at the time, but I awkwardly noticed my value in verbal relations with women. Verifiably, more guys made up my friend list than girls but most of my female friends were close friends, but no not like that. My gal pals and I shared many open thoughts and feelings, more so than I did with any of the guys, and mostly the same is true today.

Leaving with all my clothes, all my tools and all my bike parts packed tightly into my shitty blue Subaru, I ventured off for places unknown. The three pairs of downhill skis I owned were positioned securely in the roof rack, alongside my two bikes, one mountainbike and one road bike. The possessions left behind were the hopeful-someday-to-be-hotrod Camaro sitting out in my father's driveway and my dirtbike motorcycle, both machines scattered about in pieces. Much of the Camaro suspension and interior parts were previously pulled apart and stockpiled inside the car. The borderline bygone Camaro sat in the rain and snow for almost three years by the time I left town. I mostly gave up on my maybe-one-day fantasy junker hotrod, sitting there deathlessly idle in BigBird's driveway. I yanked the car to bits, and quickly became disinterested then irresponsibly flat broke to rebuild it. Maybe I'll drag the darn car westward in the future, if I have a flipping future, or who the frick knows, maybe I'll be forced back to 'Balmer the murder capital one day to stay. Or maybe, I will abandon even a fleeting flying fuck and instruct my father to sell the damn heap of metal and grab whatever minimal money he can get for it, like oh who fricking cares whatever.

The calendar found this time as December 1985. Thanksgiving had just wrapped up and I was finally doing it, I was moving the fuck away. The previous winter I skied in Europe and also took a snowsports trip to the western US, both with my naughty neighborhood friend Ryan Gniazdowski. Stateside we skied at several areas in Colorado then continued to Jackson Hole and Grand Targhee resorts, both in Wyoming and not far from Yellowstone National Park. Just standing within big mountains the previous year hooked me unlike anything else ever experienced in my life, I knew it, I knew I must live amid the peaks, I knew instinctively the need to trash my current environment in Baltimore. The only secure peace and love I knew in my heart up to that time was when sunk deep within big mountains.

Within the next few days I would choose one of the many beckoning ski towns to call the new place home. No idea where I might land, zero inclination what I would do when I got there, and I did not at all fricking care. My best friend middle sister Beth was supposed to move with me but in the end she decided to stay behind. Not having Beth by my side alpine adventuring was not going to stop me, I was going no matter what. Finally wheels rolling northwest around the Baltimore Beltway, I turned onto Interstate 70 and aimed for, hum, I have no clue where I am going, only big westward peaks.

I experienced squeamishly strange sensations on I-70 passing the exit for Alan's store but committed, I continued forward towards them mountains be a calling me.

After partially exhausting my simultaneous dual career as a fulltime drug addict and bike mechanic, recently ridding my poorly battered arms of the years-long incessant stabbing from drug needles, I cared nor planned not for any set destination. Unless leaving the deadly Charm City quickly, I knew not to make it out alive before turning 22. The year before I overdosed twice and if staying put much longer, my life would be over and soon, I knew as such. Experiencing a powerful realization following my second overdose, it rocked me into some sort of odd offbeat sensibility, decidedly choosing I would rather live, and start living right fricking now, than soon die. Skipping out on 11th grade, no college to speak of, and after the overdoses, I tried to rally upwards in life, I really tried. Regardless of unemployed and practically broke, I was off to try and create a brand new me, and would not fucking look back.

Ms. Birdy and Mr. Boyd

Lauren and Travis, my loves, pieces of me have been lost on you. Things I never told you. Questions you never asked. Specificities I unsuccessfully tried to share yet were never heard. Just like my father did for me, I pen these lasting words for you both, my beloved children, my brood, my precious. For you are, all I am, my entire world, my only factual meaning, my one singular true purpose.

Your life will spin out of control and often, yes, count on it. Undeniably, all issues will arrive as unique to you. And still, for all one can dream, my life's words here help you see things differently, perchance through an alternative lens of understanding. Reasonably my chirps serve as slight devices to somehow help develop strategies of your own, if even an oddball experiment to try for now. Of course I cannot perpetually help you, least not in person. I will not always be here to help when you need or want me. I might be around physically, however you may not desire my assistance at all. There might not be anyone nearby to lend a hand, or you may think you just want to, or need to, go it alone.

Some of our sisters and brothers believe life's purpose is happiness. I wish and pray their vision of eternal painlessness, forever rainbows overhead, and immortal bunnies boundlessly playing at their feet beams down upon them forever and ever, amen. Awhile this here poppa bird nonfictionally positioned, adversity will rise up and greet me every single fucking day of my life no doubt. Fact-one I absorb fully and remain steadfast on the necessity to handle my own struggles no matter what the what, even when the challenge put upon me comes from nowhere else but inside my own head.

Accepting the truth of fact I cannot control everything happening with me, I choose to work ridiculously hard to make a difference in the world with the time I have left. No idea how much longer this battered body and brain will last or properly function, feasibly only one more day, imaginably another 40 years. My expiration date unbeknownst to me and this effort here, my life's aggregated puzzle on paper, is meant to help make a difference in your lives whether I am around physically, mentally capable, or fricking not.

I attempt here no teaching. I intend here no preaching. Plainly my orientation is to share, just so you know.

Just so you know…just so you know who what and how I am who I am, and still why, why do I do these things? *Why*? Because I believe it fucking matters. Because maybe something within these pages helps you live as you intend to hope or dream. Because maybe something here speaks to you, by your measure. Because maybe you desire a different and unique routine, habit, orientation, betterment of presence outcome or self-discipline, by your measure. Or maybe, my word chirpings and poopings peck at you and you gain some insight or ideas to help someone else who cannot currently help themselves effectively. Then again as it may be, you are least mildly entertained by my dumb-ass life adventures and this here volume one serves as a robust doorstop, maybe the best dusty doorstop ever.

The Warmth and Hope of New Beginnings

Although most days I wear my heart on sleeve, mine has not been a totally transparent journey to you. Having an insatiable thirst for travel since first feeling wheels under my feet, most my hundreds of glorious trips I spent alone. Despite sharing many adventures roadtripping and jetsetting with travel partners, I enjoy mostly my own company for all the sunsets, all the sunrises, and all the blizzards. Sunsets making me cry…breathtaking, literal speechless salty tears falling to my lips at dusk. Sunrises blinding me with the warmth and hope of new beginnings, a new life one day at a time, right here and right now, and if only for today. Blizzards so thick I barely see the faint glow of my car headlights through the frantic flurry of the almost insignificant windshield wipers, and of course we know snow thrills me to no end, even blinding blizzards. Infallibly the adventures glorious, no matter the where, whatever the purpose, despite glitches all the while, forever and dependably.

Dare I now claim straight up…the bulk of my bird brain knowings arrive through travels and interactions with others 'long the way.

Many summits high I have climbed, many valleys low I have trekked, many dark and scary corners explored. Many surprise meanings learned, those findings found hibernating in the damp edges of total truth.

You only know what you know and frankly, your field of reference concerning me is relatively small. You never heard the historical tales from Grandpa With Ginger or Grandma Pat about who their only son was back when. Stories bearing my implosions, my slip up's, my crazy injuries, and just how it is that I became to be the person you know today. Your mom barely knew my family, and opportunities for shared tales of days past were minimal at best. With you guys in tow, we did not hang with my three sisters and their kids.

You do not know my six remaining cousins, save for a distant and almost forgotten contact with Cousin Tina, my first cousin once removed, aka my Bird grandmother's niece. So, you missed those experiences too. You have not spent measurable time with my hundreds of friends scattered around the world, many of whom I have known for more than 30 years.

Nor are there home movies showing how I stumbled into this here adult bag of bones and skin shell I occupy today.

Busy as I stayed exploring, stumbling, then starting over, so many of those details were lost as I sped from place to place. Not wanting to just wait around for anything to change for the better and have happiness magically fall into my lap, I went off and created my own new experiences. Somehow, maybe from the autonomy I gained after mother Patricia got locked up, I felt to quench some of my unsettledness by traveling elsewhere. So I did just that, often as I could. Even once beginning my habitual then dead-end academic truancy career, I withheld an internal motor and inner compass pushing me away from wherever I was. Wrestling with safe and local boredom, I ran and rolled towards adventure, albeit carrying a presumption of risk.

Hence was I, in-truth running away? Maybe. Rushing towards something better? Certainly not always although yes, sometimes off to more desirable things, trying not to look back at the bad and scary shit at home. It could only be technically described as wandering, though the minute movement began I was joyed to be going somewhere and doing something. The particular somewhere or thing often lacked specificity, just elsewise and away from home. That might sound hectic to you, but to me, it was not. That might appear hard or challenging, but to me, it was thrilling. I was intent on the journey awhile the variability of just getting up to go. Did this make me a nomad? A hobo possibly, as you both used to say? Was I unsettled and scared to stay put too long? Like a gypsy? Finding comfort in nature or resting amongst property not mine? I did not envision myself as any of those things, nevertheless partially least yes, all is probably accurate, scarcely-minimally-emotionally yes, you know...organically unsettled, frightened, unsafe, and needing to be outside is what I find when I dig deep enough and speak honestly of it.

I comforted on the move, safer outside adventuring than trapped within the idleness of four walls at home.

Multiple opportunities presented themselves daily for long back as I remember, least when my eyes and heart were open wide enough to notice. The different job opportunities, the different geographical connections, the different housing options arising, the different love interests catching my eye and snagging my heart, and the different friend experiences...the collected pieces all add up to this master tale we are about to explore together.

Crumbs
In all imaginable ways for fuck's sake, you both deserved a much better childhood and certainly a much better father than the one I offered up to you.

You did not do anything wrong to justify all the stupid shit I delivered, or not, as I fumbled pathetically through fatherhood.

My fallout heartbreak from both divorces, the questioning I had of life itself after Lexie's tragic suicide, the death of both my parents your Grandpa With Ginger and Grandma Pat, then finally my somewhat senseless other four-plus addictions you both have lived through so far, well, I apologize for my inadequate and miserable fucking parenting during these times.

I am sorry, I am very, very, very sorry for my parental shittyness. I could have done better and of course, I did not. I tried, I really tried, I tried my best. I tried my very fucking best I knew how for you both. In the end, I reside soundly to have done my best at the time. I could have put you first on my schedule, in front of everything else sooner, still of course, I did not. I was doing what I thought to collect and save for a better future for your mother, and for you both. I could have worked less and played with you more while you were both of playful age, but I did not.

Yet we still played and traveled a fuck-ton, and I am grateful to my pop BigBird for instilling in me the joy of photography as I took thousands of pictures while you both jumped, played, skied, and rolled vibrantly throughout your youth. I could have been better educated and prepared to know more about parenthood, romantic relationships, and marriage before jumping into those things, but I did not. I could have protected you better from the drama and chaos of my romantic pursuits after your mom and I split up, including protecting you from your mother a little bit more herself, although she also did what she thought best at the time. The many amazing loves lost, the women I tried to hold securely and love correctly, but alas I fucking sucked at that too, aka I could not love them properly either. The time spent trying to find my perfect mate was just more distracted busy time, which kept me away from you both. I am sorry for not putting you first when I had the chance and when I should have.

I am very, very, very sorry.

The deduction became that of utter bestness, utilizing all accumulated during my rambled journeys and wanders. Yes, often my best is beyond what expected…I might not pause, I might not stop once completing the required finish line instructions and rather, keep pushing 'til leaving things good as I can make them, by my measure. And of course we know that sometimes, I just fuck everything up.

I try time and again to do things right, although not always do I know how to do it right, and might even hurt everyone around me in the process.

I had to figure shit out as I went along because no one was going to do it for me, and there was no owner's manual I knew of on how to do life.

One of my greatest lessons learned is do best by my measure, and do not crucify myself when shit goes other than planned. I try my best try, using my best purposeful intention, results be damned. Hopefully one day you will figure out how the whole life-effort-love-balance math thing works for yourself. Let me explain. I mean to say the definition, by your means, to arrive at your own personal truth and your own state of purpose, by your measure.

Basically unearthing what you might call your self-defined meaning…the balance of living, loving, choosing where to place your efforts and how much force to exert, also what to let go of and walk away from. And as it relates to me, your dear dad, if the thought of me resides heavily inside you now, or if I really screw up at some time in the future, I hope you accept things as they were and not hold me out of your heart forever, blaming me for screwing up your childhood or even fucking up your entire life.

Although some reserve few friends claim to have a perfectly beautiful life that strolls along with ease peace and tranquility, most of us are struggling on a daily and fucking maybe even minute-by-minute basis. We are stuck and wrestle with the pains, traumas, and realities of our past. Our struggle with current days are scarily real, and most of us spend too much time wishing and praying for a different and better ideal future state. We throw most of our self-imposed inefficiencies into the pool of our own personal unhappiness, eagerly claiming someone or something else is to blame for what we do not have or what was done to us. We do this without proper planning or pre-work to help make any of our future-living dreams come true at all.

We sit and wait for a better life, better than this shitty one we have here anyway, praying for everything to magically work out and fall into our laps without accepting the fact that our life is what we make it.

What we make it…I lived to experience learn and know that we humans do some pretty stupid shit, us doing stupid-stupid shit the day's long. We all do stupid shit much-much of the time. We do and say things we do not mean or did not intend, every fricking day. We promise ourselves and make boastful claims out loud, only then to not start the darn thing at all. You've both certainly heard it from me many times before, I try to let people be stupid, aka I try to let people own their own behavior, knowing I cannot change or save anyone. I try not to get upset by their stupid shit, I try to let them carry it. Not that anyone is inherently stupid, no way, rather some of our behaviors are stupid. We're all doing what we think is right, and doing it in ways that makes sense to us. I try not to judge, blame, or assume, knowing yes of course, duh, I too behave stupidly at times. I have no earthly idea what others have gone through and I sure as fucking bloody hell do not know what they are experiencing right now. We all withhold our individually unique experiences, even as we stand shoulder to shoulder and observe the very same thing…what an odd discovery to recognize, hence a powerful one. I try to not come unraveled when I see my sisters and brothers do stuff that makes no sense to me. These, some hard-fought bird life lessons collected during my clunky flight.

The thought of you guys struggling along your way hurts me. Of course, you have both anguished already as of this writing. You have both wrestled with some legit hard shit and certainly, some of that lingers still. Please make no mistake that more hard shit is not coming for you because it certainly is. The death of yours truly and your momma might really fuck you up, least for a while. I and your mom will probably die before you so please give it much thought as you safely can before it happens. *Why?* So when it does happen, it does not cripple you much and long as it could otherwise.

We will die, and hopefully we die before you. Then with time you will start to heal, and the tears of our passing will be transformed into smiles as you remember our glorious times together, and the silly little idiosyncrasies of your forever-loving parental birds.

Your future years of challenge concern me because although recognizing you must face life on your own, it causes pain deep in my heart of hearts to know I won't always be around to help you. I might not be there, least in some small supportive role when you face the hardest fucking thing of your life, well, you might not choose to possibly include me. Hence my effort gifting you lasting pieces of me, hopefully these here my crumbs are somewhat relevant to when you might need them most.

I must ask something of you both.

Once already I requested this of Lauren and I retell the story in my podcast episode number one, whereas…at my funeral, can you please not sit down? Go ahead and cry your eyes out as needed, that is perfectly fine, and please do me this favor, do not sit down. Do not sit down. Get up. Stay up. Stay standing. Walk around. Talk to as many different people as you can. Please try to honor me in this way by spreading yourself around the room to those who also, are in attendance to pay honor and share their love with me one last time.

I want you to primarily do it for yourself, not to sulk, not to withdraw. I want you to sing, dance, laugh, and celebrate your dad's amazing life. I now advance you the notion I will certainly not get out of this place alive, none of us will. Please try to not be sunk or stuck in sorrow. I do not want you to sit, please. I do not want you to stay in bed for a week after I pass, please. I want you to go live your glorious life the best damn way you can, please. Secondarily, I want you to do it for others, for friends I consider family. So please get up to meet share and love our family. Because on that day, I will still be in the room, I will be inside of you. After my battered brain and body expire, I will live on, forever, inside of you and your children, and your children's children, forever after, well, of course, because you are me and I you. Please share yourself, and share your pieces of me residing within you one last time with our bigger family. Lastly, I want you to do it for me. I do not want you to stop, least not for too long. Please do not give up. Sure, pause and rest as needed but I want you to get up, go, and keep fucking going. Even when you hurt like hell, get up, get up and stay up. You're a lot tougher than you will ever know. I know this because I have tested all limits, and you are me. Please do this for me.

By and by in totality I have survived more days of shadow overhead than sunshine ablaze on my back. Soon I learned no one was coming to fix it for me, not a single no fricking body. I had to smile between perilous periods of pain, if even a slight smirk of neutrality. For Pete's sake I put myself through so much hell, yet to then get pelted with the truth of the handicap…it does not consume, least not forever. Slight breaks placed me outside the prison walls of pain momentarily then no, I can't, I'm supposed to be miserable for whatever the circumstances, unwittingly then guilting myself back into shackles of sadness. I lived to learn that most hard blows soften eventually, if courageously facing them.

Such undulation repeated itself time and time and time again to the point of nauseous confusion, that is until I woke the fuck up to notice it as nothing more than a silly rollercoaster.

The perpetual carnival ride was one of part-time self-sacrifice...consciously crying, bleeding, laid out broken and aghast, yet ready to right myself once the clouds part. Meaning to say, I learned to reside willfully during times of trouble, but then rushed to my feet once the sun comes out and birds begin their song.

Undeniably, not always are we so tough. We might refuse to even hope, think, or move. Days dim to night, and we possess zero reserve tries, often this an abysmal pit with no way out. I have known this hopelessness, it being a dominant force factually beyond my diction. When unable to continue, then releasing hopeful attempts of all future days, I stand to accept this curtain close as a choice of the individual. I know not their hurt, I am no better than any woman any man, my shoes fit inside no other's footsteps but my own. I support all sisters all brothers no matter what, even when saying their last goodbyes. Often, bravery and courage are fleeting forces unavailable when we need them most...bravery to trudge forward despite the shit storm awaiting us, courage to enter the snarling beast's lair of uncertainty. Embracing the transparency of ups alongside the downs, I found my way through to the peaceful middle. Much of this bird's tale is meant to help you know me, thus help know yourself, and to shine some added light upon your path in some screwy stupid and microscopic way.

I do not count on tomorrow giving itself to me freely, or even once more.

Ok and gee whiz, this is not a big book of sad tales and funeral plans, fuck that noise. I just had to put a healthy frame of reality around this picture I am trying to paint. This is factually a glorious tale of adventure and my documented discoveries of learning to live my life my way, along with some new-to-you details, my hard-fought truths, and definitive lessons learned. Yes of course documented heartbreak lives here yet while the while, for every love lost, following every struggle, after every moment of suffering, and for every tough situation I lived through, at all times did periods of personal growth, supreme beauty, and better-defined purpose follow, every time, fucking for sure every single time. Alas after somewhile wrapped up in the bliss of good times, the undividedness of this birdbrain came back together, recognizing that toughness is lurking and tracking me just over the horizon no doubt. And that is the main premise of the collection of pages you hold in your hands now, my learnings to live fully in the moment...loving, laughing, and adventuring through no matter the fricking what, even though I knew my heart will surely fracture again soon.

Lauren you may still be 22 years young when first reading this, my life's work. Travis you might still be a man of 24 years when first glancing over these pages. Quite possibly you are both now in your 30's or 40's or later, and finally have reason or the time or commitment to open this hardcover with conviction.

Reality is, whether you hit this paragraph only once or even multiple times in your life, these things I spell out may not mean so much to you at all. You may have already figured things out. You may not care to consider alternative options to your path already committed to. Although I hope this not the case, you might not give a shit at all, and any or all of that is perfectly ok. I still give myself to you with this endeavor, with every drip drop of my abilities, with the totality of my heart, no matter what the flipping what.

All you have done and how you have done it may have served you remarkably well up to this point in your life. I certainly do not mean to cast a spell on you or your offspring with fears of future trauma and rather, please consider the reality that the same things getting you here will not necessarily nor effectively carry you into your future, hah, because they probably will not, and for fucked-sake I know for fact to say, they will for-sure not.

I have to change my thoughts, my ideas, my structure, my techniques, and my routines regularly to stay relevant in this here world.

Change and death are the only truthful certainties I know of in life. The interjection usually arises…*and taxes*, but to me our charge for citizenship is just a small bothersome cash-lanes toll along the route. Change will happen and honestly, I am required to change and keep changing. So, maybe this tale provides a jump-off point for you to change a little. No not at all to change who you are, but just the same, help you shape a new headspace on some stuff weighing hefty on your aching brain or laying heavy in your breaky heart. Maybe this work serves to give you a little boost and try something new and better, or perhaps get out of something bad. Maybe still, to help you imagine and build new thoughts or routines for yourself, possibly reaching targets of your own yet to come.

It could be that you give these here pages not one solo brief glance. I do not put forth these writings to assure you read them. I offer this tale, for you to use as you desire, for your reference either when I am still here at any rate unavailable or rather, long after I am gone from this body and earth. Maybe your partner or your spouse or your child graces these pages before you, hah, maybe even your grandchild. Maybe they find some hope strength or calm for themselves within my writings here. Maybe your love will share some of this with you, prodding and teasing you to finally pick it up with conviction and read it yourself.

I cannot control another…I rest soundly in the fact I put forth my best effort with the time afforded me and did the good work I thought was correct, by my measure. This book being the most legit effort I put forth thus far across all my years of living. Occupying over three years of dedicated fulltime writing to you, here I present these my pages, this my magnum opus. This here grand piece of work most in alignment with my true life's purpose, helping my kids best I can, be prepared as they can be for their lives, by their measure.

Sharing with you my learnings, no way do I cast them upon you, these my lessons, not yours.

Amid December 2020, a lift to get me up off my ass helping Uncle Ralph in Wyoming was a gap-fill opportunity. The questions held concerning my father and various family dynamics risked going unanswered. No, those skipped life chapters have not stopped me, but do cause an awkward irritable pause from time to time. I orient to not burden you my precious in such ways going forward. Two months previous and just after his paralyzing stroke, I offered to help The Admiral if needing a hand. And of course I was serious, or I would not have said it. He assured me that he himself and his local network was more than capable, but thanks anyway he said.

Caught slightly off guard when I got the call weeks before Christmas that yes, my dad's big brother now wanted my help, I struggled with the reality of needing to put my highest purpose, this here book, on hold for a while, maybe a year or more. Whilst and beyond my conscious highest purpose project, this here book, is my subconscious get up and go booster rocket when someone is in danger or needs my help, go, just go, just fucking drop everything and go, so I did exactly that and drove straight to Wyoming.

Within these here your pages I share practices and tools constructed for myself, these tools also tested shared and working for some other brave humans close to me. My array of routines habits and rituals are perhaps overwhelming, yet not to share such the detail would be void much the narrative. My shit works for me and no fucking way no how do I suggest you attempt or operate as such. This is my shit and I intend not to preach, teach, or instruct, I intend and desire only, to share.

You will live by what compels you to function as you can, and as you so dream to exist.

Despite purity of intentional attempt, both my delivered creative effort and the grandiose page count of this here hefty multi-volumed doorstop, enclosed is the sum of my best selected brevity. Not everything is here, nor could it be possibly. The harvest of my exhausted capabilities, housed within my best skilled effort, I share with you now, these pieces of me.

Here are my pieces residing within.
Here are the pieces of me felled, seated far below surface-level.

Lauren and Travis, my loves, my precious, pieces of me have been lost on you. Speaking total pieces of me straight-up truth, although some bits may have slipped by, you are treasured to already know the best pieces of Roger Ray Bird. What are the best pieces of me you say? Oh, that's easy, just look in the mirror, they reside there, the best pieces of me are you two, no doubt. Here is that which lies between us. Here is that which comprises me, hurts me, and makes me sing.

This Here Chapter Two, Pieces of Me
Chapter two unravels and shares a small collection of things you probably do not know and facts not found elsewhere. Or perhaps here lies backstory detail of something else you already partially understand of your bird brain father. This here chapter two is the second topic chapter, bouncing around timeline-wise, yet offers a peek into a thing or three perhaps relevant to you or this bird's tale. Here I give you additional crumbs, sharing some other pieces of me with you both, just so you know.

Little Bird

Get up, get up
Get up my tired little bird
Stretch, stretch up high
High as you can reach
Extend your muscles
Extend your dreams
Extend your mind
Be tall be strong
Yes you ache, yes I know
We all ache too, try to be brave
Be brave today, and if only for today
Be brave today, and if only for this minute
Spread your wings, grimacing if you must
Courageously gathered and ready to journey
Bigger than your pain, you prepare anyway
Get up, go now, upon the edge of the nest
It's ok, trust me, jump now, just jump
Fly your flight, clunky as it may be
And as much as it may hurt
Your rhythm will settle
Things will smooth out
Smooth out for certain
They always do
Always.

And then, and then
And then little bird you will find it
And then my little bird you will find it, and see it
You will find balance and you will see the beauty of life
To try and keep trying, to start and keep starting, these the toughesl parts
To go and keep going, you find your way, you learn your path
Go now, fly, I know you can, I know you can, if you try
And then my precious darling little bird, you will soar
So soar my little bird, soar, soar high as you can.

The Most Vicious Inescapable Enemy

Every ounce of my human comprehension was entranced, sitting in our family's living room. My eyes affixed on the semi-large black box transmitting festive moving pictures from around the world, places I was sure to never visit and mostly, it was one place. One place held my attention and captured my heart more than all others pre-teen, that place below where we live, the place beyond where we can breathe. I surely arrived on time for the wondrous gaze of dreaming along with the French crew of underwater explorers as they searched around subsurface during the hour show of The Undersea World of Jacques Cousteau. Jacques was a French Naval officer turned famous oceanographer, and his was my most influential show on TV. The program rode along with Jacques and his crew across the globe on their big boat, in their small explorer submarine, and as they snorkel and scuba-dived into most every crevasse of our water world below. The technicality of the gear, the weird weightlessness, the mesmerizing sea life, and the spectacular underwater landscapes absolutely thrilled me.

The notion hit me hard around the time I was 10 thanks to the Cousteau-bestowed audio-video educational society…the world's surface is more than 70% water. So by far as much as we humans may try to dominate the planet, I unuttered to myself, undersea creatures must outnumber us in multitudes. My fascination with the land-water-math was overwhelmed by the additional elements of color, movement, and culture of Mother Nature's aqua world. Beyond what I knew heard or dreamed of on land, the bulk of this planet's offerings existed beyond my reasonable access. I was missing most of what the world flaunted for me to experience…I wanted to be an oceanographer.

For years and when given the opportunity, I would say it out loud…I want to be like Jacques Cousteau, this my first life aspiration.

Our standup-and-turn-the-dial TV had a whopping four channels to choose from when I came around to be inside watching it, a rather rare happening. Several hours of cartoons filled our Saturday mornings yet still, nothing came from the silliness of the animated shows. Alternatively, the wonderment of the National Geographic series was spectacularly riveting but never could I imagine traveling fricking anywhere, so I watched for entertainment only. And then the Mutual of Omaha's Wild Kingdom show featured beasts galivanting betwixt each other in their natural African habitat. Never thinking to see any of it myself and certainly no draw to hunt or pick up a gun existed anywhere within my bag of bones and skin so also, the show was just general entertainment. BigBird granted us time on Saturdays to enjoy the boob tube's mindless brainwashing, and early on we partook in some evening family togethering around the communal screen. My father name-tagged the TV *The Idiot Box*, and tried to shoo us outdoors instead of allowing the brain-melting sessions to plod on too long or too often inside.

A few conversations occurred with BigBird concerning my life's possibilities and still mostly he was busy, overly busy…wrangling us four kids by himself, working fulltime, going to night school, fixing up his old dilapidated boat on Saturdays, pimping his bible words on Sundays, and spent the minimal remaining free time alone in his woodshop or sitting silently in his cush den chair, reading.

Mattering none the place nor time and of course, the while BigBird was smoking his cigarettes. Still-still and only as a little kid, the evident-at-least-to-me pressure gripping my father seemed borderline horrific, well, stricken by an indistinct burden eating him up bite-by-bite and hour-by-hour, though unrevealed to us his children in any understandable manner. His extreme edginess presented early on as hatred for me and my sisters, and yes for God's sake of course this was stupidly untrue, he told us he loved us, but many times his actions portrayed the opposite. What the fuck did I know, I did not know shit about nothin', save for what I was told felt or imagined. The BigBird conversations beyond immediate needs were few, hah, never mind the fact, duh, I was one of four children clamoring for his attention. If by chance my father was in the mood to discuss life, more than half the time I was mad at him and pissed at the fricking world so of course, we missed each other on those days. When I, however rarely, might be lingering in a somewhat sunny state, then the occasion mostly a crapshoot if BigBird would be in a corrected frame of mind to chat. Many times before I gathered even the nerve to speak up, my father lost his emotional shit about something else so I scrapped the effort to even open my damn punk ass mouth.

Monthly or thereabouts I bought a magazine of specific interest using profits from cutting lawns, serving newspapers, shoveling snow, time on the clock working for my friend David Ankers' father, or otherwise hustling money as a beer sherpa for partiers attending the horse racetrack in our neighborhood. Mostly I cycled through three different magazine genres: Hot rod cars, downhill skiing, and motocross dirtbikes. For goodness sake no realistic funds existed for these silly extracurriculars, so I held lightly the scantness of the imaginative fictions materializing one day, any day, any of them, ever, and still, these some faint hopes and dreams of mine. The motocross dirtbike was believably the most plausible one-day-come-true. Other kids had dirtbikes in the neighborhood and often my vivacious jealousy consumed me. I rode my bicycle around making zoom-zoom noises on the local motorcycle trails, fantasizing…one day, one day…one…day.

I dreamed and dreamed and dreamed of racing motorcycles and for years I clung to the one-day chance dirtbikes would save me from my most vicious and inescapable enemy: Me Myself.

The earliest underground lifeline escape, aka my subsurface underwater explorer dreams, remained floating belly up lifeless in the kiddie pool though. Once the high maintenance clinging monkey of illegal street substances attached itself squarely to the middle of my back, in short order my longings of undersea explorer fragmented. In my mid-twenties I almost signed up for scuba diving lessons in Maryland then stupidly spent the money on drugs instead. My intense moto-race craving was dismissively obliterated, burnt and reduced to no-way leave-that-shit-behind ashes.

Barely able to detach from the rage consuming me over my sans-moto race future, I did rally however, then clinging to the fanciful chimera of an internationally-traveled downhill ski racer, me already idolizing many of the sports' stars although I still had never been on snow.

I mailed away for spectacular ski and motocross posters that covered my bedroom walls and ceiling for well over a decade, the room art surviving into my mid 20's. Plastic model cars occupied the bulk of my minimal inside hobby time, occupied my time intently, least before the drugs. I swapped parts back and forth, adding custom decals, jacked up rear suspensions, and created little modified works of art.

Hands Off BigBird's Shit

My father became infuriated if I touched a single fricking hand implement from his robust basement woodshop. Especially I was instructed to be scared of his power tools so I was, yet wanted to borrow simple devices like wrenches and pliers and shit. Working on my bicycle sometimes went too far and I'd pull stuff apart, me then unable to reassemble the darn thing. When I had money, my father drove me to Princeton Sports bike shop so mechanics Wilbert or Tommy could reassemble the gosh darn things for me. Once in the car but before rolling, BigBird made sure I possessed my own cash, making it crystal clear he wasn't paying for jack squat anything. My father was a great man yet emotionally taxed beyond his limits most days. Generally I stayed far away from him if having the choice or opportunity.

BirdHouse Pet Shop

A handful of cats used our nest as their playground throughout my youthful years, mostly kittens found in the neighborhood then hidden inside my sister's jackets and smuggled into our birdy house. One of our earlier cats was my big sis Laura's beautiful grey and elegantly majestic Siamese named JC, aka Jesus Christ. One of our most beloved long-time family cats was a super-sweet black and white kitty with a little black mustache against her white face background named Hitler. Although her name not at all PC, she was a dear snuggle companion. One of our cats later got attacked in our driveway by a big white fluffy off-leash free-range Samoyed dog from down the street. Kitty survived the first attack but as I remember, not the second. I watched the initial mauling and the incident was verifiably fucking horrific.

One day a dear darling doggie strayed into our world, joining our family for the remainder of his life. Schultz was the only dog we ever had, he a medium-sized mixed breed, light brown in color, maybe a lab mix or something, and named after a television character from a popular comedy show at the time, Hogan's Heroes. Schultz the TV character was a German World War II prisoner camp guard, a large innocent man seemingly caught between his duty and his heart. Our dear dog Schultz seemed to have had a hard life too, his general disposition came off as sad, still we loved him intently and many days he matched our mood. Horrifically, one night my intrinsic fears were fed when Schultz did not come home.

Straight-up tragic...the next day we found him lying in our yard lifeless, OMGosh, his poor shell horribly shredded and bloody. Speculation said it was a band of raccoons or he squared off against one of the wild stray dog packs sometimes running through our part of the city. Remarkably, the vet found a faint heartbeat and worked on Schultz for hours, shaving most of his body and stitching up the many nasty cuts ear to tail, our dear doggie especially ravaged around his neck and hind quarters. The damage was so vicious that not even the vet could determine its origin. We nursed Schultz back to health but the thought of an unknown nighttime besieging evil on the loose rattled me badly.

The Essence of Adventure

The determination arose that me and my neighbor buddies Danny Nurco and Mark Weinreich shared a special desire, a some-thing some-where sorta craving. Travis you will be thrilled to know the driver was hours of gaming, enthralled by the features of Galaxian and later Galaga, Space Invaders, a multitude of pinball machines and of course, Pac-Man. The den of retail wonderment was the video arcade ten miles away. Every so often me Mark or Danny conned one of our parents to schlep us across town for a few hours of tech play. No alternative for such entertainment existed closer to home, save for the rather encapsulating but limited action Pong game attached to our analog TV's.

The mall hosting the hideaway arcade was kid-relative far away, only accessible by big streets and wide highways, so we were at the mercy of outside forces like adults and cars, well, that is, until we were not. I do not recall which one of us dreamed it first and although my remembrance held slight hesitation and a moderate safety concern, it was unanimously decided, yes, let's do this...we would ride our bikes to Security Square Mall, bring a bike lock or two, and remain in control of our own operations. So we did, ride to the video arcade and it was glorious, truly glorious. Yes, nerve racking and hairy at times yet still, glorious. We operated under our own power and made more of our own decisions, right or wrong, chose more of our own path, good or bad, aka glorious.

Still yet, then something changed, least for me, legitimately changed. My love for the trips to the mall grew, awhile my draw to the games began to wane. Scrutinizing the ideal...hum, analyzing the validity...well, the nucleus of the matter appeared as the delight of the comprehensive journey itself, aka the adventure of travel and moreover, the essence of doing that shit with my friends, aka doing it together. Ah, there it is...my romanticism was reserved for the expedition, the 90-minute bike ride with Mark and Danny. I struggled with such the odd notion, I was no longer doing it for the games, I was going for the journey. And so recognized with intention, the initiation of my life's grand adventuring began.

Once realizing the importance of the gallivant, a new world appeared, an unlimited expanse of seeing and learning, an opportunity to meet and know thousands of cultures, still and all while also, hum...an impetus for me to meet and know myself.

Moreover the local enhancer...a truly magical episode of feeling-understanding-learning-escaping and being was visiting the nearby outdoor space of Lake Roland. Either by bike motorcycle or foot, I began my wooded wander just to be, nestled in Mother Nature's arms silent and alone, the assembled trees being the only comforting touch of a mother I had ever known. Yes sometimes my purpose to zoom alongside the railroad tracks or squeeze through the trees fast as I could on two wheels, but sometimes just to get the fuck away and sit, finding a nook either on the edge of the water or off trail deep within the woods, to sit, just fricking sit. On occasion with agenda but often not, as comforted to purely be on my stationary butt, blocking out all behind me while soaking in all afront of me...the swirling breeze through my hair, the off and away slight rolling clap of the lake water waves, the play-chasing squirrels scampering gleefully afoot my feet.

The independence once there and also along the way, the quiet thoughts I faced and the deep conversations I had, most all with myself. Travis, your inquisition of *why are you so into bikes* begins here…my need to flee the flipping chaos, to find peace, to force clarity of thought, plus the summary to speak of the long-range self-supportive transportation that my bicycle afforded me.

Then off and footbound…the captivation of walking the neighborhood train tracks by my lonesome is something I cannot adequately describe, least here I try. Until thus-then I never knew of Bonnie Raitt or Billy Bragg or John Prine or JR Johnny Cash, yet my state of mind walking those tracks hour after hour and day after day, well, such my saunter must be somewhat related to the shared emotions of these hyper talented singer songwriters. In ways unexplainable, I listened silently to the unheard concert of this far off awhile treasured connection with self, kicking the kid fist-sized railway rocks as I paced.

The shared meaning, the similar clarity, the myriad of musical ballad realizations accumulated when rhythmically stepping from one rail tie to the next to the next to the next, or atop the track itself and as it is being of itself, the aggressive what-ifs of life, this my wild wonderment showing…the image of the solo me amongst the world's multiplications.

My deep self-meetup's, the plotting and scheming and doing the damn work whatever the frick the work calls for and no matter how much it fricking sucks, well, this that and the rest of it, aka a treasured connection with self.

What *Did* I Learn in School?

The rare times in class, I believed to matter none to anyone nor the world, and gave the concern no never mind anyway, ah fucking fuck it, meaning I mainly stuck to myself. Well, I did learn to read and write at basic grade level, so there's that. The complex math I plainly avoided, awhile learned to add and subtract but never committed adequate brain power towards hand division or multiplication. Whatever core competency academic knowledge I collected, it occurred in elementary school fifth grade and prior. Once beginning my drug use at age twelve, I exercised highly selective learning, largely because of my mind and body residing elsewhere.

Mid-grade, two classes held my attention, but only because of the teachers. Unable to recount what Ms. Freed taught me in my break away creative writing class, I only know something stuck with me and mostly, it was her eyes. Ms. Freed looked into me with care, perhaps empathy, certainly with patience, and in the end, she was one of only a few teachers in my life making it remotely worthwhile for me to even show up and try, least a while. Ms. Freed's eyes spoke to me and although I could barely bring myself to believe it, her eyes told me I mattered. Also in middle school the awesome Mister Thomas was kind, patient, attentive, and although pushing me, he did it in a positive manner which didn't drive me away. Mister Thomas captured my twisted-up adolescent heart, engrossing my otherwise held aside fatherly admiration, and I desired greatly his physical take me home adoption. My industrial arts teacher gifted me slight confidence and hope along my future life path, least a while.

One of the more empowering experiences surfacing amid my youth occurred when I failed geometry.

Again the appreciation that a good teacher is game changing…my turn around retribution of sorts during remedial summer school geometry was factually a semi-religious experience. Straight away in high school, the major life enhancement I collected was proper handwriting by way of mechanical drawing class. As you both know I inscribe like a draftsman or architect, when those professions included hand stretched lines and lettering. Often I am complemented on my pen to paper scribing skills, and somehow it seems to perhaps make more of a difference than maybe it should.

Although my selected high school was a college preparatory engineering institution, several hands-on electives afforded me the confidence to try new things. Entering ninth grade I had yet to pick up a single power tool, although desiring it greatly. Laughingly, by the time my opportunity came to cut or drill something I was traumatically afraid of them, my fricking power tool fright perhaps befalling me honestly after BigBird's years of shouting and claims I'd lose a finger. And then, the feeling of a properly laid welding bead became one of my more satisfying life experiences.

Incredibly and indelibly for all I fricking missed, what stays with me today is powerful, well earned, and revered.

Shoulda

I shoulda been a motorcycle dirtbike racer. More than anything I held such desire. Concerning my fears, my insecurities and my hurts, I thought proper healing could occur if escaping my horrid home life and afforded to do what I longed for. Believing my brilliance would bubble up and blossom if allowed to try, if only given a chance to show what I could do, and not assuming where I would come up short or fearing what might go wrong. At 13 years old I became proud owner of a dirtbike bought with my own damn money, the first objective step towards my dream come true, my number one big-ass cool thing in life. I wholly believed in the possibility to live out loud as my opportunistic self and as I so desired, if only given the chance of one single fucking attempt. Alas no, such dream out louds were disallowed.

Coulda

I coulda been a high school lacrosse athlete and beyond. I held much of the passion intent and desire, the possibilities lingered in front of me teasingly, and there I loitered. I wanted to make a run at it but couldn't, neither able to embrace the sport fully nor walk away from the game entirely. On the verge of tasting the appropriate lacrosse work ethic needed to succeed at something, I hovered hauntingly, looking down at the open grave awaiting my arrival, my name headstoned by the drugs themselves.

I coulda been a nationally competitive indoor short track ice speedskater. After spending much of my life on skates, someone saw more in me than I thought possible of myself. I was afforded not only sponsorship but also scholarship to give the sport a try. My appreciation grew for the technique, discipline, and training. Awhile sadly, the legacy pain deceitfully covered my mind's eye to see.

To see if I might be worth a shit at something, on skates or otherwise. My life was too much a mess to understand that pushing a little harder might have been worth it. I teetered there, marking time for something to push me one way or another…just waiting, waiting, and waiting.

Woulda

I woulda been a car designer or engineer, maybe like the then-unknown-to-me story of Carol Shelby who rose to high performance automotive success making his own specialty models for Ford Motor Company. Supercharged by my infatuation with building those modified plastic models, I raced towards such high-octane reverie. Alongside these my pre-high school auto intentions was my father, us planning for my thrilling advanced academic future at General Motors Institute in Michigan. I was sure to later be working in Detroit for one of the main American car companies, yes-yes I saw it, I saw such clear vision for quite a while, clear enough and close enough to almost taste and touch it.

Hah, henceforward the human herding…the literal terror I faced at home, the rapid escalation of fucking fanatical fright while the clock ran down on my adolescent interval, well, fact literal I then stomped into a dismally darkened corner where perchance my upcoming substance abuse was a given. One by one my dreams fizzled, my balloons of hope popped…pop, pop, pop…my desires dismantled and demolished. One ladder step after another, much as I aspired to climb out of my shitty fucking fear-filled life, my muddied shoes slipped off the rungs and I only traveled down, down, down, not up.

Glossary

Here is the decipher of my dictional voice, my mystical words defined. With exacting guidance, I sling my speech intentionally. Then en route, viably the meanings run astray and a semantics tug of war begins.

To me, clarity and details fucking matter, so not wanting to cause any confuzzlements, henceforth here my declarative spillage, just so you fricking know.

AF. As Fuck, extreme, all the way. Attempting to present as mediocrely PC at times, hence I use AF instead. **AF.**

Aka. Also known as, or another name for. Here my lazy rudimentary grammar usage. **Aka.**

Belief. A solid state believing. For me only, a known thinking farthest past feel, an advanced thought that is now a conclusive and formulated knowing. A known certainty that I try to put forth like truth. I *believe* in trying to tell the truth, I *believe* honesty is my utmost fucking humanoid action. Belief is the highest functionally cognitive character of my eight-member Consciousness Continuum Collection, sitting on top of thought and highest atop feel, respectively. **Belief.**

Benjamins. Aka Bennies, aka $100 bills because Benjamin Franklin is on the hundred. **Benjamins.**

Clack-clack. My laptop, aka typing on my laptop. Initially named for the loose and clacky keys of my 15-year-old Trek-issued Dell, hah, the darn studly stallion is somewhat still kicking. Horrifically, several times the old Dell mysteriously shut down or wouldn't work during the writing of this here your book. Mortified to lose more of my me-to-you work, with monies I did not have I finally purchased a new Dell in early 2021 when living with Uncle Ralph in Jackson. Not casting to construct and shove pins into an instant bad-mojo killer-karma voodoo doll, but old clacky works better. Without internet at my cabin and unable to upload the newest version of this bird brain document to the One Drive cloud, I deemed old clacky a worn-out workhorse and pinned the donkey's tale on him for put out to pasture. Although the new clacky's keys don't quite clack like old clacky, I like the nearly adorable nametag so I think I will keep him and hug him and love him and squeeze him, trying not to curse out loud so fricking much at his shitty fucking mouse touchpad and limited dysfunctional hardware interface. **Clack-clack.**

Congruence. For me only…a term decoded as transparency when laid atop my core oracle, existing and remaining in alignment with my intentions or guidelines set. If I say something, I should fricking do that shit. If claiming intentions to do some sorta thing, I try my utmost to get the damn thing done, even if late. If defining how I intend to live, I do not go far outside the rules set for myself. To me, congruence means I am not in conflict with the words, actions, behaviors etcetera that I believe are correct for me, by my measure. Certainly an implication of truth and remaining core to self is understood and in play here. Congruence may associate with, or otherwise be disguised as integrity, honesty, values, morals, or what the flip ever. To me, congruence means I do the shit I say and don't fucking waffle between saying one thing and doing another, aka talking crap and walking bullshit. **Congruence.**

Consciousness Continuum Collection. My precisely defined list of eight inner core oracle descriptors, presented with outside world conscious application. I mostly hold firm the proper meanings of my bird brain diction yet as I began to write this here your book, I tripped slightly during a few moments of up and down word twister crossover. Regarding me, my clarity is critical and several groupings of similar notions arose, hence requiring pause, close attention, and delineation. Firstly, I split hairs between the words can, will, act, and able. Second was the proper separation of truth honesty and trust, with a quick to follow analysis of peace calm and beauty. Fricking fourth was the migraine-inducing exercise of spelling out the difference amongst values, virtues, morals, and ethics. Lastly came my Consciousness Continuum Collection, an encapsulation of the following clarified usages: Feel, think, believe, wish, pray, dream, hope, and faith. For me, the final set of eight sometimes interchanged concepts was the most critical group of characters to get right. I spent more than ten hours granularly scrutinizing each one in relation to the other, by my measure. After pinpointing their respective articulations, I arrived at their proper value and usage, thereafter used reliably throughout your here pages. I certainly do not intend to push these definitions to the world but want to make transparent my diction position.

Perhaps for you this is just semantics, yet to me language matters supremely and I'd rather say too much with stringency, than risk being misunderstood. **Consciousness Continuum Collection**.

Core oracle. Inferring my all of me, my central meaning, my heart brain, my main inner operating system. My body or mind does not function, my breath does not breathe, my heart does not beat nor exist apart from my core oracle. This origination zone is not a ghostlike pin and rather, my core oracle is my unadulterated truth, it is my comprehensive foundational known and knowing, well, hah…it is that which lies resoundingly within me. After much scrutiny during exploring the concepts of 'heart & soul', I instead found there to be much more to me, thus referring to such derivation as core oracle. **Core oracle.**

Dirty-ego. A self-fabricated phrase meaning the undesirable workings of yours truly. We all have ego and I believe we need ego, I need ego, healthy-ego that is. I define dirty-ego as the subconscious part of me that battles the conscious part of me, whereas my subconscious inflated dirty-ego thinks I am atmospherically better than my conscious true self. Conversely and more important, my healthy-ego feels I am least slightly better or opportunistic than my conscious self-doubting loser-loser punk-ass-bitch lowlife dropout junkie loser self. I attribute my healthy-ego as the driving force of much my motivation, envisioned life possibilities, willingness, grit, self-starting, discipline, tenacity, stick-to-itiveness, let-go-of-itiveness, and fuck tons more. I believe without my healthy-ego I would have died before the age of 19. Yes I quietly chastise the presence of my dirty-ego, and also accept the factual reality I possess it, and will never completely shake it, this my unclean and otherwise unwished-for piece of me. **Dirty-ego.**

Dream. As defined by and for me, dreaming holds a positive connotation, aka an operational sliver or slice of my healthy-ego hard at work. Dream is a partially thought-out possibility, not an unrealistic fantasy. Specifically here to say…I dream that one day I can live as I desire and behave as I intend, once I do the darn work. For me, a dream boasts associated enhancing awhile life emphasizing qualities, least a faint outline of an image desired. For illustrative purposes: I *dream* this lottery ticket I bought will at minimum pay for itself, least I tried, and the odds are possible, however fanatically slim. I *dream* one day to own a log cabin in the woods of my own, long as I keep saving the damn money dedicated towards the cause. Dream aids to comprise my Consciousness Continuum Collection. **Dream.**

Faith. For me, faith holds a positive connotation…trusting something to be, remain, or become as so thought. Faith means trying to commit to the realistic albeit far off notion. Most often my nemesis is the trickster within: Incorrectly thinking a non-reality is true, because of self-shame, self-blame, self-doubt, or unverifiable outside forces. For me only, faith dream hope and belief are internally generated and truthful can-do standings, while pray and wish are unwanted and misaligned stagnant sittings. My mind's eye views praying and wishing as sitting out on a street corner curb waiting for a miracle to fall from the clouds…waiting, waiting, and waiting. I rather intend and try to generate and sustain my own momentum instead of counting the days for some imaginary force to jumpstart my life or direction.

No suggestions, implications, or intentions to preach my notions and rather, here a sharing of my clarified definitions, be it my personal beliefs and truths, by my measure. For illustrative purposes: I have *faith* that if I stick to my plan, stay alert, and adjust accordingly, I'll be ok, or good enough anyway. Faith is a member in sound standing amid my Consciousness Continuum Collection. **Faith.**

Feel. A feeling. For me only, a sensing or awareness of an emotional or conceptual idea of something I do or do not yet understand, something not always totally defined, a suspicion possibly uncertain or unknown yet it resonates within me. For illustrative purposes: I *feel* the desire to do what is good for me, awhile avoid what is bad, but I am not sure what to do, how to do it, how to start, how to sustain it, and sometimes I'm not sure it's even possible for me. I *feel* I should go visit my neighbor to see if he is ok, because he's behaving weird and it seems like he is in some true trouble, but I'm not at all sure, I could be wrong, maybe he's just overdoing life. Feel is the floor-rank and starter position of my thinking threes, then and if appropriately, leading to *think* then perhaps graduating to the highest level, *believe*. Feel exists, however confidently, within my Consciousness Continuum Collection. **Feel.**

FUBAR. Really messed up, some supremely screwed-up shit. Literally translated as: Fucked Up Beyond All Recognition. **FUBAR.**

Hon. A Baltimore slang salutation term meaning honey, or dear, or hey you, or similar. Thousands of times I heard, "Hey hon...", or "Hey dere hon…", dere being a version of there, like hey you, hello there, in Baltimore City blue collar speak. This diction most prominent on the east side of the City but over time, hon became a revered Baltimore area greeting. **Hon.**

Hope. By my definition, for me only, hope holds a positive connotation, an intent for possible and most likely probable events to occur as desired, if I do my fricking part. Critical to hope is maintaining the willingness to endure the suffering in favor of the possibilities. Hope tightly aligns my controllable self with my intentional aspirations.

I believe the word hope is a superpower, able to sustain life even when all additional systems might otherwise be shutting down, truly, factually, fucking for real. Many times what keeps me from maintaining hope is the half-baked notion I am standing in the midst of the worst thing of my life, which I am usually not, I then realize this damaging falsehood once I do inventory and analysis. For me only, hope faith and dream are internally generated conscious and true positions that I create or take, like cooling off under a clear mountain creek waterfall, while pray and wish are unthinking stagnant and swampy conditions I get stuck in. My mind's eye views praying and wishing as sitting around waiting for a miracle to fall from the heavens, just waiting and waiting. I rather intend and try, to generate and sustain my own get up and go drive instead of time wasting it 'round town for some unknown and fucking fictitious force to jumpstart my life or action.

No attempts to sling or preach my shit and rather, sharing my clarified crap, my personal beliefs and truths, by my measure. Sometimes hope is maintained by just hanging in there, by not giving up or quitting. For illustrative purposes: I *hope* to generate the courage to meet with my boss and say exactly what I planned, nothing more.

I *hope* I can stay disciplined tomorrow and finish the work I committed to. I *hope* I can resist the urge to quit, I believe I can in-fact hold on, I can, I really *can* do that shit, damn the doubters, just hold on, just maintain, don't quit, don't quit, don't…fricking…quit. Hope is one of eight members making up my Consciousness Continuum Collection. **Hope.**

Jacksons. $20 bills because President Andrew Jackson from the 1830s is on the 20. **Jacksons.**

Jimmies. Colorful candies used atop ice cream. In Baltimore I never heard the sprinkles descriptor, all I knew of was jimmies. A regional alternative term, like bubbler…huh, say what hon? I call that bubbler a water fountain. Want some pop? What's that? Oh, no thanks, I call that pop stuff soda. **Jimmies.**

Kicks. Shoes, sneakers. Cool shoes but not always necessarily cool, just shoes. **Kicks.**

MathTest. My fabricated mash-up phrase meaning to face challenge without emotion, hah, even when verifiably it *is* an emotional situation. The ability to get the thing done anyway, without delay or excess worry. I face the activity and try my best try regardless of skill, preparation, or understanding. I attempt to enter the challenge with focused intention of effort, no matter the struggle. I walk in with a non-negotiable position: There is only one way, to try, aka do what I can, best I can. Sometimes moderate to maximum courage is required for the MathTest. Accepting the at-time reality of not possessing the necessary knowledge or talent required for maximum results or completion, I show the fuck up anyway and lay myself out there, aka just do the damn work. I fear not the possible slip-up's or results outside of my best effort. I try to leave behind the worry, stress, fear, self-blame, and excessive expectations. I try not to assume, I try not to self-judge, and I try to accept total responsibility for everything, from my intention to the final result. Sometimes this is just a *is what it is* orientation, if otherwise arriving unprepared or unsure, whether additional time or preparation opportunities existed or not. I try to not let any dirty-ego ride along, rather stick to the objective truth of the situation, therefore not worrying about embarrassment, ridicule, or teasing, aka fuck 'em all, I tried my best damn try. **MathTest.**

Monkey on my back. Meaning drug addiction. Drug addiction being the fucked-up thing fixed squarely on my back, positively positioned where I cannot reach or get to, even if I possessed long monkey arms. Decades after shaking drugs, I struggled to creatively honor my clean time. Eventually my bro pal Brian Jansen at Capitol City Tattoo in Madison inked a ratherish large commemorative piece between my shoulder blades, a Buddhist monk deep in practice. By way of Brian's expert hand, I finally traded in my monkey, for instead the inked monk on my back. **Monkey on my back.**

OG. Original Gangster, aka originator, aka founder, aka old-school, aka there at the beginning. **OG.**

PAB. Punk Ass Bitch. An accurate descriptive and legacy phrase I only use referring to myself. Punk ass bitch, aka punk, aka asshole, aka unruly and lacking much concern for others, aka a sans-empathy I don't give a fuck about anything or anybody dirtbag that was me. **PAB.**

Pimpin'. Aka pimping. Sharing selling or showing off, bragging, displaying proudly, maybe dirty-ego-presented. Something known or within our possession or on our person or presented by us. **Pimpin'.**

Pray. Referencing me myself only, pray carries a negative connotation, a calling out to a far-away figmental savior. Broadcasting silently or out loud for a miraculous turnaround, a happening outside of reasonability. A lost emotional state far outside my true self, away from my authentic here and now. I try not to use the word pray within my truthful and intentional forward-vision diction. I believe the word pray is incorrect for me. I attempt to use words appropriately. For me only, dream faith and hope are internally originated while pray and wish are inanimate hold-ups. My mind's eye views praying and wishing as spiritually stationed, awaiting a supernatural windfall to drape across my shoulders just waiting, waiting, and waiting. My endeavor rather, to kickstart and maintain my own propulsion, instead of dillydallying around and killing these here adored times-of-life for some false witness to one day happen upon me. No shoving of my shit is going on here, no offloading of these here my bird brain pecking's to you and rather, a sharing of my clarified definers, my personal beliefs and truths, by my measure. For illustrative purposes: I *pray* a miracle befalls me…*pray-pray*…yes, $10Million placed in my lap would erase all my troubles, all of them, but otherwise I'm fricking screwed. Such deposit from oh-thank-you Fantasiaville would fix everything, but I refuse to waste money on those stupid lottery tickets. Pray hovers above yet holds membership to my Consciousness Continuum Collection. **Pray.**

QPM. Quite Possibly Maybe. A mashup phrase resonating with me. Used when maybe or possibly or quite possibly is just not nearly enough. Meaning an advanced or complex stage of included individual components of the idiom. Meaning yes, for sure bro yes, aka it is as such or is gonna happen. **QPM.**

ROI. Return On Investment. Evaluating or analyzing what the frick comes back, counterpart to what is spent devoted or given away. Technically a business term and still, applicable to multitudes of life conditions top to bottom. Alongside a plentitude of business-related concerns, accurate ROI analysis requires deep work, many times traveling three or four or five steps below surface level impressions. Those shiny top-level sheathings often lay eagerly, hoping to later, hah, bite me in the ass after I assume, or idiotically behave quick-to-judge. **ROI.**

Run what you brung. An old hotrod car racing phrase meaning to just participate anyway, regardless of the condition of our equipment. Originally addressing the dilemma of competitors when something on the car breaks but the machine still runs and rolls. Although the collective racecar might not be in top notch ideal shape, we should keep racing because of the collected education by practicing and experimenting, even with less-than-complete equipment or conditions. A phrase I believe is hyper-applicable to me and my world, yes-yes…accepting the truth of change and my need to remain flexible to whatever arrives next. *Run what you brung*, I have said numerous times out loud, reminding myself to just go and keep going until physically fucking forced to stop.

Including when something on my bike or motorcycle or even human frame breaks, when the weather warms a little too much and the snow is now slow, when my elbow is torn open but I'm still 20 miles away from medical assistance, or when I discover a sticky wheel bearing right before starting an inline skate race. I have said this phrase at work, while traveling, when my daily driver car has a problem, within romantic relationships, and hah, after starting a drag racing run when the rear wheels break traction, sending my snarling Camaro sideways. Then I feather the clutch slightly while keeping my foot slammed to the floor full gas anyway, thinking I'll get it straightened out before hitting the oncoming concrete wall. **Run what you brung.**

Sans. Meaning minus of, being without, absent of, left out, or apart from. An adorable little word I learned in France and one I utilize often, elsewise my foundational diction rather sparse. **Sans.**

Slingin'. Aka slinging. A term describing us street level dealers selling our drugs. Construing the hawking, giving, sharing, pitching of things or words to sister and brother humanoids. **Slingin'.**

Sporting. Possessing, aka proudly displaying. Similar to pimpin' but not as dirty-ego showy. **Sporting.**

Thought. A thinking thought is an advanced, more developed, or better formed feeling. My thoughts are perceptions of concepts realized or not, known or uncertain, something I need to work on some more, so to believe it and not just think it. Thus an unexplored, unrealized or unknown belief, aka a strong perception. For illustrative purposes: I *think* I know what is best for me and I try to behave as such, but not always do I do it and sometimes *I* think doing the opposite is better. Thought sits confidently with my Consciousness Continuum Collection peers. **Thought.**

Truman Show. A movie starring Jim Carey. Opening as a quirky comedy, the script goes deep quickly and leaves me wondering about many more things than before sitting down with popcorn. A movie lingering longer in my think box, forcing me to reassess my truthful life situation again and again, aka check myself because everything is not always so clear. I sling the term Truman Show to mean the state or short-term residence in a clueless alternative world to that of reality or truth. **Truman Show.**

Tokemaster was my precious marijuana bong, aka smoking device. A two-foot-tall clear tube I owned for over a decade, approximately two inches in diameter with a closed bottom and an open top. About four inches from the lower end was a smaller offshoot tube extending outside the main body, only a few inches long itself and had a brass bowl affixed to its uppermost point. I installed a small screen in the brass bowl, filled the bowl with pot, and filled the main bong body with about six inches of water. The daily practice was the same: Do-not, do-not, do-not spill the skanky bong water, fill the bowl with some sweet bud, linger a lit lighter longer overtop of the weed material, plant my mouth inside the top of the bong then suck long-time.

Sucking provided the fan under the flame, burning the goods in the bowl, thus inhaling the smoke through the main body of the bong. Factually, my two-foot-tall Tokemaster afforded me a lung capacity workout, hah, on and off for 19 hours each day.

In the late 1970s I knew not an outlet to purchase such illegal devices. Nowhere I knew in Baltimore displayed bongs or even small pot-smoking pipes. Once when running to Washington DC, I saw the strangest thing I could dream of, even if tripping on multiple doses of LSD…uh, what is that? …a retail store dedicated entirely to drug paraphernalia. My reality was thrown into a tailspin as I stood there bewildered, trying to understand if what sat in front of me was real. Cautiously, I entered the drug implement den. I knew next to nothing about anything and mostly by process of elimination, I accurately presumed all paraphernalia was illegal in Maryland. I did not realize however, that in the District of Columbia and under the shade of our nation's Capital, such drug gear was totally legal. That day I purchased my Tokemaster, in addition to several packs of rolling papers for smoking joints, a few small pot pipes, and two short purpose-built metal cocaine snorting straws. Over the next few weeks I returned to DC several times, purchasing more and more drug equipment for myself and coming back to Baltimore with similar gifts for stoner friends. In this way and more, I considered Washington DC a very cool place, maybe too cool. Years later the irony amused me. Marion Barry, the celebrated two-term mayor of DC was arrested and served prison time for smoking crack cocaine on undercover FBI videotape, imaginably using a pipe from one of his city's local retail establishments. **Tokemaster.**

Toot suite. Aka immediately wise, straight away, right now, getting that shit done on the spot, and aka as our Boyd so eloquently and frequently says, "Let's do this". Originating from the French term, *tout de suite* which means the same, aka hey Zippy, hurry that shit up s'il vous plait, if you please. **Toot suite.**

Wish. By my definition, relating to this one here singular oneself only me, wish carries a negative connotation. Wish: A longing for something to materialize or disappear without doing the work, likely imagining an unrealistic process or result. A wish is something placed or erased in my desired future without acting to make the change happen. I try not to use the word wish within my truthful and for-me intentional forward-vision diction. For me only, hope faith and dream assist me where I want to go, or properly aid where I intend to detour. Me as myself, pray and wish are sedentary fly-paper settings, aka sitting ass-stuck. Within my control, I try to navigate my life one day at a time, and utilize when I need to, my believed and acted-upon faith hopes and dreams. No subliminal slingin', pimpin' or pushing of my bird brain speak meant upon you and rather, crystalizing my documented language, my intentional movements, and my truth, by my measure. For illustrative purposes: I *wish* Billy the Goat from next door would stop eating my fucking flowers but Billy's hooman scares me to death, so I will shut up and not chirp a single peep.

Possibly just a play on words or semantics by other's measure of me thus still, this an intentional preciseness I take seriously, by my measure. Wish is the final eighth alphabetical member comprising my Consciousness Continuum Collection, that being: Feel, think, believe, pray, wish, dream, faith and of course, like duh, the superpower hope. **Wish.**

Raindrop

I am not like a raindrop
or like a wave
not a waterfall
nor a puddle
not so small
but much-much bigger.

My small focused spot disappears
grandiose grace takes over
resting in the importance of the present
and also the insignificance of the past.

My shoes make but one footprint at a time
only in this moment do I truly live
pausing to see it, intending to breathe it
this beauty, this supreme value of time.

I am not like a raindrop
I am the community of water
I reside as part of the world's ocean
part of this treasureful family
part of this abundant place
alive here now, within this wondrous life.

Three

~

I Am NOT Writing a Fucking Book

Thinking not this here your book weirdly excessive or irresponsibly mistimed, I attempt an unravel of perhaps the wickedest-smart question ever, "Dad what in the hell are you doing and why now…you aren't dying are you?"

Chapter Three, I Am NOT Writing A Fucking Book ~

On a gorgeous fall day in 2017, ahh, just beautiful, barely a cloud in the sky…my buddy Ray Petro was doing what Ray Petro usually does on a workday afternoon, he was going for a mountainbike ride on his familiar trails close to home in Cleveland.

This particular path was a trail Ray knew well. He chose to ride a little harder than normal on such a stellar day, enjoying the crisp air speeding around his chosen loop but once on the bike, Ray's life direction took a horrific and tragic turn.

Neither of you met Ray Petro in person by the time I finished writing this here your book. Although not yet meeting my dear friend Ray, the man who invented indoor mountain biking, you certainly know of him, us enjoying years of riding inside his Milwaukee Indoor Mountainbike Park. Ray still owns his original bike park in Cleveland, after the second Milwaukee park then closed. Cleveland is also, by the way like whatever, where me and my slightly younger sister Beth were born.

Ray is an exceptionally good mountainbiker, after navigating many difficult riding areas around North America. For several years by the time I met and began working with Ray, myself I was working to shed some of my every day and undesirable human habits like assuming and judging. Assuming I know the deal and judging people by their appearance or general surface-level persona. Gosh dang, I caught myself doing it again on the first day I met Ray. Slipping up and judging Ray was painful in two ways. First, I was trying to live out my mantra of not judging blaming or assuming, so I lost that battle, guilty as charged. Second, my dirty-ego judgments of Ray were about to hurt me physically. I knew better but before we pedaled next to each other for even 10 feet, I assumed Ray was an average or maybe even kinda slow rider based on the size waist of the jeans he wore, totally judgy bird. I was then shocked by not only his skill but also with his unassuming speed.

Inside the Cleveland park we threw on our pads, then took off pedaling the cross-country loop. Ray was in front because duh, he knew where to go. He was also excited to show me several key features within the massive park. Ray's Cleveland sits inside an old brick factory, a ginormous brick smokestack towers over the place, and the signature smokestack is visible for miles around. Once off the concrete and rolling along the hand built elevated wood decking XC course, I immediately found myself struggling to catch back up to Ray. He pedaled away from me, him talking the whole time in a relaxed and calm voice. Ray had not noticed I fell behind only seconds after starting our ride, and hah, I was already out of earshot. I was so badly out of breath, I could not have responded coherently anyway, if I heard him or not. Ray rode with a smooth and flowing speed, placing his front and rear tires effortlessly and precisely where they should go. Meanwhile, I struggled to even stay close to my skilled leader, while banging my front tire into the plywood sidewalls almost every fifteen feet. Even though I raced mountainbikes for 17 years and nine of those years as a pro, Ray was kicking my ass. I was not out of shape, but I was certainly, out of my element.

Back outside to that bright sunny fall afternoon on the local Cleveland trails he knew so well, in conditions he expertly navigated hundreds of times before…Ray lost control of his front wheel. It happened that while going around a turn with moderate speed, Ray slipped in the leaves and fell to the ground. As sometimes happens, and the same something has happened to me myself least eight times so far, Ray fell off his bike and awoke a little while later, missing some amounts of mental recall moments. I think when we bang our heads hard enough, our brain blacks out the memory of the impact, conceivably protecting us from the trauma during such an accident, hah, absurdly serving as a brief organically occurring timeout. Logically this lapse of memory gives us a break, least a short while, until when we are capably cognizant then hopefully, better prepared to handle the aftermath of our injury. I really do not know the facts on the subject, I'm just talking out of my bird butt here. Yet based on my 100+ concussions, including nine occurrences when I either lost consciousness, lost my vision, lost my memory, or a combination of the three, based on that, I reach these here my deductions, aka why our memory lapses during a brain injury.

Ray did not comprehend much time passing during his knockout period, but something far more troubling appeared, something scarier than Ray ever experienced before, motherfucking ever, Ray could not move a muscle. Ray describes his body position as laying in a weird twister move much like the popular yoga pose of downward dog. His arms were collapsed under him, and he was unable to move not a nano body part except his mouth, well, kind of. Struggling to even breathe, although Ray could technically speak, his mouth was jammed in the dirt.

Thankfully, a trail jogger happened along shortly after Ray awoke. She asked if Ray was ok or if he needed anything. Ray spurt out enough of an explanation to ask if she could please move him. Understandably, the woman did not want to touch Ray, fearing she might make his injuries worse. Helpful jogger lady finally assisted, repositioning his front-of-face slightly sideways so he was not kissing the ground. Without wasting more time, the lucky-for-Ray lady took off, promising to get help quick as possible. Ray faded in and out of consciousness laying alone in the woods, struggling to breathe, and unable to wiggle even a *this little piggy* finger. Ray hoped silently for the rescue squad to arrive soon because otherwise, he was not sure he would survive the day.

Ray describes it as mere minutes later awaking in a hospital, tubes and wires attached across his entire person. Ray's mother and sister were standing by his side when he awoke, a situation making no sense to him whatsoever. His mom and sister did not live in Cleveland, they lived further away in South Carolina…how in the world did they get here? Ray was very confused. Despite having so many people rushing about helping him, he still could not move any part of his body. Not wave a toe, not shrug his shoulders, not even lift his head. Ray was completely paralyzed. Speculation says, when Ray slipped on the leaves, his head hit a tree and Ray laid there with a broken neck until the hero female trail runner happened along. The ambulance paramedics whisked him off to the nearby hospital when Ray was either unconscious or just missed the recall. And now after a handful of surgeries three years later, Ray has regained the use of his shoulders and some slight movement of his arms but is without feeling or functionality in any of his fingers, like living with lobster claws. Also and from chest down, Ray is exactly paralyzed.

It appears Ray will live out his days skirting around atop his electric-powered wheelchair, and assisted in and out of his at-home mechanized hospital bed. Ray is aided by his sister who is now his roommate and has a federally appointed care person to feed him, bathe him, help him operate life, and maybe someday soon, help Ray get back on a bike. Obviously, the bike his Cleveland team is building exists far beyond a traditional pedal mountainbike. Rather, Ray's bike is an electric-powered three-wheeled low-to-the-ground high-performance recumbent tricycle with off-road knobby tires and mechanically-savvy shocks front and rear. An elaborate set-up for sure, the comprehensive effort aimed at helping Ray one day navigate the trails again. Much of Ray's hope and purpose in life is the plan to get back on a bike, any kind of bike, and prance through some wooded sections once more, or thrice.

Ray is labeled a 'highly functioning quadriplegic', possessing no ability to move his torso or use his hands effectively. For Ray the former alcoholic and cocaine addict now in recovery from his abused substances, for Ray the former self-employed carpenter turned business owner and his one true passion was plainly riding his bike, Ray struggled for about a year to otherwise find meaning in his current and future reality. And then, Ray just got back to fricking business. With the help of his aide Kelvin and sister Rikki, Ray works from home giving direction to his amazing Cleveland bike park team, and Ray started a new company building high quality customizable home stereo speakers, sold online. Ray also holds mental business plans for another new operation or three. Despite the consumption of necessary heavy daily doses of nerve painkillers, Ray Petro remains incredibly active and engaged with life. Ray is surprisingly upbeat these days and I talk to Ray often. You can check out my podcast episode #7 featuring my bud Ray as co-host.

Ray speaks in detail of the accident and shares the loving and humble gratitude he still feels for being alive one more day.

The human spirit amazes me, especially the one inside of my friend Ray. Ray possesses a realistic run what you brung roll-up-your-damn-sleeves and get that shit done mentality. Several times I have blurted my skeptical words out loud, doubtful predictions of such bravery myself, if ever required to operate at partial or full-loss capacity. Maybe I am not giving myself enough credit, maybe yet hum…similar to a conversation topic Ray and I discuss in our podcast, with rare exception can we hoomans truly empathize and understand the hardship of our brothers and sisters.

Another such spectacular soul is Andre McDonald, aka the beautiful and supremely loved brother from another mother. Andre, aka Dre and I worked together decades ago at Mount Washington Bike Shop and we clicked right away, establishing a powerful connection and today we try to stay close still. Dre is one of the most joyful, enthusiastic, outgoing, and honest humans I know, even as he now operates life as a paraplegic from his mechanical wheelchair. When Nora and I flew to Baltimore in 2016 to buy the Camaro back from Uncle Charlie, we got together with Andre. The first night re-owning the car, Nora and I went cruising to meet up with some Baltimore hotrod buddies. We converged at an old favorite hangout, Mike's Pizzeria in the Pikesville community of Baltimore County.

Andre showed up for the slight reunion, arriving in his handicap-friendly van. In no time flat, Dre climbed into his wheelchair by himself and was rolling around the Pikesville parking lot making new friends, laughing about old times, and oogling over the cars. Later in the evening as we all sat inside eating pizza, Dre retold the story…racing his dirtbike indoors at a Arenacross race, the throttle misfunctioned and he landed wrong off a jump, hence taking the use of his legs away from him. Andre's positive energy seemed almost too good to be true, although I knew him to be genuine. I asked Dre how long after the accident did he accept the reality of his new life, and finally get his positive mood back?

Puzzled, Dre looked at me for a few seconds…"Got it back? I never lost it Rog, what am I gonna do? It was an accident and it happened, I never got bummed, I just changed the way I got around, that's all Rog, what is there not to be positive about?".

Wow, I thought then and now, that's an amazing perspective, and not one I am sure I could maintain, I'm not so sure at all, yet such this the shining star I am lucky to have in my life, The Amazing Andre.

Additionally, there is the outrageously witty and ginormously hearted one-legged man, Big Dave Buberl, roommates with my right coast bestie David Duvall. In the 15+ years knowing Big Dave, I never heard a negative word flow from that guy's mouth. After suffering a horrific lower leg injury in a streetbike gravel-road motorcycle accident, Big Dave was close to death before lifesaving emergency care was provided, ironically by a passing-by backwoods mountainbiker in Harrisonburg Virginia, aka a fucking hero.

Big Dave had everything to lose in that Virginia forest, but the totality of all he left behind was one lower leg, soon to be replaced by an operational prosthetic.

Perhaps some of us, hum, maybe myself included actually, would give up. Reasonably, I could not regroup after such a tragedy, yes, tenably then…lost and adrift, wallowing in sadness and misery, depressed and immobile at home but no fricking way, not Big Dave. Working a hectic and physically demanding fulltime job detailing private aircraft at BWI airport in Baltimore, Big Dave adventures around the country most every weekend on his three-wheeler Harley Davidson and has a huge smile painted on his face 24/7. Facing the mirror, my confidence waffles that I could make such a comeback.

In 2016, Big Dave and David Duvall took time off from work and delivered my recently repurchased Camaro to me. The guys drove their big truck with my beloved trailered hotrod halfway across the country in one day, a 15-hour drive. A cat and mouse game then ensued with me insisting to pay them for their time and expense, and still they refused. So I did the only thing left to do, hah, deep inside David's luggage, I sneakily hid seven Bennies for payment the next morning before I left for work. When I returned home later that day, of course I found the $700 cash money sitting on my kitchen counter. Miraculously, David found the money before they drove back east then he dropped the hot potato in the kitchen.

David Duvall and Big Dave Buberl, true rockstars both of them. Beyond further explainable diction lies the level of respect and care profoundly cemented in my heart for such beloved family members, aka my friends.

Thenupon now, what the frick is the essence of retelling Ray's redefined life story, while tagging my bro Dre-Dre and Big Dave? I divulge that several times over the span of this here life I have lost focus, I distracted, meaning I got mentally lazy. Within said stretches of easy breezy sunny days, I irresponsibly lounged. I rested assumingly, thinking the land nothing but luxuriant. I expected the simple things in life will remain for me and frankly, I took them for granted. The certain change-a-coming I dismissed, hah, I mislaid my legacy hardness, I mistakenly shunned the shadow. I turned off my conscious thought radar, I forgot some of my own hard-fought lessons. Mindlessly, I muddled my priorities, and yes to say, pathetically, I wandered past my purpose.

Ah those blissful months, the happy years…well, while the while factually I lied to myself, I lied, thinking the supreme joy will continue as-is, ah, it's fine, I have nothing to worry about, nothing big anyway, aka big dummy stupidhead hooman that's me. Fooling thyself fully, I rested placidly with my vacation noggin shoved shoulders-deep into the proverbial beach. I stayed busier than was physically comfortable, or healthy. Stupidly, I slighted my extreme need to keep first things fucking first.

I am comfortable when seeped in pain, yes, I know it well.

Work-busting my ass, sweating, bleeding, pushing hard or mashed up against hardness rests within me as commonplace, verifiably…natural. Hard feels accurately appropriate, more so than taking the paved smooth path. The hits, the hard shit, the pain, the bad crap operates on its own special frequency to track me down and crash the party at will, especially during times of massive glory and ease. Much as I desire, I cannot punch the pause button of the stay-right-here-right-now state of my glorious life, no, no such thumb-smashing options exist. Fruitless the hope…to continue blissfully as-is for the remainder of my poppa bird organic human eternity, my maybe 80-ish years total. The occasions I do spin my wheels aimlessly and saunter longer than I should, regrettably I lose the critical awareness of my peripheral vision. Those times when I miss keeping purposeful priorities up front the most, I expose myself to take a fall. When not alert, when not consciously aware and along comes a hit, often I fall hard, extremely hard.

Thereupon hold up and wait a second, I must say, I must clarify, please do not misunderstand me. No way do I mean to highlight my proprietary fear during sun's-out-season, not to cower or hide under skies of blue. I do not fear life, or doubt myself too much while wrapped in shiny-shiny placidity. But I really should live it up while I can, and I try to do just that. The while, orienting to stay alert and maintain a fun fluidity. I try to collect more common sense not less, I advance my awareness, I sharpen my intention, and I better define my purpose. So now, while I can, I have sidestepped the rats a racing speedway to pause, run upstream, and take years void of competing amongst all them other sister 'n brother rodents. Rather here I sit, sit, doing the one and only thing that truly matters, diligently tasking away on this letter to you, thus keeping first things fucking first, by my measure.

So Says You

Most of my way through writing this here your book, I asked you both for any detail I should include. Essentially your mentions had already preexisted, then I added some clarity and callouts, so thank you for the special spice. Recapped here are your inquisitions and throughout the different dusty doorstop volumes, you'll find the detail.

Lauren my precious Birdy:
1. Tell me more about your dad, I didn't know him, he died when I was young.
2. I assume there's stuff in there about the divorce with mom.
3. Why were you, and how did you become a drug addict? And how did you quit?

Travis the Boyd:
1. Why are you so into bikes?
2. How did you go from being a biker to an executive at a large corporation?
3. What was the defining moment when you chose to make helping others your priority? I remember you telling me long ago the most important thing is helping others, how did you arrive at that?
4. Tell me about the other major defining moments in your life.

This Here Chapter Three, I Am NOT Writing a Fucking Book

This third topic chapter is a sectioned collection of written thoughts and feelings attempting to clearly present the notion to you both, why this book and why now?

Singular Focus

To try, to share

A gift...this here looking glass

A story to make you cry, a tale to make you smile

A truthful adventure to perhaps warm you, perhaps lift you

Not to tell, not to teach, not to spell, not to preach

This my tale but no, it is ours, for I you and you me

Your experiences your own, I carry zero fantasy otherwise

Near the root of our dissimilar experiences however, surely exist some
alignments, some similarities, some sameness

As my grandest intention, my best attempt, and from the gross
mass of my loving heart I give you this...my story, my life, this here
my magnum opus.

Getting Good at Walking Away From Her

That's it, screw this, I am fricking done…so sick and tired of the damn arguing. I am walking away from this relationship. I am leaving her, today. Maybe not leaving her forever but least, I am leaving for now, I need a break. I regress…firstly, the last straw snapped in the relationship with your hot momma thirteen years earlier. Brutally hard as exiting was, breaking up the family, leaving the three great loves of my life, being you two and your Jersey mother bird, I did it anyway. The final decision to split with ginger wife one felt wrong on many levels, but the guiding truth star of my correct overall chosen life path led me away from my thus-then greatest of loves with definiteness. Conclusively, the marriage was over. I was absolutely certain divorce was our only possible next step because, otherwise I would have stayed. Otherwise I would have stayed. Otherwise I would have fucking stayed. I would have stayed, if thinking there was a slight hint of possible reconciliation.

Secondly, two years before this newer sick and tired arguing time, I already dropped every ounce of hope Nora and I could remain together into the future. Certainly, well, hum, let me get this right…I decided, I decided the drama-filled family dynamic game show with wife two was not going to continue any longer, no way and not for one more minute. My once dream-imagined-come-true relationship, aka my never-ending-dream-date, aka these birds mate for life, whatever you call it, needs to finally end and end soon, for everyone's sake. The mic-drop moment occurred when I soundly and with perfectly articulated clarity announced to Nora right there in the kitchen, "I want a divorce".

Walking away from women who filled my heart and helped complete my world was turning out to be sort of a tradition with me.

However, as it was this time, thirdly, my leaving her was different. Was my borderline habitual 'leaving her' track record an issue of my impatience or propensity to abandon female relationships too soon? Maybe. Was I playing out my insecurities of trust and retention after 15+ botched love relationships? Probably least somewhat. Does it go even further back to when I was still a little nestling bird and my mother left for good, or when my father dumped me in Detroit for a year, clandestinely? Earthly yes. Was I now being an idiot, was I…was I being judgmental? Probably yes, probably both, an idiotic judgmental bird. Certainly, I acquired the practice of evaluating most things in my life for the overall goodwill benefit versus investment required. I lived to learn and know that shit happens fast and rarely is that flung crap worth sticking around for, once I believe no hope is possible for change. Not just leaving impossible love relationships, but throughout varied situations of my life, I lived to know, when it's time to go, then fricking go. On this particular day however, the nail-in-coffin relationship end-of-it-all indicators commenced weeks before…the dreaded eye rolls, aka resentment, aka the silent togethering-killer. I consulted my handcrafted life notebook before walking away from this aforementioned third woman and found case in point…my rules for living item #43, which at the time said to me:

43. Connect with others who can give me advice, inspire me, and give me direction when I have lost my way.

Hum, you might think…hey dad, I don't see anything in that *rules for living* list number 43 about love or romance or marriage. Well my Birdy and Boyd, please hold that wise thought.

My intentionally-based living patterns were in full swing at that time, echo…over a decade past when me and your mom broke up and, echo-echo…years after Nora left our Coyle Parkway Cottage Grove abode for good. The arguing with the third woman was going down just before I decided to write this here your book-book-booker in earnest.

Frankly, I could not grasp what she was blah-blah-blah saying to me.

Sounded like nothing but gibberish because I was in conflict with her words, aka I did not agree with her speakings. My ears began to bleed, not really, but her words hurt my brain…me need more Tylenol, she trying to explain how this relationship should go, but yet, well, honestly, her words felt all wrong to me. No, no, no…both inside my head I was saying hells-to-the no, and out my mouth I was also saying frick-to-the no. I began to lose my grip of self-control…my emotions began to bubble up close to the tippy-top, approaching surface level and about to blow.

My thinking box decided…no way, once again I was walking away from an amazing woman in my life, once more convinced this shit is not working. I needed to do what seemed correct for me, acting out my total truth, well, minimally I needed a break. I took a timeout from this woman, a woman, well, here it is…a woman not with whom I had ever held her hand. Never gone for a walk in the woods together, had we. This time, I was fed up with a close associate, my bustling business brain Coach Sarah, aka SuperStarSarah Young who was talking too much shit and relentlessly pushing me in a way I did not want to be pushed. For weeks, Sarah was doing exactly what she felt was right, exercising her verbalized thoughts for me to do something she saw as my higher purpose, but hah…a direction I had no-way-no-faith in.

Known to me, least *for* me, that two minds pondering the same 'what's up next' question, understanding two pairs of eyes looking at the same 'what's up next' possibility, that two is better than one, grasping fully this my knowing, I engaged with Coach Sarah. Well, lemme back up a bit my birdies…seven years before I met Coach Sarah, when I was still operating at full-speed change-the-world mode at Trek, I hired my first business coach, the masterful Mister Sterling Lynk. Sterling was my mentor, my guide, my tough-love advocate. Sterling offered me a perspective on myself and on the world I could no-way not see on my own. Sterling flipped my switches and pushed my buttons, in a good way, a very good way. Sterling made me do personality and performance profiling tests, proposed challenges I never before considered, and gave me tools and techniques I would not have found on my own. Sterling was with me for a couple of years then after some big changes in his own family life dynamic, we parted ways amicably. After plowing forward and knocking shit out by my selfdom for several more years, I realized once again, I needed a perspective I did not currently have, so I hired my SuperStar Coach Sarah.

During the troubles with your mom, I also learned not to leave someone or leave a situation, until sure I did everything I could to make it work, BigBird taught me that. I do not want to look back in my life with remorse, hoping I had done more, then possibly forever regretting I walked away from something or someone too soon. Regret is a motherfucker.

So thereupon this one here, Coach Sarah genuinely pissed me off and I decided, least for a while, I needed a break from her.

On many levels, I have grown to understand the fragility of life and the limited time I have to make a difference, doing what I think is right within this here my world. I already fully embraced my found reality of staying on my critical path, that is to say, mostly not getting distracted or pulled away from my higher purpose. I guess the best definition is, hum, think-think-think…my willful discipline. *Like how?* Well, like how at work I grew to become the difficult one in the room when need be, me not willing to go along with the bullshit and rather, more than ready and able to speak up when I thought a new voice was needed, even knowing I would be ridiculed or punished. Discipline has become a large part of my DNA and although not always on top of my game, I am not afraid of doing the work, making the hard decisions, or speaking the fuck up. So, after one too many times as I sat there and listened to Sarah enthusiastically say, "You should write a book, you should write a book", I broke up with her for a few weeks, executively. Coach Sarah and I got back together again and her pushing was silenced, until it was not.

After months of arguing this same bullshit sales pitch of what I should do with my life, I finally said emphatically, "Sarah…I am NOT writing a fucking book."

Often I chuckle out loud, hah, throughout the crazy twists and turns of my life, shit just works out. There arguing with Coach Sarah, I could not see how writing a book, any book, could possibly help me move forward in my work career or personal life at the time. Thank goodness, I only took a break from Sarah and did not divorce her professionally. Sarah pushed hard for me to follow my heart, even when I could not hear what the emotional oracle inside me was saying. I look back to over four years ago and realize every fiber of my being was telling me to write this book, but the inner messaging could not be heard by my own ears. The astonishing part is that Sarah heard that message, even when I could not, bless her beautiful badgering soul.

Chips

For over a decade now, Ray Petro and I have joked about the concept of 'chips', like the implied credit of life poker chips. We move these imaginary valuable tokens around, placing them, giving them away, or grabbing ones of our own and fleeing fast with the fictitious cash-money value while we can. The referencing of chips does not always signify actual investments but mostly, Ray and I play our private game, speaking of where our limited resources, time, and efforts lie. Additionally, Ray and I share real-life learned lessons about when to pull the plug on seemingly dead-end projects or relationships.

Now then, I know many others to operate this here life as I do, and me like them. The way I view our world, and referencing thousands of real-life examples to back it up, many of us hardly appreciate what we have while we have it, yes, I am sometimes this way. It seems that imagining another life, better or worse, other than the one we currently hold in our hands is way too hard, even impossible.

We stay way too busy, we cling to life as we know it, wishing and praying our world gets only infinitely better, never badder, and yes at times I function this way and more. We refuse to give much mind to worst-case scenarios, contingency plans and what-ifs. Even given the opportunity to practice gratitude thankfulness and empathy, many times we ignore the hurricane flags going up around us and keep trudging forward, staying busy as we and me included can stand, and ignoring the proverbial incoming storm signals. Ray names the shock of major negative change in life as, 'Getting slapped in the face by a big fish'. Ray talks of having a beautiful life, already accomplishing everything to be happy and then…, *ugh*, Ray fell off his bike. Before the accident, Ray joked…if hit by a truck today and died, he would go to his grave happy that his life left behind was complete. My mention of Ray applies to other important life lessons also popping up several times thus far. As discussed in detail during our aforementioned podcast episode, Ray was gifted the opportunity to see life from two opposing views: Previously walking around able-bodied and also his current reality of relying on others to feed and bathe him.

Once more, what's my damn point? Well, I try to appreciate it, fucking all of it. I try to notice every little fricking thing: A smirk, a hint, a sigh, and all those mentions of, 'I'm fine'. I try to not take anything for motherfucking granted: Not breathing, walking, seeing, hearing, thinking, talking or even clacking. I try to do all I can, with all my force, using the totality of my will, while I fucking can. I know not when shit will change in a major fucking way, just like how things changed for my dearly beloved Ray, Big Dave, and Dre-Dre.

Never might I have the opportunity to do those simple things again, things I might mistakenly take for granted today, things I assume can wait until tomorrow.

Like catching up with an old friend on the phone, never again. Like washing my own hair, never again. Like saying I'm sorry, never again. Like brushing my own teeth, never again. Like saying I love you, never again. What are the life guarantees I can bank on? Hah, bare is the list. What securities might I imagine will always be there for me? I think to always have the health comfort and shelter I have now, won't I? Cannot I assume everything in my future will remain stable and just lay there unchanged, waiting for me to pick up and play with anytime I desire, aka my foolishly fantasized procrastination of 'someday' or 'one day'? Uh and duh, no, but you already knew the answers to those painfully real and rhetorically obvious bird brain notions.

Within my head, my heart, my core oracle, all that is within and beyond, I know only two things, two objective truths reigning extreme above others, only two, period. Now with clarity: One life absolute is death. Two is change. I know for certain I will die. I know for sure change will happen. Everything changes, period. Apart from and void of the promise for tomorrow, I assume fucking nothing and choose to put everything aside, fucking everything, so to write you both this note, while I can. Hopefully I finish here what I start without major disruption, hah, now a Roger Ray multi-volume set.

Tick-Tock...Tick-Tock

After me and your hot momma split up, I possessed the inkling to pen you a note similar to what BigBird left for me. I held a few fatherly thoughts on paper but the physically collected mass was my poetry, some slight journaling, and the individual short letters I scribbled when you were born. I had not yet sat to build the comprehensive story or even imagine the framework of such a massive body of work. After arguing with Coach Sarah about her concept, melding my life story and proprietary tools into one consumer piece, we reached a compromise. I would do it, I claimed, but first, my kids. My kids come first before everything. First I will write my expanded BigBird-styled letter to them, and only then would I start on the project she envisioned. Factually, after shouting at Sarah that I am not writing a f'ing book I said, "Who the hell reads books anymore, no way, if anything I would start a podcast...I guess people still listen to audiobooks but who the hell reads paper books?". I did not believe everything I was yelling at her, and more so, I was just pushing back. I went on to say I was close to zero-cash-money broke so how the hell would taking time out to write a book benefit the stabilization of Me-Incorporated? She clarified oh no, get a job, but then write the book during other available times. Hah, I scoffed that fable down too, no way, I knew better.

Expounding on the fantasy of writing a book for real, I faced straight-up the truth that my fingers had more to say than could be documented in a reasonable amount of time. Certainly, or so I accurately presumed, the small gap between a fulltime job and daily bird night moves would not be sufficient to say what I have to say. As you both know, I do not waffle much on decisions. Not unlike how I am also a power shopper, in and out. I carefully weigh options quickly, giving as much thought as I need to by my measure, then rarely change my mind once made up, sometimes stupidly so. Actually, the only true decision full-turnabout I recall in my entire life was the notion that Travis must attend college out of state, or I was not paying for it. Forever might I have regretted that one absurdity, had Boyd not settled in at Bucky's Madison dorm house.

I missed various opportunities after choosing alternative life paths, but not this time.

Like BigBird's stapled sheets of handwritten cursive, I write this bird's tale to you my brood. I anticipate my page count to be thousands, not just the 18 paltry pages my father left behind. Yet I doubt my written word could speak above BigBird's voice, in substance. Per always, my father's spoken and scribed words packed a punch. Side by side against BigBird's brevity, I multi-layer my deep flowing tales of relevant connection atop my core messages, henceforth my billowed page count. I doubt my ability to effectively transform feelings and thoughts into comprehensible characters and sentences even close to BigBird's. I am sure my flow and order of thought pales pathetically to a faintly similar effort of my father's, if he had found time to document his life's work in totality.

Yes, true, I am currently blessed with the treasure of time. Yet no, no extra time was handed to me, and no, not that I purchased or stole time from otherwise critical or urgent pursuits. I have chosen to make the time, to force time, and not wait for time to find me.

I shed everything that society, associates, and friends would otherwise expect or want of me. Rather than marching in line with the other rats in the race, I choose to pause, I choose to stop.

That rat race she unsuits me; she has charged me a mountainous sum.

Calibrating against my truth meter, only one singular thing in my entire fucking life has true meaning going forward…this, this, only this. Minimally, I possess a few critical proprietary life tools, for sure. Whereas so far as I soundly believe, if the foundational structure of truth and values is wobbly, the necessary nature to execute these toolbox practices sustainably, well, my attempt then crumbles. Multiple times these lessons, truths, and tools have provided the strength, structure, resolve, and habits which kept me alive. Either fabricated from within or arriving as flying objects originating outside my periphery, it would amount to mostly my aversions, my worries, my fears, and my pains constructing themselves into a formidable adversary, even on my best of days. Only when reaching into my life toolbox am I able to face and battle my monsters, push them aside, and progress forward. Akin to my shield and sword, these life tools are the hardware for defense and the implements that when faced with no alternative, I raise in my hand with which to do battle. Not just in theory did I craft and hone these objects, fuck to the no, yet through revised experimentation, time, after time, and time again.

Carrying my gear with me into challenges one after another, I gain confidence strength and momentum that if otherwise without, I would have given up. My mornings I arise before the sun. I collect, I sort, and I organize. Reviewing everything possible my day could include, I prioritize…these my tools, this my planned route. My lists then prepared, my map made, I go. Learning rather well the familiarization of traditional distractions and probable rise-ups, most every day I make least one tough decision, necessitated by change.

Yet here now, my list contains only one item. My map leads me to one place alone. Here now my one to-do, I write. I write and I write, I write for you, aka my highest purpose.

Further along your path, when these pages are the entirety of me available, I am trying to be here for you, even when I am not. Quite probably, because you are more like me than I even realize, the life lessons you need or want to learn will be sorted out and learned by you alone, sans any assistance from me and yet, I will not pause with this my share to you my precious.

Regardless, if once upon a cloudless starry night there comes an instance when you might have turned to me, maybe you will find some helpful or supportive words here.

If I look honestly into my heart, deeper than peered before, I will most likely see and learn to know the clarified choices I should make. As is self-evident, like duh, only by trying will I succeed. If I do not try, I will not reach my goal, fuck to the no way. Only by bleeding will I grow to know my limits, or find my edge, as Sonya mentions so expertly in her Friendwords piece. For me, confidence takes practice, confidence takes training. These words document the process by which I became who I am. Truly only by doing will I truly learn.

Here are my feelings, my thoughts, my beliefs, my dreams, my hopes, my actions, my inactions, my results, my adjustments, and my numerous lessons learned. The challenges have been many yet here I am, check, not dead yet. Notwithstanding, my purpose here is two things: Intent and attempt. My best intent and my fitting attempt rules over these here your pages, my intent and attempt to share, to share with you the pieces of me, with every single and last drip-drip drop-drop of love I possess.

Gut Check…Are the Dogs Eating the Dog Food?
Occasionally I paint dreams, goals, or least a few preferred faint pictures to one-eye focus on. My concentrated effort holds me mostly steady in my own shoes, by my measure. Still and truth be clear, well…stress, fear, depression, anxiety, addiction, alcoholism, and suicide have all brushed me. These evil bitter and poisonous pills had their turn, yet, here I am. It ain't easy though, not in the slightest. I prove with my resolve that I am in fact, tougher than the things hunting me. Under deep inspection of days past, the detail spilled. During earlier Roger Ray times, although the general nature of life was frantic, I thought less and ran more…I ran, I hid, and kept running. Looking over the puzzle game board of my life, yes, I wallowed negatively in thought and speak a while, and boo-fucking-hoo poor me, until, until I caught myself, zipped my fricking lip, faced my truth and took responsibility for everything in my life, regardless where how or when it originated.

I have an emotional reality that is subjective and based on feelings. This emotional reality cannot be proved on paper and yet times too far often, I would reside here, in my bird brain, full of stress, fear, what-ifs, and downright dirty lies. I create my own pain, certainly my worst pains, those crippling fantasized fears fabricated nowhere else except inside this here think box. Even after the bleeding heartache has somewhat lessened, I carry this old pain like a 200-pound backpack. My pack burdens me, heavies me down, hah…despite me knowing way better. I feel the weight growing minute by minute yet refuse to drop my sack of sadness. I carry the packaged hurts, I senselessly let the absurdity cut me time after time, my bled frights soak its straps. My rucksack I lug everywhere, creating residual pain and suffering long after once leaving the crappy emotional tempest behind.

The chaotic life is the one I choose for myself. If I am too busy to do something, it is because of my choices to make that something a supreme priority, or fricking not.

Why This, Why Now?
I am void of any clear and present illness threatening me currently. Still, I hold a supreme sense of urgency to complete this one thing before my functional health gets away from me. Even if doing nothing but this one singular act with the years or days or hours or minutes I have left in my life, I will look back on a glorious tale of living and smile delightfully. If ever were there a singular effort of where to best put all of my chips, this one wins, your book, hands down.

BigBird died in September 2008 after battling heart disease and a multiplicity of internal dilemmas due to his incessant cigarette indulgence.

Yes I was mad at him for smoking, and told him so directly. Factually I angrily blame-chirped that he was stealing the opportunity away from his grandbirds, for you to know and love your GrandBigBird.

My pops secretly constructed his 18-page letter decades before, way back in 1983, him telling me stories of how our lives unfolded before I was born or old enough to remember. My littlest sister Christy found the letter and mailed it to me, after BigBird died. I read his note only once, then I put that shit away. The pain bled through BigBird's written words was extensively horrific, by my measure. His words shocked me, comforted me, awhile hurt me. I cared no-way-not to review it then-twice anytime soon, hah...on some level, I regretted reading it once.

With nagging suspicion as I amassed these my own story-share papers, barely could I recall some of BigBird's words. So, I did it, I went back and reread my father's note. Although emotionally painful, it proved a powerfully positive exercise to experience. Odd and new-found feelings sprouted from the pages to decipher, since my eyes last searched for answers within his cursive characters years before. The acclaimed letter catalogs how my parents met, and how they became married with four bird babies hatched seven years apart. He adds how my mother's poor mental health then took her away from us, forever. My father's articulated feelings account his emotional roller coaster of sadness then faith then more sadness, as my mother went in then out then finally in for good, of the mental health institutions. Eighteen pages was not enough to satisfy me. My alternatives to learn more of the stories from my childhood are extremely limited, and fading fast. Open still is all that I will never know, ever. I feel gifted with the treasure of my father's written words, yet I hungered for much more. I believe such details help me know myself and learn my truth, by my measure.

The saying, 'You never step in the same river twice', is a damn powerful truth, written thousands of years ago by the Turkish philosopher Heraclitus.

The original quote is longer and goes on to mention, 'because it is not the same river, and you are not the same person'. I lived to learn know and believe that nothing stays the same, and even if in its same old appearance, everything ages, which alters them different, aka time changes every little thing. Minute by minute I change, regardless of my hope or desire to control such stagnation. Since changing day by day, I intend and attempt to move in a more purposeful direction, least here I try.

I hope this work serves you, and serves you well. If not, maybe this here your book makes for a memorable family heirloom drink coaster, or hell, a definitive spider smasher.

I did not have the connection with my father I hoped for. In a few not-so-emotional ways, I miss the chance I lost.

My intent is to not leave you with unanswered questions or perhaps left-out insightful detail.

If my father wrote me a 3,000-page rambling note and not just his 18 sheets, I would have read all of that shit by now, least once and maybe fucking thrice. I believe my entire being prospers greatly from BigBird's masterpiece, brief as it is, total truth.

With a limited humanoid battery life, one day my heart will expire and pump its last pump. How can I best treasure the present joys and benefits of being me myself right here right now, deeply and passionately as I can bare, and with the maximum humility I possess?

My biggest guilt is reasonably my hurriedness, my concentrated lack of awareness, and inattentiveness to the whole awhile simple beauties of life.

Ah…to smile so wide my face hurts as the butterfly plays peek-a-boo, laughing til my chest pains at the exuberant puppy romping around with the senior curmudgeoned big dog, dropping tears and falling to my knees afoot the flawless wonder of a northern summer sunset.

One day, the magical giving light will fall upon my cheeks for the last time, then conceivably, my only desire is for a slight spare moment with you both.

Alas, I care not to regret.

I care not to want for any undoing's.

I care to rest soundly that I did what I could, alongside my best try, and engrossed by my maximum best effort, whilst afforded the chanced minutes.

As with every current and forward other, today may be the last day I am able to write or speak, yes, meaning to say…today may be my last chance to hand you something of possible value for your journey.

Lives I Led

Lived defiantly, life volume set at eleven

Tried and tried, more than twice of me

Buckets of blood, treasureful scars

Running...chased incessantly

Sometimes, used up, hiding

Fragile, damaged, broken

Brushed off and took off

Dreams, all colored-in

Six figures of travel

Half-shadowed

Half-showered.

Now, only light

Giving, all I have

Lies shed, truth led

Living, all my might

More, than required

Quit lots, gained more

Basking in her, the sun

Digging, metaphysically

On purpose, with purpose.

An Isolated Tear

My life, bled well.

My time, glorious, fathoms beyond expectation.

My want, one thing, my need, one thing, same thing…to satisfy my life's one and only purpose.

If conceivably saving you an isolated tear, if imaginably softening one heartache, if perchance alone a minuscule helpful crumb, then the 6,000 hours of my intent and effort of this here book worth every second, ten fucking bazillion times worth it.

Because if isolating a split second of your darling precious-precious lovely life, if somehow providing a pause or a deeper look, for all one knows I somewhat assisted. You both now existing as the new and improved better versions of me, much-much more better. Although you both now out of the nest, my job here not done.

I care not for wealth, fame, or comforts. No more shiny possessions please and thank you though, I am trying to rid myself of some the too many. I rather want not the endless bike rides, no further the forever ski gallivants, meh…none the some more exotic globetrottings. I need not the stress-free lounge of my days, or pain-free rest of nights. Nor do I desire a new and improved great love, I have received all the love I believe to need, all the love I can perhaps hold, and think to have given away all love which was left to give.

I need not fucking walk again.

I need not fricking speak again.

I need not feel nor flipping breathe again.

I need not see again if now giving you all I can, while I can.

My focus one focus, my intention one intention, my purpose one purpose: Trying my best try, extending my best effort, to help you learn and live life your way.

Last call…why this? Maybe my increasing neurocognitive losses push me. At the time, February 2020, I still carried nagging after-effects of a concussion suffered eight months earlier, my 100th or more blow to the head, so I was not yet back to full speed. Not good enough anyway to throw myself back onto the speedway amongst all them other rats a racing. Maybe I have a bigger, deeper, and more critical narrative. Maybe I nurse regret, that one singular horrific regret in my life. Maybe I need to change what I once thought was best for me. Maybe I have more to give back to everybody. Maybe I am trying to repair my fatherly missteps. Maybe I am slightly lonely and using this as a path for increased connection.

Maybe I just love my kids so fucking much that I want to shine more light for them.

Nonfictional Novella

Hardcovers disguise the threat of upcoming storms

The teacup ring still soaks through and deforms

The story hides from itself at times, shadowed

My tale broken and rocky, a twisty-turny road

Pained to look back...the memories the disarray

The one I was barely recognizes the me of today

Not far from where I always was, always am

Here not there, working to prove what I can

Thoughts of who I would be got passed-by years ago

For every day afront, my dreams I can outgrow

Clear nights, calm breezes swirling underneath relentlessly

A story owed, telling, and shared extensively.

Four

~

Liar

Contesting rollercoaster puzzle game, aka life…parenthetically snagged by nature and the predisposed inability to tell the truth about fucking any of it.

Does trust matter if it otherwise helps me arrive where I want to go?
Does honesty matter, long as no one dies?
Does truth matter if there is no way to prove?
Does integrity befall me long as no one finds out?

Number One Priority

I care not, to be the best

I seek not, eternal happiness

And I have found no scale for difference-making.

I focus none on success, whatever that silly word for goodness sake might look like

I bust my ass...not for money, not for title, not for fame

I need not be in love to feel complete, or balanced

I would go mad if not working on some joyful thing

I need not purchase a yacht to be happy

To live on an island I own the keys to? No, but thanks all the same

I do not rush to be first, with anything

I claim not, I wish not, to always be right

I want not, to be the cheapest

I care not, to be the fastest

I will never be the smartest.

I know nothing, only what learned first, with these here hands

Others should receive all the praise, no praise not me please none, thanks anyway

I thirst not to be always moving, you know, on the go, residing in a van

I hope I am never without an address

I cannot always be at rest, such loungy inactivity is unhealthy for me, extremely unhealthy

And neither can my banker explain to me the measurement of enough.

My number one thing?

Total truth, drama be damned.

Chapter Four, Liar ~

Standing barefoot in my pajamas, and shivering nervously, I attempted some weird sort of forced facial composure, trying not to look so damn guilty in our kitchen.

I need to remain calm and resolute with the tale I just laid out minutes earlier…I can do this, this is gonna work out just fine, he will never know what actually happened, no way, I am totally good to go.

My father dialed up the Northwest Baltimore City police district. Pausing slightly…c-a-l-m-l-y, s-l-o-w-l-y, and with a solid firmness he said into the phone, "Yes, hello, I would like to report a S-T-O-L-E-N car".

I interrupted him immediately, and he was just waiting for me to do it too. "Dad", I said, "Hang up the phone…I did it, I wrecked the car."

BigBird politely excused himself from the police operator and slowly, viciously pausing…he placed the old rotary receiver back onto the big black wall box of a telephone. Akin to a Halloween movie mass murderer, my father then exercised all the suspense fear and quiet AF creepy dad shit he could muster. BigBird scared the crap out of me, like I almost pooped my pj's scared the crap out of me, I might have actually peed in my pants a little. My father, to me, resided within his angelic aura as the most empathetic, thoughtful, great-listener dude you might ever have the chance to sit down with in your life, concisely a super cool human. He was a good man, no wait, that's a lie, not true…factually my father was a great man, a caring man, a giving man, a loving man, performing many great acts for others, and BigBird did best as he could, whilst walking in those broken down and tattered parental shoes of his.

My father told me he loved me no matter what, almost every day, but…but for an otherwise master-caring and ever-helping Christian Protestant minister, charming…he sure could go into a deep dark well of intensity, and quick. BigBird could curse like a motherfucking goddamn son of a bitch sailor when he got pissed and did just that, from time to time. My father was a booming and world-class orator in his church yet at home when he lost his shit, his cursing became one big indistinguishable slur all jumbled together, like when he got mad at one of his children, calling one of us a partial name of all four kids at the same time. He probably visioned through lenses colored a moderate shade of red, getting confused which child was in the most trouble at the moment, "Be, Chr, La, Ra", he would say, "Hey you, get over here, RIGHT NOW!". And we never paused, my sisters and I did exactly what our father said…BigBird wielded an emotion-filled heavy sword of words when he wanted to, and he made his point known to us, every goddamn time. I remember only once getting disciplined with a beating from my father, his weapon of choice, his belt.

I was about six years old when I got whipped and he only laid hands on me one other time, after a cruel and provoking back and forth exchange when I was 12, and I threw my first 'FUCK YOU' in his face.

He instinctively and with major pissed-off dad force slapped me across my cheek and mouth, which I probably deserved, at the time. Shocked, horrendously hurt in a charged way, supremely pissed and now seeing red myself, I began crying and about to scream at him with the totality of my pent-up emotional background, the summarized hard and dark 10 years of household fear fright and rage then-thus far. My father had just hit me with forceable anger, and then whatever honor and respect I reserved for him was instantaneously dismantled, resentfully discarded, and for 20 years to come, BigBird and I were on opposite teams. Immediately after the monstrous slap I threatened, instructing him with maximum I-am-going-to-fucking-kill-you-like aggression, if he ever laid a hand on me again, he would be forever sorry. BigBird never touched me again, much because I was rarely home, day or night.

Back to peeing my pants in the kitchen, my father was about to teach me the biggest and most important life lesson I would ever learn.

After disconnecting with police, followed by a painfully extended four-second pause…his right hand still holding the receiver hooked onto the black wall box, him gazing at destination-none with the hollow aura of totally depleted hopelessness, my father started to speak. Like typing every s-i-n-g-l-e scary letter of every s-i-n-g-l-e word coming from his mouth, BigBird began by addressing the wall, slowly turning to me as he talked, burning a hole in my retinas with his intensity as he explained, "Ok, here is W-H-A-T we are G-O-I-N-G to do".

Oh fuck, what the hell had I done? The entire world as I knew it came crashing down on my idiotic 17-year-old skull in an instant that morning. I really thought I could get away with it. I barely practiced any pre-planning with the big fat stupid lie I tried to pass off on him. I only cooked it up the night before, the dumbest story ever told anywhere in the world, then I mindlessly went to bed. Shit, I was not getting away with jack squat fricking nothing on this day, fuck, I was in real trouble now.

I spent almost fifteen minutes that morning, mostly as I laid in bed after getting rocked awake by my father, me telling him the ridiculously elaborate tale of how the front end of his car is like now totally smashed in, almost undrivable, and I have no earthly idea how it happened. I was sound asleep as it began, "Roger, Roger, Roger…what happened to the car?". Purposefully dragging along a strewn-out and loose stringer of words behind me to acknowledge him as he sat on my bed, his entire being a mere few inches from my face, I woke artificially slow. I started to sit and said nondescriptly, with my signature but at-moment held aside hidden smirk, "I have no idea". Hum, I gathered confidently…this is going to be good, this is going to be really good. I thought I was rather convincing actually, explaining to BigBird perhaps what transpired with his car, the family car.

I began to lay it out…about 8pm last night I drove the car to the ice skating rink where I worked, but side-step clarifying to BigBird who was now all up in my grill and shit, that I was not on the clock last night. I went to like only skate that's all, and innocently hang out with my like totally awesome never-been-in-trouble-never-ever-never-before friends. I was inside the rink for the entire two-and-a-half-hour public session, like I didn't go anywhere no not at all, me just like skating around, you know, hanging out, like totally cool, no biggie, nothing out of the ordinary happened at all like not at all, totally chill.

Once the peaceful skating session ended and finally time to drive home totally like slowly, no big deal, I walked outside to go home and I noticed, oh for heaven's sake, darn it, look at that, gosh darn it…the silly front end of our poor little car was smashed in, almost like dead center, like somebody crashed it into a telephone pole or something.

I continued idiotically…jeepers creepers, that is horrible, what an unfortunate circumstance. With a scary AF calm and suspecting smirk, BigBird who was still sitting on my bed said, "Well, how do you suppose T-H-H-A-A-T-T happened?".

I replied rapidly and with an innocent puzzled inquisitiveness, "I have no idea".

I continued with mounting bird brain brashness and boldness, "It was like crazy, I had the car keys like in the pocket of my coat and my coat was like sitting on the rink bleachers like the whole time, so gee whiz, I don't even know, gosh, I guess, like, well, maybe, someone must have like sneaked over to my coat while I was skating around, and like stole the keys or something…so weird, I totally did not see like anyone creeping around near my coat or anything, but they must have like took my keys, gone outside, like took the car for a joyride, wrecked it into a pole or like something then brought it back…like I mean, it's like so weird because they like totally parked it in the same spot, locked it, and must have like come back inside the rink, and like put the keys back in my coat."

"Then like when I walked outside to drive straight home and saw our poor little car like all smashed up, I wasn't sure I could even like drive it home at all, but didn't want to like call you and maybe like wake you up. So I like got in the car and tried to make it home, and it was like totally fine actually. Like it's not even really like that bad actually, like not really at all, really, like the car's ok. So, like yeah, that's totally like what really happened." Yup, I thought, I am good, like that was rather good, I am done. Now he can like leave my bedroom and go back downstairs. There it is, like I totally did it, end of story. Yup, I like totally nailed it. "OHH-KAYYY,", he said, "Is T-H-A-T what R-E-A-L-L-Y happened?", "Yup, that's what happened", I replied. He did NOT repeat himself. "Ok", he said, "Then let's go downstairs R-I-G-H-T now, call the P-O-L-I-C-E right now, and report the car S-T-O-L-E-N, right now". OH MOTHER-FUCKER, I did not see that one coming, fuck me, hum, well…but then quickly this here dumb-ass lying-like-a-rug bird brain shifted into big dummy stupidhead mode and confidently, almost proudly, and now sounding like a little playful puppy I replied, "Ok!.".

So he told me to get up, right N-O-W, and come downstairs, right N-O-W, because we were calling the P-O-L-I-C-E, right N-O-W. Ok cool, like whatever dude, this might actually be fun, let's go do this, I thought cockily. I chucked my bedcovers aside and popped out of bed right after he got the heck out of my way. Super-cool, no big deal, I got this, I just need to hold my line, I can do this, solid, I just need to stay solid, should be no problem.

But I was beaten over the head with a tree-trunk-sized stick of truth that morning.

Prior to our truth-or-regret-gameshow in the kitchen, my father, through this here bird's mind's eye, despite his hair-triggered yelling, mostly maintained an unconditional love and support for me, no matter what, even as my drug use heavily escalated over the previous five years. BigBird seemed to back me up no matter what I got into, well, and perhaps too much the support. The birdhouse rules nonexistent, the consequences rare at best. And oh yes for truth be clear's sake, BigBird dismantled and discarded some of his own emotions, minimizing the concern and parental covering for me after I dropped out of high school, more than a year before this kitchen gameshow.

Comprehending the convergence of me dropping out, my father not once presented as bitter, zero resentment billboarded across his face, sans any scolding sent my direction, nor even a single I think you're making a mistake comment spoken or implied.

During the parent-student-vice-principal mid-day meeting that spun out of control quickly and the house landed on top of me, within minutes we signed papers to entirely remove me from the Baltimore City public school system.

Once the trio of amigos in the room agreed this was happening and happening now, BigBird scooted back in his chair, figuratively and literally. Walking out of the prestigious Baltimore Polytechnic Institute doors with my father by my side, after driving me home and dropping me off, BigBird went back to work, and then just left my life the hell alone. He left me to fuck up as much more shit as I could possibly conjure up. Glaring intently at the now drawn-out years gone by, hum, well, he tried to do what he could. He did what he could even when I was being a supreme punk. He did what he could even though the minute he helped me, I was into something else and screwing more shit up supremely. Well, I guess BigBird did not let me be entirely, he did not abandon me as I once believed. He stayed the fuck out of my way yet numerous occasions BigBird still bailed my pathetic punk ass out of jail. He came to rescue me multiple times as I lay broken somewhere there in the woods bleeding across the ground, after a friend ran to our house or called to tell BigBird that his little birdy-boyd was busted, and he retaliated none after I stole more than a hundred dollars a month from his unsuspecting wallet, for motherfucking years.

Throughout all my supremely dumb shit, he stood lovingly, supportively, and strongly…beside me. Or he stood defensively close in front of me, shielding me, the best he could. Or he stood a mere few inches supportively behind, trying to catch me before I fell, then motor-assisted me with his tower-of-strength hand on my back when I tired.

BigBird did that, and did it all the while, as I stumbled through life with my youthful dictator-like stupidity. When I would sneak off trying to hide from him, even then, once I got into a place I could not get out of on my own, he would miraculously appear at the precise moment I needed rescue. BigBird had a Spidey-Sense and knew when his little birds were in serious fricking trouble.

Once getting the itch of his parental seventh-sense intuition, BigBird came flying in, every time the situation warranted, every time I truly needed him BigBird was there, BigBird was fucking there for me, best he could.

Refocusing back in on the supreme hot mess I just created there in the kitchen, by mid-day that day, my father could not even look me in the eye.

His supportive stance now gone, decimated. Fleeing from my father was his loving fortification I saw felt and could draw on for all breathing days prior. Rather, beginning the monumental day after my wreck the family car and sling stupid mindless lies about it wildly all over the damn place incident, my father seemed to talk to the shoes on his feet much of the time while speaking to me. The disheveled communication between us would then continue likewise and run as such for the bulk of the next two decades.

There in the kitchen, as my father tried to explain, along with a side-dish of disgusted instruction…he did not care about the damn car. He would go on to say he's glad I'm safe, and his disappointment lies with the fact I couldn't just tell him the truth, rather I thought the need to lie about it. The shattered trust my father displayed to me that day hurt me, it left a deep scar and poked a hole in my heart I would remember clearly, vividly, the exact detail of it, still to this day. Supportively, my father gave up on me once out upon the lying kitchen gameshow floor. Back then, and right there, I gained a resulting deep-rooted although parttime-lived respect for truth. Another 30 tumultuous Roger Ray years ticked by before I embraced the veritable essence of living truthfully.

Of all my strong standing foundational life cornerstones, truth rules. Truth comes first and truth paves my path to living factually aligned with my other core oracle priorities, aka my eight documented personal life values. The truth-or-regret gameshow in the kitchen afforded me an opportunity to learn another foundational life lesson: The damn thing is not the fricking problem. I wrecked my father's car, the fact presenting itself as being the initial thing, but wrecking the car was not the problem. A much bigger matter than the damn car appeared quickly, I lied about it, and then the damn car barely fricking mattered. The damn car was no longer the truthful main focus, just a distracting technicality, like taxes. The lie was the true problem and a big problem at that because my dishonesty destroyed my father's trust, aka decimated.

Several times before this here kitchen-gameshow-day and often after, I viewed the damn thing as the problem. Rapidly I lived to learn, the fricking problem is the resulting maneuvers, what happens next, the residual fallout and mostly, how I handle the ordeal.

Throughout every arena of my life, the learned lesson of the damn thing not being the fricking problem rang true, and I believe always will.

Same-same at home, work, and generally out there in the big ole wide world of ours, the thing is rarely, if ever, the true problem. I also gained additional new-found respect for other people's feelings that day.

I mostly bounced around doing whatever the hell I wanted, until stepping onto the stage of the gameshow kitchen, hence-past ignoring the polluted wake behind me. Not to say I was always taking advantage of people, nor was it about my inability to practice effective empathy. Alas then right there on the spot in the kitchen, I first discovered what true disappointment felt like. The infamous day was a definitive moment for me as a one-day-to-be-semi-decent-human. Not only did I lose much of my father's respect, but he then turned his back on me, even though the worst of me was yet to come.

Clearly, I was oblivious to the level of hurt and true damage a singular lie could embody, until I saw my father wear it on his face and on his sleeve after the morning gameshow con-concluded. Quite frankly, up until that point I rarely gave truth any exploration in my con-conscious mind. I stumbled through life, doing whatever I needed, to get whatever I wanted, while the while trying to just keep moving.

At first, lying was easy. Lying was the easiest thing to do in most situations and as a result of slingin' all them lies, I got what I wanted most times. What was once the easiest thing to do soon became the most wicked stressor of my life. The snowballing of untruths, notably during my 13 nonstop years of illegal drug transactions, both the slingin' and the buyin', created runaway rhapsody. Well hum I'll stand to say…my lies melted down most of whatever trust others reserved for me, and created some dangerous situations I could not always get myself out of.

And then it was my ridiculous fib, actually my asinine fib…that stupid shit cut my father down to the bone that day. Only one other time in BigBird's entire life did I ever see him get so serious, factually forlorn and downright distraught as I'll describe it, appearing as a mere shell of a dad…weakened, hurt, stagnant, powerless, dumbfounded, awhile helpless.

I believe the culmination of punk-ass-bitch Roger Ray moments came together there in the kitchen, and although it is certainly an assumption on my part, my father felt like he perhaps failed with me, because I was growing up possessing such widespread nonchalant defiance, throughout the while a preferred favor for the scattering of untruths with mindless ease.

As a punk teen, then boiling over into same-same as a punk twenty-something, I had no earthly idea how extremely damaging untruths would later fall upon me, once the flow was reversed. As a husband and father, I watched the top-to-bottom truth-honesty-and-trust life dynamic then play out like a malevolently cruel joke. If afforded the slight moments required to slip my foggy and smudged judgment goggles over my eyes for a hot minute…the feeling of hurtful reads like hateful, at times.

Sitting in this here life-reflective kiddie pool and soaking in my own stenchy-swamp of tears, things come 'round full circle to where I feel my pop BigBird's pain, more than feel his pain, I taste it, more than taste his pain, I bleed it. You might claim here comes killer-karma or a bizarre-o strange payback, although I care not to judge the mirror with that seasoning of self-blame and still, I have slept with such.

Now having bedded down with BigBird's same pain, having carried that hurt, having bled those tears, I can taste the feeling of a heart that has fallen out of the bottom of its box. Now that heart is just a blob, a bleeding lifeless blob, laying unrecognizably there in a heap of dirt, and I am sure this, not to be unlike what BigBird felt back when because of me, his only son.

A New Connection, A Truthful Path

None did I recognize at the time but because of that one singular interaction between me my pops and the cops briefly on the phone, henceforth I would spend the rest of my life striving for truth.

Primarily, aiming for truth in thought and feelings within myself, truth in my written word, spoken word, intention, behavior, action, and the later-learned dynamic, my *Trifecta of Ugly*.

Shining the studio lights back onto the kitchen gameshow floor, "Ok", BigBird continued, "…here is W-H-A-T we are G-O-I-N-G to do." After admitting I wrecked the car and my father hung up the phone with police, I received instructions on my next steps. Your Grandpa with Ginger continued to explain…I was not allowed to drive HIS car for the next six months. I had to find way to a junkyard, collect the correct parts to fix the front end of HIS car, buy the parts myself, and bring the parts home myself, unaided by him or HIS car. The car will be repaired by me alone and to his satisfaction. To be clear, I was not allowed to drive HIS car for the next six months. And to be double-crystal-clarity-clear, I had to buy the parts myself with my own damn money.

We were done talking and I was dismissed, now I could leave. With my tail feathers between my bird legs and feeling the 39 porcupine quills of my take-home prize from the truth-or-regret-gameshow still dangling from the skin on my neck, I went back upstairs to change my slightly wet pajama bottoms.

Walking away with a slight zip in my step though, relieved the entire ordeal was not any worse. Strangely, I felt stronger climbing the stairs. Admitting I screwed up before things went too far with police, I believe I saved face, least a little. And although not yet absorbing the extent of bleed-out from the cavernous hole torn in my father's heart, I felt some slight satisfaction and warmth from him because he was clear, direct, swift, listened to me fully and faithfully, and BigBird was fair. My father did not make me feel stupid that day. My father did not call me a worthless irresponsible idiotic teenager. My father spoke not a single hint that he was ashamed of me or I was a bad person. The facts and next steps were clear and double-triple-clarified. Never did my father ask to the why, the how, or the what of the banged-up birdmobile, because none of that detail shit mattered. My father dealt with the facts at his feet, not tangling things up worse for either of us to trip on by way of emotions or assumptions. Instead of blaming, my father laser focused on the issues. My father only spoke to the two true objective core truths. One: BigBird focused on, was emotionally sharing about, and spoke directly to the lie I told.

Two: BigBird spoke in clear, specific, and exacting terms about his expectations of me fixing the car, and then repeated the two key points I should be sure to remember.

That was it. After years of being a total fuck-off, I anticipated the straightforward and tangible project, albeit a non-negotiable one. I liked working on cars, so it was no hardship for me to do the work. Within a couple weeks, I secured the parts and began to fix HIS car. The damage was regrettably worse than it looked, yet I was able to do all the work myself. My father checked in regularly and although he never lent a hand, I did sense some feelings of approval that resided slightly below his surface-level emotions and far away from the expressions on his face.

Hyper critical to note: The damn issue is not the fricking problem, Level 2

If BigBird instead yelled and called me names, I quite possibly would have yelled back, and the calamity conclusive could have been physical, or worse. Perhaps if my father screamed and name-tagged me stupid, comprehensively not trustworthy, pathetically and pathologically unreliable, punk piece of shit, I could never drive his car never-ever-never again, I had to now start paying rent or move out, for sure certain I would have felt like my father was not being fair, not fair at all. I quite possibly maybe would have resented such an irrational hotheaded blow-up, BigBird theoretically exploding and attacking me, labeling *me* as the problem, punishing me in other unrelated areas of my life because he's steaming mad about the damn car and the stupid lie. Then, the fricking problem has zero-not-nothing-zippo to do with the damn wrecked car or the stupid lie, yup, the fricking problem is then 103% about his no-nothing-loser son. So, truth be clear as diamonds, all-of-this-all-of-it came down to one critical, and viably life-or-death singular maneuver: How my father handled me and these here *my* issues, to own and carry myself, by his measure.

Forthwith, the encircling outcome of the entire ordeal relied on one person and one act...how my father dealt with the issues. Meaning to say the objective truths, aka the facts sans emotion. I have used this example to guide me and steer me literally hundreds of times at work, hundreds, literally. I slow, take a breath, maybe investigate more, ask additional clarifying questions and go see with these here blue bird eyes first before saying a goddamn word, period, least I try like hell and execute as such most the time.

Digressing briefly with bolstered boldness this here bird brain broadcasts...across every path of my life, the peaks high and the hollers low, one of the definitive top breaker of relationship ties both home and work is that motherfucker, resentment.

I guard this gem, my hand-held learning of resentment close to my loving heart, watching for the creep of it and trying to avoid at all costs...resentment. As a close cousin to untruths and similarly able to strike down, yes, same-same as lies, resentment kills. At the then-that there time alongside my father in the kitchen at 17, he side-stepped the unfairness factor, hence bypassing the channeling of resentment throughout my entire structure. Well, hum, factually my father jumped over the stream of unfairness and avoided it altogether.

Wow, this outrigger runs deep…collectively dissecting my father's discipline of me, or lack thereof, I might splay open my judgy thesaurus and call him a softie. Hum, is what I am about to say really true? I believe…yes, true, my father not once overreacted in response to anything I ever did or said. Moreover, he let me learn critical life lessons the dumb way, aka he let me be to learn shit by way of my own. Outside of this here your book I have claimed, and maybe even sitting somewhere within these flaps I say, I resented my father for not being tougher on me. Now upon deep and clear thinking I realize that's a lie. I said it, and felt like I meant it at the time but I do not now mean it. Such was said without thinking deeply and making sure that shit was true before I let that horse free from the barn. I do not resent my father. I was looking at him through those damn foggy and smudged judgment goggles of mine.

Here now I arrive to a finish line of sorts with my slow-down surmising, aka examining resentment, oops, wait, maybe not, there's another thing. The bitterness of unfairness is one of the worst taste testings I have ever attended. Unfairness is, obviously, an emotion packed-full with judgment but it's real and for the majority of my lifespan, the bubbled-up and boiled-over emotions of unfairness controlled me and thus, the little hellion is unavoidable. To me and for me-myself, by my measure, unfairness is resentment. Like the silly saying of lookup resentment in the dictionary and there you'll find a picture descriptive, a photo of unfairness. I might not be making sense. For me and resoundingly, I can perhaps possibly, and effectively, cast aside unfairness…push it off, sidestep it, or even discard it entirely when mindfully regulated.

However, when I do not effectively manage my thoughts and emotional reactions, when not mindfully driving my own proverbial car of life, unfairness can devilishly jump behind the wheel and slam its foot to the fantasy floorboard for an irrational joyride while I'm not looking. Speeding ahead and then slightly over the horizon, the pesky little bugger can easily and rapidly transformer it's hidden beastly self into full-blown resentment.

Echoing…I believe resentment also kills, it certainly kills romantic relationships. I have seen and felt this relationship execution by resentment play out specifically least two dozen times, both in my own life and within the lives of others close to me.

Interchangeably, and definitively, I am certifiably ignorant on more things than not. I skipped and cut and quit those forced learnings, thus omitting the treasured and illustriously revered books and teachings and shit from my reality. Yes, I fumbled through most of what lay waiting for me outside the institutional walls of the academia detention center, hence learning this here life the bird brain way. Only with these here my hands do I know retain and practice anything, and not fooling myself I know jack-shit because of reading one of thems theres books ones or twos of thems theres times.

So then, and to present the truth…I have found not much worse exists in any sort of relationship, home or work, other than that fucker resentment.

Yes of course, similar destructors romp around too like distrust but getting all granular about it and shit, once romantic trust is in jeopardy, what does distrust blossom into? Many times, distrust jumps in the passenger seat with unfairness as they speed off into the sunset together, off towards the land of resentment.

But holy heck, resentment begins so easily and starts out so small, within just a cross look, implied negativity, or even exclusion, then capable of beanstalking into a full-blown Abominable Love Monster.

The Damn Issue is Not the Fricking Problem, Level 3. Once again and as it could have gone south, not the darn car nor the darn lie or even the loser son were the problem. The problem would have been if my father over-reacted or didn't listen to me or didn't believe me or wasn't fair. Utilizing my Trifecta Of Ugly, not judging assuming or blaming, and listening fully do I detour level 3. Mostly at work I practice as such, to be more like BigBird, listening fairly even to the lies, supporting, and respond appropriately.

The job completed to the customer's satisfaction, and I was free of the looming auto body repair contract. There was no fanfare and I do not remember hearing any thank you's, which I clearly did not deserve. I walked away feeling a great level of satisfaction for mending the physical fence previously torn down by wrecking his car. I knew the emotional pain of the untruth I stabbed him with ran deep. Yet I walked away from the experience holding a net positive, hoping BigBird would forgive me one day for the big fat lie I puked all over him. Stopping him immediately on the phone with the police was a knee-jerk reaction, because although ready to stick to my untruth and play it out til the end, once hearing the words 'stolen car', I had to pull the stopper on this charade. Never anticipating him to call the police and rather, assuming just a slight argument between my father and I would ensue. Resoundingly though, once the police got dragged into it, I felt guilty and was flooded by an immediate responsibility not to waste their time as well. The moments my father and I spent tangling over his smashed-up car was the first thing we connected on in several years. Sadly, it would also be the last thing we would effectively communicate on for more than fifteen years afterward.

Oddly, the situation created a treasureful connection between us I would have missed otherwise. Although an incident based on conflict and hurtful untruths, BigBird navigated the challenge extremely well, with respect and grace.

I humbly admit not practicing even half of the fatherly fairness and patience myself that BigBird exhibited with me, every day for the entirety of his relatively short life. The previous sentence is a truthful statement, truthful because I hold the same calibrated gauge in these here my hands…knowing how my father treated me, aligned to how I treated you, by my measure. I should have been a better father to you both in your formative years, much-much more like BigBird was to me. Birdy and Boyd, my precious, I sorry, I very-very-very sorry.

Early on amid my truth pilgrimage, during the slog under the moon when I could not yet see clearly where I was going, I tried to identify and hold court with my non-negotiable position of truth period, both from others and the world in general. Quickly I learned to laugh teasingly at myself, recognizing this as pure organic judgment. I just had to wise up some more, toughen up a bit still, and accept the untruthful world as such.

We humanoids seem to have a dysfunctional inability to do life sauntered in truth, and although you could claim this to be judgement, I have found it to be fact.

Now I travel zestfully, I rest soundly, I work reliably, I play joyfully, and I try to judge not, not myself or others, for I am…no better than any woman any man. We carry our truths buried inside, and I claim no superpowers to see other's pain, nor possess an ability to inspect the scars of my sisters and brothers.

This Here Chapter Four, Liar
Chapter four's semblance of words shares my prioritized orientation of staying aligned with my learned truthfulness. For me, echo…preciseness matters. When precise, sometimes I get pushback scoffing's from others, and they validate their dismissals of my precision as shaded terminology under the umbrellaed palm tree of semantics. When spending hours or multiple hours zeroing in on my embracement of a single word, I aimlessly allow others to hold their judgments of splitting linguistic hairs within their own hands. So what about it anyway, what are the separators amid my premier life value of truth honesty and trust?

Truth: An accurate reality without variance. Sometimes I sidestep or withhold entire revealed truth shares yet still I do not intend act or speak untruths, aka speaking zero none of them there lies.

Honesty: To do as said fully, and if said, my saying is my commitment. I believe honesty runs beyond truth because if honest, then no parts of truth are held back or avoided, aka supremely virtuous.

Trust: A comforting sound belief of moral orientation. A lower-level foundation principle, more of a conclusive understanding of proper goodness than the actionable movements of honesty and truth.

Then possibly, because of relinquishing untruths, I am somewhat inflexible, aka rigid, maybe. Because now putting truth above all else, am I otherwise missing slight wonderful opportunities outside my personal fact of case circle? Perhaps the staunch truth line I try to walk is a form of judgment itself, maybe.

Throughout my lift-ups and mine many the downs, I suffered much more irreparable harm and cast similar hurt myself when I chose to practice or play along with untruths.

For the wonderfully beautiful things I miss now, for anyone I lose, for those I cross while remaining on my truthful path, I accept these sacrifices because, pints have been bled from the otherwise resulting lies.

Arriving here, standing firmly in place and aligned in truth, this being my living intention: Total truth, drama be damned.

Learned Truth

Life gets horribly mixed up when untruths are spewed, and it happens so quickly. Lies hurt, lies dismantle, lies divide, lies ruin, and lies are capable of taking a life. Before I hyper intentionally placed the factuality of my truth honesty and trust dynamic on the life virtues operating table, often I did not realize I was lying until after the words had spilled out of me. At times and by chance, such realizations of truth delinquent slipups only arose later. Even still, I might not understand my doings or writings or speakings as lacking core truth, because they once appeared superficially correct.

Once the untruths were set free unto the world and the little ponies running for the hills, I never felt like I could recapture them, so I let them go. Mortified to be judged, and giving thought only to manipulating the present moment in my favor, I saw it as too late to change my falsified statement, because the unbreakable lying bronco was then past the fence. Meaning…I attempted no take-backs or come-cleans or eating of crow, because of fearing embarrassment.

Ridiculously, I recognized some of these released fibs that if not herded quickly and returned to the ranch of delusion, would grow up strong and fast on their own and factually, hurt me much worse later.

Ah the truth, so ridiculously easy to practice, yet so incredibly hard to do. I habituated within the lies I told myself, the lies I shared with others, and the lies I played along with almost every single day. Do I lie now? Yes but rarely, only once in a while, mostly the self-defeating lies whispered into my own ear, but I try hard not to. Do I sometimes catch myself in a lie and immediately take it back? Yes, and I try not to let the defrauding statements slip out to begin with. I learned to try and slow all my thoughts, all my spoken words, all my written words, and all my actions in this regard, best I can.

Verbally calling myself out or typing as having told a lie can be belittling if I associate self-judgment along with it. It certainly takes courage and humility to face my lies and to own up to them. Yet most times these days when opening the gate of speak action and word, I grab my untruths before they have a chance to clear the corral. Once I started doing this in the late 90s, I have now flushed most fear of takebacks and rather, wear it as a badge of moral bravery. Same-same similar to other associated references in this here your book, I try to regulate and manage my truth as if it were a 'MathTest'.

MathTest…walking in to take my Roger Ray MathTest, I know the material or I do not. No essays apply, no multiple choice available, no curved answers, and no curved grades possibly exist on my MathTest, there is one way, there is one answer, period.

When walking into the proverbial MathTest exam room, I try to arrive prepared best I can. Accepting and anticipating the fact I do not know everything nor am I capable of doing everything myself, I try to rest easy upon what I do know and not stress out too much about what I do not, aka not fearing my wrong guessed answers, aka putting forth my best honest try, aka it is what it is.

I attempt minimal to no emotions once sat down at my MathTest desk, aka just do the damn work, no fluff. The resulting score of my MathTest is somewhat irrelevant to me if I arrived to the classroom prepared, did my best, and left my emotions waiting in the hallway. If I worry, if I stress, if I fear, if I self-blame, if I set too-high-bar expectations for myself, if I assume, if I self-judge during the test or after getting my grade, and if I blame someone or something else for my less than desirable expected score, then maybe I'm in the wrong damn class.

Bottom line is this, I use my crude idea of MathTest as a reminder to leave the fricking drama out of it, meaning to speak and act honestly without allowing for the sprawl of controlling conditions. I try not to fear embarrassment or ridicule because I either showed up and did my best, and spoke my truth, or hah, I let my emotions walk into the classroom and take the fucking test for me.

Now exiting MathTest, am I conditioned to fabricate untruthful statements as I go along, usually to appease others, hence avoiding conflict, and tricking myself outside thine the reality realm? Formerly absolutely yes, until I dug down to the bottom of my well of truth, then clawed my way the frick back out. Now I do not at all fucking care in the slightest, because total truth is so flipping freeing, and easy, and lacks drama, by my measure. Not that I expect anyone else to tell the truth because that's on them, not me. Must I lie? Fuck to the no way. Not even sometimes? Fuck a duck not. I do not know of a single instance I need to ever lie, not here in the real world anyway. Really, not ever? Maybe a few situations appear and I think it better to change the truth or truncate corners but in my years of truth experimentation, and challenging the truth within truth, I have not found any such legitimate locations or occasions to lie, period.

I have yet to find a single acceptable example of the need to tell a lie in our real world, period fucking period.

Punk Ass Bird...Truthfulness on a String

During the first two decades of occupying space in this big old unforgiving world of ours, I did not give much mind to who I was, more or less what I was becoming. Before completing middle school, any plans I had for my life's future got thrown out the window once I became a fulltime drug addict. Pre-teen, my three sisters and I mostly raised ourselves. Amid the exposure, I told lies to gain acceptance with kids in the neighborhood, trying not to be the last one picked for Whiffle ball. I was meek, more shy than bold, and not yet tall. Since disliking ball sports, they retaliated and disliked me right back, although ball games were the primary pastime in the 'hood. I was the last to be chosen for teams and sometimes, the larger group of kids played without me or started before I could get there, thus leaving me as odd man out once I showed up.

Liar 95

Although giving it no conscious thought then, I felt I had to lie. I had to be cooler than I was, or I might get shut out of the play.

Try to imagine, but I am certain you cannot envision…playtime outside was all there was. I was not a recluse bookworm, I held a horrific allergy to homework, and all my friends were out of doors. No internet, no computers, no mobile phones, no texting, and the only video game in the house became less exciting than playing Go Fish.

If not manipulating the truth least somewhat, I feared being unaccepted by the majority of kids and honestly, being shunned from play was not an option. If omitted from games, such meant there's nothing left for a bird boy to do. The only thing interesting to me involving a ball was the local number one sport lacrosse, aka 'Lax' yet alas, I sucked at that too.

If relying on neighborhood peer acceptance and inclusion based solely on my ball, bat, kicking, running and glove skills, I might as well have moved to fricking Alaska and become a salmon fisherman.

Surrendering to the unsettled humanhood and separateness before reaching my teens, the resulting synthesis was that of a pledged drug addict. My factual world then got thrown on its head, I had no choice, and fuck more, no route existed except to assume the role of drug dealer. The economics of pure consumption was not sustainable for me, and the inevitability seemed a foregone conclusion…me a sure-to-be unemployable dropout. I believed it incomprehensible to just use the substances without also trying to profit from them, awhile stretching the quantity of goods further at the same time. My inventory turns, asset management, gross margin, cost of goods, net profit, cashflow, budgeting, forecasting, and general fiscal responsibility skills were already forming at 13 years young. And then deception, cheating, and flat-out lying seemed an associated necessity, while trying to survive the rough and tumble illegal drug trade in Baltimore. I was not an intellectually stupid kid. Mostly I was on the run, not caring to observe any instructions or ideas, from anyone. Quickly however, conflict arose, mostly at school. Starting out I lied to my father, claiming I was sick and couldn't leave my bed Monday through Friday.

Not remembering how I discovered this next manipulation, hum, I think one of my sister's told me…eating raw uncooked hard pasta makes me vomit.

So for a couple of months on and off, I puked after waking and my father did not argue with my want to stay home. Next, I either hid in the house, tricking BigBird I already left, or I exited on time but strangely, never even found my way to school. After the pasta puking no longer passed my father's stay-home approval, I might but rarely in fact head off to the halls of institutionalized ivy early enough, logged in for homeroom, but then left school property for the day. The commixing problem was, duh, my escalated drug dealing. I had street business to do and substances to consume, while also school was rarely fun or nonconfrontational, mostly due to the fallout of my truancy and homework allergies.

The pressure of lies, hustle, and coverups from my untruths had built steam…I was getting reckless, and this disheveled turmoil was taking its toll, fricking inside and out. After quitting school, I stole money and goods from my jobs, especially during my junkie years, and there appeared no end in sight. That is, until my overdoses began which frankly was the beginning of the end. As is said, with the end of one thing along comes the opportunity for new possibilities, new beginnings, and in my case, the chance for truth.

A decade after I dropped out, my chirps to BigBird grew truthful, but a wide breadth of estrangement already laid between us. I feared perhaps too much damage was already done, and it was looking like my father and I might not ever reconnect.

I rallied hard and gathered the angst from my missteps and missed opportunities, trying like hell to make up for lost time away from BigBird, and attempting to regain his trust. Almost 20 years of total truth later, my father appeared to let down parts of his guard, believing some of what was coming out of my mouth. I think he needed to see and feel my truthful behavior in order to honestly believe it. I so desired that BigBird could have reveled within more breath years, while holding total faith his son's words and actions were trustworthy.

Neither me nor him were able to bask in those enjoyed glory years of trust and togetherness later in life once I got my shit together. BigBird died not long after him and I rejoined the same team again.

My commitment to truth and aversion to untruths, the number one of my eight personal life values, first became officially documented before the breakup with your mom in 2006. The commencing polished honesty sentence I built in my values document is not an entitled noble statement but rather simply, unspoken righteousness that brushed me to my core.

Personal life value #1: There is truth honesty and trust in everything I do.

Good Dad Shit Zoom-Out
My father did not lie, anyway much as my uninformed kid perceptions experienced. BigBird's emotions were clearly stretched to atmospheric levels, taxed in aspects I could not adequately estimate at the time of my youth. The verifiable hand-to-hand war with nationwide social gender norms my father battled, well as closer to home, Maryland State social services aka child protective services, to keep his four kids held back and out of our otherwise intended foster family homes, was a challenge I could only imagine should have destroyed most mortal men. Zooming out and viewing the totality of reality for a side minute, none of that strong good dad shit surprises me, because I intimately fucking now know where the energy and commitment comes from. Not just comprehending the source of fatherly drive and dedication to care for my children but I see it, I feel it, I taste it, I believe it, and I hold it in both these here my hands every goddamn day. I lived to learn and know, when it comes to you my children, I will work myself to within a nano of death and I have, eat little to none and I have, sleep little to none and I have, sacrifice every square millimeter of everything I am and everything I possess just so you are taken care of and I have, best I know how.

Without one singular doubt and without hesitation, fear, or regret, I would step in front of a speeding truck, cross a storm-ravaged river, guzzle a gallon of sulfuric acid, dive into a pool stuffed full of hungry-angry alligators, just to safeguard or help you my children however I can, no fucking doubt about it.

Veritably, my cognitive diction does not empower me to properly describe how far I would be willing to stretch for the benefit of you. I know not the proper words yet this chirp.

If the factually formed Devil pimp-walked our true earth, if I could ever contract a deal with the Prince of Darkness to give up my future and beyond, and if for goodness sake there were ever such a silly little thing, if I could then assure your heart would never break...I would cut off my own finger, all of them, chop off my own hand, both of them, dismember my own arm, both of them, even decapitate my own fricking head for you my preciouses.

If assured you would never be sick or face unfairness, I would welcome a life-ending 30 year cancer battle to enter my bloodstream. I would do anything for you my children, motherfucking anything, so it's no wonder BigBird was able to do what he did, no fricking wonder at all.

What was Left Lying in the Nest

Never a football game played on the TV in BigBird's house, not any kind of sports game. I guess it then somewhat stands to reason organized ball held no notable space in my heart. Also mentionable, no beer bottles ever sat in our living room. I never saw beer containers in our house, ever. I never saw BigBird drink a beer or even hold a beer bottle or can, ever. I never saw my father drink alcohol, ever.

Oops, well shit no, that's not entirely true, the only fermented Devil's Water I ever saw BigBird consume were the small sips of wine during some oddball church functions. I guess I was there once or thrice during his administered open holy communions, him sharing the drink as commemoration to JC's blood, but that's it, period. Well, oh shoot, wait a darn minute, I do not think that's a true statement either, although I am talking out of my ass in church, aka I do not know my words upcoming as accurate, but maybe the purply liquid was actually grape juice, yes I think so, wouldn't it be grape juice if little kiddos also walked forward to sip from the cup? It must be, I do not believe my father the father would let kids drink wine. I was never once a communion kid, hah, never mind the fact I was traditionally truant in church anyway...yours truly the punk-ass-bitch bird preacher's kid.

My father was a dyed-in-wool smarty-pants moral character. The only somewhat non-controllable behaviors I ever saw from him, aka his addictions, was the love BigBird had for his kids and grandkids, helping others, and his incessant reading. My father sat there reading almost every day.

BigBird leafed through book after book while sitting in his study for hours, in the evening and during any spare time on weekends.

Alongside BigBird's three uncontrollables, I swung the opposite direction with one of his things. For seventh grade homework I fake-read a fictional printing but the drugs already had their hooks in me so meh, I didn't retain the words, failing the associated book report assignment. When I got my homework paper back, my teacher asked me with an overtone of disapproval, "Did you even read it?". I occupied the opposite range of the spectrum and far-far away from BigBird's love for reading, especially that fiction stuff. I don't read fiction, least I haven't beyond the seventh grade.

Decades beyond my youth, when Travis you were eight and Lauren your little cutie pie self was still five, being it earlier in 2008, aka the year of BigBird's death, my father told me some of our family background. FYI he died on August 28th. As I drove him and his beloved dog Ginger to the family cabin in Michigan, I learned several things new to me. Keep in mind this was more than a year before I would see that illustrious 18-page letter of his. So, for the first time, no actually, not for the first time, this was the only time my father spoke to me about what happened in the way back. And so, flabbergasted I was to learn my father drank heavily for least a year after his baby birds went to bed every night- what the fuck? While my mother's paranoid schizophrenic mental health played a cruel Jekyll and Hyde peek-a-boo with BigBird, my father enabled alcohol as his coping mechanism, although he masterfully hid it from me at the time. I never questioned BigBird's moral character, certainly not when I was younger.

I never assumed he was doing anything except what I saw him do right there in front of me. Other than him ignoring doctor's orders and smoking his cigarettes there near the end, I had no reason to doubt my father's honesty, so his alcohol reveal was ridiculously out of order amid my brain. One singular weird occurrence could have tipped me off to my father's parttime closet-drinking, but I missed most of the clues. Clearly, BigBird used alcohol as his emotional crutch when unable to stand on his own mere mortal two feet.

I was in my late teens, long time past my father dealing with the direct unruliness of my mother's poor mental health. One morning in the kitchen of our third Baltimore area Ken Oak Road house, a rather large half-consumed fifth-sized jug of vodka sat all by its lonesome in the middle of our counter, not far from the fridge.

The cap neatly affixed to its bottle, no drinking glass in sight, and no blood splashed about or anything.

Precisely, the lone storage of vodka was absolutely positively without a singular hesitation, the weirdest thing I ever saw in our house growing up, akin to a far-away random item cast adrift at sea on the kitchen counter. The booze bottle was radically out of place in BigBird's nest, like a horrific murderous crime occurred the night before and now the scene with barrier tape removed, everything cleaned up and put away except someone forgot one small little detail like blood still on the ceiling, or hah, the bottle still on the counter.

I maintained the notion for almost 30 years, thinking one of BigBird's friends came over the night before and it was their booze.

They brought it with them, so I imagined, then mistakenly left it behind. Factually, seeing alcohol in our house was so bizarre that the occurrence definitively rattled me. Strangely, my father slept in that same morning. Sleeping in was radically out of routine for my father who every day woke before we did, except for Beth who went off to work at 4:30am, her exercising the racing machines at Pimlico horse track.

Elsewise BigBird was either making breakfast, getting ready for work or steadily fixed within his reading chair in the morning. His big cush chair resided in his study, aka his home office-style work-lounge room adjacent to the kitchen on the first floor. BigBird's study led to his bedroom a little further still away from the kitchen, and I never remember seeing my father in his chair when not holding a book.

I never said a word about the bottle and not a single hint ever presented itself to me either, least until almost 30 years later when BigBird spilled the beans as we drove to northern Michigan. Later in the morning after the freakish unveiling of the fifth on the counter, after I heard my dad rustling around, the vodka bottle vanished.

I was lurking about to see what would happen but missed the revealed exchange, me trying to unravel the bottle mystery and next happenings after BigBird awoke...I wondered what would become of the extinct Dodo bird sitting there on our kitchen counter.

I ignored another associated clue...my littlest sister Christy ran away from home the same week. Although I can spew assumptions about my remembered circumstances why Christy got the hell out of Dodge, it serves no purpose so I will zip my mouth and curl my fingers away from this clacky keyboard. I remember what I knew of why Christy took off but the facts are half-baked, because I never talked to Christy about it, so I will not share partial thinking's.

During my time still in the nest, did my father lie to me about his then emotional unraveling? Not by my measure. Was BigBird untruthful concerning the at-time hammered bender happenings around us? I do not see it as so. Far as I was concerned at the time, and as far as I know now, I do not perceive that his drinking affected me in any negative way. Oh sure, maybe some of his yelling was a resulting by-product of his Devil's Water consumption, maybe, but impossible to know. However, if his drinking or other behavior not known to me at the time led to life-altering changes, I would reverse my statement and say I believe I had the right to know the truth at the time of any such happenings. Beyond my believed right to know surrounding any altered days, saying it would have been his responsibility to tell me unprovoked so to remain an honest big bird, I see that no harm befell me.

Yes sure, he could have sat me and my sisters down, telling us everything about our mother before BigBird died. Honestly, such a share could have been least a partial mistake because of the pain and fear, especially what I imagine my older sister Laura felt after what my mother did to her. BigBird did not lie because I found nothing he said to contain anything but core truth. Was he honest? I believe so yes because in the parent-child relationship with me as a nestling then fledgling before I flew away, I did not need to know everything if it did not affect me. He needed to help protect me the best he could, that was his job, and in retrospect, I now believe he did it rather well.

Maybe some life-altering happenings occurred, you know, stuff I would have preferred to know about but mostly, those details are long gone. If it may have been I questioned him about the vodka bottle at the time and he lied to me, well then, he would not have been truthful. If I asked him about Christy running away or his sleeping in, or the bottle itself, I assume he would have told me the truth, or told me he chose not to tell me the complete facts at that time and therefore he would not be lying.

Under the age of 26, I said lots of stupid shit, shit I didn't know what the hell I was talking about. Yes also in those years I judged my father harshly but most such times, I had no idea how to yet form thoughts correctly.

Now as a parent myself, although for decades I railed my father for lots of shit he did not do for me, now I recognize clearly that I cannot do it better, oh wait no, that's not true, that's a lie because for-fact-one, I did not and cannot do it even close to as good as BigBird did.

I made it my job when younger to judge and blame my father and of course, duh, those judgements and blamings were lies. I did not know the facts of my father, of my mother, of the world, of myself or of almost fucking anything, and therefore I was incapable of defining, more or less speaking the truth.

Roger Ray Untruthfulness

The effort spent to understand my untruths, more importantly and specifically the truth within my untruths, finding the honest core meaning behind the lies required a voyage deep within my core oracle, aka diving deep into my emotional abyss and deeper still. Referencing only the truthfulness inside and explaining best I can, my lies fall into seven categories. This shit is relevant to me and my life only. Not a single implication upon another human otherwise. These here are just my bird chirpings or as you may desire to consider them, these here my bird poopings.

How do I lie?

    ONE: I lie to restore strength and confidence within myself
    TWO: I lie to cover up, avoid, and detour undesired situations
    THREE: I lie to please, comfort and serve, trying to ease other's journeys or suffering
    FOUR: I lie for betterment of position for myself
    FIVE: I lie to gain respect, power, and money
    SIX: I lie to hurt, harm, and retaliate
    SEVEN: I lie because I am relegated outside of reality.

So Onward and Therefore, the Ridiculous Untruths I Spew
Spewed Untruths 1.0: The Pin and the Cushion

We are trained and conditioned to lie, we are both the pin and the cushion. I do not remember being pissed or resentful once discovering my father's flat-out lies surrounding Santa Claus, Rudolph, the other sled-pulling reindeer team members, the Easter Bunny, or the Tooth Fairy.

Appearingly, the world prefers to categorize these made-up characters as playful and harmless myths, allowable legends, or acceptable fantasies. Still in my mouth is the bitterness of fatherly shame from flat-out lying about this same shit myself, for almost a decade. I claim due to an initial mindlessness on the subject and later as a play-along at the time, I chose not to battle the fabrications and instead, continued to sling them legacy lies. As some sort of small parental consolation prize though, I am proud of keeping most other untruths from befalling you, except two or three vacationing internet inventions and a couple half-baked irresponsible promises made long ago.

From the beginning of my childhood, I cluelessly played victim to the historical untruths pelting me. Once discovering adults lied to my face on a wide variety of subjects, I backed up trusting most everything grownups said. Once parenting and giving the issue conscious consideration, I assumed a shameful however assumptive position, carrying along the untruthful traditions. I chose avoidance of presumed disappointment, therefore not squashing your holiday or under-pillow tooth compensation dreams. I challenged such notions internally and ran the ROI...if I followed my mounting beliefs of total truth, thus coming clean about these early mythical characters in your lives, would I in fact hurt you? In the end might I inflict more damage by way of my idealistic total truth reveals than just letting the fibs flow? I saved the toddler tears and possible single-digit-aged heartbreaks, skirting aside my idealistic commitment of sans-all-lies and maintained radio silence.

Once you started to question the validity of this Santa dude, I got off the hook least twice when Travis jumped in to argue the fact, "Of course he's real, otherwise who ate the cookies?"

I hated making up such outlandish lies for a seemingly cheap entertainment factor. I can only talk out of my ass here so therefore this is not a believed learning or knowing but rather a thought...if I were a single father and operated freely, I would not have lied. For a handful of years, you guys played along but as the suspicion grew and when questioned, I maintained the charade of stupidity, "Yes he's real...", although I hated the falseness.

Spewed Untruths 2.0: One Thing I Will Not Lie To You About
The last lies I told you were untruths about Santa, the Tooth Fairy, the Easter Bunny and, "No sorry Travis there is no internet where we are going". Clearly I heard the early-on questions of why me and your mom broke up. I held my position securely, until you were both seventeen. Handfuls of times I said, "I choose not to tell you now, I won't lie, but will share with you anything you desire to know, everything, when you're eighteen". I clearly and precisely chose my response, avoiding speak of the matter, me presuming the harm too advanced past your emotional ages, and no fricking way was I going to lie to my children about that, fuck no, not about *that*. I discontinued parental breakup details censorship with Travis first, when he was seventeen. Once he asked me a question I could not wriggle my way out of, I knew the time had arrived. I figured 17 was close enough to 18 and I spilled the beans. About a year later Travis clued Lauren in, then I shared the same file of hundreds of emails with lil' miss Birdy.

Then the reason why me and your mom divorced was truthfully on the table and thankfully, ginger mother bird finally came clean with you both.

In August 2014 we went on a family vacation to northern Michigan, near where my father's family's cabin once sat. Only days prior, I bought Clifford the big red car and we drove eight hours northeast to a rental house on the same lakeshore where the Bird family had spent time for the last 80 summers. The Boyne City weather was too chilly for swimming and although we stayed busy, I falsely claimed no available internet existed at the rental, because of wanting to play instead of casting you aside or giving you an out. By the second day no one seemed to care, and we developed our card and board game skills together.

That was the very last lie I told you both…August 18, 2014.

I have not lied to either of you since, period.

I will try to never lie to you anytime in the future, period.

I am radically confident there will not be a reason for me to ever lie to you, fucking period.

Spewed Untruths 3.0: Selective and Subjective American Law Enforcement

A minimum of twelve times I sat in traffic court, and I was instructed to lie. The traffic violation process system offers me four basic choices.

1. One. Pay the maximum citation fine from home, accepting maximum penalties, and submitting payment online or through snail mail
2. Two. Attend a court appearance with or without representation, enter a guilty plea, pay the maximum fine, and accept the maximum penalties
3. Three. Attend a court appearance with or without representation, enter a not-guilty plea, thus gaining the opportunity to speak and be considered in front of the judge same day
4. Four. Attend a court appearance with or without representation, enter a not-guilty plea, and request a jury trial in the future if available

If I know myself guilty and lack comments, I will not extend the effort to attend traffic court but rather mail it in. If possessing remarks or believing circumstances influence my case, I go to court. Either through direct instruction from the local government prosecution officer, or from the judge directly, the explanation I receive is to plead guilty if wanting to pay the maximum fine and leave.

So, as instructed, if wanting to discuss any circumstances with the judge, ONLY a not guilty assertion on my part is allowed. If requesting to be heard and considered, I am forced to plead not guilty, I have no choice. Often times I admit my guilt but prevalent details exist, hence requiring me to plead not guilty and therefore forced to lie, I have no choice. So then I lie, and I hate it.

Hate is a strong and rarely used word for me.

The prosecuting government official clues me in that if I desire leniency, a reduced fine, lesser driving demerit points applied to my license for years, or a possible dismissal entirely, only when under the not guilty umbrella can such considerations be made. Five times or more I have entered a guilty plea then became educated on the spot by the judge, as the highest sitting person in the room instructs me, well, maybe I actually mean the opposite. Once picking up on my intent, the judge informs me the court cannot consider my request to speak unless I retract my guilty plea and enter a new and opposing not guilty claim. So I change my plea, because of having something to say, but I hate it. I desire to share my circumstances but am forced to lie about my non-acceptance of guilt. I am not asking for an exception to the court process, hah, no way, I am just playing along. The entire system operates precisely this same way every day and has so as such for 50+ years. Although I am assuming, most traffic violators in attendance seem to inherently understand the court lying process, or as it is the court lying rules, the rules to lie, or the lying guidelines are then explained in short order. Maybe my assumptions are wrong and the traffic court violators are not so tuned-into this lying process, but rather they roll with it as part of the bigger lying game of the world, IDK.

Now circling back slightly to wrap-up my truthful use of the 'H' word, when aligned in truth, more often than not for me, hate is a lie. To me, the word hate is primarily a hot reaction not a tempered response, generated by emotional thoughts and fueled with assumptions and judgments.

Regarding traffic court, I hate being told and forced to lie, only then afforded the rights-based opportunity to speak.

Spewed Untruths 4.0: I Promise, I Swear
Perhaps more echoes…I try not to use the words promise or swear except with the successive word try: I promise to try and I swear to try. To me and for me, if I use swear or promise and dig into the truth of the words I just spewed, I realize I am unable to promise or swear anything because of the wild uncontrollable variability of life, aka my runaway rollercoaster life, start to finish. Even when I cannot possibly imagine any issues will arise to keep me from such certain tempting statements, I lived to learn and know the exact opposite, aka do-not-do-not fucking say it. For me, echo-only three things can I ever promise or swear.
1.   Total truth, I will one day die. I promise I will die one day. I swear I will die one day.
2.   Total truth, change happens. I promise change will happen. I swear change will occur.
3.   Total truth, I can try. I promise to try my best try. I swear to try my best try, that's it.

Spewed Untruths 5.0: Could Be the Biggest Lie of All
Perhaps the tallest and most unconcerned lie I ever told was announced out loud to a mass of family and friends, and hah, I did it twice. I promised to have and to hold until death do us part. Yes absolutely at the time of the holy matrimonies I wanted the marriage, I wanted the promise of togetherness and safety and comfort and love for the rest of my days.

I was simultaneously bothered by the language of the legal marriage contract audible, the first time administered by BigBird himselfdom when I married your hot ginger momma bird.

Whereas and about…I cannot promise I will not litter unintentionally or intentionally, I cannot promise I will always stop at stop signs, and I cannot promise once married I will never separate from my spouse no matter what. So maybe I should not have gotten married but my unadulterated embracing of truth had not happened yet, not yet either time with my two great loves. Besides, everybody else does it, the marriage thing. Well, thereupon fuck no, if not saying I do, if not promising to your momma, then tragically your little bird feet would not have ever walked this earth, so in this case, that lie was totally worth it.

Mind the Gap
The opposite of truth presents itself in huge varieties of ways, not always initially or reasonably transparent. One such falsehood is ignoring reality and marching blindly, you know…plowing forward without much thought, wishing for a better result falling from heaven and landing in my lap, despite how well or not I am facing my proprietary facts of life.

Much ado the extension of feelings or thoughts…the words or actions stewing within me or cooking around me and about to bubble up, but I consciously choose or behave to walk on by, chanting my la-la-la-I cannot-hear-you's louder and louder, as my perjury pot about to runneth over.

'Mind the Gap' is a famous marketing slogan from London's subway system known as The Tube. London-proper houses a well-developed and well-used underground subway system, much like New York City. In these places especially, more people need to shuffle around than room exists on surface-level streets for them to do so. Henceforth their primary transportation systems are underground. Both the NYC and London underground hooman-moover systems are surprisingly thrilling, the while slightly intimidating, until getting the hang of how the covered-up people circus trains work. Of course you know more of this now, after our fantastic subway guided trip in The Big Apple, January 2024.

Minding the famed British gap means maneuvering the open voided space we step over, between the edge of the concrete platform at tube stations, and across to the on-rails stationary lip of the tube car open door. This glorified gap is not a big space to navigate, about a twelve-inch measured foot, but if not mindful, bad-bad things could happen. Mind the Gap is proprietary to London awhile to me, I use the phrase often within my thought-heightened world as reminder and reference to life in general. I joke to myself, sometimes saying out loud, "Mind the Gap", as I run amuck…intentionally watching for details meanings or extents I might otherwise ignore or overlook, if not aware of them or while perchance lacking respect for them. The multitude of gaps in my world could hurt maim or even kill me, if operating absentmindedly.

Alertness and awareness…a legacy life saying suggests we keep our heads up and eyes open. As The Tube reminds, also I truthfully pay service to keep my head down, awhile these here blue bird eyes on the lookout. Heightened alertness and awareness, 'cause shit is gonna come at me from any known or unknown direction, even from an angle entirely motherfucking incomprehensible.

I count on a 'oh shit' occurrence going down nearby, viably at any fucking second now. Yes, certainly the physical dangers out and about abound…moving too fast and tripping on a curb I didn't see, walking around a corner too fast while looking at my phone then running into something or someone, and the wild variability every single damn time I climb into a car.

Then also the silly things too, like being so deep into the conversation at a restaurant that I don't notice the last three bites of food I just scarfed down were from a piece of undercooked chicken, true story…mind the gap.

Or not triple-checking to measure an outrageously expensive piece of wood before cutting it too short, true story…mind the gap. Or Travis not paying attention while dancing with scissors at 2 AM then rushing to the hospital for stitches, true story…mind the gap. Or while not being an attentive and supportive dad or husband, me dismissing the unrest of the household and cockily proceeding with my bird beak buckled, not speaking up or acting on the bad vibes. Only to find out my wife or girlfriend was cheating during those earlier suspecting but silent times, guilty, true story…mind the gap.

When driving, I transpose myself into a real-grownup-life Mario game, constantly charting and maintaining more than one quick escape route. My Baltimore buddy Jon Balk echo-taught me that over 30 years ago. Across most zones of life I try to slow down even when going fast. I attempt to maintain some playfulness no matter the specificity of the engagement so to breathe, stay loose, practice alertness, and hold onto least a minimal right-here-right-now and nowhere else mindfulness. My attempt is no skip-overs or shortcuts, being truthfully intentional, do real things right, and do not rush to do false things or fast. And yes, I am sure to check and make sure all restaurant poultry holds no pink before shoveling it into my face.

Chicken Little, Time, and The Boyd

Chicken Little is an illustrious lil' chick but quite notorious for his frantic running around claiming the sky is falling-the sky is falling with great frequency. The extension of his barnyard family realized in short order, that the loudmouth verbal spewing's of the junior chicken were made-up untruths. The farm family tuned-out the dishonest rhetoric of the attention-seeking ego bird until when the sky actually does fall, although the boisterous biddy tried to warn them, no one believed anything the cockerel was cackling.

When truth runs too far the wrong way and for too long, we lose track of what truth means and sometimes we doubt every word from the mouths of others. Heck, under such grey clouded skies of the habituated untruth culture, sometimes I wonder if I can believe my own thinkings…mine the few accuracy of thoughts, misaligned to the lies of the many.

Processing untruths can be a cost-benefit analysis…weighing the pros and cons of outcome, trying to reach an analytical or emotional decision of allowing untruths to survive or rather, fighting vehemently against them low-down lousy lies.

Both regarding my first-person self-experiences and referencing the many untruthful humans I have spent moments of my life with, although easy to say and hard to do, untruths are a choice. Yes indeed, I admit carrying my own life-long habituated dishonest speakings and actions, that is until I discovered my way and chose truth. I also recognize much of our terrestrial lies bubble up somewhat subconsciously as just the way things go and just the way things are, aka it is our organic human nature to lie, or so I presumptively judge and blame but observe. Our reactions to the world's untruths dishonesties and unfairness' are more aligned with assuming judging and blaming the surface issue, rather than ruling out emotions and calibrating our position back to truth. Hence we then jettison the opportunity to correctly focus on the core problem. Conclusions are made, the hurts arrive, and the pains settle in, all because of our unauthorized reactive behaviors. The damage arrives in ways not intended and even, the results are sometimes downright regretful.

Time. Some human nature commonalities include taking shortcuts, doing things the easy way, quick to judge, easy to blame, and even embracing subconscious assumptions. Yeah sure, you might believe the previous sentence is me assuming and judging right there, but this is my intention of a pure and learned truth share. Why not save time and make snap decisions about a person or situation instead of being patient to diligently sort out the truth first? I have done as such guiltily many times, assuming I know the facts and believing myself to be true without even fucking thinking first. It takes time, energy, patience, and tenacity to get to the bottom of things and not detour, and time is precious for each of us. When not slowing to practice truth first, the soupy shit just flows downhill from there.

Our dear Travis the Boyd now takes the stage…final exams during junior year at MG high, watching as one guy, one of the more popular dudes in school, is handing test answers to another guy in exchange for money. In what sounded to me like a split second, Travis' commitment to his personal truth pushed him to act outside of social untruthful norms, to act, just jump up and act. Perhaps act impulsively, but Travis' truth honesty trust and fairness reigned supreme as he snatched the sheet of cheat answers, marched it forward and slammed it onto the teacher's desk at the front of the room. Travis made a split-second critical decision, to do what he believed to be correct by his measure, only to then be bullied his entire senior year. Sometimes, truth carries a hefty price tag, sometimes this toll is downright fricking expensive. Maybe the truth payment worth it, perhaps not. I am incredibly fucking proud that Travis acted on what he knew in his heart to be correct.

Thankfully, things were not worse for our Boyd senior year but by my measure, they were bad enough…"Hey Bird, snitches get stitches and you'll get yours".

I now make my gambles and place my bets on truth, fuck the fallout. Although in fits and starts I sometimes think the price I pay for honesty is too great. I run this assessment in my head until I get a migraine and have to lay down. Generally in defiance to lying norms, thereupon fuck the lies…if uncertain, if risking, I try like bloody hell to stay on my side of trust, meaning to maybe sometimes withhold a truth detail or three but tell no lies.

Yet anyway, I've been snagged and gotten stuck within the emotional trauma of betrayal before, me not able to drop my blame and judgments to refocus back on truthful reality, and I'm sure to be there again, least a while. Over a handful of times I've shook my head nonsensically…I just can't, I just can't, I just can't understand the attempted justifying words like, "In ten years I'll look back and it's like it never happened so who cares, you should just get over and forget about it, he didn't mean anything to me, it was just sex."

I just cannot understand that reasoning, true story…more migraines. However then providentially, I lived to learn the judgements and blame I carry only hurt me myself as others gleefully skip forward, them continuing to spew their untruths like tossing out gifted mini–Tootsie-Rolls to the crowd at a 4th of July parade.

Finally…finally…I finally learned true forgiveness. Never ever never before in my life have I experienced such a powerful and instantaneous release of pent-up negative emotions, once feeling the result of verifiably forgiving others. I did so by just doing it and it was so ridiculously powerful, the forgiveness, like rebirthed religion, or so I gather.

Here now I self-puzzle…what is the root purpose of lies? To shortcut? To gain without having to do the work or carry the load? To avoid a tangle, to side-step a confrontation? To avoid the pain of truthful reality, ours or others? To steer clear of uncomfortable conversations, then instead fabricating blissful but untruthful happiness? Hum., if lying or avoiding truth, using years or decades to hide from lies, awhile covering up with more fibs or attempting to bury untruths deeper, hah, does the camouflage provide justification? So some of my sisters and brothers seem to believe. That right there is my assumption, while also my lived-to-known truth. I believe untrust comes down to time, trying to save time, trying to make time, or gain time, because time is money, right?

Soundly near the end, when I find myself more alone than together, my spent exploits detouring truth or managing untruths is much-much the greater payment than just working through truth itself straight-up to begin with, so says me, by my measure.

In such untruthful regards, I lose the time I save.

The T-Bird Truth Laboratory

Travis arrived in the Coyle Parkway kitchen on the evening of his 20th birthday, immediately working away on his bright red festive cake. He chose, not surprisingly, a boxed strawberry cake mix and I suggested a slab of organic strawberry preserves between the two layers of double-decker delight. We immediately engaged in a vibrant chit-chat per usual, catching up on his school and life. I was happily working on the opposite side of the counter, fixing up our main course of ground beef tacos, thrilled about the upcoming evening with the pseudo-Link, our own birthday boy Boyd. This time found me pleasantly surprised that over the past few semesters, Travis was spreading his wings to other minor interests too, like drama and psychology. Especially, my intrigue was the academic review of his human nature class.

Previously, some deep and fascinating conversations occurred between me and the Boyd, corralling his psych teachings, learnings, and assignments. Muddying the water slightly during such verbal exchange however is the dynamic of my open blabbering mouth, in conjunction with my firm position on a few things Homosapien brain and behavior related. Most times when our chatter turns to Travis' psychology homework and projects, I catch myself incessantly approaching a tone of knowing, preaching, and advising…yuck, yuck, triple yuck. I attempt to zip it, backing up from what I have found to be true and allow Travis to form his own learnings without argument from me. There in the kitchen on his 20th celebration-of-life day however, me and the Boyd embarked on a captivating path of truth what-ifs and a warmer-upper topic of intention versus result. As told to me, Travis finished his latest psych homework and chose 'yes it's ok to lie sometimes' as his stance for that paper. Jeeze, it seems the kitchen is my personal truth laboratory of sorts.

I might have caused my lip to start bleeding right then and there as I narrowly missed biting my tongue. With a playful rhetorical tone, I asked Travis if that particular *yes it's ok to lie* paper had already been submitted. Immediately I recognized that my words formed a supremely dumb fatherly judgement notion as they unthoughtfully spilled from my mouth. It was gone, the assignment already submitted. Travis supplied a short summary of the homework and I tried to slightly change subjects, so I did not slather my learned life treasures concerning to lie or lie not, upon my male mini-me.

At the same time, Travis agonized with his own slathering of that Bucky-red frosting, trying to have it stay put on the sides of his self-baked cake. He did a fine job in the end and the cake was scrumptious. Seemingly firm on his final answer of untruths being perfectly acceptable in some cases, Travis was amusingly fascinated to hear why I might believe the opposite to be true. Sitting there with zero judgements in tone or body language, Travis first listened to the same story I have certainly told you both least once before. Choosing to divert or later cautiously approach the truth issue from the side door, I began with this short example, before I possibly jumped into the truth rabbit hole.

A man gets cut with a knife and the injured man dies. Is the other man who held the knife and cut the now-dead man guilty of murder?

Travis easily answered, yes, he's a murderer.

Ok, I went on…the once-injured man is dead, a result that cannot be reversed in the real world. If the man who held the knife was robbing him, stabbed him, and now the man is dead, yeah sure, put the dude on trial. But what if the man who held the knife was a doctor performing surgery, trying desperately to save his patient's life? Intention…the doctor intended to save the man and let us presume the doctor did everything he could, but his poor patient died anyway. Intention…the robber intended to harm the man and the most harm possible resulted. Intention.

In this regard and others, I try to lead with intention instead of being fixated on results.

My point using the intent versus result example before chasing Alice down the hole of quandary was twofold. One, on the surface, things initially appear a certain way and if we choose to, we can view them and accept them as-is. Some things are as they appear, cool, no worries. Alternatively, when we slow down, maybe even pausing or stopping before accepting things during first glance, it might be discovered that there is more to learn than what appears to be laid out in front of us. Not always but sometimes, it pays to be inquisitive. Perhaps some things deserve a deeper and more cautious look, considering that there might be more below. I do not mean that we should question everything, because that is no good. Nor should we be cynical, argumentative, or judgmental at every turn, no not at all, because nobody likes a pain-in-the-ass other person. Rather, while trying to pause, while thinking below the surface to not judge too harshly or too soon, can we move forward with more thought? More thought by learning, looking, asking and listening before we assume and blame at surface-level? Maybe in this way we can become more kind and try to do less harm. I share several examples of this elsewhere, both with the kid's time-out scenario and the business lesson of Go See For Myself.

Two, and next, grabbing first glance of things as-is, many times we scramble to find the easiest way in or out of an assumed situation. Sometimes when in scramble mode, we imagine a creative way to move forward or exit. During that creatively scrambled time, we do not always care if our thoughts words or actions are truthful because things are so darn stressful. Because scramble mode is in fact, inherently stressful, our priority quickly becomes an issue of urgent resolution. So to resolve things under the stress of time, we grab whatever we can to better our position, even if what we grab are lies. Travis mostly understood where I was going with all of this and then, the gameshow began. We dropped the challenge of resolving intention versus result because somehow after meandering slightly, we landed on the freewill argument.

Wanting to move away from 'freewill' before my brain started to bleed into the tacos, we went back to the discussion of truth.

Boyd asked me straight-up if I agreed with his homework. Not necessarily trying to be right, I answered directly that I disagreed with him. The assignment presented a person on their deathbed pleading to a friend to use the soon to be dead person's money in a certain way. Quietly, the healthy person-erect thought of how the money could be used to help more people in a better way. So, would you lie and promise to place the soon-dead friend person's money where they instruct, but rather do something else with it you believe to be correct? Travis said he would lie, so to better help others, but also lie so to try and protect his sick friend's feelings. I said…*well*, I could not guarantee I could even access their money on a whim. I could not promise the dying wish could be properly executed anyway because I imagine pre-planning and permissions will be required, so I would not lie but promise to try. Hoping to keep this chit-chat short, I wrapped it up from there because a larger notion stewed in my brain cauldron. Proclaiming then directly, I said I have not found a single situation anywhere in my current life when I need to or want to consciously lie. Travis then perked up like he was about to win a million dollars, literally.

I was not implying he was wrong and rather, trying to explain that in my 36 additional years on the planet than our birthday boy has gainfully gamed, I lived to learn know and reside in my firm position of truth above all. "Ok, ok…", he feverishly began, bouncing up and down in his chair like he does when he gets really excited. After Travis attempted to capture me within a couple proposed but failed ambushes where I would lie, his body began to slump like he just lost nine games of Connect Four to me in a row, which duh, we know would never happen in the real world. Finally, T-Bird catches me in a slight snare trap with this made up quizzing gameshow question.

The doorbell rings. There is a strange man on the front porch with a gun. The man asks me if Travis is home because he is here to kill Travis. In this game show question for a million Monopoly dollars, Travis is in fact that moment, standing not far behind me in the kitchen, out of sight from the potential murderer. Now the question is…would I lie to strange man on porch with gun?

I asked Boyd, me then attempting to qualify the exercise, is this total fantasy or real-world shit? So, as I continued with my qualifier of an inquisition, if this is fantasyland, if I answered no to strange man with gun standing on our porch and hunting my son, if by answering no, Travis is not here, would the man instantly turn around, walk away, and *POOF*, would the man then vanish? Would the man then disintegrate before even stepping off the front porch, never to be heard from or seen ever again?

Travis answered the qualifying question as yes, in that case you could regard this as fantasy…the guy would vanish if I lied. Ok, I went back and answered the original question after the new understanding. Well, if we are acting things out in a unicorn-led world than the one we live in now, and this man would vaporize if I lied, and he could never possibly come back, then yes, of course, I would lie and possibly avoid having Travis killed today in my kitchen by strange man with gun. But, but what if the answer to the qualifying question I asked Travis was no? What if…what if this is not a scenario for the stage of a fantasy alternative-universe, but rather this is real and happening right here and now? I perked up and got ready to throw gloves down on the birthday Boyd, aka to vivaciously share my scholarly counterpoint. I went on to say that if this shit is real and about to go down here and now then my answer is no, I would not lie to strange man on porch with gun.

I would instead tell the man yes, Travis is here, swinging open the door and waving my bare-knuckled welcoming hostess-with-the-mostess hand, please come in.

Birthday Travis appeared shocked, his blue bird eyes grew larger by multiple sizes, him anxiously awaiting my open-door hosting-thy-murderer justification. This entire exchange was fantastically animated and energetic, worthy of an awarded feature first night on-stage performance.

I know a fucking thing or three, so let me drop a pin on my position of truth here. There might be as much stuff I do not know as stuff I think I do know, and probably so. Sure, I've mostly been a free-range wandering punk-ass-bitch-bird since seven years old, so I admit some valued worth of my various collected crumbs during my saunter.

The book-learnings from the so-says-somebody's however, that shit escaped me entirely, whatever no bother none better. Realistically I am 5th grade schooled but I recognize the edumacation of just living, and so as such are the results of brainwashing by my beloved pal Laird Knight during my podcast episode one, meaning my lived experience. Certain I have enough space on my cranial hard drive to download double the knowledge into my head because only half of the available storage space is used up, and yet, I do know the following as pure fucking truth. You two have never resided there, you guys never attended school there, you never walked in to buy or sell drugs there, and never even visited there accidentally, but we live within a tough environment, upon the surface of a relentless world, and with some ferocious characters lurking about. There are people willing to do the craziest fucking shit that you could not even bring yourself to imagine, horrific things for fuck's sake I could not even speak of.

There are a couple select words I have not once used in speech, on paper or screen. I hold these words far from my mouth and clacking fingers. I keep these words locked away, not because I lack their definition or that their true meaning escapes me but rather, I do not use these words because I DO know their meaning and I DO know the vicious damage they wield. I believe never ever there be a reason for me to speak these words, well, hum…being realistic, and honestly, if I were backed into a corner under attack, defenseless, with you my most precious-precious dangling in danger…my children, I am likely to do most anything, and quite probably would, if it would truly save you, true-truly. Even as a hyper-intentional human, I recognize I am still a wild beast, unable to always control my thoughts, my feelings, my emotions, and my actions.

Which is my point entirely…backed into a corner.

I once had a fucking loaded handgun shoved into my fucking face, by a guy I obviously knew a little too well, and verifiably his big fucking semi-automatic had pumped bullets into human flesh previously, I smelled the residual but recently fired gunsmoke for fucked sake, just six fucking inches from my fucking nose. Once that fucking shit happened, well, my reality fucking shifted. The guy said he should fucking kill me right this very second, I knew he would, and he had just-cause. It went down right there in my Ken Oak bedroom, with four dear friends barely off to my backside, my father and three sisters futzing about downstairs, and worse. So anyway, well, I CAN say this with absolution: Once that fuck-shit happened, once that fuck-shit happened I straight-up learned fucking lots from the experience. I remember it vividly, still, I can smell his sweet stinky gun, fucking still.

Then elsewhere, after I was lied to, after that, so to bring me to my knees without a fucking micron of fucking hope, I remember forever how I felt, exactly how I fucking felt. And after I watched friends and strangers alike gasp their last tragic breaths and die right fucking there, right before my fucking eyes, and maybe I could have fucking saved them but I fucking didn't, until I experience some of that shit, any of that shit really, then it would be easy to claim what I would or would not do about an armed man on my porch, hunting our T-Bird. So, yes, I would fucking welcome strange man with fucking gun from fucking porch into our fucking house. Then what?

I would try to somehow hint without lying to strange man with gun that maybe Travis could be somewhere else in the house, and not currently hiding behind me right now in the kitchen. He was downstairs earlier. I would then try to wordlessly conspire with an unsuspecting Travis to help me trick the man. Hopefully, skillfully, and successfully, Travis and I would then overpower him together, gaining control of the gun and other potential weapons. Hopefully rendering the man bound and temporarily imprisoned until police arrived to safely remove him from our house, but, hum…but during the struggle, the man might get hurt which would not necessarily be my intent. The man may even suffer fatal injuries which would not be my desired outcome, well, um…but maybe, in a split-second flash, I might not hold back potentially fatal blows upon the hunter of Boyd. Because what if the man lives, is arrested and convicted and serves time in prison, even a long time but then gets out, only to come after Travis again?

If and when he comes back for Travis, and he quite possibly maybe might, what if I am not around to help?

So what if I initially lied and said no, Travis is not here and the man left? Well then, Travis would have someone out there hunting him down and I know better than to fucking fantasize that it all fucking works out peachy fucking cobbler after that. Because THAT fantasy shit of real problems and threats just going away is not our real world, and I have seen that horror slasher flick before. I believed our odds would be better to deal with the situation on the spot, rather than leaving the fate of Travis' existence to chance later. Tragically still, what if strange man with gun returns years later and if not first finding Travis, harms his sister spouse or child, or worse? Uh yeah, fuck to the no fucking way, that shit ain't fucking happening on my watch. Travis might have still died that day if I had told the truth and the man came inside, but probably fucking not. Probably I would have died too or first, trying to fucking protect my son. Thereupon fuck it all anyway if then, if it was actually my time to die that day, well, then hopefully either immediately prior to or immediately after my heart stops, strange man with gun, well, hopefully his heart then stops too because I fought like hell to save my kid.

Then maybe Travis would have lived. Keeping Lauren and Travis alive will forever be my top priority, my first non-negotiable effort no matter what, even before my own life, fucking period. As it may have been, both me and Travis died there in the house that day, and stranger danger gun man walked away un-found forever. Maybe, I fucking doubt it, but maybe. Just remember if you will, T-Bird's intensity and quite possibly his already-possessed bottled-up rage, especially as displayed to those at his 3rd Degree Black Belt test, with the frightening sounds of the pads from his ridiculously fast and violently unrestrained kicks, and those now-turned-to-rubble three concrete blocks trying to but unsuccessful in their tres amigo attempt to absorb the Boyd's fury. If I ever get into another street fight that I cannot weasel my way out of, I hope like bloody fucking hell my son is with me. If backed into a corner while living in the real world, I think Travis and I would both have a better chance of not dying by facing this situation here and now, together. So, would I lie?

Maybe if it were the aforementioned fantasyland, but probably not while living here and now in the real world. Probably not here in the real world and most likely, definitely not.

Straight-Up Truth, What It Is and What It Ain't

Judge. For me, judging is lying. I do not know the entirety of another person or their hardships, period none. If judging, I assume I know their story. I then jump to conclusions and form opinions without knowing the truthful narrative, aka I assume I know everything there is to know about them. When I form an opinion either in my head or out loud of another person or situation without knowing the entire verified backstory, I am fooling myself, aka I am lying. What if stuff appears certainly a certain way but is not verifiable? Then I try to stop, and shut up. Delicately then I proceed, listening, observing, listening sum-sum-some more…maybe asking questions, while wriggling to keep my lip zipped. I have been burned badly more than 20 times in this regard, judging, within a multitude of conditions and I wear some of these judgy scorched skin scars still. I try hard not to do this. Judge.

Blame. For me, blaming is lying. I have no higher power than anyone. I am no better than any woman any man. At best, I am only as good as my worst mood awhile my worst behavior on my worst day. I am not and might not ever be again what my worst behavior *was* but in totality, I am no better than my worst behavior, period. Make sense? Meaning, I do not lie to myself and pretend I never did the bad things I did. Concurrently and moreover, I am technically capable of sheer savagery and try not to lose grip of this beastly truth, period. Of course, how can I propose culpability if I do not know everything? And how the fuck is it that I could ever truthfully believe I know everything? No, I am no God, not even close…acutely I am a stumbling and bumbling wild beast with a darting monkey mind. On some level I could argue I will never know everything there is to know about another person because I am not them. Many times when I blame, I avoid accepting my part in reality and therefore, I am avoiding the truth. Avoiding the truth is also a lie so I try not to blame, aka lie. Blame.

Assume. For me, assuming is lying. When I have not looked close enough and I pass on the opportunity to uncover the reality of the situation, I assume. Echoing, I go see for myself when evaluating a situation and do not rely on word fucking one from another. Similar to when I accepted testimony from one of you and assumed what I heard was total truth, then punished the other one based on the words of your sibling. During your mid-youth, I then performed a hard stop of all second-hand attestation, all. This spawned from my honestly learned business values, not from me disbelieving you guys, no way not at all. I try not to assume, I try to deal with facts as I learn to see them myself and not base my beliefs on the words of others. Assume.

Hate. For me, when claiming I hate another person, I am lying. I do not truly know other people, none of them. Heck, hah, sometimes I struggle to know myself. All times I do not know everything there is to know before assuming judging or blaming. I know very little, period. Many times, the more I think I do know, is when I know the least. An eastern teaching suggests to maintain a beginner's mind, aka walk into situations maintaining I know little or nothing, until only then later learning hand-first. If I think I know someone or something so intimately that I claim hate, I am certainly lying, certainly. Even when I might say to hate myself or my life, I am lying.

In this case and many others, my emotional reality drives, thus controlling me, as my technical reality takes a back seat. When my emotional reality is commanding the helm of my head and heart, I am barely if at all, capable of speaking or behaving truthfully.

Regarding my sisters, my brothers, I am not them, I do not know them well enough to judge them, and at the bottom of the hate barrel is judgment, a factual untruth beyond my own civility. We speak and act based on our truths and sometimes our truths do not transfer, align, or even crossover. I try to let people own their individualized behavior, echo-echo...even if stupid. Assuming I know their life, then blaming them for acting inappropriately, and judging their personhood based on what I heard or observed them doing is not dealing with truth, but rather this is a lie, by my measure. I do not know anyone's backstory, even if they claim to have told me every little thing and I think I understand them. But fuck to the no, I do not know how they carry their pain and no one I have ever met shows their core hurt. If I hate, such emotion is my dirty-ego thinking I am better than they are. We try to do our best in situations and if I stop there, it's unrealistic to think I will behave in the same ways others do.

Blah-blah-blah thereupon fucking holdup a damn second.

Here are my facts. Who do I know best, besides but perhaps not even myself? Duh, not my bestie, not my GF or spouse, but it is you two my children. I know my children best because I am you and you are me, we are of one blood above all others. But. But, but duh, I do not know you, I am not you, I do not know what you know, feel what you feel, think what you think, experience what you experience, or believe what you believe. So how can I honestly know the core of you, duh, I cannot claim such nonsense. Therefore if I do not know the ones I could know best, then how the fuck is it I so cockily claim I know anyone? I fucking don't, period, amen, and end of sermon.

A powerful saying borrowed from eastern wisdom states, my best teachers in life are my enemies. Meaning, the people I do not jive with can help me see another side of things, another side of myself, that is, if I am patient enough to look closely, and listen honestly. Ah the lies of Hate. Hate.

Owning It
After the long-ago morning in the kitchen when I lied to BigBird about wrecking the family car, I became increasingly serious about truth. That one lie, that one stupid lie created a paradigm shift between me and my father. Using that one lie as my emotional rocketship away from BigBird, I robbed myself of the relationship that he and I could have had. I also and factually stole from BigBird a better relationship with his son that I am absolutely positive my father would have fricking preferred. Within much of my life so far, I have practiced much excessiveness, and much avoidance. I take truth seriously and I think for good reason, least for me myself, and by my measure.

The Life I Lead is the Life I Make
Why did I previously strive to be correctly positioned as others requested of me or implied? Meaning it was me clamoring to be appreciated and valued, both at home and at work...oh yeah, and in love too.

Sure, I desired acceptance, awhile hoped to willfully survive and of course, aimed to provide. Such fabricated photos of striving and approval are the epitome of the American Dream defined, go ahead, look it up.

Thus the assumed culture of where I belonged or hum, I guess it was my self-defined culture, my constructed culture…middle-to-upper-class-punk-ass-whitey…anyway, my perception told me that my place in the world mostly demands that I hoist myself onto a higher step every year. Therefore I believed the necessity to multi-task, push, shortcut, and fight to reach my next northerly rung, aka climb the ladder, aka get ahead, aka this here rodent was nothin' but another rat a racing.

The subliminal but understood human tide coming in at my ankles expected me to do better and gain more, or be swallowed by the sea of irrelevancy, or so I once believed. Splashing around in the shallows of the rat race, after a while I was reaching so far ahead that I became entranced, dragged away and drowning in the swirling current of self-serving lies.

What a fucking horrible and tragic underwater sinkhole. Truth be relatively clear though, I did not claw or battle or cheat life so much to proceed as most speedily allowed. Yes I was running, but not so much striving for what's ahead, rather at the beginning, hum, I did not slow because I was being chased from behind, on the run from my legacy monsters, mostly fleeing my technical motherly monster. Yes and correct, then with absolution, enough never was. Much of the fuel for later demands and pressures for ahead-getting were marital. I competed amongst peer rats but motivated none to embody the socially revered Hollywood millionaires, the Silicon Valley billionaires, or serve to artificially please my work bosses. Rather, once married, my charged drive bubbled-up at home, my go-go-go cracking open Pandora's Box and sneaking treats to feed my little dirty-ego hiding inside.

I do not need to always be right, fuck to the no. I would rather be wrong and learn something real about myself, and learn something real about the world, than stuck thinking I know anything. I am thankful not to rely on taught testimonials, the words from foreign books implying to tell me that once read, now I know what I know. I lived to learn what I know by doing and at times, I stood trial by fire. There is a simplicity and humble nature to truth…much of the manageability I carry around with me now is when I openly admit to myself, and to the world, I do not know much of fucking anything. For what I do know, I come by way of honestly, my known truths bled well. So why do I focus on truth now, why the hell do I care so much, what changed? Because I have lived in the alternative world, in the helpless world of untruths.

I cannot survive in the land of lies and woefully, I will not survive in the land of lies. The factuality of my self-built world required me to leave the nest of my dark grey reality. Only when knowing that I do not know, then and only then can I learn.

That Which Tethers and Divides Us...The Dance of Romance

I absolutely love being in love.

I am a much better me, when in love.

I learn and grow in new and different ways, when in love.

Easy and good togethering time when true, is magical.

Easy and good togethering time when untrue, is magical.

Easy and good togethering time whenever I can get it, is magical.

Some of my romantic relationships seemed easy, until they were not.

Some of my romantic relationships seemed real, until they were not.

Some of my romantic relationships seemed hard, and they were.

When I shut up, listen, accept, allow and forgive, perchance can we stay together.

When totally and truly togethering, my togethering requires total truth.

When togethering is untrue, I truly struggle to stay together.

Here I sit living and trying to love correctly, while keeping my functional shit together.

Here I sit living and trying to love correctly, while not pushing my loves too far away.

Here I sit living and trying to love correctly, but alas, I possess the incorrect spice.

I love doing right in relationships.

I love when relationships feel right.

I suck at relationships.

One supreme challenge is echo-keeping my functional shit under operational control in other areas of my life, simultaneous to when things get out of order in the romantic union. Truth be crystal, the foundational relationship disorderliness challenging me is my own doing. Minimally I own a 51% participatory role. My love suck factor is not from lack of trying though. Over 30 times I tried to bring the correct spice to the love kitchen but alas, I suck at it and hum...think-think-think...just why is it that I suck so expertly?

Maybe I lie to myself that I am capable of operating effectively in love.

Maybe I lie to myself that my legacy pain adhesion has been flushed out properly.

Maybe I lie to myself that my emotional instability is even qualified to be in love.

Maybe I lie to myself, thinking my expectations of my partners are realistic.

Maybe I lie to myself, convinced my partner will leave so I sabotage.

Maybe I lie to myself that I am an effective communicator in love.

Maybe I lie to myself that I am capable of long-term sustained love at all.

Maybe I lie to myself about all of the above self-blaming excuses.

Maybe it is just the way it is.

And maybe it is something else.

I try, I really try to respect the small things I do that bother my partner. I try to adequately communicate and effectively regulate my opposition to my partner's small things.

I have lived to learn and know these little things can equate into big problems in the relationship. I try, I really fricking try to do my best. I try to know myself intimately before rushing too far or too fast ahead in love. I try to communicate up front with my partner so to hopefully avoid problems later. I try to not ignore the little things. In spite of my preceded intentional tries, I echo-suck at relationships.

In the movie Good Will Hunting with the wicked-smart Matt Damon and the ultra-wise Robin Williams, rest in peace Robin, a famous scene in the movie is when the two main characters finally connect in a deep and meaningful way after a slow and dysfunctional start. Robin Williams plays a clinical therapist and describes his wife who battled cancer and he goes on to say, "…She used to fart in her sleep, one night it was so loud it woke the dog up, she's been dead two years and that's the shit I remember, wonderful stuff, you know…little things like that, those are the things I miss the most, the little things only I knew about."

Redemptive Love Religion
About a year after I divorced for the second time, I found an extremely powerful romantic relationship quote on Pinterest. When Google searching unrelated a few months later, I then found another one.

The first saying made me ball my fucking eyes out, total truth, me holding it high as the preeminent love saying ever heard of or known, fucking ever.

After stumbling upon the second, a profound, well, precisely a stupefied happening occurred. The coincidentally shingled writings hit me like double successive lightning bolt blasts directly to my loving heart, if for goodness sake there were ever such a silly thing. Shockingly, immediately, and forcefully, I pushed back in my chair after I realized the same author wrote both pieces. The irony surprised me in a non-understandable and unexplainable way. My tears flowed instantly with heavy uncontrollable force.

Jumping up cloaked in extreme subservience, I stumbled around for a few minutes doing laps through the great green room and kitchen just shaking my head, attempting an expositional and interpretive walking meditation.

The depth of the cumulative two writings brewed inside me quickly, and the immediate impact of the newfound supreme relationship truths almost brought me to my knees. I was weakened by the force of now seeing I knew nothing about true love, absolutely fucking nothing, after reading these two separate pieces. Still today five years later, my legs quiver, humbled by this pair of small word collections to the likes I have never seen.

The first saying was ridiculously powerful, smart, insightful, accurate, true, and sat there profoundly as its own sort of love religion. Although many things are easy to say and hard AF to do, now and again I run across or create a saying, thought, or process that seem supremely smart, far beyond really smart. Such was the case for me concerning these two pieces, and then some.

Besides both romantic truisms ringing my brain bell, they made me immediately think of both ex-wives, and how wow, holy fuckballs, I missed something critical in love.

In association, late in the union with your hot momma, before I finally decided it was over, we were getting couples marriage counseling from Doctor Mike, our third couples' counselor who tried to help us stay together. Doctor Mike was superior to any therapist before, far superior. We only connected with Doctor Mike later and factually, after it was too late. The doctor was mystically magical with his skills and both me and your mom agreed, perhaps if we found Doctor Mike earlier, he might have helped us save our marriage. I absolutely felt the same after discovering these two documented quotes as I did regarding Doctor Mike, my stardust desire was that I found these love religion scriptures earlier, they might have contributed to rescue one of my marriages.

Of course life and love aren't so easy to will or wish new days, imagining I can change just because of reading a collection of words, no fricking way. So, I am not committed to the notion of any other outcome from reading these alpha characters yet sometimes, I do encounter something that actually changes me profoundly. I have successfully brainwashed myself before, changing my perspective over time because of reading or viewing the same thing day, after day, after day for weeks or months, legit. I would examine the powerful piece, digging deeper and deeper into myself, an expedient effort to say the least. Maybe if I found these two writings earlier and kept them in front of me, reading them daily for weeks or months or years, I could have changed my perspective, seeing and learning different things and finding clarity of love truth over time. Here now, the first love religion scriptures reading.

"If she's amazing, she won't be easy. If she's easy, she won't be amazing. If she's worth it, you won't give up. If you give up, you're not worthy. Truth is, everybody is going to hurt you; you just gotta find the ones worth suffering for."

"Wow, fucking holy hells bells", I said to myself out loud the first time I read it, and I say the same thing silently every time I have read it ever since.

Now, the sacred second scripture.

"You may not be her first, her last, or her only. She loved before, and she may love again. But if she loves you now, what else matters? She's not perfect, you aren't either, and the two of you may never be perfect together but if she can make you laugh, cause you to think twice, and admit to being human and making mistakes, hold onto her and give her the most you can. She may not be thinking about you every second of the day,...
...but she will give you a part of her that she knows you can break, her heart. So don't hurt her, don't change her, don't analyze and don't expect more than she can give. Smile when she makes you happy, let her know when she makes you mad, and miss her when she's not there."

Oh my fricking good-googly-moogly lord, my eyes as before...tear flooded. If that ain't true gospel love religion right there, I don't know what is or could ever be. Holy hell, my emotional well leaks tears for the dozenth time reading these revered scriptures. Absolutely astonishing. I decisively worship these two supreme love writings and Lauren, seems the same or similar should be true for guys.

I do not incessantly stalk love quotes but still years later, I have found no better intimate insights than these two. The author is modern-culture world famous, but tragically we lost them to a bizarre cancer in 1981. I was and am a ginormous fan of them for more than 30 years before I found the two testaments I share here. The creator is not a pure writer per say, he's a musician. The reverence of the recurring still surprises me a little, no not surprised these are his words, not at all, but I didn't view the guy in this holy love light. However and yes of course it shocks me none, because this singer-songwriter exists in a class by himself...deep, insightful, creative, sharing, giving, loving and reigning supreme, Mister Bob Marley, the Rasta reggae jammin' jam-master himself.

My Varied Past with Both Vibrant and Subtle Untruths

I accepted some untruths people told me, both at work and amid the outside world, until I didn't. My unmindful allowing afforded their lies to have life to begin with, and that was my choice. At times I let the lies lay, not accepting them, pretending to ignore them. Repulsively I walked around the invisible dishonesty buckets like steaming vats of toxic waste, refusing to allow them to rest autonomously in my consciousness. Day by day over my lifetime I grew increasingly suspicious and my confidence weakened in my ability to believe or dispel words actions and notions that felt questionable, by my measure. The untruths I did let in, I did so hesitantly. I operated my life this way until I could not anymore, and then I decided.

> **I choose to make my world one of truth honesty and trust.**
> **I choose to be factual over being liked.**
> **I choose to be genuine over being loved.**
> **I choose to be alone rather than lie or lied to.**
> **These things I choose for me.**

My Lies

I lied about my mother. I was embarrassed. I felt disadvantaged, oddly weird, a bitch-boy unicorn of sorts. Many people wanted to know where my mother was and what happened to her. My dishonesties were those of avoidance and omission, not speaking untruths. I never wanted to address the question about my missing mother, it was a painful question and an even more painful answer. I lied about my schooling and substance abuse. Never lying directly about my limited education drugs or booze but also many times I was not entirely honest. I believed it best to hide the truth I dropped out and shoved needles in my arms, fearing torment, blame, ridicule, omission, rejection and worse.

When hiding the transparency of me, hiding the truthful parts of me, I feel unqualified to be living…unmerited…someone not good enough to be standing erect in these here my shoes right now.

Untruths hurt me. Perhaps I arrive to my resulting painful place from lies honestly, maybe not. When my mother first got sick, no one told me anything. I knew something was tragically wrong but zero information was offered, even when I asked. I felt adrift, alone, shunned and omitted. Attempting to sort out my castaway situation of unknowing, I many times wondered and emotionally wandered in the wrong direction, then hurting myself more. Residing in such hurtful and shadowed places long enough, then finding out the truth much later, most times the damage already done, aka irreversible pain and distrust.

I believe I am much the same as my sister and brother humanoids…these here times it is often hard to find the truth in others. Like exceptional customer service, which is also rare and difficult to see, even when experiencing it. At times I accept the lies and shitty service, shrugging my shoulders in submission as just the way things are. The value of both the world's truth and great service is at times lost, because my expectations are so low. After a while I lose vision to see a different and truthful path….how sad it is that I accept and learn to expect shitty service within a world of untruths. How does this happen, that I rollover claiming it's just the way life works?

Even when exposed, if the story or purpose serves the server and situation, the truth really no longer matters in the eyes of those entertained by it.

Trifecta of Ugly: Judge, Blame, and Assume

I maintain a documented collection of rules for living, which is only one such life tool in my carry-everywhere life binder. My life rules are a dynamic numbered list of approximately 60, regularly adjusted and refined over the last 30 years, mostly one-liners, and entirely self-fabricated. My list helps ground me, keeps me honest, and guides me. Each morning I sit with tea and read my collection, helping to properly orient myself for the day. My current #4 item states "Do not judge, blame, or assume, period". I gave my current number four item a nickname, the 'Trifecta of Ugly'.

When I judge, I feel ugly, inside and out. When I blame, I feel ugly, inside and out. When I assume, I feel ugly, inside and out. Deep inside my core oracle, I desired not to judge blame or assume but in truth, I was not functioning as intended. Recognizing my trifecta of ugliness, I decided to change. Managing and regulating unintentional actions was hard for me. Managing and regulating unintentional actions over time was hard AF. To factually live as intended, I leaned against my Trifecta of Ugly, even if getting cut, burned, or broken by it, or worse. I could not live out loud misaligned to my core oracle, I had no choice. Aligning my behavior with my intentions was futile until I verified my truth, committed to living honestly, and did the fucking work.

I cannot, I cannot, I cannot live misaligned to my core oracle. I will die if I do not live fully engaged with intention. I cannot live untruthfully. Illustrating my Trifecta of Ugly lived learnings I share four experiences, nametagged as the following.

1. Subway Wars
2. Moms on a Plane
3. Sugar Bomb
4. Go Ahead, Take Your Best Shot

Dropping assumptions was hard, and is still today hard, but not as much. Not judging was a tenuous challenge and now, such undesirable behavior is mostly gone. Discontinuation of the blamings was extremely hard, but rarely now do I blame anyone for anything, myself included. Not by wishing or praying will anything in my life truly change, yes here I echo…only when I rise to intentionally live truthfully, can I truthfully live at all.

Judge Blame and Assume, Trifecta of Ugly example 1.0
Subway Wars

Per usual, the morning subway car was rather crowded. Mostly we kept to ourselves, not too much excessive look-at-me-everybody-I-am-very-special-and-important loud-tone public chatter and otherwise, no out of order unruliness or uncontrolled ruckusing going on, thank goodness. It's Monday, cold as shit outside, gloomy, there's been no sun for weeks, windy as hell, and none of us seemed to be enjoying another rat race commute into the big city today, certainly not fricking me. One stop after another, handfuls of people got off the train and mostly, the same amount of human rodents scurried back on to replace them other rats a racing. Some vacant seats were still available, only but a few, when the mid-30-something year-old father walked onto our sub-surface train car with his young kids in close tow behind him. Almost immediately, my fellow train mates looked up and gazed accusingly in the father's direction.

His kids were being assholes, running up and down the aisle, weaving in and out of the vertical handrails, yelling and playing wildly as they chased each other around inside their private makeshift jungle gym. Remarkably, the father just sat there clueless doing nothing, and how in the hell does he think this shit's ok? The other passengers began to whisper their aggravation, no longer docile in their own little worlds. I heard the volume of whispers increase, now soft conversations both behind me and to my side, "Who's kids are these?", "Where are the damn parents?", "Somebody should say something".

There was a brief and awkward pause before it began, the words passing around and people pointing, "…he's over there, that's him, that's the guy…". The ridiculously rude father sat there motionless, entirely tuned out, his head leaned way back in his seat and his eyes closed, like he was trying to take a fricking nap or something while his little hellions destroyed everyone's morning…are you fucking kidding me? I couldn't believe this guy.

The little brats ran by me again, carelessly bumping into several people's knees, their wild arm movements flailing care-free like floppy windmills and almost ripping the newspapers out of the hands of two fellow frustrated commuters. I tried to take a few deep breaths and not lose my fricking shit, but it was not working. Finally, this crap had gone on too long. I took one for the team and made my way towards mister dickhead, a couple other people getting up to approach the guy too, just as I started to move. I was farther along than they were, so I kept going and got to the dude first.

I wanted another ten minutes of damn peace and fricking quiet before facing the brutal winter wind and the stupid walk to my shitty little cubicle inside my big shitty office building downtown.

I tapped the bad dad on his shoulder, "Hey…dude… your children are running wild and making it impossible for us to enjoy a little quiet time before work, can you please do something before one of us yells at your kids, or worse?". Ridiculously, the father was slow to respond, gazing up lazily, like he wasn't even interested in doing anything about it at all, practically dismissing everything I was saying. The lack of responsibility for his brat pack was offensive. Hah, I thought to myself, almost mumbling my threat out loud…there's gonna be a real fricking problem here in about a hot second or three, no doubt about it. The kids are being little brats, but, well, maybe I shouldn't be so quick to blame the kids, nah, screw that, they are bona fide brats, and their dad is a rude and inconsiderate asshole to just sit there and let his kids run wild. How in the hell is this guy even allowed to walk around? I'm surprised he hasn't been put in his place yet, but maybe his time is now.

This bullshit just ruined my damn day and is starting to ruin my damn week. I'm sure it's exactly the same for everyone else on the train, everyone else just sitting still and putting up with it, not doing shit and obviously too scared to speak their mind, well screw that, not me, I wasn't scared. This fricking guy just messed up everyone's day on purpose. I couldn't believe it and I wasn't going to let the nonsense continue any longer, I was trying to capture just a few minutes of calm before jumping into another crappy work week. Also, since no one else was willing to get up and do anything about it, I figured I would help them out, doing what they were thinking but too scared to say or do themselves. "Yeah…", the father said, not even bothering to tune into what the hell his little punks were up to at the moment. "Yeah, you're right, I should probably do something, I just don't know what I'm supposed to do, I'm sorry, I just don't know…we're on our way home, we just left the hospital…my wife…she…their mom…their mom just died…".

Oh my fucking god, I couldn't believe it…I pleaded with the man, "Oh my gosh, I am so very sorry, I'm…I'm such an asshole…what can I do, what can I do to help you guys, anything, anything at all". Now melting down and horribly ashamed, I scrambled my brain to try and think of what I could possibly do to help this poor man. Instantaneously I saw this broken family in a new light, the father absolutely destroyed and understandably so, his kids obviously wrecked in their own way, struggling to know how to act after their mom just died, and holy shit, I couldn't believe I was being such a dick, in the mirror I spy…ugly angry bird.

My assumptive and judgmental emotions formed immediate opinions, and I was certain I knew everything going on, certainly I thought to know enough of what I needed to know, and I felt absolutely positive of these beliefs. I didn't even pause to consider anything else was happening except what I saw right in front of my face. And then I took it even further, I stood to act against the bullshit that was destroying my day, starting to wreck my week, and maybe then standing for the other times in my life I never stood before. I was fully engulfed in the events staring me in the face and I was aggressively going to confront my understood reality, while sticking up for some of what I believed to be wrong in the world, aka ugly angry bird. But more than confronting, I was reacting. I reacted with accusatory language, and might have even continued in an explosive manner.

And then, I immediately performed an absolute and opposite reversal of my perspective. Five seconds ago I was mad as hell at the guy. I viewed him as some off-kilter human just sitting there tuning out the world, a shitty dad, separating himself from reality, shirking all responsibility for his kid's antics, a horrible person, and a man I was almost ready to physically attack, aka ugly angry bird. Then in a split second I realized to hold no idea what the hell was really going on. I was the clueless one and I was wrong, I was so ridiculously wrong, aka ugly. Exiting this Subway Wars story now, to me and for me, the absolute and immediate turnaround of perspective is a critical realization and one of the most valuable life lessons I have ever learned, or ever will.

When in presence or observing others from afar, even remotely, when simultaneously engaged and focused, while mindful of true truth and real realness, I try to fully embrace and positively keep front of mind, the single solo one and only true fact of my precise perceptibility in regard to the other person.

I know zip-zero about other people's true reality…their deepest feelings, pains, hang-ups or fears. I know naught nor could I. I know absolutely diddly-squat of what truly matters in their brain and heart, and I never will, ever. I know zilch, even when I think I know everything, and even when they claim to have told me all there is to know about themselves, still I fucking know fucking nothing, fucking period.

This complete thought reversal experience is known as a paradigm shift. Paradigm shift, a complete turnaround of thinking, at times the brutal opposite realization of perceptions. Paradigm shift, the presence of reality on the furthermost opposite cusp of judging blaming and assuming, aka the Trifecta of Ugly.

Subway Wars, liner notes
Three real world life experiences follow shortly to additionally round out my collection of four Trifecta of Ugly examples. Subway Wars as stated is one Trifecta of Ugly example, plus the three upcoming adds up to four, basic math right? Except, my four 'real world' examples are not all mine. One of the four is not mine. My four 'real world' examples are not all truths. One of the four is a fabricated story, aka fiction. Showing my hand, exposing my trickery, I now throw my Subway War cards on the table.

I never worked in the big city. That's a lie, aka fiction.
I have never occupied a shitty little cubicle. That's a lie, aka fiction.
I never worked in a big shitty office building, fiction.
I have never traveled on a usually crowded morning subway car, fiction.
I have never encountered a bad dad, letting his little hellions play wildly and chase each other around on their makeshift jungle gym, fiction-fiction. I have never taken one for the team and approached a parent to threaten them because of their children's behavior, God forbid, and certainly never considered beating up a father because of his unconcern for the inconvenience his kiddos are causing me or anyone else, fiction. If I ever did such things, I hope someone hits me in the head with a big fucking hammer, nonfiction.

This prior first piece of four titled Subway Wars is a highly embellished fictional tale I use to clearly explain the concept of Trifecta of Ugly by way of a paradigm shift. I borrowed and stretched the story from the masterful Mister Stephen Covey, originating from his globally acclaimed gamechanger of a book, Seven Habits of Highly Successful People. I did not read the book but heard the tale and retold the story so many times, after verification I share it here with certainty to its origin and intent. The Subway Wars story is the only fiction in your entire book so please process the piece as such and try to reorient yourself back to truthful reality.

I am sorry for the fictional tease and scaring you that your dad is a closet inconsiderate asshole. I struggled slightly to write that piece with such callousness but I hope you can shake it off. The additional three Trifecta of Ugly shares are 100% first-person lived total truths, down to every waterbottle squirt, every mouthy grandmom, and every 'I should kill you right now' death threat. For everything I experienced, for the understandings I adopted, for everything I try to do or do not, I believe my learned Trifecta of Ugly is my most revered and implementable truth ancillary above all others. If I made the proper time for the opportunity, I could author an entire book titled Trifecta of Ugly and speak solely to the matter of judge blame and assume.

Judge Blame and Assume, Trifecta of Ugly example 2.0
Moms on a Plane

The plane trip was scheduled for four hours, nonstop. The Delta flight attendant informed us…this was a full flight, please put as many items under the seat in front of us as possible, and please do not fill up the storage space overhead so to leave room for others, as we piled into the plane. She continued with her announcement and it was not all good news, there is a long line of flights waiting to leave before us, we still have to de-ice before we can push back from Detroit and start to make our way to Salt Lake City, the maintenance crew is on their way to fix something before we can leave, and please take our seats as soon as possible so we do not delay things anymore.

Most passengers around me spoke and behaved with agitation, but not me. I was flying out west to meet my pal Shawn for a few days of work-skiing in Park City. Shawn lived in Utah and he worked for me at Trek. I did not have to worry if our flight arrived late because Salt Lake was my final destination and I had no concerns for connecting flights. But immediately, most of the passengers moaned and complained about their expectations for the rest of their day. I rolled my eyes a little but otherwise silenced my brain and formed no judgmental thoughts or opinions. Lauren you were about two as I sat there on the plane, blissfully listening to music through my earbuds and reading a book resting in my hands, while many of my fellow passengers mouthed off with spirited negativity.

I rolled my eyes slightly once more and ran through some thoughts. I had been traveling regularly for work, years by then, none of this was a surprise and actually, I learned to expect major disruptions as part of business travel. I also try to plan accordingly, not pack my schedule too tight, presuming some delays somewhere. It's a clear truth who is a seasoned business traveler…they sit in the front of the plane, they know how it works, and they possess shiny dangly tags from their luggage. I was a frequent flyer too. Not trying to judge but I giggled a little that day, how a couple handful of passengers were being so darn negative while also possessing many more miles flown than I did.

Overall, I thought they should know better but I didn't judge them, maybe they are mad about other parts of their lives. Overall, the mood on the plane was stressed. Almost everyone was in their seats with seatbelts buckled but it appeared we were still waiting on a few more passengers, because a few seats remained vacant. Also, the door to the plane was still open, even though the flight attendants were trying to hurry things along.

A couple of additional passengers arrived, huffing and puffing as they entered the plane. Seemed like they were running to catch this flight before the door closed. One was a single mom with two little kids under the age of five, the smallest kiddo infant was strapped into a car seat-type carrier. Not that I knew if the mom was married or not, I mean to say she was the single guardian child handler at the time. The mom was literally sweating from her face, the older kid was slightly rambunctious and defiant, and the woman was struggling to even hold her belongings as she shimmied down the aisle, heading for the back of the plane.

I was in a window seat and the two seats next to me were already occupied. I wanted to get up and help the woman but she seemed technically ok at the moment and besides, I didn't want to disrupt my two row-mates unless a bigger issue warranted. Hah, one of my shoulder neighbors was already snoring soundly. I felt completely horrified for the taxed mom because Andrea and I had already traveled with you guys on planes so I somewhat understood the challenge of the single mom. Andrea also took Travis on a plane to California by herself when Travis was still a baby, less than one year old. So, I could mostly appreciate the struggle and the stress the mom was feeling, but also realizing the hardship is one greater than I factually understood. When your mom flew with the baby Boyd from Baltimore to see her brother in San Francisco, I knew it was not an easy expedition but I was not there, I am not a woman or a mom, and I am not your hot ginger momma, so I did not know what I knew about single mom flying realities.

Forever before this day I accepted and still embraced the junior humanoid cackling and banging as a beautiful symphony of youthful discovery, the kiddo sounds as entertaining to my eyes and heart wherever I go. The technical crying and carrying on of children, either my kids or someone else's has never really bothered me because I try to fully grasp the love I have for you both, keeping it in mind as I watch parents struggle with their own kids. The main thing tugging at me most when traveling with your younger selves on planes was the kiddo disruption to our fellow travelers. I felt horrible for the other flyers when you would cry or carry on. I struggled with the bother and inconvenience it perhaps caused. I also put myself into a pickle, ugh, the dilemma of shielding everyone else on the plane while unnaturally telling you to shush or here, play with this, me however attempting to keep you quiet. I tried to spare fellow passengers the audible disruption of beautiful kiddo development in action but I never remember anyone ever mouthing off to us when you guys would cry or yell or throw a slight fit. I never did hear anyone complain about you my kids inside an airplane. Specifically in planes, I go overboard to put everyone else first, and believe I forever will, I am hard-wired this way. I have a few hyper relevant airline empathy examples I will share later in the chapter but for now, back to Moms on a Plane.

The single mom from Detroit to Salt Lake finally made it to her seats about ten rows back from where I sat.

Our main hatch door was closed, maintenance fixed the problem, the crowded line of planes is clearing so we should be able to get in the air quickly, so said the flight attendant over the speaker, and the weather is improving. Next, the captain got on the small confined grumpy group public announcement channel to share his glee…the winds shifted and he believes we should actually arrive in Salt Lake a little early. Wow, I thought to myself, what an amazing turnaround of circumstances and now, the previous negative assumptions and judgments sitting in the seats around me should be relaxed and no one has anything else to be upset about.

It was a precious little cry, soft…I imagined the infant cooing about ten rows back to be a little girl kiddo, gazing at her momma and her wriggling little baby fingers reaching out wishfully, pudgy little fists squeezing to be picked up and held. The bellowing baby cries floating through the plane were truly wonderful and it made my cheeks smile out loud. It was a lovely sound. Least a dozen full grown professional experienced men and women business frequent flyers then belted out extreme verbal frustration because of the baby's cries. I had to imagine but I am only assuming, that many of these loudmouth negative travelers are also parents themselves…the situation baffled me a little. The baby continued to cry for a few minutes as our plane backed up and we headed for the de-icing pad.

I heard the mother desperately trying to calm and quiet the baby while the older kid started to complain about something and I started to physically sweat myself, mortified and feeling horrible for the single mom. I felt some of her mom pain, and wanted to help but there was nothing for me to do at the time, our plane was moving. The negative business traveler chatter intensified as the baby continued its moderate-toned cry. Most of the cantankerous people were irritated because it was still early in the day, it's a long flight, they planned to get some sleep but with 'that baby' crying, their sleep will be disrupted, or so they said out loud to everyone else on the plane who did or did not at all care to hear their affectless inner thoughts. We made it through de-icing and briefly sat still on the tarmac, second in line to take off. The baby quieted and it sounded like the little kiddo was sleeping. The entire plane grew very still and quiet, as most people settled into attempted shuteye mode. The single mom must feel incredibly relieved and hopeful their little one sleeps soundly for the next four hours.

The baby started up its cute little cries again and least four passengers from around the plane yelled out, "Oh my God", "Are you kidding me?", then least one gracious and kind comment coming from the first-class section announced publicly, "That's fucking bullshit". One of the shouts blasted almost straight into my ear, flying forward from a boisterous woman directly in the seat behind me. I felt horrible for the single mom 10 rows back and maybe…hum, is this true? Not sure but I might have factually felt worse for the passengers that were verbally upset by the baby, than I did for the single mother. Yes, I believe I felt worse because of the ridiculous embarrassment for the rather inconsiderate behavior of my fellow frequent flyers, but I am judging and blaming.

I spun my head around and peeked over the top of the back of my seat to look at the woman behind me mouthing off about the baby. The lady behind me was maybe early 60's amid her years, dressed very sharply in fancy business attire and was already working on her laptop with spreadsheets in hand, someone I assumed was a seasoned traveler.

I knew the woman's voice from her previous public conversations but had not looked at her until I peered over my seat with embarrassment for her and her snappy comments about the baby. I knew the woman's voice because earlier she was going on and on, proudly telling someone next to her about her new granddaughter, pulling out pictures and everything. This lady previously shared to the world she had three kids and two grandkids so I'm surprised mouthy grandmom wasn't a little more empathetic for the struggling single mother in the back of the plane. I continued to stare back over the top of my seat until our eyes met for one-one-thousand, two-one-thousand, then I turned back around slowly, attempting an intentional shame cast upon her, and kept my judgy nose forward for the rest of the flight. I had glared at the loudmouth lady behind me and fuck to the yes, with weighty disapproval. I assume she recognized my negative look but she was not deterred and repeated herself after I turned back around, "Somebody better shut that damn kid up or I will".

I thought of the single mom ten rows back. I wiped the beads of nervous sweat from my forehead. I thought intently of Andrea and my eyes welled up, trying to imagine how hard it must be to travel with little kids on planes all by her momma-self, feeling guilty I was not always there to help her.

I wiped the right tear from the top mound of my cheek, and just let the left one fall.

Lastly, I thought of the daughter of the mouthy lady behind me, a mom herself. I thought of the mother of a newborn baby girl who had the woman behind me as their mother. I thought of the grandkid of the lady behind me and that baby's mother, and although assuming, I was rather sure the lady behind me would not be telling her daughter to 'shut that damn kid up', if that 'damn kid' was this lady's own granddaughter. I bet the mouthy lady behind me would not even say out loud what she said, even if she thought it or meant it, if it was her own damn grandkid doing the crying. I sat there as we took off, Trifecta of Ugly sick to my stomach and I thought deeply.

I thought, and quickly knew for fact how I felt.

I felt ashamed to be a business traveler.

I felt ashamed for the times me myself lacked proper empathy.

I felt ashamed for the times I lack empathy, the times I barely resemble being human.

I felt ashamed to be human.

I felt ashamed.

I felt very, very ashamed.

Judge Blame and Assume, Trifecta of Ugly example 3.0
Sugar Bomb
One of my best friends back in Baltimore was John Riley. He was my best man at the wedding when I married your mom. John Riley worked for Trek for about nine years in Maryland and in 2001 when he got a promotion and moved to Wisconsin, I took over his job in Baltimore. John was also Lauren's coach when you guys did the mountainbike program at Camrock during middle school. Six years before I met your mom I quit drugs, and five years before I met your mom, I started racing pro on the mountainbike circuit.

John and I did a lot of stuff together, especially ride bikes. One day after I turned pro, John and I went on a mountainbike ride. We had to pedal on the street for a few miles before we got to the trails. The ride with John this day was a hard training ride, not an easy casual ride but an intense fitness ride. Later in the day when we were riding home from the trails on the street, I got into some trouble.

We were riding on a busy narrow road and I was in front, John behind me by about twenty feet or so. The road had no shoulder so our position was precarious at best. Trying to get off the section of dangerous road soon as possible, John and I were riding fast, about 17 MPH. Most times training and racing, I pushed hard and intently focused on the task at hand. John and I were hauling ass down the road, teetering the very edge of the street surface. The cars were doing 40 MPH or more and whisking past less than a foot from the end of our handlebars. Minimal margin existed for error. Just as one of the cars drove by, the passenger screamed loudly, very loudly into my left ear and I ran off the road.

The blast of verbal malice startled the fuck out of me. I was previously totally in the zone, focusing to stay relaxed and pushing hard, only about a mile away from where we could escape the blacktop and dive onto a dirt trail and into a park. Post-scream, while miraculously, I did not crash. I got back on the pavement quickly before hitting any obstacles in the small grass ditch, but I was still rattled from the shock of the shriek, and barely could I ride a straight line. There was nowhere to pull over and try to calm down for a few minutes, so I just had to keep going. I was extremely frazzled but thankfully, neither did I cause John to crash. Not intending to brag, yet to say I am rather steady when riding. I worked hard for years to minimize excessive body movements on the bike, so not to waste energy. I cannot accurately describe the extent of pure fright I felt when the car passenger lashed out at me, it really-really-really sucked, so I'll abandon any further descriptive attempt.

I tried to settle, so I didn't wobble and risk getting hit by a car. After a minute or two I was holding a smooth line again but saw the long flow of cars start to slow down in front of me. There was a stop sign ahead and by the time John and I approached the mostly-stationary stringer of autos, about 15 vehicles laid waiting in line to go through the intersection. Oh shit…the screamer car was stopped third in line, creeping along slowly and waiting their turn. I knew I would pass the car in the right-hand gutter before they had a chance to drive away. My pulse was still artificially high and I saw through their rear window, the passenger looking back and bouncing around. It looks like a dude, and it appeared excited dude guy was preparing to yell at me again as I rode by, because it seemed to work so well for him the first time, or so I boldly assume.

Quickly I reached down and grabbed my number one waterbottle, opened the squirter nozzle, and held it ready in my left hand. I was preparing to spray the guy in his face if he tried to scream at me again. By this time John and I were going about 20 MPH, a speedy fast number for a mountainbike. I was still seeing a slight shade of red from the previous incident, but didn't want to flat out retaliate if the guy was willing to let it go. Because I was going so fast and the car was stopped, it would be a split-second decision if I sprayed the guy or not. I quickly processed…doubting I had enough time to accurately decide. I prepared not to do anything, but held my waterbottle #1 ready, just in case.

I was almost alongside the car and the passenger jerked his head back and forth quickly, a seeming attempt to time his assault correctly. I took aim, anticipating engagement but also receptive to let this shit go, if possible. As I got up to the open window and right before I zoomed by, the guy stuck his head out and started to scream. I squeezed my bottle violently just inches from his face, rapidly filling his mouth with a forceful spray, almost half the contents of my bottle, more than 10 ounces. As I whisked ahead, I heard the guy gag violently on my squirted bottle contents and choked it out all over himself. The whole thing happened within a second or three.

I shoved my number one bottle back into its cage, and oops, I suddenly feared for John behind me. With cars zooming past only a foot away, I could not turn around and make sure John was ok. My ears pinned backward for sounds but also I was speeding up and trying to get to the trail fast as possible, anticipating car passenger retaliation very soon. I was quickly relieved to hear John's familiar giggle-laugh saying, "Roger…", and I assumed my riding partner's slight amusement awhile slight disapproval that although I didn't start it, now I'm picking a fight. FYI, my number one waterbottle contained plain water.

The traffic was really moving now and I became concerned, knowing the car would pass me again before I reach the off-road trail. Now John and I were really hauling ass, times two. As expected, my road rage playmate came flying by and the guy was violently cursing me, "You fucking asshole…" as a sealed full can of, I think it was beer, zoomed past my head about eight inches in front of my nose, barely missing me. Ok, this shit just got real. I was enraged with a weird mix of reactive emotions, both fury and fright, but mostly sky-high fury. I couldn't hear John behind me but because of the competing velocities between the car and bike movements, I assumed mad car guy did not assault John first as the vehicle sped by, rather probably waiting to assault me, least I hoped such was the case.

Currently now looking back under review I see the following. One, regrettably, I put John in harm's way. If he got hurt, it would have been my fault. I should have let that shit go earlier, mostly because of the confined opportunity to escape off the narrow busy road, and because I was gambling with John's safety too. Two, in short order, I blame-pulled mad car guy's chain and although I was slightly frightened, I was simultaneously thankful the speeding can aimed at my head wasn't a speeding bullet from a gun. Baltimore's one murder per day average forced me to keep top of mind that handguns were scattered about. I avoided the thought to consider truth perhaps rightfully, and did not give consideration of possible handgun retaliation when I first sprayed the guy, but absolutely I should have. I blame-reacted when spraying, instead of thinking. Three, the guy escalated the issue to a new level when he…uh, well no, fuck that, that's a lie, the guy didn't do this, I did, I escalated this shit. After the loaded soda-beer bullet barely missed me, I definitively blame-decided not to leave this one alone but I probably should have. I was not thinking and let my raging emotions steer my behavior, aka reactive dumb angry bird.

There was a traffic light ahead, right before the turnoff for the trail where John and I could escape. Oh wow, the traffic light just turned red so there would be one more exchange before this battle is over. I felt rather sure I will get the better of him, certain they will not catch me once I hit the trail. Pretty much the same shit was about to go down as what happened at the stop sign.

I saw the car stopped ahead of me and because of my speed, I believed I might pass them before the light turned green. My rapid traffic calculator found an opportunity with no conflicting crosstown traffic and I planned not to slow. As I approached, I could see the passenger spinning around and looking at me through the back window.

Two additional complexities arose beyond the earlier stop sign altercation. One, I knew the guy was going to fire at me again. I expected it to be another full drink can pitched at close range. Two, I was absolutely going to fire also, me not guessing the matter like the previous stop sign incident. I prepared my ammunition as I motored towards their stopped car. I saw the passenger lean back in the front seat, almost laying back on the driver's shoulder. The passenger's arm was cocked and I assumed he was about to fire at me with full force. I grabbed my number two waterbottle this time. My number two bottle is a larger 24-ouncer and completely full of my sugary-sweet and sticky sports drink mix concoction, Cytomax.

I neared their rear bumper and was moving at maximum speed, when I cocked my arm back myself. I was about to fire and I saw the passenger about to release his shot, seemingly right on time and I did not think he was going to miss this time. And no, you might be surprised to learn that I did not open the squirter nozzle on my large bottle of liquid cotton candy. As I approached the window, I could hear inside the car. The passenger wasn't saying a word but I saw his loaded arm move towards me at high-speed. The driver was laughing hysterically, I assume because I previously soaked his passenger, said passenger who it appears is steaming mad at me. I quickly flipped the entire wide-mouth lid off the bottle and tossed the whole thing inside, the bottle spinning and bouncing off the passenger's shoulder, exploding its pink goopy splatter everywhere inside the car. My pitch had some speed and spin to it…I briefly saw the bottle absolutely cover the inside of the windshield and entirely cover the driver too. I heard the driver's cackling immediately cease. I put my sugar-bomb launch hand back on my handlebars and sprinted with fury through the just-turned-green light, frantically speeding for the turnoff into the safety of singletracked woods. I slightly panicked…first, if caught, I fully anticipated the driver to run me over, literally, because of his sugar shower rage, or maybe this time these boys might possess a gun to then point and shoot. Secondly, I thought if I might be able to get away safely, the car would instead choose to aim for John. I realized too late that I fucked up supremely, me putting John Riley directly in their target scope.

Perhaps one of the most joyful experiences of my life occurred next. I guess John was watching this road rage bullshit develop from behind and he respectfully stayed out of the line of fire. Just as I turned off the main road, John caught up with me. John and I shared a few holy-shit type of words and we sprinted down a side street and around a corner, intent on making it to the upcoming singletrack trail before hearing or feeling another shot or bump-bump of us under their weighted wheels.

I assume but I believe John did not appreciate getting caught in the middle of that stupid and possibly very dangerous road rage street fight. I carry a slight emotional scar from the matter still. I was ridiculously embarrassed that I took it so far and the entire ordeal could have easily ended in true tragedy. Over the next few weeks, my rattled emotions intensified and I made an extremely serious life decision.

In mid-summer 1991, I absolutely decided I will try to never let my ugly, assumptive, judgmental, and blaming reactive emotions spin so far out of control again. I will try to let shit go, even when people get in my face. I will try to deescalate, laugh it off, walk away and drop aggressive behavior from my forever future. I will try to be the bigger person and not lay hands on anyone. I will try to let other people carry their own behavior and I will try hard AF to manage and regulate my own, despite what others do or do not.

Try, I will try to remain on the emotional high road and walk away, even when other people are losing their shit, and even when they want to kill me, it's just not fucking worth it.

For the next 26 years I would operate as such, me letting shit go, and avoiding such confrontations entirely, well, that is, until mid-summer 2017.

Judge Blame and Assume, Trifecta of Ugly example 4.0
Go Ahead, Take Your Best Shot
It was the middle of the summer 2017, home in Cottage Grove and as an overview, Mother Nature mostly graced us with stellar weather to frolic around in that year. I was riding my road bike a ton, struggling with some behemoth life decisions. Often I use road bike rides as self-consultive mental therapy sessions and certainly such was the case for the previous ten years before this time, ever since 2006 when I moved out of Starlight Lane. The longer the bike rides the better too, because with such heavy shit on my mind, I had more time to try and think some of the things through. In 2014 when I was trying to figure out if I should quit my 20-year job at Trek or divorce Nora or both, I pedaled my road bike over 8,500 miles within nine months, or about 240 miles per week. Truth be clear though, I was also doing a lot of long-distance rides because of the complex ponders, so the miles added up fast. That summer, I did 32 bike rides that were more than 100 miles each and my longest ride was 301 miles, completed in 19 hours, leaving Coyle Parkway at midnight and arriving on the sidewalk at Nora's sister's house in south Minneapolis the same day.

The additional frequency of rides well as the additional duration also meant for additional complexities. Beginning around 2009, I noticed a dramatic increase in the number of distracted drivers. Over 15 times between 2009 and 2017 I almost got hit by a car on my road bike, mostly as drivers looked down at their phones instead of looking up at the road. Out of the 15, I had four close calls that easily could have killed me. Besides the few near death experiences, most other near misses I did see them coming. Perhaps the distractedness of drivers could have flabbergasted me as they somewhat-mindlessly piloted their 3,000-pound rolling death machines while texting. Perhaps I could have been mad because of their silly multitasking behind the wheel, while my life sits inches off their front bumper like an insect to gobble up. Perhaps I could have called them names or even given them the finger as they cut me off, their front fenders practically brushing my hip while they are doing 20 over the speed limit, eyes down. Perhaps I could have considered these people inconsiderate, reckless, lacking basic operating mental capacities, or even lacking basic concern for human life. But no.

No, no, and no...I know not their distraction, their worry, their struggle. I try not to judge them or blame them, not even for their potentially harmful or even lethal behavior.

I must come clean on something. I am assuming, but I believe because of mixing time alongside cars while on my bike in Baltimore, I grew to develop a self-preservation defense mechanism. When riding my bike in Baltimore, if I didn't have to stop at a stoplight or stop sign, I didn't. Many times in Baltimore, for me, it was safer to get the hell out of the way of the cars whenever possible. I have seen people get hit on their bikes as they sat there at a stop sign or stop light. I saw more people on bikes get hit standing still than moving. For me and mostly, the continuous movement is a defensive maneuver that keeps me out of harm's way more than stopping and starting. I believe I became habituated with my continuous movement ways. When I lived in Baltimore, I rode my bike tons more than I ever will in Wisconsin, cumulatively. The population of the Baltimore metro area ranks near the top 20 in the country, around 2,000,000 people. The population of Madison proper is about ten times less than Baltimore, around 200,000 but the Madison metro area is around 600,000. Still, I am extremely challenged to observe the functional meaning of stop signs and stop lights in Wisconsin, not kidding. I have consciously tried to observe these legal traffic devices but my body physically rejects the notion, and I no longer try to fight my natural instincts to just keep moving, staying safer and staying out of motorist's way.

Of the 15 or so times between 2009 and 2017 when I almost got hit riding my bike, most of those 15 times I absolutely positively would have been hit if I was not super-alert and was not maintaining continuous movement. Actually there's a high probability two of those times I absolutely would have been killed if I wasn't still clipped into my pedals, eyes up, nimble and moving. The close calls escalated greatly in 2014 and beyond. Least five times during that period, I had drivers curse me out, chase me in their cars and throw things at me because I didn't stop at a stop sign or stop light. And to be clear, every single one of these least five times escalated and could have become road rage altercations, hah, but not why you might think. To be double-layer clear, every single one of those least five times had nothing to do with close calls or me mouthing off. Every single one of those least five times, I was nowhere near the driver who then came after me. But rather, the driver saw me from the other side of the street or somewhere else, and I was nowhere near being a hazard or threat to them or anyone else, not kidding. I was apart and away from their path of travel and the driver became so judgmentally concerned and enraged that they chased me down.

I don't get in anyone's way when I keep my movement on the bike continuous, actually it's the opposite, I am staying out of everyone's way and do so smoothly, quietly and safely. But in these five instances the drivers, all middle-aged to older white men, felt the need to come after me. Mostly, although a few of these guys tried to physically hurt me or stop me so they could try to beat me up, I just kept rolling and did not react. I did not react to their threatening and intentional attempts to hurt me and on some level I maintained a moderate amusement of their out of orderliness and hypocrisy. Hypocrisy. I am rather alert and aware of many small details both within myself and out in the world, not only while on the bike. I think, because I spend so much time riding my bike on roads, I have grown hyper alert to driver's movements and one thing I notice more than looking at their phones while driving, is that barely anyone driving a car fully stops at a stop sign, barely anyone stops, for real.

Factually-actually, for over two decades I kept a mental scorecard of this illegal behavior, motorists not fully stopping at stop signs, and I state emphatically this to be a truth of my life experience: Less than 5% of motorists come to a complete stop at a stop sign when there is no conflicting traffic. To me, a complete stop in a car means the car lurches backwards slightly when a complete stop occurs. When performing a complete stop and inside the car, you feel it, and when outside the car you see it, a slight lurching backwards. Most drivers, as I have keenly observed for multi decades, slow greatly but then just keep going, maintaining forward movement the entire time and never truly stopping. So when these five hothead dudes came after me, I kept in mind they themselves are probably not stopping either most times when driving their cars, so the notion of them judging blaming and attacking me is slightly amusing by my measure, aka hypocrisy.

After a few too many such incidents, I developed a new strategy. I assembled a verbal comeback for the next time somebody in a car chases me down, screaming at me and threatening me because they saw me roll a stop sign, nowhere near their path of travel. My planned remark to their contemptuous language or behavior:

Do me a favor, I won't try to read your mind and how about you don't try to read mine? I won't try to read your mind, imagining I know why you are chasing me down. I won't try to read your mind, imagining what other situations you have going on in your life to possibly motivate you to behave like you are behaving right now. I won't try to read your mind, possibly skipping far ahead to judge you or blame you for your actions.

I won't try to read your mind and assume I know anything about you or your thoughts. I won't try to read your mind, then judging or lashing out at you and call you names after your assault of me. I'll try not to do that, I'll try not to do any of that. So how about we share that respectful intent, and you not try to read my mind? How about you try not to read my mind why I rolled past that stop sign nowhere near you? How about you try not to read my mind, and assume you know the reasoning behind my behavior? How about we do that? Do we have a deal, can we agree on that? Because that's what I would like to do.

I rehearsed that speech and held it ready for years. Many times the verbal address sat on the tip of my tongue as I approached or rolled through all those wide-open stop signs, but the circumstances never presented themselves for me to share that well thought-out comeback. I was still riding my bike hundreds of miles per month so the opportunity existed, but I became further detached from emotional reactions following the long-ago road rage incident in front of John Riley. That screaming car passenger incident had a profound effect on me and I literally changed my core perspective of other people after that, not only people in cars. I came close a couple times to implementing my mind-reading pact but chose to rather say nothing and just pedal away or wave happily, giving them a condescending, "Hello, thank you, thank you" smartass wave as I rode off.

Furthermore, although I believe my still-held snapback is both accurate and appropriate, I embrace the honest but harsh reality of our modern-day world. People these modern days appear more stressed than relaxed. More people these days I observe reside in conflict mode and factually, more than ever in multitudes hold concealed carry gun permits. By default, although I am assuming and judging, fewer people these days would put up with my somewhat cocky comeback and I might get shot more easily than ever, because duh, nobody likes a smartass.

So yeah, although I held that well-crafted word collection, I was less and less likely to need to use it. Less inclined to spew those words because of my conscious avoidance of confrontation with road-rager's behind the wheel, well, but then, it happened.

It was midsummer, late July, a Tuesday, echo-calendar year 2017. I was riding my road bike south on the rural Oak Park Road, negligibly leaving the Cottage Grove township boundary and crossing route 12. My planned excursion was a 50-mile loop to the sleepy little town of Edgerton and back. Oak Park is a simple north-south road, very quiet, not much traffic, and just rolls along through farmland. Route 12 is an east-west two-lane 55MPH major thoroughfare, one lane going one way and one lane going another, but no median or curb in the middle or anything like that. Route 12 is not a highway, just a highspeed road connecting Madison to many small eastern towns like Cambridge and beyond.

The afternoon sky all blue, beautiful, and the traffic on route 12 was steady but not crowded. As I pedaled the sleepy Oak Park southbound, I looked least a quarter mile in each direction down the cross route 12, since having clear view both ways. I noticed a safe opening in the flow of cars perfectly sized for me as I approached. I know better not to gamble across busy or highspeed roads so if thinking the timed situation a slight hazard, I loop around in small circles before adventuring through. I do not-do not risk my life at intersections. I do not behave irresponsibly or in a reckless manner. Truthfully I state, I am extremely calculated. Knock on wood, knock-knock, I have never been hit by a car. Almost 1,000 fellow cyclists die on American roads every year, including some people I once knew.

I ride more miles than most people I know so I remain thoughtful of the truthful hazards, and of the hazards rapidly increasing because of mobile phones. I ride with clipless pedals on my road and mountainbikes so my shoes are locked in, similar to ski boot bindings. If I stop and put my foot down on the ground while riding my bike, I have to unclip my shoes so by default, when I restart I must clip back in right away. Handfuls of times in my life, when trying to speedily clip back into my pedals, needing to mentally envision the small lock-in cleat affixed to the bottom of my shoes, aligning it exactly with the pedal hiding out of sight under my foot, doing all this by feel as I keep my eyes up and try to get going fast, sometimes I miss.

Once living hyper-intentionally, my elevated awareness has collected educated bits of most things, alongside the build-up of my 20,000+ hours riding my bike out in the world, so far. I have fumbled atop my pedals before, coming close to contacting a car when not clipping back in accurately, an otherwise mundane job for a seasoned cyclist. Since I ride a fair amount, I recognize the increased chance for a mishap. Most times I stay clipped in because it's safer, much safer. When I miss reentry into my pedals, forward acceleration then stops, and I put myself squarely in harm's way. I can ride for three or four hours while remaining clipped in through congested urban areas, until pausing for food or the bathroom. I stay locked into my pedals at busy intersections by balancing in place, or leaning against a pole, or holding onto a public urban trashcan. I intend to stay locked into my pedals, hence avoiding the risk of falling when restarting, but oops, sometimes I miss clipping in speedily when it's my turn to proceed, aka a legit danger with impatient cars all around me.

A silver pickup truck was paused at the stop sign on Oak Park, heading the same way I was going. Watching cross street timing, I knew I had a safe gap, so I spun by on the right and within the small available shoulder, past the stagnant pickup, and proceeded smoothly through the intersection. Often I calculate the audited seconds when passing an obstacle, counting down until a car crosses where I just was, to check if I judged safely. That roll across route 12 was almost a four-one-thousand space, plenty of a safe gap for both me and the crosstown traffic cars.

I was about a quarter mile south on Oak Park beyond route 12 when the altercation began. No other cars existed anywhere near us on Oak Park when the silver four-door truck sped up from behind, the driver laying on the horn, and the horn remained laid-upon, pinned and blaring. I imagined this the same pickup sitting at the stop sign a couple minutes before. Yup, I glanced back slightly and recognized the truck, but I could not slow down or the truck bumper would hit me because it was practically touching my rear tire. I prepared my legacy mind reading speech but hum…in short order, I recognized this person was perhaps too pissed-off for me to try and speak to them as planned. Oh yup yuppers, I was right, the situation quickly became crazily confrontational.

I was traveling about 25MPH, with now my head pounding from the incessant horn blast. I rode steady, making zero movements sounds or gestures towards the aggressive truck, no way, I knew better and learned that sugar bomb lesson long ago. I was holding my line and hoping they would eventually speed around, probably shower me with some curse bombs then maybe throw shit out the window, like has happened multiple times before. Oak Park began to incline and a turnoff road was a slight ways ahead on the right, near the crest of the little hill. Once on the hill, I could not see oncoming traffic which was a concern, although maybe not a direct peril. Things should be ok long as the truck stays behind me or passes quickly. The driver of the truck, a red faced whitey-colored man, let go of his blaring horn and started screaming violently out his open window…fucking asshole this-and-that, pull over before I hit you this-and-that, so I planned to turn onto the small road upcoming on the right, the tiny Milo Way. Before I made it safely to Milo, the truck pulled around and cut me off, blocking my lane completely and most of the other side of the road too.

The entire area was wide open and exposed, nowhere to get away, so I knew the need to deal with this silly-ass shit right now. I skidded to a halt and stopped my bike at an angle before impacting the truck but barely, and put both feet on the ground, now feeling vulnerable and insecurely disadvantaged while not clipped into my pedals. Oh boy…I immediately thought of my old hothead boss Jeff from Mount Washington Bike Shop in Baltimore, aka Trina's boyfriend. Several times when I later worked for him, Jeff got into fist fights with store customers in our parking lot. Jeff would come back into the store afterwards panting, sweating, slightly disheveled, proudfully cocky, with his bike shoes in hand and each time spouting his worldly wisdom, "Always take your shoes off".

Jeff meaning to instruct me: Always get out of my bike shoes before throwing down. Because the pedal cleat on the bottom of the shoe protrudes, barely could I solidly stand more or less dance around in cycling shoes securely while fighting. I never exchanged punches while in bike shoes, but maybe my time was now, right here. Briefly I thought of Jeff, and as it may be shortly upcoming, the need to take my shoes off in the middle of Oak Park Road.

I was decades before however, pre-committed not to engage with guys like this and make similar stupid shit any worse. I landed about four feet from the right edge of the road, straddling the bike in the middle of my southbound lane and the truck was now blocking both lanes. If a northbound car came at us over the hill doing the 55MPH speed limit, we all might die because the oncoming car could not possibly avoid hitting this rage-filled truck sitting in the middle of the road.

The unrelenting verbal assault continued, with similar elevated horn volume and agitated combativeness by the way…stupid fucking asshole blah-blah-blah, but the outraged guy never spoke specifically to why he was mad, what he thinks I did wrong or anything of the likes, he was just calling me names. I guess it really didn't matter, I knew what set him off, it was me rolling across route 12 as he waited behind the stop sign on Oak Park south for traffic to clear. Keeping my stuff facing into the distance and outside his field of vision, I rolled my eyes because of the un-gluing going on beside me. The guy became more enraged, wildly jumping about in the driver's seat.

As he bounced around, oh wow, oh no…I saw why he was not getting out to tangle with me fisticuffs, and I was thankful as hell to still have my shoes on.

I watched his hands carefully to see if he might reach for a gun. I am totally judging but it appeared to me this burly dude dressed in camo might own a gun, or twenty.

The belligerence snowballed from there, him screaming at me with spit flying out of his mouth and he said with hell-bent force, "I should fucking kill you right now", he said that exact phrase twice amid his multi-minute raging rant. I was scared to death, but no, no way not at all concerned for myself. I tried to speak up, perhaps interrupting him but hoping to water down this emotional wildfire, least a little.

Once finding a slight opening in his violent ramble, I jumped in repeating sternly a few words with military-like respect, "I hear you sir, I hear you sir", me trying to diffuse this mad-mad man. He kept one hand on the steering wheel the entire time, while his other hand waved around wildly pointing at me and shaking. At first I was trying to get the dude to leave me the heck alone, so I stopped my bike and unclipped, willing to let him unload on me entirely, like whatever who cares…do whatever you want dude I don't fricking care…throw shit, spit on me or even push me over whatever…go ahead and dump on me as you will, but then bro, just let me get back to my bike ride.

But uh yeah, hard no, fuck that noise, soon as he used the word *kill*, it was a brand new fucking game. Ah yeah, I thought to myself authoritatively, *kill*?...really dude, *kill*?...are you fucking kidding me, that shit ain't fucking happening. Meaning, he should have never used *that* motherfucking word, no fucking way, not fucking here, not fucking now, and fucking not with me, fucking fuck to the no. That shit in my book, as I argued within myself, that shit is entirely fucking disallowed. The out of control dude just crossed my damn line. I believe then he saw my smirk. I readied…my posture sprang to attention, my chest outpuffed, and my left hand sitting atop my handlebars formed a hammerfist.

I grabbed and held back some additional reactive thoughts at the last second, before they almost spilled out of my mouth, although I strongly desired to throw the words at him out loud. So I instead said inside my head…there ain't no fucking way I'm letting you go there dude, no fucking way, no fucking how, and I knew exactly what I had to do next.

Not mildly did I concern myself with anything he was blah-blah-blah saying or might do, I didn't give a shit in the fucking slightest, I only cared about not making life worse for his two little kids in the back seat.

I got more and more scared for the kiddos as I watched the bottom lip of his daughter quivering, then the darling little girl crying quietly as her dad screamed his death threats at me. The junior gal was about five and the little boy maybe three or three and a half, both of them super-cutie-pies. The kiddos were secure in their car seats and my heart melted entirely…me wanting to reach in and grab them, taking them straight home to their momma. After his second 'I should fucking kill you right now', I said similarly as before but with an elevated stone-stern-tone, "I hear you sir, I hear you, and if that's what you feel you need to do then go ahead, take your best shot", as I clipped back into my pedals and just rode right the fuck around his truck defiantly, continuing then out in the open, me casually strolling straight down Oak Park. The guy spun his rear truck tires on the pavement coming after me, almost hitting my left side as he sped past.

I am rather certain over my entire life I have never encountered a more out of control violent person anywhere than this guy who screamed, "I'll be right back with my fucking gun!", as he raged by in his big silver pickup truck directly south on Oak Park Road. I was surprised he didn't hit me and rather, he honestly seemed to be rushing home to get one of his probable 20-something guns. He sped ahead of me then hit the brakes suddenly and I thought…oh fricking hell, what now? Hah, but he did not stop, no not at all. Rather, he was aggressively slowing down to make a turn and sadly, *sheesh*, he turned right on Milo Way, then speeding down the mini road. "Oh fricking great…", me now having a legitimate outside-voice conversation with myself, "…that's just wonderful", speaking with my defiant but highly amused surrender-giggle, "…he lives right fricking there, oh well whatever, this won't take long". Milo Way is a brief dead-end road with only a couple farms residing down that lane. Nowhere existed to hide from this guy, and I expected it only a few minutes before he caught back up to me, and I safely assumed he will have his gun with him this time, as promised. I really didn't give a crap if he had a gun or not, no way, not the frick at all, I just hoped he didn't still have his kids with him when he comes back to shoot me.

I rode south on Oak Park Road, taking a slight drink of water and a nibble of an energy bar from my jersey pocket. "Hah…", I laughed to myself out loud, "last supper".

Like most bike rides, I was not carrying my phone. My phone is an unnecessary weight to haul around and an entire unnecessary distraction to be tempted by. Regardless, I would not have called the police anyway, there was no time I figured, and I wasn't going to spend my possible last fucking few minutes of life fucking fumbling around on my stupid motherfucking phone.

Although my thoughts raced briefly ahead, me half-ass considering an attempted duck and cover to run off and hide somewhere, the area was really way too exposed, and besides, I truthfully didn't give a flying fuck.

No, forget it, just forget it, it wasn't worth it, nothing was worth it.

I shifted my brain waves.

I focused on my breath.

I gazed skyward.

A red-tailed hawk soared elegantly, his head pivoting around and looking down for I'm sure, ground mice lunch. I sat up, stretching high and no-handed, my fingers wriggling and attempting a make believe belly play-tickle of the hunter bird overhead, thankful as all get out for these precious moments of appreciated birds against blue sky. Nora revered the red-tails as her guardian angels, and I transposed myself in Nora's place, reaching out for a chanced or even slight, deity interlude.

Hello birdy, hello there, could you possibly collect some of heaven's love then come get me? Birdy can you lift me, birdy can you carry me? Let us fly away, brushing our wings against the sun, together. I picture us near the daytime stars and far-far away from here, far away, far away but together.

My hands slid gently, purposefully, and precisely back onto the bike's handlebars. I consciously relaxed my shoulders, bringing my chin up, extending my chest out, rotating my hips forward, and precisely settling in oh so comfortably…perfect, just perfect…this my place, here my space, now my grace.

If I could, I would unhurt those I injured, un-find those I lost. If I could, would I locate or hold true what I lack now? Perhaps not…maybe I know not what I had, have, or might.

Factually embracing my composure like never once in this here life like fucking ever before, then overcome by a huge warming smile, I thought humbly these exact things…what a beautiful day, such a beautiful road, oh this great ride, just great, this ride my life.

Late July 2017 was a hard time for me, emotionally, fucking exceptionally fucking hard. In late July 2017, I didn't care if somebody fuck wanted to shoot me or run me over or whatever who the fuck cares. Yes sure, I threw gasoline on his emotions ablaze there at the end with my 'take your best shot' teasing, but the heart of the matter was truly something entirely different all-to-fuck-gether.

Additionally, besides the something else fuck of the matter, I wasn't going to fight back, no way forget it and not even, I just wasn't. A full 26 years earlier in Baltimore after I launched the sugar bomb, I decided not to engage with anyone, even if they were physically in pursuit of me, even if they were trying to kill me, it just wasn't fucking worth it. My fighting days were over. I was way, way long-ago brain and heart-tired, I really was, and, well, and well, it just wasn't worth it.

Five days before this phoenix hunter bird blue sky bike ride, meaning that precisely on July 20th in 2017, something pushed me to the point of not caring to put up a pinky finger fight to even fucking stay alive. So although yes, true, around that time I was still working with clients, riding my bike, parenting, and trying to be a good husband, I was ruefully indifferent about one more days' time.

This chapter four concentrates on truth and smack-dab here specifically, the focus is my learned assimilation, the Trifecta of Ugly, aka judge blame and assume. So not to disrupt the honesty pond or muddy the truth stream, my 2017 emotional challenges are more appropriate and best saved for later, probably reserved for your upcoming volume two chapter thirteen already titled The Other Side, all of it mostly already written.

Sitting here now modern day and thinking back, was I assuming the role of sacrificial lamb just pedaling along on Oak Park south, unconcerned for what would soon arrive behind me, probably my enraged executioner? Hum, no, I do not believe I was necessarily trying to trip and fall onto my exposed self-sacrificial sword blade but rather with lucidity, trying to disengage from the guy. He didn't appear to be winding down his rant, so trying to save his kids from more ogre screaming, I rode off, irreverently detached from thoughts of harm coming my way, aka ah fuck it. Additionally, it seemed crystal clear the guy intended to come back, and I would rather face him now or soon, hence my take your best shot tease. My preference would be to get this shit over with and now, instead of having him hunt me down at some inopportune moment within time forward.

Knowing that if I ran, perhaps some other day he happens upon me, possibly when you guys or Amelia or Nora is near, and I knew I would never take that risk, no fricking way, no fricking how.

Trifecta of Ugly: Judge Blame and Assume Wrap-Up

The habituated human privilege to judge blame and assume shines brightly in front of me as hyper-apparent. Once initiating even a slight regulation of my dirty assumptions, I discovered conditions even worse than first believed, dang, I was missing additional underlying problems which contributed to make assumptive matters even more troublesome, many times a worse outcome for everyone. Ancillary intentions to manage the Trifecta of Ugly also arose like, my attempt to respond instead of react. To me, responding comes from a fair and rational thinking brain capable of pausing and holding comments consciously, least a while to listen more, learn more, and enquire more. Reacting rushes in from a pushy drama-filled emotional brain needing to blurt shit out right away, without thinking words or repercussions through before speaking writing or typing.

Regarding then Subway Wars, my examination here is others' pain, trauma, fear, and life conditions. I imagine that most others are like or the same as me, I prefer not when people assume they know me or guess to know what is best for me, trying to read my mind or the sort. I try to practice basic common courtesy, putting myself above no others, envisioning everyone I meet a mother, a grandmother, an aunt, a sister, a son, a little brother, a spouse or a child because we are all related, aka one blood total truth.

Concerning Moms on a Plane, even if never trapped in the same challenge as others before, I have a related experience from which I can draw. In most ways, I try to linger on the low side of humility, sometimes teetering on the verge of beating myself up unnecessarily. I'd rather think slightly less of myself than place my rank or order above others. I mentioned earlier about my excessive efforts to put others first when on planes. I mean to say the following. Never once in almost 40 years since I began flying have I reclined my seat when someone is seated behind me. Not even when the someone seated behind is a junior-sized-small-unit-kiddo. I do not place my elbows on armrests when someone sits next to me. This kinda sucks on the rare occasion I have a middle seat but I tuck-in this my kindness, consciously. I do not talk on the phone when in a plane, period. I only rarely talk on phones inside airports or public buildings, only when far off in a corner by myself, so to not disturb anyone.

Referencing oh then the Sugar Bomb, I was judging blaming and assaulting the guy who yelled at me. First he lashed out, I snapped back, which put us then on the same level, I was immediately no better than him, him then no worse than me. Beyond me judging what he did or did not do upon review, I now here focus on my own behavior, inherently knowing I cannot control others' actions. What went through my head at the first stop sign? I decided in a split second not to be abused further or taken additional advantage of by the car passenger's screams in my ear, so instead of trying to talk with the guy, laugh it off or avoid him altogether, I fired back. Instead of using my words, I used my fists, or rather my bottle-squeezing left fist…truly the definition of unregulated childlike reactive behavior. Maybe car passenger dude recently suffered some horrible trauma and he needed to vent, so he did it in my ear, IDK. Or maybe he's just a bit of an inconsiderate non-thinking monkey-mind bully person. The frightening speed to which that one shout could have escalated straight up to vehicular manslaughter is horrifying.

I thought the passenger sugar bomb guy was wrong to yell at me…I quickly blamed him, and I snapped back without thought or care for what could possibly happen next. I lived to learn and know that little things are capable of snowballing fast, unless I me myself is the one to jump out of the situation and genuinely deescalate or end it. My rageful dirty-ego did not allow me to plainly pedal past the stop sign with patience and not spray him in the face, once I heard his secondary scream start to wind up. Only today and decades later do I now see…I should have slowed with traffic and stopped, pausing far behind the shouting car once I saw the passenger's head spinning around looking for me in anticipation of, ding-ding…round two.

I should have diffused the situation in this way and resignedly waited for the car to drive off ahead of me, thus avoiding all engagement. Nothing else would have happened except my dirty-ego would have been mad I didn't have the opportunity to fill the guy's face with judgmental opposition water. My thinking brain would have known better and realized my upcoming optional behavior was unfavorable, factually incorrect behavior. My actual behavior being ridiculously confrontational and demanding to win, thus I sacrificed all opportunities to be right, I sacrificed all opportunities to operate correctly, I sacrificed all opportunities to remain aligned with my foundational core morals, by my measure.

Lastly, within Go Ahead, Take Your Best Shot, it could be the same role-reversal as me in Sugar Bomb.

Evidently the angry father in the truck felt my behavior was wrong and he too had to lash out. Unless I unnaturally stopped behind him at the intersection to begin with, I do not see what I could have consciously done differently to avoid or calm the dude. Well, with the exception of not teasing him to take his best shot. My best shot mouth-off was a total reactive verbal geyser of judge and blame. My reaction boiled over and jetted out of my mouth because of his steamed double-down use of the word 'kill', right in front of his legitimately terrified kiddos. Although held-aside extenuating circumstances pre-existed within me, once more I was willing to fucking die for the benefit of the children. Although my taunting streamed from my core intent of protecting the kids, still my behavior was purely instinctual, judgmental, blaming, and perhaps even, suicide by rabid dad.

Once I began to effectively control my assumptions, my life improved dramatically.

'The damn thing not being the fricking problem' lays heavily atop the Trifecta of Ugly. Let us use our wild whimsical imagination for a minute or three, making believe that one day Travis might have sprayed Lauren in the face with a big soaker-style water gun. Lauren screams at Travis and then runs to find me, crying and screaming as she runs. Then I punish Travis and put him in a timeout while deceptively throwing the darn water cannon in the trash. Lauren tells me her version of the deadly water gun assault story and I believe her.

Travis then yells at Lauren, saying he has a different version of the story and then I start extending the time-out minute meter because I proclaim Travis is arguing. I assumed what happened, Travis does not feel like I listened to him or allowed him to speak at all, I emotionally reacted and judged Travis, and I punished Travis based on my blaming assumptions.

The whole ordeal ran quickly beyond the base issue. Initially, the darn thing was the water gun but then, the true violation was the poppa bird's inept governance of crime and punishment.

A conscious and responsible handling was available to me in regard to the water soaker incident, but I did not possess the necessary skilled parenting tools back then. I sorry my precious, I very sorry. I am so-so-so sorry for all that stupid timeout punishment shit I inflicted upon you both. I am regretfully and terribly sorry. I was a fucking shitbird dad in several ways no doubt. I was doing what I thought was right despite my bad dad lack of skills, at the time. I so-so sorry.

Assumptions and judgments spin an especially sticky web throughout every orifice of my livelihood. Only after thousands of hours invested on the matter have I learn the honest maneuvering of my orientation…dropping the striving towards the assumed fantastical, avoiding the judging of the competitiveness within my measure and compare contests, steering clear of the misguided wanting, letting go of the untruthful self-shaming and self-blaming, and facing headlong to overcome the inexcusable that is my avoiding.

I also wholly accept the total truth within the sole responsibility of my own balanced peace. Foundationally, I try to own my feelings without influence.

I try to own my thoughts as existing free and clear from a master external thought maker. I try to own and hold true my beliefs as unequivocally known to me. I try to own my actions, even when I fall asleep behind the wheel and allow my monkey mind to drive.

I hold not, nor can I impose my nonexistent superpowers of change over any of my sisters or brothers, despite my desire and attempt to intrude…me trying to fix or save people. Yes of course, the intent and attempt to help others is an otherwise desirable trait. I lived to learn and know that when stuck, we need to hold ourselves accountable to sort out the fixing part on our own. Many times I have languished deep within the moments when I cannot effectively navigate life myself. True-true, during my I need help emotional down times, I do not always ask for support, nor now and again can I admit anything is wrong at all. Even when others see my pain, I might deny my suffering, sick and tired of hearing myself complain, and cognizant that everyone else has their own shit to handle or that I'm too proud to admit I cannot do it on my own.

At interval I silently hope for the simplest yet most complex of all support…please just hold my hand. Just hold my hand, and let me be the one to let go first. Such hand holding could help lift me up and out of my mini hell at times, and has. My gal pal Tara Lobreglio is a Jedi Master in this regard. I need to know I am ok, and that at the end of the day, if still feeling feathers-ruffled or unsure, a hand is there for me. Alas here between lies the truth…not always can I have such hands at my beckon call, not always exists the necessary tough love from others when I do not see clearly, and the challenge of my habituated aloneness day and night will be fixed by no other. Romance or not, I hope for occasional support to help me make and find my way through the crappy hard shadowed times of my life, times holding me back from the sunny better days coming for me ahead. My living to learning to knowing has produced the realization such balanced calm is internal, or least it is my challenge to open up, or ask for help, if even for a slight hand hold from TLo, or a glorious GrizzlyBearHug from Travis the Boyd.

Summarizing the Trifecta of Ugly…sure, I still judge blame and assume slightly now and then, but I try to shine a light on it brightly so to improve my practice. When getting caught, I try like hell to stop short of acting or speaking to it. When observing others how I might identify as behaving unfavorably, I try to say either strongly with my internal voice or softly with my external voice, "Looks like they're dealing with some other hard shit in their life that's messing them up right now". I try to walk on by, letting them carry their own behavior. My intent begins with dropping assumptions, and my world just grows sunnier from there, when I can factually do it.

I do stupid shit much-much of the time, maybe the every-days-long, much ado my makeup as a complex and untrained bird-like beast on the loose.

Sometimes You Have to Let People Be Stupid

If I see behavior misaligned to what I believe is appropriate, I may silently to myself judge the conduct so to steer clear of their actions, realizing conflict-a-coming. I try to not assume judge or blame them as a wrong or bad human person, no way, but rather they are just being themselves. Plenty of times I perform stupid maneuvers myself but does this make me foundationally a bad person? I believe not, and I try to maintain a similar or same position in regard to others. If judging, I do so of their surface action or speak that I observe hand-first, not my assumptions of the motivation laying hidden behind their human bag of bones and skin curtain. When I stay on task precluding the judging blaming and assuming, I release any possible frustration inside me. Thereby I let my sister or brother person carry their ideas on their own, without much effect upon me.

If lined up against the theory of attachment, my concept of judge blame and assume is the opposite, this is releasement, and I am letting people go from my emotional grasp who do not share the same thoughts or movements as me.

If I spend critical time effort or stress worrying about what other people are doing wrong, I believe I am facing in the opposite direction of where I should be looking and going.

When my sisters and brothers from other mothers drive cars attention diverted, when drowning their unseen sorrows in drugs and alcohol, when struggling with their out of sort emotions, I have no idea what's deep down wrong. All I see is surface behavior, all I *can* see is surface-level maneuvers. I try not to lie that I am any better or possess the right to judge anyone in any manner, for fucking anything, because I am fucking not. I try to let my assumptions judgments and blaming go. I don't waste time judging, or attaching, or being bothered with people who scratch me unpleasantly. I try to walk away.

When not steering clear of unwanted interactions, I try to play a game: Smirk and bear it. I stay silent and let others mouth off while they wriggle inside their own little invisible box. Am I factually then lying if ignoring, leaving their dysfunction alone, or refusing to accept reality, me doing nothing while their unfavorable actions play out? I believe not. I trust this is my sense and sensibility smartly going to work, I rely on this as my humility and compassion on point. Much the world seems to thrive on this blaming and lashing out, almost like hooked on the drug of what they feel others have done to them, unfairly. This shit is dispensed to us through fricking social media contrived feeding tubes, urging us to divide then fight with each other. Fuck that, more the attractiveness to live off the tech grid at my cabin in the woods as I do now while writing and podcasting. Such my laboratory for hooman behavioral discovery, alongside the experiments and explorations began when I entered the illegal drug trade at 12. I went in and out of so many different situations, houses, cars, neighborhoods, side doors, windows, crawlspaces and relationships that for the most part, I saw most of what was out there to be seen...the real, the wrong, the truth, and the downright dirty lies.

But more than saw, I felt. More than felt, I tasted. More than tasted, I understood. More than understood, I bled. I bled the truth, I bled the lies, I bled the cheat, I bled the sacrifice, and I bled the razor thin line of death.

My ambition…let the undesirables stay carried by the carrier.

Even when others pass out unpleasantries akin to old moldy lollipops on a rainy Halloween, I try to let that shit lay in the gutter, I want not the spoiled chagrins. I have a choice to let my sisters and brothers' words or actions or implications bother me, or not. I have a choice to allow myself to grow rattled or frustrated or angry, or not. Even when I think others push me or make me or force me, I know too-too well that this ship has one solo rudder, and I alone stand behind the helm. Unquestionably here, a primary fortitude is fully accepting responsibility for my thoughts, my actions, my feelings, and my behavior, best I can. When running amuck, hah, much the reveal is my Trifecta of Ugly insufficient management, which with practice, I can greatly improve. I must embrace my accountability, trying to shield or shed myself from the sticky emotional shit thrown about this land, everywhere I fucking go.

For me, a component of proper existence is patience versus rushing. Many times, if striving to gain, little to no time exists for waiting or pausing. Even if or when striving, I attempt a temporary maintain, aka do not upshift, aka do not increase, aka briefly hold current speed so to remain thoughtful. I attempt first the thinking then the acting, versus acting then thinking. Comically, an old phrase I've heard is ready-fire-aim, aka acting before focusing. I try to avoid speaking too soon, rather pausing to gather thoughts first. Hah, yes although I appear to operate contrarily, aka just go, aka just jump, aka huck and hold, factually as Friendwords Sonya says, I do analyze, however quickly.

Sometimes afraid of missing something, I lose the portion of my thoughts that operate my common sense.

Here now is same-same or least not far removed from my long standing notion on shopping discounts, aka buying stuff on sale. Just because it's off-price, I don't buy it unless I need it, can use it, and want it, aka the purchase makes sense. Not only need it, but I can use it fully or adequately within a proper time period. Many purchases are impulse anyway, which could be my untruthful non-thinking reactive brain waiving around my debit card, or least this here is my impatience defined. Even as retail buyer I attempted such discipline. If the item promotion is over, I know I am better missing out on the slight sale margin I could have gained if previously purchasing more quantity. To me, some slight missed profit dollars is better than losing major margin dollars later when the consumer demand dries up and I am left with a three-year supply of Sea Monkeys.

The truth is simple. No recall is required when speaking total truth. The truth is freeing. I am weightless and transparent when truthful. The truth is easy. The truth, so ridiculously easy, but so darn hard AF to practice.

During my hyper intentional transition to total truth, of course I botched the attempt time and again. Reorienting, my focus was heightened thoughtfulness, slowing down my mouth and typing fingers, thinking more before speaking or acting, and try again.

Currently my routine is repeatedly restarted every day, if not every hour. I train, I practice, I role play and experiment, I try again, I try again and again when training to tell the truth, and even when attempting to shed assumptions or functional addictions, aka lies.

As otherwise is the same, where I reside is the place I know best. What I know best I fall back on most easily, and for decades what I knew best was untruths. Through practice I lived to learn and know truthful change as better than rigid distrusts. Trying not to judge but seemingly, my cynicism once pushed me towards untruths. At times it's fun and engaging to challenge others and the world, aka to untrust, aka to be the rebel, aka to fight. I see that sometimes, untruths arise as I fight change and I try to be mindful of this truth. Without entirely realizing, I might remove myself so far from truth that my position becomes too easy, too inviting, and I begin to find comfort there, because of the familiarity. Truth seemed so hard when living apart from it for so long, until it wasn't.

Does success constitute integrity? I have seen successful sister and brother people lacking integrity. I had a boss who preached transparency and demanded brutal honesty. After some years I finally grabbed my balls and shared with them a hard truth, outing one of my peers who blatantly spoke defrauder statements publicly, and now here I'm judging, but I believe the peer person lacked integrity by my measure. Immediately upon my fibber peer reveal, my boss spun around snarking at me with his finger in my face, "Roger, never let the truth get in the way of a good story". Uh, say what? I was flabbergasted, those words were entirely incongruent with my main operating system. I then got the fuck out of there, I quit that job, much in favor of truth.

For me, there is a simplicity to living truthfully...
An easier life
A more peaceful life
A better life, by my measure.

Last Known Truth
I attempt to live intentionally. I cannot promise or claim I will absolutely live intentionally. My ability to live intentionally is not one of my two absolutes. The totality of my world minute by minute is a weather forecast...boisterous, variable, aka chaotic and ever-changing. How well I operate this here life peacefully and with purpose is no responsibility of a subcontractor.

My navigation is up to me.

My life asks me to attempt...do my best by my measure or let go of the bother, let go of the worry. Truth is, even when visible indicators push my sails opposite directions, no one nor any condition has as big of an impact on me as my own ability to orient my mind this way or the next, to steer my own damn ship and just fucking go get after it, that is all ~ truth out.

Five

~

Kicking the Elephant Out of the Room

I did not arrive here by my lonesome, no way, certainly not supported by my own wit, skill, or grit. Countless people and experiences carried me, influencing the me I am today. Here my intention to give props, both the gold star praise alongside the thumbs down, to the countless determinants shaping me.

Need it or Want it, Give it Away

We wait until everything feels right, before letting ourselves be happy

Then another thing comes along, and we try again

Why do we want, yet will not give?

Give the time, give the words, give the chance?

If wanted or needed~

Give it away.

Need It or Want It liner notes found in chapter-end footers section

Chapter Five, Kicking the Elephant Out of the Room ~

Shivering wildly with bizarre weakened emotion, I stood but barely, fearful to face the heavy threat of supernatural presence lingering just off my back.

Not necessarily trying to camouflage my hurt, I held onto the darn bike wheel with my left hand while wiping away hurtful tears with my right.

Amid the franticism of my worst workplace altercation ever, I turned to find my beloved payroll peers tasking away busily at the other end of the shop, not otherwise positioned alongside their bike work stations near me, but at their individual ski benches farther away. When laser focused on reassembling the darn bike hub, and just before Sonny kicked my work stool out from underneath me, I failed to notice that Tommy and Wilbert had returned from the warehouse.

Sonny's puffs of blowoff frustration filled the entire space of workshop sound, him storming towards the lunchroom with sacred stool in hand. I stared in Tommy's direction, but then glared desperately at Wilbert, trying to decipher some silent but insightful looks from my friends at the other end of the shop. Tommy seemed to know better, like he had been on the receiving end of that same rage before himself, so he kept his back to me the whole time and worked away diligently on the ski bindings he was mounting. Not a peep came my way from TC that day. Wilbert faced my direction but barely looked up, a small downward smirk on his face and slightly shaking his head back in forth in disgust because of Sonny's outburst on me the new kid.

I wanted to get a big Buddha bear hug from Wilbert, but both me and my lovable coworker stayed frozen and far apart, knowing if Sonny returned we would both get yelled at for hugging, at the time.

I loved these guys so much and best they could, Tommy and Wilbert tried to protect awhile teach me. Tommy was mostly quiet, and definitely bowed down to Sonny every time his work boss was near. Usually about two steps behind Wilbert, figuratively and literally, Tommy seemed happy to have his more dynamic counterpart Wilbert lead the way. Tommy Carter aka 'TC', was maybe fifty years old at the time, a tall skinny and extremely pleasant black man, mostly with a signature cigarette in his mouth anywhere near an outside door. He loved talking about hot rod cars and every chance we had together away from under roof, TC's favorite pastime was encouraging me to ride wheelies on my bike.

Wilbert was about five years younger than TC, maybe more. Wilbert was incredibly joyful and animated but in a ridiculously deep and self-inquisitive way, like a middle age black bicycle mechanic Buddha, complete with a slightly rounded Buddha belly and everything. Wilbert mostly wore his heart on his sleeve when talking to our work team, except when Sonny came around, then Wilbert would cover up his outward playfulness. Everybody loved Wilbert Wilkins, everybody. We consulted with our in-shop Buddha for his wisdom and advice on all things.

He was an utterly amazing and lovable man, and could have charged us thousands of dollars for often as we turned to him for his wicked smart and life guiding words.

Wilbert owned a big dual cassette radio old school fifty-pound boom box and we listened to it every day in the shop.

Wilbert's box was plugged in at his bike or ski bench station yet still sat readied, locked and loaded with its required eight fresh D cell batteries, primed to travel and prepared to party. Protected from dirt and dust by a perfectly draped and brand new daily clean shop work rag, and with a personality of its own, that cool boom box was mostly slightly loud, with Wilbert's symphonic classical music filling the back of the store, spitting out an occasional and slightly diverting NPR news report.

Tommy and Wilbert worked at Princeton Sports for quite some time. Sonny was white Jewish second-generation owner, taking over from his parents who started the business long before. Tommy began working for Sonny's lovable mother Lucille, then TC stayed put when Sonny took over the business. Tommy Carter worked for Sonny or shop mom Lucille longer than I had been alive. This was the only job Wilbert ever had after he returned home from active fighting in Vietnam. These guys had stories, both of them, but for the most part they kept their mouths shut at work, and heads down.

Even now I cannot name that tune, the indescribable feeling of flushing and melting I experienced, standing there crying after Sonny stormed away with his famous field goal stool. I was timid and nervous as hell working for Sonny at my first fulltime job, my first bike shop job. I felt rather absolute to soon get fired at any minute, because I barely knew what the hell I was doing. Nobody told me anything, just punch in and get to work. But I started to do better, and began walking around a little taller, both on the street and inside Princeton, especially because of the support and shared wisdom from Mister Wilbert Wilkins, Mister Wilbert Wilkins my beautiful Buddha.

Hard Audit

I never violated the sin of cardinal law and removed a sacred lunchroom stool again, so this was the one and only time Sonny accurately yelled at me in anger. It may have been that Sonny was trying to make a powerful statement, like I better pay attention or else. Not that I was necessarily aloof, but enrobed with a constant personal odor of marijuana, maybe Sonny Davis felt like he needed to set me straight more than I could have done on my own, and maybe he could do it before I seriously messed shit up.

Sonny never made me feel like a worthless piece of shit humanoid, just entirely slow, incompetent, and held me in payroll servitude as a nearby play toy emotional pin cushion. If not withstanding such incandescent discomfort at Princeton Baltimore, I might not have learned to deal with such workplace uneasiness as much, impossible to say for certain. Without a doubt though, my resulting work had to arrive consistently completed in a high quality and almost perfect state, no exceptions. Concurrently, I was under a severe time crunch well as a hard audit on costs so honestly, there was zero margin for error. With the factors of hyper awareness, quality, time, and money reigning supreme as equally paramount, this is perhaps where and when much of my perfectionism spawned.

Not to-do's

Barely bold enough

Barely brave enough

I just went

I just went, figuring shit out as I journeyed.

The sum totality of my eventualities is what I lived to learn and know, with these here hands

Much of my collected learned experiences were the birthed pickups after observing others miss their intended result

Cataloging my plentiful to do's, perhaps more critical is here my collection of not to-do's.

Teacher Test Answer Key

Sonny taught me many valuable lessons, both direct instruction plus some less obvious hidden-meaning-type-of-things. Surprisingly as I learned later, after long gone from Baltimore then returning to visit Wilbert in the shop, an outlandish turn of events occurred. Sonny gave me a tell-all account of our time together so long ago. He laid it out, admitting his maneuvers as deliberate efforts to do work stuff his way, to do shit the right way. I was floored Sonny took the time to level with me and speak truths of the past. Once showing his hand 20 years later, the uncovering was a shocking revelation. The session included a borderline-insulting period of his uncontrollable laughter, while taking my decades-long questions of why…the Roger Ray ponders then answered and explained. Sonny's come clean session still goes down as one of the more joyful surprises of my life, though it still stings a little.

Deviant

Although the object of Sonny's hidden instructional deviation, for me that unsure 17-year-old punk ass bitch, the field goal incident rocked me to my core in a hurtful and negative way. Immediately I wanted to run away and self-punish, reinforcing what I already withheld and then what was forcefully spewn upon me…I was nothing but a worthless piece of shit loser-loser dropout addict lowlife loser. What I walked away with and carried top of mind into my future however, was something dramatically more upbeat and profound in its deeper meaning. Despite the certainty I was getting fired after Sonny angrily kicked the stool straight out from under me, I stayed at Princeton Sports Baltimore for another two years, learning many of the most valuable work skills of my life.

Sonny did everything his way, and made sure the 15+ fulltime employees working for him also did things Sonny's way.

Yes he was a bit of a tyrant, but as I recognized later, Sonny Davis was one of the smartest and most positively influential people in my entire life.

Funny, funny Sonny.

This Here Chapter Five, Kicking the Elephant Out of the Room

Qualify-claiming my effort as impossible to share all the helping hand learnings offered me in the last fifty years, here I focus on the notes of most interest or value, by my measure. Chapter five is your fifth topic chapter, specifically heretofore dedicated to my friends, family, bosses, employees, and even strangers helping get me to where I am today. Initially I planned to place this collection in position number one, not five, so to give proper first accreditation rights. Yet once cooking up the idea of Friendwords and the submissions rolled in, I knew in my heart of hearts this here elephant needed to wait patiently in line, now position number five.

Here I give you these additional pieces of me…here resides a critical collection of honored learnings from situational discoveries and human relationships, my shared results from the most influential people in my life, aka a healthy smackerel of what lies between us.

Not Entirely Original

No I am not

How could I be?

I was birthed and raised by others

Raise myself? Hah, I would have died

I live not squandered in a cave, nor hiding under a bridge

I am not deaf or blind, I recluse none off-grid

I am a wild and wandering creature

Every word or meaning I touch or sense, I absorb

Every seeing and implication, sticks to me

All meanings not mine, some borrowed, some free domain

I try to give props where due.

Many lessons learned from others

Some up's, some downs

Both equally valuable gems, the do's, the do-not's.

Defragmenting Mortal Corporal

Collecting a thing or three while stumbling along this here life path, I traditionally attempt for my own sake to clarify and summarize my intentional preserves. Within the multiplicity of varied theories, concepts and learnings flying around both outside and within my brain, I strategically try to retain the ones most meaningful for me, aka that which I self-identify as highly useful. The best collection tactic I developed, best for me anyway, is to abridge my most valuables. I gather the sum and substance of me, write that shit down, keep that crap visible to my face, and reexamine my compliance regularly. One such summary I call The Four P's, aka my four criticals. My Four P's are the top four highest level overall functional baselines I have found to work for me, aka an encapsulated list serving as focused reminders to operate this here life most effectively, by my measure: People, Perspective, Purpose, and Passion. Later I utilize my Four P's as guided organizational structure for sharing my absorbed lessons.

Book Burnings

By the time I turned 31, I legitimately deciphered only one book, the famous business printing of *Customers For Life* by Carl Sewell. True-true, over a decade earlier while held captive inside the mid-grade academia complex I thumbed through Ray Bradbury's *Fahrenheit 451*, but absorbed fricking none of that shit. F-451 was the only required school assignment book I ever picked up with slight intent but still, one I mostly defied. The 20-years-plus since paging that there my first book, that being Carl's Customers, nightly I absorb a wall full of nonfiction works before falling asleep, oh good grief, now self-illustrating how truly small my world and thoughts really are.

I inheld the wonderment to read once I pulled my head out of my ass but amid days prior, such cranial conjecture thwarted as I surrendered myself to the snagged stagnation of the drugs.

The compounding self-sabotage was adequately exacerbated by my, echo...habitual school truancy beginning at 12 years old. I joke with self, hah, I could have dropped the scrimmage of keeping cadence with the structured academic process, if contrarily making the staunch commitment to read incessantly. Alas I honor the journey itself as my greatest work.

My greatest work, aka this here life...an unimaginable adventure without getting up to just go live it, twain the time frolicking beneath sunshine, alongside the stints cowered in shadow.

Life Verses

Some poem-stylized pieces that are littered throughout this here your book were fabricated under the clouded influence of self-doubt, heartache, or some varied form of confrontational discovery, perhaps even during a tequila or red-wine-induced drinking binge.

These influences too, I honor and credit the resulting work, hence the learnings I would not have otherwise found on my own. Some unknown-to-me notable person once said we should write while drunk but edit when sober, I presume the suggestion to mean the best capture of creativity occurs during storm, but better the cleanup under bluebird sunny skies. My collection of short writing pieces is vast. Over half of these poetic-style works written while distressed and under simultaneous influence of the Devil's Water, more than ten years ago now. You'll find the gross of these works one day, many of them triple-saved electronically, both down here on terra firma in my laptop and backed up on external hard drives, well as preserved high in the OneDrive cloud. Currently I possess least five books of paged paper writings, them being my Ted Baker brand daybook journals. One more is the published poetry Nora transcribed shortly after she moved in, printed in a legit book format, a black square bound piece with a picture window and a pronouncing sticker, 'Live a Great Story'. Lastly, you will find more Roger Ray written ramblings within a large black leather three-ring binder enclosing the typed and printed poems, there most of the writings ordered and numbered. Perhaps in the truest sense of the phrase, these writings are the pieces of me. Much of this here your book is the assimilation of such efforts, your father's collective heart bled through word.

Herding the Chapter Five Elephants: The Collected Indelible Effects On Me
Introducing…The Bicycle
Gregory Wells was my earliest best friend in school. Many days long we passed notes back and forth, him teaching me foundational meanings behind different bicycle parts. I didn't know anything about bikes and Gregory knew everything. His note tried to explain what a 'gooseneck' was but I did not understand, until his artful hand penciled a masterful drawing in the next note…oh, now I get it…a handlebar-holder stem thingy.

The infatuation I gained for bicycles back when and the same I am still absorbed in today, definitively came from my childhood friend Gregory Wells.

Gregory lived in a rougher neighborhood than me, the condensed apartments of Cold Spring. From the stories, he had his hands full with local goings-on once exiting the public transportation bus from school. Handfuls of times I journeyed to Cold Spring looking for Gregory but the area was much tougher than I could handle, so if not seeing my beautiful bicycle-genius friend immediately, I hauled butt out of there. I perceived Cold Spring in north Baltimore a threat because I was a skinny little wimp, not yet tall, and being my pre-drug years, not yet had I collected the later-to-come courage to cockily enter any car, any house, any neighborhood for my intended purchase of illegal substances.

When Gregory's teachings began, I was still riding my father's shitty Montgomery Ward adult three speed bike. BigBird's whip was like a cheap department store ten-speed with assigned skinny street tires, but with upright flat handlebars and a small thumb shifter attached to a gears-controlling cable. Yes, you may have caught the fact BigBird's bike featured the highlighted rear wheel hub with internal planetary gears, mentioned elsewhere. Once I saved up enough profits from my grass cutting business, I bought my first off-road BMX bicycle.

Gregory coached me through the entire process of customizing my new two-wheeled whip like I had dreamed of for years. My magnetic attachment to the bicycle was a diverting lesson aside my allergy to school teachings. The two-wheelers became a flickering flame of my desire and I absorbed the real-world value, yup…not only the enthused travel but a one-day dream of possible sporting participation. Gregory held my high admiration the entire time we were together and still to this day.

Regrettably, Gregory and I did not spend much time together outside of school. We kicked around a little and rode bikes together a few times, but rarely. He was bigger than me and a great rider, especially when we navigated the small motorcycle jumps on some local dirt trails. Gregory went on to attend Northwestern High School while I went off to Poly, so we separated after leaving middle school.

Throughout this here book I attempt to explain the life altering and healing powers the bicycle has afforded me. Initially the self-powered two wheels offered me transportation, independence, escape, exploration, and extended periods of self-inquisition. Of course we know the later resounding athletic affects and career path the bicycle gave me, without restraint. Although trying to find Gregory over the years, my search has been unsuccessful. If nothing else, I would like to thank him for what he has done for us, teaching me so expertly about bikes, injecting in me a passion for two wheels, and providing a livelihood I probably would never have found, if not for my beautiful bicycle friend Gregory Wells.

Enticing the Mechanic Within

The times easily amounted to over 20 when I sat in the Ankers family living room stuffed with Ankers children, watching the hyper-popular English comedy TV show, *Benny Hill*. A few blocks downhill from my father's house was the Ankers household, a ratherish loud and vibrant place where if I did not stay alert, I would likely be knocked over by one of the six boys running by, or have a broom shoved into my hand and put to chores by the house boss momma Sylvia. Time around the 'teley' watching *Benny Hill* on the boob tube with the Ankers was enchanting. Me there pleasurefully within the small TV room, now part of the family unit…both parents and all nine kids laughing hysterically in unison for an hour, literally rolling around on the floor together from the televised potty-mouth humor and buildup of silliness in the air. Miss Sylvia and Paul Ankers Sr. accepted me into their home, into their family, well as into their business.

The second born boy in line was David, about my age. David's big brother Paul Junior was the oldest and younger than David was Steven, Peter, Daniel, and Adam, in that order. Maybe Daniel was older than Peter, I forget the exact arrangement but Adam was definitely the youngest…the boys also had three sisters, all the girls older than David. David and I enjoyed blocks of quality time together when I wasn't spending hours with my next-door neighbors Mark Weinreich and Danny Nurco. Usually when around David Ankers, his slightly younger brother Steven was with us too, except when David and I were off and about miles from home riding dirt bike motorcycles together. The other Ankers boys were mostly too young to tag along on our expeditions but when on the family compound, most all boys were involved in the brotherly play as one. Especially with the four younger boys, I assumed the feelings of surrogate older brother, and I loved it.

Mister Paul Ankers Senior, although a radically intense not tall in physical stature British wild man, was ridiculously patient with me, thereby providing an undeniable comfort not offered elsewhere. Mister Paul Senior and his amazing wife Sylvia were both born in England, and I was told Mister Ankers previously served as a mechanic in the British Air Force building and maintaining airplanes. At about 10 years old I began working for Mister Ankers alongside most of his sons at the family automotive machine shop business in Baltimore City, Ankers Automotive. There I learned to properly use my hands…turning a screwdriver on a tight screw without stripping it, proper handling techniques of box combination wrenches, ratchets, the non-negotiable torque wrench, base mechanical lessons, and detailed specifics within a mountainous list of operational what why's and how's. Through my eyes and within my heart, the relationship I shared with Mister Paul Senior was so magical because he made no assumptions about my skills or knowledge.

Rather, he reviewed expectations with me quickly and effectively, without any judging to either my lack of knowing or my possible expertise with various things, he assumed nothing. Mister Paul Ankers Senior not only gave me the highly coveted hands-on opportunities and lessons my father refused to offer or participate in, but Mister Ankers also paid me cash money and paid me well. Mister Paul Senior never yelled at me or even implied a cross tone, not once, awhile simultaneously chastising his own kids and maybe even slightly slapping them upside their head from time to time for not paying attention. A certain type of respect existed between Mister Ankers and me, a respect that I highly appreciated, and quite frankly within like every single second of this here life, I revere.

When on the clock at Ankers Automotive, I not only became infatuated with mechanical workings and custom fabrication, but developed a romantic relationship with performance automobiles. Disassembling and rebuilding greasy carbonized engines was thrilling and minute by minute, I was learning something brand new. Many days I would have preferred to stay, building wild internal-combustion creations the whole night long instead of going home to bed.

My thrill and passion for cars then blew wide open the day a radically sexy and low to the ground yellow Italian De Tomaso Pantera sports car rolled into the shop, and I lent a hand rebuilding its assigned Ford 351 Cleveland engine.

Operationally, the Ankers business was a heavy-duty machine shop featuring multiple *Bridgeport* milling machines weighing tons, giant drill presses, lathes almost twenty feet long, and metal shavings filled almost every inch of the old brick two story mini factory. I aided with the machining and resurfacing of automobile brake rotors and drums, assisted with cylinder head valve jobs, well as joining in on the random machine shop games. One particular job sticking in my mind was fabricating hundreds of stainless steel tapered pins, only about three inches in length and perhaps a quarter inch diameter on the thicker end. The narrow end received a precisely placed hole that was then chamfered, while the larger end was machined on the Bridgeport to develop a four-sided flat head configuration, so able to use a small open-end 5mm or so wrench on the flats.

I knew this was no automotive piece but only at the end of the job did I learn, the components were tuning pins for large musical harp strings.

Sadly, I fell out of touch with the Ankers but much later reconnected with Steven through Facebook, only to learn that my main family connection David had passed away. The lost Ankers connection reinforced once more the importance of beloved humans in my life, and motivated me to try and better stay connected with people. The Ankers afforded me an extended loving family, a nurtured automotive passion, a hands-on skill set, an involved set of cooperative parents, an incredible job for several years, and a deep rooted thrill for all things mechanical. Resulting from my relationship with the Ankers, I was later able to hit the ground running as a bicycle mechanic, tool-handling-wise. Prior to the consumption absorbed within by way of the bicycle, because of fondling that sexy yellow Pantera at Ankers Automotive, I then focused the entirety of my pre-teen life sights on becoming a car designer.

Simmer Down Grasshopper

While my first fulltime work boss Sonny ordered me to speed up, Wilbert counseled me to slow down. Not slow my hands or feet but calm my mind and assumptions. In a more traditional home family dynamic, a son might seek advice or counsel from a father. BigBird appeared too unavailable, too far away from me emotionally, and too far from the action. Mostly, I disregarded my father's word relevancy to any of my life situations. Wilbert was my work family team captain and quite literally functioned as my first life coach, operating significantly beyond what a father could accomplish trying to effectively advise his male offspring. The focus, calm, recentering, and methodical analysis that Wilbert practiced and coached me on was one of my first and most valuable life lessons. Much as I jumped ahead with presumptions fears and imagined negative outcomes, Wilbert expertly pulled me back, him not afraid to tell me no I was wrong, but he delivered such words in extremely loving and inflating ways.

For slightly more than forty years exactly, although easy to say and hard to do, I have tried to slow, strip away the emotion and focus on the immediate issue at hand, my initial offering coming by way of Mister Wilbert Wilkens. Practicing this focus, and tossing emotion to the side has served me extremely well over this here life. The same exact practice is one of the key life and business lessons I share with others and coach them on heavily. Wisdom, patience, slow down and look at the heart of the facts is what Wilbert taught me best, and not by his words but within the hand and examples he lent me. Wilbert had a healthy loving heart, a vibrant finely tuned thought process, excellent delivery, and like many other people in my life, he seemed to care for others more than he cared for himself.

Wilbert was my life counterbalance and much of Wilbert's charm was the critical timing of his shared heart when I desperately needed it…needed it, not necessarily wanted it.

Once graduating high school in 1963 and at the age of seventeen, Wilbert began working for Lucille Davis at the original Princeton Sports on Park Circle in northwest Baltimore city.

Wilbert survived four years of combat in Vietnam before returning to his job at Princeton. Assuming and judging but somewhat because of his beautiful and sexy Buddha type soul, it is no wonder that Wilbert fathered nine children. Wilbert worked for the Davis family at Princeton for 50 years before he finally retired. I am honored and blessed to have spent a few precious years working alongside this amazing man. I should have stayed in better touch with him, although I visited Wilbert handfuls of times after we worked with each other last, but by my measure I allowed too much a gap to form. I believe my main pickups from Wilbert were orientations of reality, not assuming, and dealing with the pure truths without freaking that some other crazy scenario might play out. It's about dropping assumptions, controlling controllables, and keep going until someone forces me to stop.

It would be interesting to hear from his family, the people he grew up with, his buddies in Vietnam, and hear from his nine children, to hear about Wilbert, the kinds of wisdom and love he shared with them, just like Wilbert did with me.

True to fate, in early November 2018 I received a message from friend and former coworker Corey Adams. Corey and his brother Torrence both worked at Princeton Baltimore, and Corey told me Wilbert had passed away. Wilbert was 72, blessed with sixteen grandchildren and I am positive he spoiled those kids rotten. Wilbert was most times a big kid himself and the overflowing passion he shared with others was infectious. November 2018 found me as still an emotional tumbleweed, not yet pulling my shit entirely back together, less than one year after wife two Nora moved out.

I was not yet my fully functioning self, still wallowing in my private vault of hurt within the big empty BirdHouseSouth.

Yes I had the cats with me but my heart still bleeding, missing terribly my beloved but now gone four humans and the big reversed mohawk ginger canine. Initially my tears of sorrow fell for the time passed between Wilbert and I, and the void of me telling him how much he helped me when I really needed it. Of course I had to attend Wilbert's funeral, and began looking for a plane connect to Baltimore, but the turmoil in my head and heart distracted me. Although desperately wanting to pay respects to Wilbert, I waffled…not wanting to leave town in the middle of some solo revenue generating work projects, nor just fly in and out of my old home 'hood without visiting my many other friends. Conversely I knew to remorse if not attending Wilbert's funeral, even if only knowing a few people there and stealthily zipped in and out of town. I wanted to just get up and go but before entirely realizing, the service time had come and gone, pathetically I blundered. The weighted burden hurts my shoulders still as I carry it around, missing the opportunity to say goodbye to Wilbert properly, well as meet his friends. Funny that my main takeaway from Wilbert was to strip away negative thoughts and that is much of what kept me away from saying goodbye to him proper.

My shame is heavy that my true respect faltered when perhaps it mattered most, by my measure.

Still, and forever, I carry my treasureful memories and love for Wilbert Wilkens, Wilbert Wilkens my earliest life coach, Wilbert Wilkens my beautiful bike shop Buddha.

Sonny's Way

Sonny Davis left me with a multitude of critical life lessons, extending far beyond customer service or workplace practices.

1. Remember people's names. Learn at least one customer's name every day you are in our store, so Sonny one day barked at me. The notion was somewhat ridiculous, not much removed from his other unrealistic expectations thrown my way. Sure, it sounded like a good idea, I fully embraced the value and the why, but missed the how and the what. Sonny never hinted towards any techniques, but just do it. I found the assignment as stated lacking so much critical substance, that I struggled to sort out my approach and I could not develop a plan to run with.

The directive puzzled me entirely for one whole hour, then I stopped thinking and started doing, doing it my own Roger Ray rudimentary way.

I assumed Sonny held a specific process working best for him, or maybe he factually sucked at it and wanted me to do better. Since the name retention challenge was my first direct order of how to operate at the second level, you know, the next level above the daily execution of tasks, I would love to have known what his method was but he never clued me in on that one. My initial process was maintaining a small pocket-sized notebook, writing names down with a special associated identifier.

Still I remember my very first entry, *JIM: 25" Blue Fuji* and for the rest of my life I will recall Jim and his tallish 25-inch-framed blue Fuji brand 10-speed bike. I intentionally built and sustained relationships, as I believe Sonny implied. If I saw a person and believed I knew them, I quickly referred to my little flipbook and looked them up before calling out, "Hi Jim, welcome back", for sure a positive opening move when taking care of repeat retail customers, even after a long hiatus.

I literally carried around and utilized my back pocket customer identification notebook for over a decade. I re-wrote it three different times, when either overly full or indistinguishable, as I jotted down notes on the go at different places of work. Later, I transitioned to a hybrid version of note-taking within everyone's electronic contact fields containing personal info, likes and dislikes, family member names, dates, etcetera. The more I utilize my notes the better I retain the memory, and still after 40 years I remember many names of people I have not seen since. I lived to learn and know, both at home and at work, quality of connection matters most, and remembering people's names is a valuably-related skill.

To clarify that last passage…for me, and especially in the job place, the primary importance is effectively navigating boss and coworker relationships, not how much I know or how well I do my work…these words feel odd to clack them out, but such is my experience.

This gets-along-well-with-others challenge is enhanced greatly when able to remember people's names, however I can possibly do it. Layered on top of life detail notes is my say-it-seven-times routine, all oriented towards name remembrance. Soon as I learn someone's name, I try to repeat it back to them, and use it least six more times before leaving their presence. It feels weird when doing it, repeating their name, but I ignore this slight embarrassment for two reasons.

1) One, everybody loves hearing their name, everybody. It is a small dopamine shot in the arm for their dirty-ego, everybody. So although they might think I am being weird repeating their name seven times in a two-minute conversation, deep down they really enjoy hearing it, everybody.

2) Two, and next, along the same lines and although they would agree I am weird, once they understand what I am doing, or I flat-out tell them my weirdness is because I am trying to remember their name, then wow, everyone is flattered by the care, the time, and the energy I am spending to respect them that way. The exchange is weird on the surface but when on the receiving end, it feels flattering. I have worked hard to not be afraid to feel weird, even when absolutely acting that way.

2. Stretch goals, even unrealistically so. The one thing I wanted to know more than all else was Sonny's lofty workload expectations of me. We never discussed the damn stool, nor did I no-way need to go there. My two main tasks were bike assembly builds and general tune-up repairs. Each of the two main operationals generally occupied one hour each of my time. So, in an eight-hour workday, I could typically work on eight bikes from beginning to end. Every day Sonny expected me to do 12 bikes or more and reminded me constantly. During the curtain pullback two decades later, Sonny pridefully said he knew I was always capable of more. He demanded 12 instead of settling for eight and we laughed in unison that I typically produced 10 bikes a day because he pushed me so damn hard. In short order however, I did recognize the value of stretch goals. My later Trek boss Jb calls it 'pathological optimism' but regardless, the concept is basically the same…set off on course for the moon, and land high up as I can on the closest nearby star.

3. Super-specific details, there is no other way. Sonny instructed, summoned, and demanded exactness down to the clock's second hand and the one cent penny. Claiming I should be able to perform a task in 16 minutes, he said to expect his return in 15 of them there minutes and 30 of some more seconds, and by the way he will have no time to wait once he comes back. Sonny was never late and his estimates were never wrong. Preciseness was shared up-front in expectation, practiced then finally followed, or else. Laughingly, for the remainder of my life I have not yet found anyone providing so much detail beforehand than Sonny did, and such clarity I greatly appreciate.

4. Show me. Sonny was hands-on. Often, after I answered his question, he started walking while pushing me or spinning my body around, trailing me or dragging me along to show him what I was talking about. Not that Sonny doubted me, nor was he calling my possible bluff.

Sonny wanted me to show off my work, egging me on to take pride in what I had done, although I assume he saw the maneuvers a thousand times before, and could probably even do the job himself if necessary. Strangely, he would be almost inquisitively specific, like pretending to have me teach him what I was talking about. In the end, I believe Sonny was reinforcing accountability in a non-accusatory manner. To show me that yes, in fact he is paying close attention to everything I do. That he's not paying lip service to what is said or heard, that he does care to see it himself and not just hear about it. Sonny was making sure tasks were being performed as stated, so as to control overall business quality and waste-free efficiencies. His approach was neither judgmental nor blameful but rather, Sonny appeared to circumnavigate operations with general transparency.

Later in life amid my big boy work career, I adopted a similar tactic to help remain on task and drive accountability. I was not necessarily doubting what people told me but after a handful of times when work family members did not speak total truth, I began to use Sonny's tactic, show me. Initially people defended and even resented my show-and-tell request but more times than not, they were not factually prepared or operating properly from where they claimed. 'Show Me' became a critically valuable technique throughout every aspect of my life.

5. Radical respect. Maybe trying to covertly flirt with the ladies, but Sonny went over the top being kind and helpful to women, more so and before the men. Later I expanded upon this base lesson…when greeting a retail couple I speak, look to, and shake hands with the woman first, even when the guy is the only one talking. When emailing texting or sending a message to a shared account, I try to address the lady of the house first before the guy.

Sonny respected all customers…walking around the sales counter after completing the transaction, placing every bag or purchase no matter how small into the shopper's hands directly and genuinely, not indifferently handing it to them overtop the counter. Sonny respected all customers…hustling back and forth from the counter to the front exit, opening the door for our shoppers, especially the ladies. Sonny respected all customers…loading every bike or large item into their car for them, especially the ladies. Sonny respected all customers…sincerely thanking every shopper for their business, even the smallest item and no matter the person. The genuine honor felt from Sonny's thank you's were truly heartfelt and clearly, he appreciated every retail dollar spent at his store. Sonny demanded everyone on the clock behaved Sonny's way.

If any of us missed doing work his way, Sonny did not pause to bark his orders across the crowded sales floor. I believe his absolute commitment to the shopping experience was appreciated by the customers, although sometimes they were slightly shocked by Sonny's shoutouts. Sonny never told me rules or instructions on the importance of taking care of customers but rather, led by example and implication. Sonny implied numerous times…this business is nothing without customers so therefore customers are everything, least that's how I deciphered it. Beginning with Sonny and for 40 business years to come, I learned to put the customer first and slather the same customer-first importance upon everyone I worked with. Yes I instructed my retail teams to clean or organize or unbox and price product, but if a shopper strolls in, everything gets put on hold, everything, because of how Sonny taught me to put and keep first things first, the customer.

6. No limiting presumptions. Masterfully, Sonny would lead shoppers around the store daily, collecting the different items he believed they needed in his arms for them, especially during ski season. Sonny loaded them up, even if he didn't know them that well. If objections arose, Sonny respectfully allowed for items to be removed from the stack, but the customer never had to worry about adding to their pile, Sonny already did that for them. Yes, Sonny's approach was surface-level presumptive but factually his technique was the opposite. Sonny knew what people needed in order to have the best experience and he collected said items, making sure his customer set off well-equipped to enjoy their activity to the fullest. I lived to learn and know this retail tactic as critical because once managing people and businesses, mostly until salespeople are trained experienced and confident, but not always, they are afraid to ask for the sale. Rather, many retail employees negatively service both the customer and the business, by assuming their shopper cannot afford to purchase everything they truly need, hah…or the salesperson is too timid to try. If the customer has a negative experience out in the world because they are not adequately equipped or properly prepared, they often blame their timid salesperson, and I have seen as such myself more than 50 times.

   Sonny would drop the heap of gear on the front counter, assuming the customer was buying everything because he not only believed, but he knew for fact they needed each item so to have the best experience. Sonny was the master of subliminal closing of the sale. Easy to say but hard to do…helping our sisters and brothers be ultimately prepared takes a lot of work, and many times proper preparation demands more gear than was initially expected by the consumer.

There is great power and value when the salesperson is the expert, and in-fact eminently amid these here tech times, sadly such dynamic is dwindling.

Sonny masterfully led by example to help people prepare for everything, even when they don't know what they don't know or think they won't need it.

7. Go, start now, do not wait. Sonny gave clear simple and only enough detail to get moving sooner than later, expertly leaving people to do their jobs once boss man delivered his words. Sonny had his hand in most things throughout the business, and managed his time well. He announced brief instructions and walked away, even though his directives only included half the total information required. Without wasting time oversharing, Sonny avoided fluff…additional instructions will be supplied when needed. His approach was conflictual for me because I like to know everything up front, but as things appeared, seemed he was focused on saving precious time. I believe Sonny influenced some of my get up and go, aka jump, just go attitude in this regard.

8. The answer, is decisively, yes or no. Before Master Yoda instructed the world there is no try only do, Sonny demanded completion of tasks, or else. Sonny made no time to squabble over possibilities, he just wanted shit done.

Although I stand in opposition today to the idea there is no try, Sonny helped me quickly assess, accept, or admit swiftly if I am or am not the right person for the job, even if learning by way of burning at the stake. When not crystal clear on my abilities or resources to perform certain tasks, most often disaster follows. If committing to something, I try like hell to get it done. If thinking I cannot do it or don't want to, I attempt to say so up front, hence not over-committing or putting myself in a tough spot. My 'lates' I keep track of, those things I adopted but have not yet completed. Even if late, for me, to do is better than to promise and do not. Not always do I accomplish this intent adequately, but I am thoughtful of the issue, and I try. In these ways and more, I see the positive residual impact within me from the learning so long ago learned Sonny's way.

9. Surprising support. Factually I believe this was the younger Alan's doing not the elder Sonny's. On three different occasions when I arrived at my hotel for different mechanic or manager trainings, all supported by my employer Sonny and Alan at Princeton Sports, a welcoming fruit basket awaited me with a personal and motivational card attached. Such seemingly small but emotionally significant actions subliminally pushed me to proceed with increased intention, sophistication, and determination than I would have otherwise when attending the event, absolutely so.

The supreme value of a surprising gift or exceedingly thoughtful gesture exceeds all stupendously glowing descriptive language I possess.

Bounce Back
On February 7th in 2022, at 4:21 pm, I sent Sonny's eldest son Alan Davis this email message, verbatim.

Hey buddy,
> Just wanted to say hello. I hope your Monday has been a good one and I hope the forecast of your week upcoming is also looking good. Wanted to let you know I'm thinking of you. How's Sonny doing these days?

Hugs to you all.
Roger

Initially, I did not see my note bounce back, crap…the email address I had for Alan was old and invalid. After noticing the boomeranged error message, I copied the written characters and forwarded them to Alan through his Facebook account via Messenger, so I believed. However stupid and precisely, I screwed up and the message never went through. I was distracted and juggling one too many simultaneous tasks instead of focusing on that one there singular important thing, my 'How's Sonny?' message to Alan.

The behind-the-scenes intention with my note to Alan was maybe in another day or two, I'll share this chapter five opening story with Sonny if he felt up to it.

Thereby letting Sonny know before it's too late, how critically important he is to me and how much he helped shape my life in a multitude of positive ways. Minimally, I wanted Alan to read it himself and maybe provide an executive summary report to his 89-year young dad Sonny.

Two days later, and before I realized my Messenger note to Alan never went through, on Wednesday morning February 9th 2022, Alan posted on his Facebook wall that Sonny passed in his sleep the night before. Uh, say what? I cannot…gosh dang…what the? I was speechless. The afternoon subsequent to Alan's wall share, on that Thursday, the memorial service announcement for Sonny was posted on social media. The next day Friday February 11th I attended Sonny's memorial service via Zoom. The following day Saturday February 12th I did the one and only thing I unequivocally had to fricking do next, yes, fuck to the yes factually, I began driving to Baltimore, wheels rolling at 4am sharp. Determined, I was on my way to pay honor to Sonny, planning to attend the post-funeral open house visitation event, the Jewish family shiva service in Sonny's home. And so I did, spending three treasureful hours with Alan and his wife Jackie, Sonny's daughter Sherri, and Sonny's second wife Judith who I had never met. Did I instinctually jump into my car partially because of the scar from missing Wilbert's funeral three years before? Slightly. Did I place Sonny in higher regard than Wilbert so to not waffle and miss the opportunity? Hum, maybe so but with margin. Uniquely, each Sonny and Wilbert hold different places in the field of my history and in the court of my heart. Mainly, and somewhat to honor the associated miss of Wilbert, I was not going to sit by and sidestep the chance to say goodbye to my other and perhaps main Princeton Baltimore influencer Sonny. I believe, however for goodness sake spiritually possible, Wilbert understands me and my actions, by my measure.

My relative short time spent with the Davis family during Sonny's shiva was spiritualistic. Nowhere else in the world could I imagine being at that moment. I would have regretted not paying my respects to Sonny and spending time with Alan if I did not go.

My time, cost and effort to show up was so damn worth it…my fond farewell to the man who taught me more than any other human contact in my life, period, fucking period, yes, my now-gone beloved boss Sonny The Tyrannical.

Godspeed Sonny.

The Many Surprising Attributes of Sparkling Cider
When Princeton Sports of Columbia big boss Alan Davis then sponsored my send-off to the New England Cycling Academy, aka NECA bicycle retail school in the late '80s, neither myself nor Alan imagined my net learnings would supersede the anticipated specialty bike mechanic instruction. Collectively, I have attended over 20 such multi-day seminars trade shows or teachings in my last 40 years of business. I might learn a little at said events or I might learn lots, the net gain varies wildly. My overriding take-home practice is to summarize and keep close at hand my best lessons secured, instead of mindlessly putting the workbooks away on a shelf or deep within an unmarked decrepit box, likely never opening them again.

I honor my opportunities and greatly respect the attained schooling, wherever collectible.

The away-game happenings cost substantial money and take me away from valuable time with my work family, so I challenge myself to maximize the impact upon me and the gainful results to my business. Many great ideas are presented during these gathered thought shares and the vital responsibility, by my measure, is finding the specifics working best in my world, and retain said captures as judicious elements of my personal operating system.

And then there is my book reading practice. I underline impactful words on the in-process sheets as I go. Then reviewing all the influences within, I form my influenced takeaway summaries on the rearward available blank pages in paragraph form. Also, I maintain a master life handbook and carry it with me most places I travel, my *CoolShit ToolKit* all-of-me binder housing the best of the best thoughts and practices I intend to implement, pulled from wherever or whenever thinking them up, seminars and night dreams included.

Not by accident will I navigate this here life as desired, my thoughts intentions and actions must be purposeful.

I opportunely absorbed more prizable life knowledge than anything else at the NECA Fit Kit schools, far beyond bike mechanic techniques thanks to Alan The Awesome, and the handfuls of days in Vermont net resulted as legitimately life changing for me.

Zombie Zoo

In Vermont, the week-long NECA seminar pitch began slow, but built steam fast. In the first few minutes I learned a new word I never heard before, habituation. The word was explained to me in a profound and impactful manner. Habituation…we are often entranced in our same old routine, driving our cars to work every day and barely paying attention to what is around us. Yes, if another vehicle pulled out we would hit the brakes and avoid the accident but basically, many times we operate our lives on autopilot, not in-tune and connected to what is tangibly at our feet, aka the opposite of consciously attentive. Almost 20 years later, I would realize an encapsulating state of habituation is closely opposed to the concept of mindfulness.

The room exploded in laughter when the question was presented, "How many times has a customer arrived in your store to pick up their repaired bicycle, and after you cannot find their bike or any associated paperwork, the customer realizes they are at the wrong shop because these places all look alike?"…ha-ha-ha, obviously, the exact scenario previously played out with other students, not just like it had with me already multiple times. Additionally, another mutually experienced, now comical and rhetorical question was, "How many times has a customer walked in very excited and asking if your store was new because they lived here their whole life, drive this street every day, but never saw your retail outlet before…no, you explain, the store has been here twenty years". Hah, that same shit happened almost every week with me at work. Great examples and ones directly applied to our lack of attentiveness…we do not operate our lives heads-up; we rush around as more mindless than mindful.

The bicycle school bottom line teaching was, make your business back home stand out in multitudes of ways and minorly brainwash your customers with your store brand, best as possible.

Although not always navigating mindfully, I adopt and hold in high regard throughout most areas of my life, the attempted operation not to be stuck in a zombie-like habituated state.

Immediately following return home from the New England seminar, I adopted a personal code when driving to look beyond the curb, and still do. When driving, I scan the side-to-side landscape, cognizant of the terrain and barns and buildings and beautiful sights I never noticed before although traveling on the same roads for years. Habituation.

Match Point

When someone sends me a long note, I should send them a long reply. If communication is short, I should match their brevity, so the NECA seminar shared with me and others. I believe this approach to be correct. People are showing how they prefer to communicate, least on this issue. Perhaps they are situationally enraged or enthused, but once practicing this lesson, I realized the criticality of the teaching. If someone pours their heart out and I respond briefly with a one word 'Thanks', well, I consider my response as inadequate and quite frankly, Roger Ray rude. I am only speaking to my behavior here, that being how I respond, not judging someone's response to my long or short note sent to them prior. With intention I care for their effort to reach out to me. I try to match their style so I hear them appropriately and respond correctly, by my measure. Matched communication effort.

Sorry, What Did You Say…I Wasn't Listening

I should listen twice as much with my two ears, while speaking half as much with my one mouth. Hah, this truism received laughs as well from the NECA bike school class. Talk half as much as we listen, or more, I was told, and it made good sense to me.

Speaking, I hear what I already know, or better sort out what is currently thought. Yet when listening, I hear something new, thus then afforded the chance to learn.

The two ears one mouth lesson sparked a decade-plus personal research project of listening do's and do not's within me. Ultimately I assembled a proprietary list, me considering the tuned coordination of my ears and mouth as critical. Said elsewhere but for me, I place higher importance on my ability to hear and be heard, aka play nice with others, than the quality of technical responsibilities I perform, no doubt. Although altering my listening behavior has not been quick or easy, I get better at it every day, and only through concentrated effort do I make any positive adjustments at all. Sorry I couldn't cook up an eight letter acronym for my list upcoming.

Better Listener Bird List:

1. One. All Systems Go. First things first, before I can accurately speak or listen, I make sure they are free, aka I do not want to assumingly pressure them. Do you have time to talk, I usually ask…how long do you have? Or are you ready to have this talk now, so I might say. Years later my Trek big boss Jb praised me openly when I started pulling this with him, him claiming it as unique. After getting on the phone with my boss Jb, several times I immediately asked if he had the time, hah, and sometimes he said no, but chuckled out loud that no one ever does that…them asking first before speaking. In general, I inquire if there is anything to make sure we discuss, or something to avoid. At times, only when asking if they have time or giving them an out do they admit their unpreparedness or inadequate availability. I try to respect and honor their time and expectations. I do not like others assuming I have unlimited time to talk, or they presume I lack the opportunity to communicate with them in detail. I ask first then listen.

2. Two. Shut the Fuck Up. Once a person is speaking, I try like hell to let them say all they have to say without my interruptions. Even if I do have something to say, I try to keep my mouth shut until they are entirely done. If I develop a mental comment while they are speaking, I find paper and pen to make myself a note, or write it on my hand, toot suite. Sometimes I interrupt, but I get better at staying silent day by day. If I interrupt, they will likely lose focus and might not say everything they intend. I do not like others interrupting me so I try not to. I shut up and listen.

3. Three. Listen with My Eyes Listen with My Body. I attempt control of my negative or unsettled body language, so I do not distract the person who is talking. I orient my eyes on theirs and try like hell to stay still, thus drowning out nearby disruptions. If I distract, they might too. I try not to break up their train of thought or delivery so I can better listen to everything they have to say. I do not like others tuning out when I am deep into my delivery so I try not to. I settle and listen.

4. Four. No Plotting- No Scheming. Once they are speaking, I remain focused on what they are presenting, and not to what I am thinking. More accurately, I attempt not to think at all but absorb. If beginning assemblage of my side issue thoughts, or preparing my immediate comments, too much noise exists in my head, I cannot honestly hear their words. My goal is not to prepare a comeback, no way but I attempt the opposite, I aim to listen understand and comprehend. I keep paper nearby whenever possible and once quickly scribbling my notations, I drop my pen then clear my brain to focus intently on what they are saying. Aside, when intentionally preparing for upcoming conversations, I begin with pen and paper on hand so to on-the-fly collect my thoughts, then clear my brain fast. I do not like others thinking too much while I am talking thus not hearing me accurately, so I try not to. I scheme not, I listen.

5. Five. Five One Thousand. Five seconds of silence is a long-ass time but I believe the discipline is critical, me counting to five after they stop talking, before I speak or begin to think. I want to allow them to say everything they intend. Why? Because sometimes they are not yet done. If I pause, I will not cut them off and I can absorb everything they said. The pause is unadulterated respect, like I learned from the ridiculously kind and considerate people in Japan. I pause my response- I listen.

6. Six. Keep it Zipped. Even if they falter, I try to keep my lip zipped and wait and wait and wait. Easy to say- hard to do, but I believe the behavior worth it…wait, just wait. Keep my mouth shut even when the person is struggling to find their words or thoughts. I should not suggest or attempt words for them. I do it sometimes but try not to, and am getting better at it. I do not like others finishing thoughts or choosing words for me, so I try not to. I double shut up and listen.

7. Seven. Sell It Back. Pitch back to them what I hear, so to gain confirmation before I speak. Especially handy in romantic relationships or when conflict exist, me making sure I comprehend correctly what they intended to say. I am no romantic expert but hah, perhaps I am versed on my deprivations, aka I know what I supersuck at. I do not like others interpreting my words opposite of what I mean, so I try to listen intently to theirs, and confirm that I heard them correctly. I sell it back and listen.

8. Eight. What's Next? Do not leave without who-does-what's-and-when's. Once confirming agreed-upon follow up happenings, I do not, do not, do not leave a conversation without clearly defined to-do's. I try to confirm that what I just heard actually has a chance to occur. I need to hear what is planned to happen next by whom, when, how, how much, how little, or maybe I misunderstood during the meeting. If leaving a talk and we all are not clear on what comes next, I have not heard enough. With nothing clearly decided, why did we have the talk? Were we talking just to talk? Sure, sometimes I purely listen, me not proposing solutions and there are no resulting action items but sometimes follow-up is necessary, especially coming out of business meetings. I have been the asshole many times because I won't let people go until clearly understanding what happens next. I have attended way too many wasteful conversations and I try to never participate in those again, best I can. I do not leave without documented next happenings, thereby I listen.

To speak and be heard, this no simple task. To accurately hear what is said, a downright arduous effort. Without intentionally operating this here life, I will surely stumble bumble and mumble.

Drinking with the Devil

Moderately flabbergasted by his words, I questioned to clarify what I just heard, to which he said, "I pressured you to drink so you would open up". I reeled back slightly, "Like truth serum?", I puzzled my boss Dave and he replied, "Yes…", he said, "…exactly, truth serum". Wow, I never knew his incessant pouring of booze at our small intimate corporate dinner parties was meant to verbally open up and splay his management team. Our big boss Dave was hoping to have me and my two peer district managers speak the truth and spill our guts about the business, us probably saying more than we would have said otherwise if not for the booze. Hum, I thought, he's sneaky, sneaky but smart. This was my first indisputable big boy job working for Performance Bicycles in the early 1990s and the smart but sneaky alcohol pourer was Dave, our Vice President of Retail. Performance was a powerhouse of an e-commerce operation, while the company also owned and operated about 20 corporate retail bicycle stores scattered around the country.

To me, this employment gig was a big boy job because it was not a local homegrown business, but rather a nationally successful organization escorted by a real paycheck and structured payroll bonuses.

Dave, so I was told, was one of the management partners previously running the old Herman's Sporting Goods stores in NYC, now with locations around the country and simply called 'Dick's'. Dave is a retail guru, a hell of a nice guy and obviously, duh, super-dooper-sneaky-smart. I was recruited to open the new Performance Bicycles store in Baltimore as general manager and did so to great success. Then a year and a half later I was promoted to Eastern District Sales Manager for the United States, responsible for a dozen-or-so stores. What quickly became routine…me and my two peer district sales managers were flown into Chapel Hill North Carolina for dinner at Dave's house, ironically the same town where your momma would later go to college at UNC, but her and I would not meet for another several years. Immediately once arriving at Dave's place, the drinks flowed freely.

I barely drank alcohol but as I would also repeat this same personal weakness later in life at my other big boy job, I let myself be pressured into drinking. The evening included talks of work and of course, the conversations flowed easily as the booze. After the second drink or so, more truthful details emerged, thus proving Dave's initiative as correct, or per minimum, effective. Funny, the alcohol never seemed to totally empty from our glasses even though we kept drinking. Thankfully, Dave was the kind of guy like Sonny who later divulged the intent behind his tactic.

The challenge of remaining in my boss's good graces and not fall overboard while drinking, then drowning or eaten by sharks in the shallows of the executive lagoon was contentious at best.

Thought I could…adequately serve my own intentions and withstand someone convincing me to drink because I preferred not to, but humph, also I did not want to lose my job. Further still, once I had a little of the Devil's drink in my bloodstream, I reveled in my mounting legacy numbness, however begrudgingly. More, more, more…I was pushed to drink more but and although pathetically, I already knew I had enough. At the time I could not see it but now I do…I should have respectfully declined and told Dave and his wife no, but thanks anyway, I am an addict. Well but hah, I wasn't going to do that shit, I did not want to show my weakness, so I kept my damn mouth shut and gave in to drink.

Alcohol is a depressant, directly attacks the nervous system, kills brain cells, diverts rationalism, and erodes the link to thought and thinking which quite literally can change us into someone we are not.

I never heard the story of a man beating his wife to death with a baseball bat while high on marijuana, have you? No, never careening a car into oncoming traffic and striking a minivan, killing the entire family of seven inside after snorting cocaine or even shooting heroin, nope. No other drug creates such humanoid disorderliness, no, none, none other, period.

Alcohol, like anything, when consumed with control is manageable, but unlike every other earthly substance except Methamphetamine, when consumed to excess or unregulated, booze turns people into the Devil themselves.

I lived to learn and know that especially when attending work functions, I drank slowly or phantom drank or for goodness sake just left early. Leaving the Dave alcohol-captive evenings, I would not drink until forced to again, yup, until when later returning to 'Chapel Thrill'. Categorically I hated alcohol, hated. Now modern day sober for 12 years, 9 months, 5 days and counting, no longer do I give a single fucking fuck when it comes to protecting my truthful alcoholic history, so I speak up and say no booze no way, thanks anyway, ain't gonna happen…I choose to no longer dance with the Devil or drink his dammed Water. Ghoulish Brew.

Don't Fuck With People's Money

So I observe and dare to claim, money is some people's number one thing, other times it is number eight. An interesting inquisition to be certain, and one I have given much time and thought to over my lifespan. Being it the human value proposition against our money earned, and why is that exactly? When I began managing businesses and was held responsible for teams of people, I dug deep into the notion of what motivates some to do what they do. Specifically I was puzzled by the tireless work ethic versus the opposite, those with a seeming total disregard for the job. Some work family members were consistently on time or even early, while others were most days late. A certain breed of human sister or brother is focused, you know…optimistic and energized while working, compared to those who somedays seem to care less.

First I explored what motivates people, them able to arrive on time. After much research of my own studies and experimentation, I found the motivation of money to drive on-time arrival generally resides lower on the list, beyond condition number five. However, I also quickly learned that the number one move by me their manager causing disengagement detachment and even defiance, is lowering my people's pay rate. More than yelling, us worker rats are personally offended when our pay is reduced. Factually, I only performed the payrate cut malfeasance once, before realizing the radical managerial out of orderliness but for decades, I watched others struggle with the technique horribly.

I learned hand-first myself as the boss to never cut pay, then was also stung by the realization from the other end, when it was done to me.

If thinking it's time to demote someone thus cutting their pay, I believe everyone is better off if I help them realize this job is not for them, aka I help them resign…good luck in your future endeavors. Simultaneously as I understood this workforce dynamic, my big boss at Performance Dave summarized it best, then the issue as stated was shining-star crystal clear to me, "Don't fuck with people's money".

The Year of Living Magnificently, On Purpose

In the summer of 1985, I first arrived in the Canaan Valley of West Virginia for a mountainbike race.

Instantaneously, I knew the almost-hidden geographical gem would forever play a role in my life, I knew it as fact. The raw beauty and magnetic draw of the valley is entirely irresistible. The Canaan Valley town of Davis was and still is, magnificent. Davis West Virginia not only pulled me in tight, but Mother Nature holds me close to her wholesome bosom every time I return. Yes, the cumulation of raw outdoors is amazing, truthfully magnetic…the mountains, the rivers, the rocks, the muddy but not limiting terrain, the small swinging bridge in the middle of nowhere, the spectacular sunrises and sets. Layered atop the mystical valley then is the people, the pizza, the racing, the racers, the natural spring popping out of the hillside, well, the sheer splendor of it all.

Honestly though, the one thing initially hooking me, the one thing reinforcing that I could never more separate this place from my loving and awe-inspired heart, the one thing was actually a person. One human drew me in more than Mother Nature herself, them supplying the comforted human accoutrements to invite me to come, stay, and return often. He was, he is, the king of fun, Mister Laird Knight. Laird's positivity, his infectious energy, his encouragement, the supreme racecourse challenges he presented to us, his competitive fairness, his structure and presentation to create more of a happening than just an event, his shared support and love with me, all of which he gifted openly and willingly as the local race promoter. The racing platform he offered to the world completed the value proposition of a life well-lived, by my measure.

Several times over some years Laird mentioned…asking if I noticed a particular patch of flowering Mountain Laurels off somewhere in the valley, or the awe of that freshly-build beaver den. He would comment on the depth of the clear running river, or the precarious conditions on the far-away hidden narrow swinging bridge. I laughingly scoffed my response…hah, no dude, I was racing, I didn't see anything of the sort. Puzzled, Laird would look back at me with his head cocked seriously somber and say, "But why not?". Laird was a racer too, he went fast too, he focused too, so how was it that he saw what I did not, on the same damn course? Learned to realize, I was missing some critical life experiences as I zoomed by.

The connectedness through our shared activity, Laird and mine the racing, was something exclusive to what I had experienced then-thus far, even after already completing more than a dozen races elsewhere before entering Canaan Valley. There in Davis West Virginia I found by chance true comradery, a factual community and honestly, friends I knew would last a lifetime. Without the racer family I discovered thanks to Laird, sure, I would have continued to race elsewhere but in Davis West Virginia I found a second home. Such the dynamic of togetherness was on scene void without Laird, meaning he brought the fun together for us all to share. Clearly, for the first time in my existence I met a lifeforce unlike any I had met before.

Laird offered me a lens to see life's beauty and possibilities through my own eyes, no matter the hardship.

Even up to modern day I retain the lessons learned from Laird, these and others, the suffering of sport is forever worth it and she Mother Nature's beauty is there awaiting, even when I might not see it or feel it, her waiting for me to pay attention.

Concurrently, also residing in Canaan Valley, another amazing soul entered my life who has influenced me greatly to go ahead and be my wild self, him being the beautiful lifeforce Mister Chip 'Chipper' Chase. I first met Chip as he ran through the woods across the relentless rock beds, through the mud, and in between the raindrops with his old-school thirty-pound video camera black box, him filming the racing action as us the racers raced and raced around. Besides Chip's wild fervor for life…his hoots, his constant positivity, his expert and forever available helpful hand, Chip is more connected to Mother Earth than any other human I ever met, literally. For least the first decade after I met him, I never saw Chip wear shoes, never ever never. Chip is a wildman awhile kind, gentle, patient, and wise. If appealing music is playing, Chip is dancing, of course barefoot. Given the opportunity, Chip will rip off some Appalachia riffs on his harmonica, joining a traveling bluegrass band on stage. His animated body movements and story-telling rivals all. Some may think him a goofball but my perspective of Chipper Chase is adrift from the silliness others might judge him of. To me, Chipper is living boldly out in the open, creating sunshine wherever he goes, not only an admirable character trait but one I am jealous not to perform much more often than the slight times I do. Travis had the pleasure of meeting Chip when we attended the local Canaan mountainbike festival together in 2016.

Both Laird and Chip reside in my mind and heart as the epitome of perspective. Reinforcing an earlier mention of my Four P's, aka my four criticals, one of my Four P's is perspective. Laird and Chip represent perspective…people who operate with an emphasis of flexing their fun and light heart, not so darn worried about the impressions and judgments of others. Laird and Chipper, the kings of fun.

Lessons Learned…My Four P's, My Four Criticals
We each have our unique personal operating system, be it favored situational conditions, reputed values collection, or proprietary life-balance metrics structure, however loosely gathered and often held inside. For me, I have lived to learn and know my true life priorities, shared here now with you both in order of importance.

1. One. People and our interwoven connectedness, we need each other. How others positively affect my human connection skills.
2. Two. Perspective, maintaining a well-rounded playfulness, a fun and light heart, a staunch viewpoint of reality and possibilities, awhile a functional healthy-ego. The impact of my intentional orientation, because of other humans.
3. Three. Purpose, clearly identifying, documenting, and keeping visible a primary orientation, my number one north star, my guiding personal values, my bottom line why, etcetera. My defined why what and how.
4. Four. Passion, not letting go of my cool things, my therapeutic and fulfilling hobbies, the stuff providing me light, even when most everything around me goes dark. The influences upon me impressing the retained cool things I do.

Now operating from the foundation of my Four P's, henceforth I layout my remaining chapter five ciphered influences, collected and categorized in accordance to my four critical areas of a life well-lived.

PEOPLE
The First of Four P's: My Influenced Gathering of People-Related Lessons
People and Our Interwoven Connectedness, We Need Each Other
How others help me find the depth of value atwix my sisters and brothers.

People. Becoming of a Politician
My ignorance concerning politics was genuine, mostly I knew absolutely nothing about governmental maneuverings and moreover I did not give a fuck, until I did. On a global and National scale, I was only engaged with the obligatory surface-level democratic voting process but otherwise, I cared for governmental goings-on none.

Once getting slapped upside my face with the big local fish of bureaucratic injustice affecting me directly however, I instinctually stepped the fuck up.

I picked a fight with a formidable adversary, a high ranking Baltimore City government official already on their underhanded political path pursuing a ludicrous initiative. Thankfully, perhaps my greatest strength was not knowing what I did not know. Recognizing I needed backup, counseling, and some expert guidance, I called up the authoritarian master on the subject, the national figurehead for mountainbike rights, Mister Tim Blumenthal. Graciously, Tim not only counseled me but he also showed up in person to walk the jeopardized bike trails in question, shoulder to shoulder alongside yours younger truly in Baltimore. Mister Blumenthal also suggested I shift my focus away from my current target of the conflict itself, dropping my battle implements and focus on creating a mutual win.

Barely acting with thought or purpose previously, the bulk of my effort prior to seeking counsel from Tim was opposing and even bad mouthing the ridiculous effort of the City government to ban mountainbiking from my local Baltimore trails without properly or legally notifying the affected parties, namely us mountainbikers. Such injustice was not something I could allow on multiple levels, but I knew I needed help. With Tim's support and guidance, alongside my peer advocacy champions in Baltimore, aka 'my Joe', aka Friendwords Joe Surkiewicz, and his wife Ann Lembo the lawyer and our other super-pal-dude David Tambeaux, I slowed down to effectively enter the lair of the beast. I invited myself to be a sitting member of the Friends of the Watershed Committee within the Baltimore City Department of Public Works.

Sitting down at my first participatory City government meeting, I followed my plan to a T and blew up my dirty-ego, smiling at the lady directly across the table who proposed the initial injunction, making friends with her before she even realized who I was or the group I represented.

I took no personal offense to her adversarial claims, that mountainbikers are gangs of nature-ravaging terrorists who practice cannibalism on human infants while riding their two-wheeled off-road hellion vehicles on her long-time favorite walking trails, near her house, on her property, aka her sacred cow the trails, but technically that land is City watershed public access property. I left my intentionally-cast-aside battle emotions sitting on the hallway bench outside the DPW committee meeting room. Me then and there practicing a calm cool methodical process, taking no offense to any unsubstantiated claims, and I drove forward to create something beautifully synergistic, and open for all local public access outdoor land users. Mister Tim Blumenthal, then director of the International Mountainbike Advocacy organization aka IMBA, provided me with a few hours of invaluable hands-on political coaching unlike any I ever knew. Tim's shared wisdom of slowing down, putting aside emotions and dropping the need to be right, all for the sake of creating a shared win-win scenario, well, these have been some of the most valuable and utilized collaborative lessons throughout my life.

People. Let's Deal With This Shit Right Now
Surface level and technically, this hallowed life influence belongs in my 'purpose' category. Because it being, the most substantial moment in my life when I did something I did not want to do, but proceeded anyway because it was absolutely the correct action, aka the right thing to do, aka congruent to my personal life values, damn the damage unto myself. Rather, I place the item here in the people category because of the demonstrated lifting, propping-up and love shared between humans, and the revered lesson I carry with me still.

Travis you were five. Lauren you were still three years old. Less than two years into the biggest and best job I ever had, Trek global director of retail, and during the same period when my boss John Burke believed I was doing awesome work, him regularly showering me with praise, well, one day I strutted into Jb's office and quit my damn job. My words came out of the blue and Jb had no idea what was going on. Told elsewhere the detail, but the lasting effect I gained was dealing with issues here and now. Here and now…knowing for fact shit isn't going to clear itself up magically because of extended time, miles traveled, or a desire to put it out of mind. John taught me hand-first, I can run away but my problems will follow me wherever I go, so why not stay and do battle with this shit right now?

I recognize and pay honor to…if dealing with the brutal reality of known facts, casting aside the drama fear and dirty-ego, splendor has a chance to occur.

In this my example I offer to say…if not emerging from my own frantic shell of emotional disorderliness, putting truth first and admitting to Jb how alcoholically fucked up I was there on the spot, he would have noticed my out of orderliness some short time down the road and fired me. If I forced Jb to read my mind or form his own assumptions based on my surface behavior, I am certain I would have lost my job long ago. By not telling Jb everything, I would be making his decision for him, a ludicrous maneuver defined.

Rather, I allowed my boss to see and know the entirety of me, helping me if he so desired, which he did, and I remained in that same exact role for another eight years. A couple handfuls of my direct report coworkers experienced related hardships in their lives and luckily, they were transparent enough with me. I exercised the opportunity to pay it forward, me behaving supportively and remaining flexible, helping nurse them through their life struggles while keeping their jobs. Only by way of the amazing John Burke did I deeply comprehend with these here hands the unadulterated value of truthful transparency and supporting each other no matter fucking what, aka sisters and brothers all.

People. Body Readings
Part way through my time at the Trek office, an outside instructor arrived to teach a two-day course on better communication. Immediately I forecasted my attendance to be valuable and oh boy, I was right. Many gems were shared which I absorbed and the main remembrance was a big one...over 50% of the way we humans communicate is not by way of what words are shared but through our eyes, voice and body language.

Since I lacked much of the formal education my peer humans sentence served, I was thrilled, well, candidly blessed, to learn such monstrous factual jewels.

The best chance we have, to understand and be understood, is primarily participating in face-to-face communication. Immediately, the class of maybe 40 people in the Trek office looked around at each other, seemingly for validation with what we just heard. I am assuming but I believe most of us inherently read into the depth of the truth-share lesson and collectively brain-scrambled on how we would manage the spoiler of the punch line...texting sucks the most, next worse is email and oh boy, these were the two primary forms of communication we participated in at the time. I began rethinking not only how to increase face time with people while decreasing email, but also began playing guessing games with myself...how could I dramatically better the effectiveness of my otherwise non-negotiable electronic communication? No way could I stop emailing or texting, such notions were unrealistic but how could I use my new knowledge and do online conversing better?

Originally I attempted to heighten-clarify what I was trying to say and explain how I was attempting to say it, aka how I was feeling, hoping to be better understood. The problem arising was my messages grew too much in length and although attempting to do better, I likely lost people and probably did little to nothing to improve my e-voice. Although self-recognizing my intentional long-windedness, I also accepted the reality that at work, less is more. If I can share critical points with less emotion, I could be better heard and then much as possible, fill in quickly afterward with a phone or in-person get together. Perfect example is this here your book, and its towering word count as I attempt to be clearly understood. Here my pages runneth over and feature even intentional crossovers, factually knowing if I am slightly misunderstood on one page, my faith rests to bring things back around thereafter on a future sheet, thus clearing away any earlier misunderstandings. Here I do not claim more is better but that it is what it is, aka this is my best focused effort share with you both.

Chapter FIVE

Still, collectively here in this volume one edition two, I spent over 1,300 hours shortening, condensing, or somehow assimilating more words into fewer, knowing such effort as highly valuable. Within and intentionally I slashed to-be verbs wherever making sense to do so, and I attempted no direct duplication. Much because of that Trek two-day communication seminar and whenever possible, primarily I try to talk face to face, second will be a phone call, third an email and lastly a text or brief message.

Comprehensively, I try to operate this here life top to bottom with intention, starting with the specificity of my words and of course, using my thoughtful readings and giving's of body voice.

People. More the Merrier

Profoundly, one of the most lovable humans in my life is my dearly departed friend Chris Kegel from Milwaukee, aka Friendwords Noel Kegel's father. Chris' business smarts extended far beyond my ability to even capture a mere percentage of his knowledge through my words here. Much of Chris' charm was the love for all humans he wore on his sleeve. Every time I left Chris' presence, I felt more open and appreciative of all people. Laughingly, following only a few minutes with Chris, most times I challenged my inadequate patience and consciously attempted to shed my attachment to any people rubbing me the wrong way. I never saw that Chris had issue with anyone, nor anyone with him. Not that this reality baffled me, but I was hit with the purity of his acceptance, I could do so much better, I could be kinder, more merciful, generous, and humble.

I believe my favorite Chris-ism is: The More The Merrier.

Several times over the last two decades, I paused to contemplate the ramifications of opening up various events, both home and work…opening up to multitudes of people and mostly I referred back to Chris' famous saying of 'More the Merrier'. Atop every occurrence, I realized Chris was ridiculously correct that yes, the inclusion of having more people around and not fewer makes everything better for everyone. After wrongly pausing to set or adjust invitee limits with events, I reoriented and most times put it out there for the world…come one come all, the more the merrier. I maintain the notion to open, doesn't matter…more the people means better the party.

Once determined to open a second DreamBikes, I focused on Milwaukee. Intuitively, I met first with the one who I knew must come first, Chris Kegel. Within only a handful of minutes into our first meeting on the matter, and as I explained my vision of DreamBikes Milwaukee, Chris gifted me with the most complementary phrase I could imagine. "Well Roger, sounds like you're Doing The Good Work". When first hearing Chris' mention of 'good work', I immediately received his words as a sort of religion, and a perfectly articulated phrase of my purposeful intent when I started DreamBikes, that being my attempt to step the fuck up and help others who cannot effectively help themselves. To me, Chris masterfully led by example…acting out his part, aiding his home family, his work family, his community, and his bigger world.

Never once when anywhere near Chris, even when he was too sick to stand and near the end of his quick fight with cancer, never once did I not feel that his natural aura was anything else than life is a party, come one come all. Chris further inspired me to smile more, laugh more, help more, and do my best part for all. Chris influenced me by silent example to act more purposefully, more lovingly, more globally inclusive, and be more inviting.

People. I Like Smiling, Smiling's My Favorite
My first conversation with Mister Dave Mitchell on the phone then immediately, I declared a compulsion to meet this man. More so, certain I must work with him, he was that good. Not only has Dave taught me much-much but to boot, I savor the fun-fun splashing around in his stupendously dynamic learning pool. Dave is a renowned public speaker, legit, a leadership coach, business coach, and much-much more-more. I hired Dave when I was at Trek and we collaborated on a handful of various projects. There was our retail sales skills training program, keynote speeches to thousands at our annual sales meetings, and more in between. The multi-faceted skill set of Dave Mitchell is ridiculously impressive. Hugely his draw as I experienced, and perhaps my biggest gain from Dave was, his lead by example lesson…sharing and teaching through story.

Although perhaps missing a career opportunity as standup comedian, Dave seems to do quite well slinging his humorous workplace wisdom. From Dave I learned that the slated message is better heard, retained, and later applied by our scattered monkey minds when delivered to us by way of an engaging and real-world narrative. Certainly influenced by Dave, I cooked up the notion within this here your book to open each chapter with a relative life thumbprint story, thus sharing more associated details with you both my precious, section by section. The blossoming results from his vast work experience, layered atop his psychological education, Dave taught me that positivity matters. Well, you might think that duh yes of course, but no, there's more. Especially on the retail sales floor, one of the most powerful forces in the world available to us, influencing the betterment of the surrounding mood is to use our face, literally. This critical, technically the second most contagious facial expression so says Dave, is smiling. Although this river runs deep, here I'll skip a stone on the surface.

When we smile, others can't help but to turn their frown upside down.

Especially during an uncomfortable or even negative exchange hooman to hooman, just by smiling the overall mood changes, yes, literally an uncontrollable reaction. This new learning, a kissing cousin to the infectiousness of yawning landed upon me powerfully and gave me an entire new lens. Twice reinforcing my chapter-opening notion is that if you want it or need it, 'it' being positivity itself, share it openly, aka give that shit away.

People. Don't Point Your Butt at Me
Dave Mitchell shared his fantastical gold nugget of delivering crystalized communication as intended, me adding the notion of not wishing or praying for variable human understanding. I worship Dave for this life lesson that I utilize every day, yes every day. Here again and for me, preciseness matters. Definitively, I operate this here life more effectively and am a better person because of this learned word precision from Dave Mitchell.

One simple word placed or misplaced can wield a heavy emotional hammer.

I cannot begin to recount the thousands of times, even tens of thousands, that I have misused this word both at home and at work before Dave Mitchell straightened out my uneducated ass, one simple word, the three-letter word 'but'. The use of the devilish little three-letter word 'but' negates everything said before it. As an example, how does this sentence feel…"I love you and you're pretty and you're awesome but you drive me crazy." To me, ouch, that hurts. The times something like that was said to me, I immediately became annoyed and defensive, maybe worse. Dave's offering…instead of using 'but', use 'and'. Alternatively to waving the 'but' around, how does this one feel…"I love you and you're pretty and you're awesome and you drive me crazy."

I humbly accept the mention of crazy and no, this does not make me mad nor defensive and I might want to reply like this, "Ok, well, thank you, I love you more, you're cute AF and you're pretty awesome yourself and fair enough right, I'm sorry for being a parttime asshole and right back at ya, sometimes you drive me nuts too…smooch-smooch." Haha, to me this version is not bad, and I accept it as a conversation and not a blaming accusation. The 'and' adds or continues the talk, not reversing forward momentum.

Both at work and out in the wild, this simple three-character word has screwed me up possibly more than any other singular word ever spoken or written. I have experimented with this notion thousands of times and so far, Dave is right, the word 'and' is better than 'but'. Dave explained there's barely an application where 'and' cannot be substituted for 'but'. Most times, 'and' saves the day because it does not reverse the conversation.

People. I Already Blew Out My Candles

My helping mindset and outstretched hand were long-ago established before encountering this powerful influence upcoming. The imprint, I believe, is perfectly layered upon my notion of rising up and trying, aka give it my best intentional effort no matter the perceived or tangible outcome. Here the deep emotional inspiration arrives through a cinematic story of one person's ability to change the world. The movie, *Pay it Forward*, kicks my ass every time…the story of a small boy who withheld both a big brain while a huge heart. The movie shakes me a little, motivates me some more, validates a fair amount, and hurts me in an unexplainable way, well, the hurt somehow related to my homeless bat shit crazy mother I think.

Intrinsically I observe the value of doing the right thing, by my measure.

Within the arena of familiar irony itself, the main movie character believes he failed, that his idealistic street level plan did not work, that none of it worked. The rollup however, showed quite the opposite. My summary claims one passionate person with a basic but worthy aspiration can change the world and perhaps is the only thing that can, if and when able to just get started. A simple but true and tenacious effort can produce remarkable fucking results, this one of my most awesome learnings ever.

PERSPECTIVE
The Second of Four P's: My Influenced Gathering of Perspective-Related Lessons
Perspective: Operating Truthfully this here Playful Heart
How others aided my healthy-ego, the possibilities of life, and my learned lack of assumption.

Perspective. Close the Door on Your Way Out
Once promoted into the regional sales manager role for Trek and we moved to Wisconsin, the job was an everyday flurry. One day I needed help, so I went to see world sales manager big boss Joyce Keehn for guidance. "I don't know, what do you think?", was her response. "Well, I'm not so sure but maybe I can call Mike back and talk it through with him, trying not to piss him off from the start…", I replied. She slightly nodded her head up then down, and told me to close the door on my way out. Hum, seemed she did not have time for me, although her office door was most times open.

More shit was flying around in my region from top Boston to bottom Virginia, much-much drama while pushing company directives upon my outside sales reps and bike shop owner customers, and the next day I walked into Joyce's office yet again. I explained my dilemma and Joyce in return laid out her solution, "I don't know, what do you think?".

Hum, I yanked my head back, thinking she was fucking with me.

Truth be firm however, her response was super appropriate given the situation and manner of my inquiry. I answered in detail, suggesting what I did think should be done amid these circumstances. Joyce did not verbally respond, although she was paying direct attention. Supercool boss lady Joyce slightly nodded her head down then up, then down, and told me to close the door on my way out. Day three directly-reporting to Joyce was much the same…drama with my customers, human efficiency issues with my 13 outside reps, and I had more problems to solve. Not sure what to do, I popped up out of my office chair and headed to ask my boss Joyce her advice, oh hold up wait, I caught myself and laughed out loud, omg haha…I spun around to sit my ass back down. I knew exactly what Joyce was about to tell me, and I chuckled at the lesson learned. Her technique rather sly at first but poignant and humorous, teaching me however indirectly to think for myself. With my untrained eye, I first believed the need to ask Joyce most everything. Within a few days however, I learned she would rather have me think and act for myself, of course consulting with her on decisions truly worthy of collaboration but the variance was mostly for me to decipher. Joyce's approach was extremely effective and in short order, the realization of making shit happen on my own was soundly in place. Certainly I learned the earliest version of this think for thyself lesson when I was four, once my mother spilled her marbles across the floor, backed up by my entry into the drug trade, when then dropping out of school, then once coached by bike buddha Wilbert Wilkens, but Joyce drove the point home expertly.

Joyce coached executively well and led by example while also, she gave me the biggest job move-up in my life, promoted from outside salesperson managing $10M of annual business in Baltimore and DC, to east coast regional sales manager. I was then responsible for $100M of Trek product going into partner retail stores yearly.

Joyce is the sole reason we moved to Wisconsin, because of the new regional manager job she offered me, requiring my presence in the Waterloo world headquarters office. The knowledge gained, the lessons learned both good and bad, well as the future opportunities afforded me, well, that shit happened because Joyce believed in me. If not already working in the Trek office for Joyce, I doubt Jb would have then later recruited me for the Retail Services director job. She and I met weekly, especially since I was new to the role. Maybe I have a warped sense of reality, but I believe I am more heart-open than the average hooman male, so it's not too surprising that me and my first female boss got along so well.

I have been called 'a fucking girl' before, and disparagingly, because of my up-front emotional style of communication.

Similarly, at neighborhood parent game nights and parties etcetera, I hang out with the moms more than the dads. I am more so interested to discuss children, kiddo ear infections and dinner preparation ideas than the awkward time with guys as they but not me drink beer, watch football, and brag about the strip clubs they go to unbeknownst to their wives.

I lived to learn and know if I am told to just go and make the best decisions I can, I fricking don't wait but go. Early on, Joyce once again reinforced the value of focusing on the issue and not the emotion. The application lay in my hands to sort out and establish my own baselines, but the value of setting aside the drama to first deal with the true issue is something I still utilize most every day of my life. The delicate balance of asking permission versus begging for forgiveness is a razor-thin line. Here much the reason I try to communicate in an excellent manner, so the dynamic of do that shit directly or check with someone first is not so much a mystery. Joyce Keehn handed me the leadership opportunity to join corporate America based on my skills and whatever growth potential she saw in me. Thankfully for the three of us, me and you two my brood, Joyce cared zip-zero none for the existence of academic diplomas or business certifications, of which I echo-had none.

Perspective. Everything We Need is Already Inside Us All

The opportunity we have at any time to learn something brand new, like gardening, understanding seismic activity, or how to install solar panels, yes, why not? Learn several basic foreign language phrases in a few minutes to save a life, why not? Yes, for fact all of this shit is most def possible.

What I select to manifest will not bubble up randomly and by accident, my intentional commitment is needed, well as everything else I fucking got.

My number one solidified overall reminder of such truisms is the John Travolta movie, *Phenomenon*. The amazing limitless potential this flick offers me is the reality that we ourselves are capable of more than we think or try. Profoundly I echo a key shared concept from the movie…change happens whether we like it or not. Everything is changing, everything, even if just getting older and not yet eroding, change is occurring constantly whether we wish desire or fight the opposite. Also that we and everything around us is as one, we are connected, we are related, because we are all made from the same one thing, energy.

Even as we graduate from life to the other side, we are journeying, forever adventuring…what an exciting concept and what a fantastical thrilling expedition, a veritable phenomenon.

PURPOSE
The Third of Four P's: My Influenced Gathering of Purpose-Related Lessons
Purpose: My Guiding Orientations
How others help me with the specificity and quality of what I am doing and why.

Purpose. To Get Somewhere…

My future state I cannot leave to chance. I am unable to presume or pray that shit works out, much because of from where I came. I need to purposefully rise up every day and operate this here life intentionally, trying to be exact. Minimally, I must begin with a verifiable, if not measurable, starter plan. Awkward as it is to admit but I believe back when, at first the drugs saved me from the fear I ran from throughout my youth. Ensuingly in short order however, the street substances were determined to kill me.

My intense structured athletic training then saved me from the drugs, because if otherwise out and about on my own, my haphazard daily wanderings would have led me back to that legacy door of shadow, me hiding from myself and cowering from the world under the warm blanket of the drugs. I needed the challenge, I required transparency and I demanded self-accountability. Surprisingly, my first athletic trainer, 'Coach Troy' Jacobson taught me that speed does not always matter…quality matters, correctness matters, at all times matter. For years I did not have a bike computer to gauge how fast I was rolling or how far I had traveled, such concerns were not participants in my plan. Quality equates to time and workload not speed, so Coach Troy taught me. By default I discovered not to do shit half-assed and don't think I am smarter than the plan. I learned during my time with Coach Troy, in order for me to get somewhere, I gotta do the darn work but do it correctly, and adjust constantly. For me, duh, unquestionably these critical life factors stretch far beyond bike riding. As I lived to learn, if I am doing something, do it to the best of my ability, exertion be damned. Coach Troy says one of the biggest mistakes athletes make is not training hard enough on their hard days and not going easy enough on their easy days. Rest is also, part of training. If always going hard or medium-hard, I cannot effectively recover, thus sacrificing my overall performance. Even when feeling invincible, I dwell within my discipline to rest on days planned, so I don't fuck up my hard workdays.

If I act correctly, I go further and achieve more towards what I am oriented.

Daily I show up to the front of house curb with a plan. I do not aimlessly wander, I do not float along wherever the winds of whimsicalness might carry me, willy-nilly speeding slow or trailing fast, traveling short or long intervals at random but rather, I set out hyper-intentionally and adjust as I go. Only with a map do I have the chance to arrive where I am going, the roadblocks detours and work-arounds be damned.

Purpose. What Are You Doing, Exactly?

During my almost 20 years at Trek, the specificity of my different roles mattered greatly, because if I did not know what my boss expected of me, how could I possibly deliver?

Rhetorical...I couldn't.

The drill-down detail that Joyce shared with me surely came from elsewhere but together, we mapped out the exactness of the critical four worker rat categories: Responsibilities, tasks, standards and measurements. Like most bosses of mine, Joyce did not spell out from the get-go everything she expected of me, least in a language I understood, by my measure. Yes I had a job description and some guidelines were in place, but after a few related back and forth conversations, Joyce shared with me a valuable tool, one I would surely use for the rest of my life, not just with myself, and not just at work.

Joyce taught me that responsibilities are the requirements assigned to me so that I keep the paychecks a coming, aka the maneuvers at work they pay me to be in charge of. Tasks are the moves I have to make in order to achieve my responsibilities. Standards are the verifiable details of how I will perform my tasks. Measurements are the objective metrics that show how well I execute my standards, and I can pinpoint-publish these measures, aka I can prove it. The process here is so simple yet this tight order of how one thing leads to the next is not far disassociated from the Franklin-Covey organization's book titled *The Four Disciplines of Execution*, aka *4DX*, and its withheld lesson of 'predictive measures'. More on *4DX* later. This mental orientation of RTSM that Joyce passed on to me, aka responsibilities tasks standards and measurements, has served me well for almost two decades now and I am certain will continue to do so, long as I use that shit and work the process...learn, adapt, change and repeat.

Purpose. Land of the Rising Sun

Driving around with peer senior manager and country tour guide, I informed the dude I needed to pee, and now. The only nearby option was a new car dealership, so I went in to use their facilities. The supreme attention, the helpfulness, and the accommodation inside the auto dealer building was rather ridiculous. I apologized that I just needed their bathroom. Believing I was trapped in The Truman Show, I shook my head trying to wake up from this overly-kind alternative universe. The new car outlet staff in Japan bent over backwards to welcome me, saying it was their pleasure for me to visit them and use their amenities. They were alarmingly friendly, gave me a cold bottled water, asked me if I wanted some free freshly prepared food, and never tried to sell me anything. It appeared the staff existed for one sole purpose, to pleasurefully serve all people, and for any reason the served human desired.

The extreme fanatical respect and formality practiced were somewhat shocking and frankly, gave me more hope for our world and for humankind.

My first trip to Japan in 2005 produced a new and interesting world lens, one I never knew or heard of before. Crazily, the atmospheric gap between standard culture operations of the USA and Japan is something I am not sure I can adequately put words to, but here I try.

Directly, the time then arrived for me to attend dinner with several Japanese Trek retailers. Gratefully I was coached beforehand because when initial greetings occurred, besides the extreme kindness grace and respect, we exchanged business cards. In Japan, business cards are a HUGE deal, ginormous. The five-minute business card inspection routine was genuine: Literal minutes of fondling, gazing, and inspecting microscopically every atomic particle of the card front, then back, then front, then back, technically the workover was more careful than handling a newborn baby. After experiencing the extreme formality and respect practiced by the entirety of the Japanese culture, well, I then tried to do even better than I had been trying to do before...more respectful, more gracious, more patient, more empathetic, more kind, and more gentle. I overdress for funerals and post-Japan I believe I forever will. I use formal salutations whenever and wherever possible. Japan reinforced to me that time is always available to be kind and more importantly, all that little shit really fucking matters.

PASSION
The Fourth of Four P's: My Influenced Gathering of Passion-Related Lessons
Passion: Not Letting Go of My Cool Things
How others help me maintain balance by utilizing my therapeutic and fulfilling hobbies.

Passion. Pushing Off From My Ears
No way can I adequately explain my long-ago glee for the first ever West Virginia National mountainbike event scheduled to occur on my favored east coast racecourse in Canaan Valley, summer 1988. Although generally humble but confident of my possible result in WV, for this event I was uncharacteristically cocky, truthfully envisioning myself winning the expert class. The pent-up National series excitement, both the mass of people and the notoriety was electrifying. The pros took off and our huge expert field was not far behind. Floating on cloud nine, I led the expert class of racers into the ridiculously rocky West Virginia wilderness and within ten minutes, I was catching and passing the slower pros. Trying to semi-loosely monitor what was happening behind me, within twenty minutes I could not see anyone in pursuit and my multi-minute lead was extending. Knowing the course and conditions good as anyone, I executed every correct effort at every juncture...every barely rideable downhill, every get-off-and-run-through river crossing, every treacherous teeth-rattling rock garden, and every shoe-swallowing mud bog. Not trying to necessarily out-pace myself mentally, but my race was proceeding swimmingly. Cautiously, once the race began I slowed my mental roll and did not envision any given result, so not to jinx it. At the time and before turning pro, I had amassed a high level of fitness and there in Canaan Valley aka God's Country, I was laying it down on the muddy line.

And then, less than an hour into that West Virginia national series race, when all I had to do was not make a mistake, my left knee area grew increasingly sore as I pedaled. Never had I felt these pains before, ever. I had not injured or experienced any trouble with my left knee in over eleven years. The pain did the opposite of lessen and every five to ten minutes, I was required to stop pedaling momentarily, because my left knee was locking up.

Minute by minute, I knew my competitors will be thrilled to approach me from the rear as I struggled to simply stay on my bike, not laying down in the mud screaming in agony like I wanted to.

With only about five miles to go before I would win my first national mountainbike race, the former second place expert passed me. The guy was a factory-sponsored bleach-blonde California bro who just walked away from me as I tried not to quit. One mile before the finish line, and through the literal pain tears in my eyes, I watched another expert racer pass me. Brushing my shoulder up against the checkered flag in third place, I collapsed on the ground, screaming for someone to get the paramedics.

I was lifted and hauled to the ambulance, they wrapped my knee with ice and offered to transport me to the hospital. Although tragically upset about my third-place finish, I simultaneously accepted the harsh realities of racing, this was not my day. The medics commented their probable prognosis of torn ligaments but I scoffed, hah, no way dudes, I did not hurt that knee recently so how did a ligament injury just creep up on me? It became a slight conflict, them claiming I must have fallen on it and maybe not realized the extent of injury. Hah, I said, thanks for the crystal ball forecast and I took my ace bandage, ice packs, and hobbled away using my bike as a crutch of sorts. Barely able to walk on stage for the awards ceremony, I knew my knee was wrecked but still couldn't understand what was wrong. A friend drove me the three and a half hours home to my father's house and next day Monday I went to the hospital, resourcefully using the crutches I already owned from a previous left broken ankle.

After a drawn-out doctor's appointment complete with CT scans, the outcome was I tore my iliotibial band, aka IT band, the tendon extending from my hip to my lower leg running across the outside of my knee. I could not understand the doctor, "Torn, it's torn?", I asked. Yup, torn. This was one of the most bizarre injuries I suffered, strangely one without any impact. Three times a week I dragged my ass to physical therapy and I was told to find a good bodyworker. "A what?", I said, a bodyworker they said, "...what's that?", I asked. I had no idea. Within a week I found my first-ever bodyworker, aka sports massage therapist, a wildly skilled Baltimore lady named Stephanie. Weekly I worked with Stephanie, paying her cash and she was ten times more valuable than my physical therapist. Stephanie explained that my IT band became damaged because of overuse. I snapped back, "It CAN'T BE overuse", yeah I ride a lot as I went on to explain but I want to turn pro someday soon and I will need to ride much more, it can't be overuse...it just can't be. My life aspirations sank. Visions of drug needles danced in my head. Tears flooded both my eyes, and I slumped forward. Stephanie backed up a little to say that yes, my body is able to handle the hours and training miles but if I didn't stretch and alter some of my activities, I will get hurt again. She rephrased herself and said my IT band suffered from a high volume of repetitive movement, and more so a lack of stretching. Far beyond concerned, I was scared to death, and afraid my mountainbike racing career might be over before it even began.

Three months later, I was still hobbling around on crutches. Stephanie was a real pro...comprehensive and wholesome. First things first, I received an expansive lesson on stretching.

I needed to vary my repertoire and because of spending 20 hours a week hunched-over and bunched-up on my bike, walking became part of my new healthy body training routine. The walking and some related stretching practices were for the benefit of my spine, which I never had problems with but Stephanie claimed I will, if I don't care for it. Much of the intentional work on my human machine focused on the hyper-problematic hamstring area, well as opening up my hip and chest-shoulder pectoral zone. When I walk, as Stephanie explained, my back receives healthy stacking treatment, which counterbalances my time on the bike. Next came a collection of critical and life-long biomechanical positioning instructions, which I still carry with me and practice today. Shoulders are my main problem area. Stephanie gifted me the learned knowledge of pushing my arm attachment points apart from my ears, and pulling them back from my chin, standing tall thus keeping my wing joints relaxed and healthy. This practice is one I would check myself on tens of thousands of times since. Also, learning to relax my upper body while riding, even under extreme loads, I keep my bent elbows loose and maintain a light touch on the handlebars.

Slightly later still, my indoor ice speed skating coach Lyle drilled me to regularly check my crunched-over and in motion skating position for accuracy. Quickly I planted both elbows atop my knees and reached up with my hands to make sure my closed fists comfortably touch my chin. If not, my body was not compressed enough for effective speed and aerodynamics required when on the ice racing the long blade skates. Through repetitive check-ins of my correct position, I assure my best effort through proper biomechanics. Over the years while skating, I checked myself hundreds of times since then. Here and definitively, by way of Miss Stephanie and the masterful Mister Lyle, my introduction to body scan mindfulness occurred, way before it was a thing.

Such correctiveness created a grounded understanding of my body.

The torn iliotibial band was a gruesome injury, the one and only major injury I ever suffered that was entirely avoidable if I would have known better beforehand. Every single night for the next 25 years I stretched and intently cared for my race machine, aka my body. Athletically, I believe no way could I have achieved what I did without such learned outside knowledge. Over three decades later and thus far, knock on wood, I have avoided overuse injuries, aka neglected and unstretched soft-tissue damage, because of the foundational and cherished body-guiding instructions of bodyworker Stephanie and Coach Lyle.

The Not-To-Do's
The Dirty Underbelly of Influenced Life Learnings.
Many excellent life lessons have been granted me from others, as shared prior. Now upcoming, hah, my underside lessons learned from others, the what NOT to do's.

Not-To-Do: Deflatable Words
Words lift up, words inflate us. Conjointly, words break down, words belittle us. Delivery style and tone can also destroy moods, relationships, and self-confidence, regardless of what is spoken or implied. I do not remember everything my friends, bosses, or coworkers said or did, but I sure as hell remember my resulting feels after their scorns, outbursts, or ridicules.

I remember the burn, the scour, and I have the emotional scars to prove it. As the Trek outside sales rep in Washington DC and before we moved to Wisconsin, I was in our nation's capital visiting one of my biggest bike shop customers during open store hours. I walked upstairs to their second story looking for the owner, me hopeful to write some business with him. Well and no, there would be no business order writing done here today, the boss was in a mood. Bossman store owner was agitated with his staff of about five salespeople. Evidently owner dude instructed two or three of the crew to paint the wall alongside the wide public steps from the first floor of the retail space up to the second level…holy hell, I felt like I just kicked open a bee's nest…"You fucking monkeys can't do anything right, come over here, look at this, how easy is this fucking shit, here is how you paint a wall…", but the boss rant wasn't over yet, "…I bet you fucking monkeys don't even know how to wipe your own asses, do I have to show you fucking everything you stupid fucking monkeys.".

Oh boy, I tried to help diffuse the situation but boss was having none of it. So I then commented that I did not want to get in the way, so I'll come back tomorrow, but retail bossman barely heard me. As he started up his yelling again, I headed for the door, while sympathizing with the staff. I caught two work servant employees before I left and offered some supportive type words, "…Try not to worry too much about the yelling" I said, "…he won't fire you because of how you're painting the wall, he's obviously mad about something else today." They shrugged their shoulders indifferently, commenting it is what it is, seems like they have dealt with similar outbursts before. I felt horrible and wanted to assist but the boss was too far out of sorts. With me there pressuring him for an order, I was not helping matters with my presence, so I left. My previously experienced wisdom was accentuated by the day's observations, do not scream but try to listen, don't blow up but ask questions, don't assume but rather try to better understand, and if you're losing your shit, go the fuck home or go ride your bike.

A few years later, a similar incident occurred except this time, I myself was the stupid fucking monkey.

It was mid-July and we lived in Wisconsin, but before little Lauren birdy was born. Most of the workplace was quiet, meaning the Trek Waterloo headquarters building. The bulk of Trek management was out of the office and currently about 4,000 miles away, them attending the Tour de France bicycle race. Of the five domestic sales managers total, only my pal Gene DiMenna and I were working stateside. Just months after I got promoted to Trek eastern regional sales manager, I was having trouble understanding the bike inventory reports. As things seemed to me, we had a discrepancy with the balance of inventory between the three different warehouses across the USA and in particular, the hyper-popular city hybrid bike inventory values were fluctuating wildly. Besides having questions, I also held some ideas for maybe ways to help make the inventory report more workable for everyone.

Needing assistance, and not knowing who else to best ask for advice, I went to seek counsel from my former sales manager boss Gene DiMenna. Gene was awesome, we did lots of lunchtime road bike rides together, we traveled alongside each other for work around the world, and I spent some time with Gene and his wife Mary bopping around Madison.

I trusted Gene, he was super cool and like me, Gene was not afraid to speak up when an uncomfortable but necessary conversation was needed. I was not so bold around the office yet, me still trying to find my place and my pace. The other Trek managers were in France, entertaining bike shop customers during our gifted thank you vacation to them at the most prestigious bike race in the world. The only person I thought to ask was Gene.

Our nationwide bike availability had been greatly challenged lately, sales were high, but supply was strained. After three-too many irate phone calls from my sales reps and their area bike shop customers, I went to ask Gene for help. Perhaps I was missing a hidden-to-me fact understanding the availability reports, but regardless I had no good answers for my customers one way or another. I wanted to understand our inventory reality, so I could responsibly reply to the ten-plus phone calls a day on the subject. My hesitancy asking Gene for advice was not wanting to cause a stir, because it was common knowledge these hybrid bikes were in short supply and mostly, we had to wait and be happy with what we got. Still, the reports were not making sense. In those days the intel came by way of a six-inch stacked paper bike inventory printout that magically appeared on my desk every morning, I assume from the overnight bike forecasting elves.

After only barely comprehending my concerns, Gene jumped out of his desk chair enthusiastically and walked out his door while motioning for me to follow him, "Let's go…". "Oh no, Gene let's not, I only wanted to ask you, I do not want to bother anyone else, please let's not", but my plea fell on indifferent ears, Gene was already in motion. "Oh no big deal, they'll know what to do", was Gene's attempt to comfort me but it was barely working, I had a bad feeling, oh shit this might not turn out ok. Weekly we joined in a sales manager meeting but otherwise, our boss Joyce insulated us from other senior managers. I knew most higher-up's pretty well as Baltimore and DC sales territory representative during the first four years of working in the field, and I got along with most everyone ok. But around the building, sometimes the scene was rather intense awhile now and then, quite on edge.

As we walked towards the upper-tier executive offices, I was happy to let Gene speak first. My peer sales manager did not get very far though, oh no, not far at all, and then, all I wanted to do was run away.

After only barely comprehending our intentions, senior exec guy jumped from his desk chair screaming withering words, walking out the door while yelling at us, "Jesus Christ you fucking guys, you just don't fucking get it do you?". He was very pissed off, holy hell I screwed up, this was a huge mistake.

He paraded me and Gene throughout two thirds of the building, screaming and cursing the entire way, wildly carefree for the fifty people or so we passed along our path. I felt bad for my coworkers and I imagined most of them felt bad for me. Peer rats who were either engaged in meetings or on the phone, but every single one of them had to pause and look over at us as he screamed his 'fuck this' and 'fuck that's', 'fuck-fuck-fuck', and 'you fucking guys' throughout the office. I was nothing but mortified. We stopped at Mary's desk who was our bike inventory forecast manager, an incredibly awesome lady who I really liked. Regrettably, he was also now screaming at Mary.

After a few more 'these fucking guys,' he stormed off and left us in Mary's hands. Immediately I realized it would have been better if I had earlier approached Mary directly before going to see Gene, but I did not want to bother her, nor had Mary and I built much of a working relationship yet. More than anything, I was just asking Gene for advice or some magic decoder insight. I was thrilled to exit the ridicule train as senior man left the shouting scene. Also horribly regretful I was, to put everyone through such drama, me especially annoying the higher-up's. Although the screaming hurt horribly, he didn't attack me personally but rather I got scooped up in a group conflict so technically, it was not bad as it could have been. Besides, maybe I should have just shut up and settled with inventory life as it was. The lessons I lived to learn and know was to think through things better first, not to scream but listen, don't blow up but back up, take a breath and ask more questions, don't assume but try to better understand.

Fifteen years later, I found myself at workplace verbal odds once more. "No you're not, Andy says he is not getting what he needs out of you, what's the damn problem?", my boss was not yet full-blown screaming at me, but clearly I was in hot water. "That's just not true, I met with Andy this morning and he told me straight-up that we are fine" …I was almost begging for them to slow down and try to understand me, but it wasn't working. Their volume increased and before long, I spun my head around to the side and away, calling through the open office door to their assistant, "Can you please call Joslyn and ask him to join us?". I held the vivid realization that Joslyn's intervention was then required there in the corner office, both for boss' sake, and certainly for mine. I respectfully excused myself to go use the bathroom and waited for Joslyn to arrive, before sitting back down. Mark Joslyn was the Human Resources director, hyper diplomatic, and a hell of a great guy.

After almost 20 years with the company, somehow I found myself standing on shaky ground. For the last decade I served as global director of retail services and concept stores, but a very short while before that day I had transitioned to a newly created position, 'Retail Fixer', me helping our most financially troubled customers one-on-one. After Joyce was forced to retire early because of bizarre health problems, I then answered directly to the big boss for twelve years. Then in the brand-new fixer role, I reported to Andy, me for a short while working in the financial services department.

Once Joslyn arrived and the three of us sat back down in boss' office, not much had changed with the lingering mood except now I had an intermediary, and a witness. The meeting went nowhere and it ended when I made a veil threat, then I waited in the building atrium for Joslyn. My first question for Mark as he then approached me, and perhaps my only hope to understand this mess was, "Mark, does it appear to you that I am set up for failure here, I do not feel like I am being listened to."

In my mind, a rush forward with assumptions and judgments did not allow enough room for realism and truth to join the conversation.

The lessons I lived to learn and know in this regard…do a better job listening, ask more questions then listen more, don't assume but try to better understand. Also I collected the necessity to check myself at the door every day, even when working for myself at home.

If my mood is shit, I might need to call in sick today, aka go the fuck home or ride my bike or work in the garage or go for a hike. A mental health day of sorts might be in order, a better decision for my customers and staff and an even better call for myself. Sure-sure, many days I'm able to reorient myself to the better as I go, catching myself while reflecting, or perhaps get a yummy snack to calm me down before I mess shit up. My bigger lesson learned is that sometimes, everyone involved is better off when I stay home or leave early, when able to identify I am having a shitbird day. On numerous occasions I was on the emotional losing end of what was trying to be said or implied, and I'm sure to be again. Mostly I walk away with the receipt of their message, you know, how the delivery made me feel. How it made me feel...the times I felt overridden by the emotions of the other person, them disregarding the meaning of my words or even attempted outcomes. Decades later, I vividly taste the historic recall of such tirades. Recognizing fully what deflates me, I attempt to regulate what I myself spew as hard emotional rain upon others, yes, those being my tear-down deflating words.

When messing shit up, usually I know it. Not always do I need an earful of rant from my boss telling me what I already know. As a boss myself, I try to praise the good and not just seek out the bad in others. Praise words build up, they lift emotionally, like..."Nice job with that, your customer was being a jerk but you handled it perfectly, I'm very proud of you...", that kind of thing. I try to build up, not tear down. Even subliminal praise can lift and carry me a while. Many of my former coworkers did it well...Lex Wallace my development manager for DreamBikes paid me random personal praise comments, creating a glow within me that would otherwise be missing. More modern day, the Starbucks Monona staff does it similarly well, I hear them often paying small but significant compliments, "I love your shoes...", "That's such a beautiful necklace...", "You are having a fabulous hair day aren't you?...". Wow, such a simple thing and such a powerful lift using an easy everyday ordinary phrase.

Such use of lifting words is infectious and immediately changes moods to the better. If you want it or need it, give it away.

Not-To-Do's: Home Matters, At All Times Matters

They answered the phone, but immediately hung up on me. I didn't even have the chance to say hello, so I called back. This time they picked up, said hello, but sounded annoyed. Yup, I was correct, annoyed..."No Roger I am sleeping, it will have to wait until tomorrow", so said Chris the general manager of the Fairfax Virginia Performance Bike Shop location, one of the DC area stores in my sales district. Chris worked for me. I oversaw all the Performance east coast bicycle stores from Philly to Chapel Thrill, years before I worked for Trek. My phone call was for the benefit of Chris and his store business, as him and I had earlier agreed. Although Chris was now agitated with me, proudly I was calling him to meet up and drop off some much-needed bike inventory.

I had just returned to the DC area after marathon-driving a large truck to North Carolina and back, hours earlier picking up new boxed bike inventory from the main Performance Bicycle Stores, aka PBS warehouse...bikes that Chris and our surrounding stores desperately needed. Around that time, the six DC area Performance stores were low on bikes.

Since the company I worked for was having delivery problems, I rented a large 25-foot box truck from Baltimore and drove south myself. I talked to all the store managers before I left, and we agreed to have me make the trip. Chris' store in Fairfax held the largest warehouse space so we agreed that after I returned from North Carolina, Chris would help me unload at his store, and we would then distribute the bikes from Fairfax to the other locations the following day. My trouble was, Chris was not at all interested in sticking to the plan.

Although I sat there in DC with a truck full of bikes, Chris' store was already closed and it was sounding like he was no-way not going to unload these bikes with me tonight. No, I didn't have keys to all my dozen-plus stores, so I was at the mercy of the managers in such regard. Chris was refusing to meet me. I was flabbergasted that he was not as excited as me to unload these sought-after bikes. Following my arduous run to North Carolina, I believed Chris should be thankful I took one for the team. Problem one, Chris viewed the situation through an entirely different lens than mine. Emphatically he repeated himself after I questioned why he wouldn't meet me to unload the bikes.

"Because it's two o'clock in the morning Roger, I am not coming back to the store until I am scheduled to be there at 10 am, goodbye, and do not call me back".

I admit only seeing the at-time situation from my proprietary perspective and frankly, I was mad at Chris. Believing him to be insubordinate, I was waffling between the pre-plan of disciplinary action I would take against him soon, or if I should now drive home to Baltimore instead of trying to sleep inside the cramped stinky truck cab, parked there in the Fairfax parking lot. I might claim this as an example of what NOT to do, ignoring your boss like Chris was doing, but um no, hum and hah, this life learning was a weird one. Now stepping afront the mirror, I was expecting, actually I was demanding that one of my guys gets out of bed, leaves his family and meets me at his store right now, at 2am. Was I behaving unrealistically, like Chris claimed? Did I not see the error of my late-night demanding ways, or was Chris an uncommitted employee, aka a bad manager?

Well then and no, this lesson is one of what not to do, learned by my own hands. Although I had zero concept of the 'idealism' word at the time, or even for goodness sake knew what the term meant, I began to associate with the notion. I expected others to feel, see, and act like me. I expected Chris would want these bikes to reach his inventory fast as I myself desired it. Not only did everyone working for me think and operate differently, we all view the world alternatively and for sure do not want the same outcomes, and, well, we also make different amounts of money for the different responsibilities we have so hells to the yells and of course, we hold dear different sacred cows.

Not until December 2005 did I learn the critical lesson that home life matters, at all times matters, because relationships of the household are often unrepairable.

I will have different jobs, workplace conflicts will come and go, but I learned the hard way to not forsake relationships at home. The alternative bossman-lens learning fell upon me profoundly, and thankfully I sorted that shit out before I chastised Chris for not meeting me at his store at 2am.

Not-To-Do's: Perhaps the Most Ridiculous Workplace Story Ever Told

My trajectory with Performance Bicycles was tracking steadily uphill for about three years, until I got fired. Layered between big boss Dave and myself when I served as east coast district sales manager at Performance was my direct report boss, I'll call him Kip, our director of stores. One day out of the blue and matter-of-factly, Mister Kip offered me a relatively large salary to race mountainbikes professionally for Performance. I was slightly flattered while perplexed, not understanding how such an arrangement could possibly work. I pushed back slightly, oh thank you, but I would not be able to properly represent the company on the race circuit and keep up with my multi-store responsibilities simultaneously, I could not even bring myself to try, I don't want to do either job half-assed.

Oh no, Mister Kip quickly clarified, he was not proposing I do both, only one. He wanted me to resign from the sales manager role but stay on the payroll, me then racing bikes for the company instead, but with a lesser salary, about one third the pay. I was perplexed, and here's where it got messy. My boss Kip was still dancing around the core reveal but I tried to rip the band-aid off this passive aggressive game we were playing. I mentioned to Kip in my best puppy dog voice that my last evaluation was stellar, so what changed...where am I doing a bad job? Mister Kipper said I am not doing a bad job at all. Hum...I wanted to know what the problem was with me continuing in my district manager role, because that's what I preferred. Kip tried to convince me I would be happier racing for the company than remaining east coast sales manager. Stunned, I thought myself extremely stupid that I could not figure out how this shit was happening...how does my boss think he knows what is best for me or what I might prefer regarding job responsibilities or pay?

Kip was attempting some sort of backdoor covert maneuver, while I pitched my best respectful inquisitions one after another, trying not to end my day on an unemployment note. In short order, the scene became revealingly obvious that I was probably getting fired anyway, so oh the hell with it...I questioned Kip directly, certainly more directly than he was conversing with me, by my measure. We danced around a few more questions, then Mister Kip finally spilled the beans...well, he found someone he liked better for my job than me. Unprovoked, Kip quickly described them, "...a very attractive smart young dark-haired woman from Philadelphia, ravishing...", he said. What the fuck dude, I almost said out loud. Then jerking my head back and OMG, why the hell did my boss Kip just brag about how attractive she is, like are you fucking kidding me? I froze, uh, um, say what, I was speechless. Glaring off into the distance, I tried to form a comprehendible response to whatever the hell that shit was, whatever the fuck he just said, because of not sure what was happening anymore...my tongue was tied in a non-loosening knot.

Kip spoke first, and oh my God I could not believe his words..."I have a problem", Kip said, "I am a love addict and I cannot resist falling in love with women".

I have never heard such an outlandish workplace ordeal before, but more than heard it, I lived it. Maybe if smarter, I would have challenged the asinine atrocity.

Mister bossman goes on to tell me that if I don't accept the proposed mountainbike race sponsorship proposal, I am no longer on the Performance payroll. I clarified, and why? Because my boss is putting his newfound Philly friend into my district manager position starting immediately. Briefly, I questioned this person's credentials and experience. Crazily, Mister Kip was honest and said she did not have much experience but it didn't matter, he really liked her for the role and plans to work with her closely, she will grow into the job and eventually do very well, so said Kip.

Uh, really dude, or so I almost blurted from my face but instead, I began to shut down, me then flooded with the feelings of disgusted unfairness. The asshole in me almost popped out, and only barely did I bite my lip and not ask Kip these types of words like I wanted to…what did his wife back home in North Carolina think about her husband's decision to replace me with his new gal pal from Philly, gal pal his the ravishing one? No, I did not go there, choosing instead to wrap things up at Performance and get the frick out toot fucking suite, me figuring the fricking fight was not worth the flipping prize.

I had no shot to play in this managerial game anymore, my boss Mister Kip decided he was done with me, it seemed I was not his type.

After admitting his love addiction and dark-haired preferences, we exchanged a few more sentences, Kip trying to justify why he was replacing me, but my boss still avoided veritable honesty, by my measure. One last time I asked a clarifying why and Kip summarized it best, because she was a ravishing dark-haired female. Here my commitment to not date anyone I work with was clearly strengthened, as demonstrated by Kip, thank you very little not so much. Within this bizzarro gameshow also I learned hand-first that some very smart and talented people sometimes behave stupidly, duly noted, thank you for the lesson of what not to do, Mister Kipper.

Not-To-Do's: Owning It, Hand-First

"We are having a meeting tomorrow at the accountant's office", my boss who I'll call Randy informed me. "Just me and you?", I asked. "Scott too", Randy said. Hum…I almost repeated my question with alteration because Randy's tone and slight vagueness concerned me, but I tried not to be a dick, so I rolled with it. I attempted collection of additional critical information, by my measure… "What do I need to prepare or bring with me to the accountant's, store sales reports for the year or what?", but Randy already walked away from me, him almost ignoring me, weird, and slightly rude…oh well, I assumed the conversation was over, Randy is being Randy. I guess I'll figure it out tomorrow.

Typically I would not walk blindly into such a meeting but rather arrive prepared. In this instance however, my boss gave me no option.

Scott Basil Beeson acted as marketing manager, and I served as the general manager of our three-store bicycle retail chain in Baltimore. Randy started the business almost thirty years before. I assumed me, Randy, Scott, and our accountant are meeting to discuss upcoming business financial forecasts. I checked in with Scott to be sure he knew of the meeting which he did and the next day, Scott and I arrived at the accountant's office on time. Accountant dude walked up to greet us, inviting Scott and I to come join him in his office, I assumed Randy was already in there. We walked in and hum, nope, no Randy. The accountant started speaking official meeting words and I interrupted him, "We need to wait for Randy...did he call, is he running late?". "No, Randy's not coming, it's just the three of us today", accountant dude informed me and resumed talking. Slightly irritated this guy is plainly rolling along, I interjected, "Why is that- what is the agenda, I cannot imagine we have anything to discuss that precludes Randy".

Randy, much as he claimed he wasn't, was a micromanager, especially when finances were involved. Maybe I was being a slight dick, but I really wanted to know what the planned conversation included. Well, quickly we found out. With some sort of random silly excuse, or maybe I should be nicer and call it 'reasoning', the accountant informed Scott and I that both our salaries were being cut by 25%, starting immediately. Trying not to jump to conclusions and make the accountant out to be the bad guy, I peppered him with questions of why and how and why, but he could only say, repeating himself several times... "Ask Randy, it was his decision". I joked that I would very much like to ask Randy, but Randy is not here. I requested we get Randy on the phone right now so we are hearing the same thing, but the accountant said no, he had other obligations and had to go. So with nothing else left to discuss, Scott and I left. After a brief interluding bitchfest in the accountant's parking lot, Scott and I drove back to the main store to have a word or three with Randy.

Then without near surprise, Randy pronounced, "Ask the accountant, it was his decision", and that was mostly the end of it. I believe Scott had a new job lined up within two weeks. I lingered slightly longer but once me and your mom discussed it, I fucking quit that otherwise awesome general manager job. This period was springtime 1997, before me and your ginger hot momma got married in August, and before I got the job with Trek same year October. That summer I took a huge step backward with my job responsibilities, working parttime as a bike mechanic for the awe-inspiring Alex Obriecht at Race Pace Bicycles in Ellicott City Maryland, racing mountainbikes most every weekend, and I planned to get a new and improved fulltime job at the end of the summer.

Emotionally, I would have preferred that Randy fired me than cut my pay 25% without reasonable explanation.

I assume Scott felt similarly. Of course I know not of what Randy expected after slashing our pay, but whatever he might have thought he would get from Scott and me, he did not get, not for long anyway. Yes I did my job after the pay cut, but barely. I felt wronged and mostly, began to wrap up loose ends with my three store managers, finish my company projects in motion and plan my next work role, hoping to quit and separate the fuck away from Randy, soon as possible.

Elsewise under my own watch…when one of my work family team members is struggling, I try to give them ample opportunity to cure, making the conversation a two-way style discussion. Even when shit is painful or embarrassing, I try to responsibly own the words I use, alongside my decisions and actions, especially if I screw up. I have lived to learn and know not to fear ridicule or public shame too much, aka ah fuck it. I accept the knowing that if not honestly holding in these here hands responsibility for everything under my watch, and even some things outside my control, no one else will. I learned to know my attempted drama avoidance will possibly result in a later and worse result, so better to deal with shit up front, directly and fast. My old boss Randy, he was doing what he thought was correct by his measure and I cannot fault him for that.

The wise words of my previous big boss Dave from Performance rang in my ears, and immediately I learned hand-first that Dave was precisely correct. Especially after Randy did it to me, I do not screw around with people's money. I would rather fire them than cut their pay because of how the maneuver made me feel. Even when I moved people around and they landed in lesser responsibility jobs least a while, I did not reduce their pay, I sucked it up because I knew better, in the long run my actions and added expense were worth it. Worth it to keep my peeps happy instead of putting a sword to their back and make them walk the plank, aka I knew better. Once torn down by a pay cut of same-same responsibilities, I could not rally and do the same job as before, no way. Lesson learned. Thanks Dave for properly setting that non-negotiable benchmark for me, and thanks to Randy for helping me learn hand-first the thing not to do: Don't fuck with people's money, period.

Not-To-Do's: Watering Houseplants

During my 18 years working in an official capacity for the bicycle company, over 100 times I was out and about somewhere in the world with peer senior managers and-or one of my various bosses. Over 30 times, maybe double that number, I purposefully avoided the expected or even mandatory evening company dinners and afterward social events. Sometimes I ducked out of the group dining area before dessert was served, or snuck out after I made a brief appearance, maybe even without eating. Instead of being where I was supposed to be and doing what I was supposed to be doing, I went off on my own, walking around town or sitting in my hotel room doing work, watching TV, or sleeping.

I was not being anti-social, I was attempting to avoid being forced to drink alcohol.

I steered clear of the work gatherings because of the stipulated consumption of Devil's Water, aka over-consumption of alcohol and the resulting negative effects booze has on humans, and especially the negative effects booze has on me. Decoder ring on the matter…stipulated, aka mandatory. There was a good old boys dynamic that I didn't fit into, even with my once female boss Joyce. If I wasn't currently drunk, or if I couldn't talk hand-first about golf, or if I couldn't tell wildly outlandish comedic stories and get raving praise, or if I couldn't effectively fake it and act drunk for the rest of the night, I was odd man out.

Even simple two-person after work dinnertime events proved to be disasters for me...joining one of my bosses in their hotel room as directed to watch the favorite football team play Monday Night on TV, I was ordered to drink multiple drinks. Oh come on now, wait up a darn Milwaukee minute...was I really forced to drink, or is this my overreaching sensitive emotions? Nope, straight up and legitimately, I was forced to drink because my boss was drinking. I was not allowed to avoid the non-entertaining-to-me football game and retreat to my room, no, no way, and I was not allowed to slow sip one mild Coors Light beer. Alcohol was part of the life entertainment factor for my bosses and even when I commented, "No thanks I really don't want to, I don't like beer that much", I was then pushed even harder and called wimpy girly wussy kitty cat names for not drinking enough or fast enough.

After we moved to Wisconsin, on this upcoming particular occasion I helped to host an international multi day conference of about 30 people. On the last full day of the event we all went out to dinner together, to Eldorado Grill on the east side. I was the main organizer and presenter of the seminar and worked ridiculously hard for weeks to prepare and execute an excellent event, by my measure. The scene at the Mexican restaurant was a joyous affair and we arrived to awaiting pitchers of margaritas on our dining tables. I drank water and got a CocaCola. In short order, the flavored jugs of tequila were refilled and everyone grew increasingly loud and buzzed. My boss at the time handed me a drink, I said no thank you. They insisted and I took the glass. I wandered off and set the glass down...hopefully, I would not be found out.

I presume my general body tone and attitude were sober, rigid, and more serious than silly or stupid. My boss found me without a margarita glass in my hand and handed me a new one, frosted and filled. I said no thank you I do not like Tequila, it makes me sick, which was a lie. They said I have to drink and I have to loosen up and I have to keep drinking...have to. Their tone was extremely serious. Immediately I believed my job was in jeopardy. Against my own intention, I drank the damn drink and surprisingly enjoyed it, my first ever consumed margarita, especially enjoyed it after I became heavily buzzed. Knowing I was approaching a dangerous situation, I wanted to go home but did not find an opportunity to escape, by my measure. My boss forcefully made me drink more. But no, wait up a sec, I am to blame here, not my boss. I should have stepped the fuck up and spoken the truth...I am an addict, I cannot drink, it is bad for me, very-very fucking bad for me. Rather pathetically, I did not speak because I was afraid of being ridiculed or even demoted or fired. Would I have been fired for not drinking? Probably not but possibly yes, fired for disobeying a direct order by my boss who does not at all mess around with that insubordination shit.

Although trying to avoid my boss heavily after consuming my second tequila drink, and I then dumped almost an entire drink into one of the houseplants inside Eldorado Grill, my glass was refilled once more. Everything became a blur after that and factually, damn it...I do not even remember driving home that night. Certainly, a portion of the world has not been negatively impacted by alcoholism, but I have. My not to do is...I try to err on the side of safety and do no harm, not assuming I know people's situation, neither their strengths nor their weaknesses. Although I am unpopular when I do it, sometimes when holding decision making powers, I organize events without alcohol or declare it buy or bring your own because I have lived to know that categorically, the Devil's Water is evil, downright fucking evil.

Chapter FIVE

Heroes: The People I Owe My Life to, Literally, and So Do You.

Kathy Burnham is one hell of a cool chick. I highly admired Kathy the first time I saw her in middle school. Kool Kathy went on to be our main cocaine dealer in the area. I openly reveal, as mentioned in my addiction book, she was the cocaine shop boss that I lost my Red Line bike to, and who pressured me to pick up the handgun with New York in the house. Now she's just Kathy Burnham the hero. Least one time, maybe twice, and perhaps even thrice, hard to know for sure, Kathy grabbed my life back from the clutches of the other side, bringing me out of an overdose. I would have certainly died if left on my own. Kathy unequivocally saved my life. While shooting cocaine with or without mix-ins, I lost consciousness. Not sure what kind of care or aid she administered but after I passed out and laid on the floor, Kathy jumped into action, aka hero, and revived me. I awoke on the ground, then brought to sitting, getting slapped in my face repeatedly and freezing cold water sprayed in my eyes, cold compresses wrapped around my head, and more. Kathy who was in the right place at the right time so long ago, Kathy who pulled me back from the greedy grabs of death.

Without hesitation to this here mind's eye, Kathy saved my life. Otherwise yours truly would have been a long-ago distant memory no f-ing doubt.

Beth the hero. Beth helped me get away from the drug needle in my late teens and early 20s, when I could not do it myself. Much because of the love for my best friend little sister, I cared to try and live, for her benefit, not mine. Because Beth cared more for my life than I did, she was able to perform ten times the work I could have ever done on my own, to save my beating heart from extinction. Once telling her of my wanting to quit the needle, Beth became slightly more aggressive, awhile loving. She kept me at home when I tried to escape. She blocked me when I tried to run, and when I wriggled away, she did not judge but kept doing her best to keep me alive. With Beth at home babysitting me, I began to see a slight spark of life light. Without Beth, I would not have made it. My middle sister Beth Bird DeLaRue, 14 months my younger, my favorite sister Beth, my best friend Beth absolutely saved my life no doubt.

Mark the hero. For months…for months Mark showed up at my work and collected me, escorting me around the rest of the night, driving himself physically between me and my needle. Mark's self-appointed mission: Roger was no way not touching a drug needle tonight, and he took this responsibility very seriously.

Even when I tried to sneak away, hide, run, trick him and lie, Mark tracked me down and brought me back from my own dead-end affairs.

Mark kept me close and watched me carefully night after night, knowing my addiction was more in control of me than I was of it. I suppose if the role reversed, I might have attempted similar maneuvers but such was not the case, I was the weak one and destined to put myself out of my own misery, if not for Mark. Only because of his vision and tenacity to help save my life did I survive. Mark Weinreich, my next-door neighbor when we moved to Whitney Avenue in Pimlico, and my best guy friend for most of my younger years. Mark Weinreich absolutely saved my life no doubt.

Mike the hero. More than helped me, Mike journeyed far past the end point any friend should be expected to travel, aka hero, all for the benefit of me when otherwise I was happily content to have the drugs take me away forever. We were buddies, but Mike had friends he connected with on a deeper level than with me. Nightly for months, Mike showed up with Mark after my work shift, to make sure I did not shove another needle in my arm that night. If not for Mike Welsh, I am not sure Mark would have joined to help save me, at the time. Mike was the one who initially took a stand against the shadow following me around, and showed up to do battle when I myself couldn't.

Unequivocally I state, without Mike I would not have quit shooting drugs, no fucking way, no fucking how…no way I could have done that shit on my own, I tried, I really tried. Mike Welsh, a good friend when I was growing up, who for some reason went way out of his way to save me no doubt.

Only then could I survive such a death-avoidance challenge, only when telling those around me I'd rather live than die, only after asking for help was a future for me even possible.

Coach Troy the hero. Never ever fucking never would I have become the athlete or person I am today without Coach Troy, fucking no way never. The bike afforded me the opportunity to transpose my otherwise deadly addiction into something livable. My cycling coach Mister Troy Jacobson grabbed me, held me tight, and gave me a reason not to let go of this possible new life I began to taste. A possible new life, a better life, a sustainable life and a life without drugs, that was the option but there was no guarantee. Only…only after my attempt to put cycling in front of drugs did I have a chance…only because of Coach Troy did I think a successful pro athletic career was even possible.

And only because of Coach Troy hounding me, screaming at me during heartrate extremes, encouraging me and not letting me quit did I stick with it, and only because I stuck with it did I not go back to the drugs.

For certain I would not have connected with cycling at the level that made the proper difference in my life without Coach Troy, no fucking way. In the early 90s when I barely knew what the heck I was doing or where I was going, Coach Troy Jacobson sponsored me, gave me direction, sheltered me, mentored me, picked me up, comforted me, pushed me, and saved my life no doubt.

Sonya the hero…Sonya taught me how to live amidst the turmoil of life, while maintaining peace calm and composure. Sonya Barton-Plavcan my sports massage therapist bodyworker, Sonya my spiritual coach and friend afforded me a mindful path, at the exact time I needed it most.

Sonya pulled me out of the emotional gutter, she held me tight, and placed me squarely on course to find my own virtuous life.

Before the marital shit hit the fan with your momma, I was meeting with Sonya weekly. When amid my highlight, aka the limelight of my life, Sonya knew me intimately. She released the pent-up physical load I bore from racing off road motorcycles and then, she tried to lessen the stress lingering within me from both work and home. Typically my bodywork sessions with Sonya ran 90 minutes, aka an hour-and-a-half of paid abuse on the massage table. During my lay-there-and-take-it physical beatings, we verbally examined a few world affairs here and there but mostly, we discussed details of our lives. With no one else did I share so much intent time or depth, talking about every stumble, every victory, openly sharing with her every goal and every heartache.

Once learning of the infidelity at home, I began drinking heavily, starting that night. Much of what I put myself through during your mom's affair, Sonya was aware of. Eight months later, seeing that no marriage existed worth fighting for and I moved out of Starlight Lane, my drinking intensified. Sonya watched as the flame of my inner light lessened to a mere flicker, then grew dark throughout the hell of the divorce. In short order, I was drinking myself to death. If the heavy consumption of alcohol didn't kill me soon, some related tragic accident would probably shut my eyes for eternity. When not at work or caring for you guys, I was living drunk much of the time.

Full of embarrassment self-doubt and shame, I tried to hide my alcoholism and most of all hide it from Sonya. Sonya and I shared much-much mutual admiration and despite the fact she probably saw clear through me, I was not going to openly admit how bad things had really become with my drinking. I thought it best not to reveal the stupid stuff I was doing wrong in my life, I did not want to disappoint her. Also I coveted the positive praise she showered me with, every time we talked. I wanted Sonya's support and admiration, and well, factually more than wanting it, I needed it.

Around then and barely able to wrangle one week at a time, the only hope and strength I could locate was my few days with you guys, my time off on my motos speeding through the trees, and my 90 minutes with Sonya. Sonya finding out what was truly going on frightened me, I feared losing her friendship. I believed if I lost my connection with Sonya, no way was I strong enough to stand on my own two feet. Unequivocally, I had already inflicted irreversible neurological harm upon myself with my drinking. Additionally, I had decidedly ciphered an unworthy romantic future with your mom, and then, astonishingly, Sonya stepped forward.

One day during a bodywork appointment, Sonya gifted me a truly magical object, a collection of words to the likes I was unaware-existed here on earth, a book, *A Path With Heart* by Jack Kornfield. Sonya showed me the way back to living, self-reliance and inner strength. Sonya grabbed me, she pulled me up off the ground, and helped me reconstruct these here two legs back underneath myself, to soundly stand again.

Without Sonya compassionately showing me the literal path back to being myself, for fact I would not have survived.

Sonya Plavcan saved my life when otherwise, I had mostly already given up.

Bret the hero. We were eating pizza inside his store late one night after closing. No one else was there except Bret and me. He took a phone call and wandered away from me. I started choking on a crust and ran outside to try and clear the blockage. It happened fast...the incident was embarrassing, and scary as fuck. Bret was engaged with his call on the opposite side of the sales floor when I hastily exited the building. Unaware of my condition and casually strolling over to the front window, Bret glanced around to see what I was up to. He then saw me; I was choking badly. Myself unable to clear the lodged pizza crust, I tried everything, I did everything possible, I knew so, because this has happened before. I was gasping what I was sure were my last breaths, already oxygen deprived and close to unconscious.

I have never-ever-never seen a human move that fast before in my life, fucking never.

With 150% effort, Bret cleared my airway, literally saving my life. Bret Gave my friend, coworker, and at-time Trek Madison west side store manager. Minimally eight times I have MAJORLY choked on food and large supplement pills, then feeling death's hand grab mine tightly. Each time, starving myself of oxygen and suffering massive headaches for days afterward. This episode with Bret was truly life threatening and despite my best efforts, I could not clear the captured crust.

Ready to give up trying to find air to breathe, and about to be knee-then-shoulder-then-face-down on the damn sidewalk, Bret saw me. From where I was, I possessed zero ability to go back inside, I tried to open the door but lacked the focus, and the strength. For what must have been three long minutes, I frantically gasped and gasped, punching myself below my ribcage trying to unstick the pizza crust, unable to breathe. My head felt like a gallon Ziploc freezer bag with the air vacuum-sucked out of it...I foresaw no hope and fell to my knees. Knowing I wasn't getting out of this one, I quickly stood, went back to the storefront and tried to open the door. When Bret looked out the window, I saw him and put a hand around my throat to signify I was choking. I certainly would not have lived another day if not for Bret, total truth. Bret Gave, my hero.

Marianne the hero. Feeling like I was unfairly alone, sitting on a small bizarre floating and melting iceberg, I needed some help and I needed some relief from the pain in my heart and the fears in my head. The medicine was designed to comfort and save me from the turmoil in my brain, but the pills almost killed me as I planned my own suicide for almost two years. Once I started seeing Doctor Marianne shortly before Nora moved out, my new clinical psychiatrist determined I was one of those people who at first feels relief on these certain anti-depressants but then the opposite effect kicks in. If I had stayed on those pills much longer I would be dead, total fucking truth and definitively, Marianne also said the same. I tell the story in detail within your next book volume two.

Marianne is an amazing woman and literally saved my life, when I was otherwise powerless against the dead-end thoughts in my head. Dr. Marianne was my new psychiatrist right around when Nora and I broke up. I had been on and off anti-depressants starting when the real troubles began with your mom years earlier.

My overall self-confidence well as my general security in romantic relationships was heavily damaged and for a while, I refused to take any sort of medication. I hated pills, all pills, well no, that's a lie, I was factually scared of pills because of my legacy addictions. I finally gave in after the stern advice from a previous therapist Suzanne and I found some short-term relief with the antidepressants. I then mostly put the mood pills away after the divorce with your mom. Alcohol then carried me for about four years until once together with Nora, and we both stopped drinking in April 2011. After Nora's similar decision as Andrea's to travel outside the marriage for romantic comfort, or least a sexy hook-up, I then went back on the antidepressant pills.

Not realizing what was going on inside me, I was on autopilot to end my own life, planning this bird to be high speed splattered against that large rock wall at the end of the bridge in Lone Rock Wisconsin, well, that is until Doctor Marianne saved me, she legitimately fucking saved me no doubt.

Kevin the hero. Kevin my dear cabin neighbor friend and all-around sweetheart of a guy, Kevin my hero. Not so much of an outspoken in-your-face kind of dude but he stepped way outside of his comfort zone, aka hero, to save me from choking. It was summer 2019 and we were on a road trip together, visiting his niece and attending a concert, seeing them Turtles the Trampled By Turtles band. We were at the breakfast nook in a St. Louis hotel lobby the day after the concert and I started choking. Once again, scared and embarrassed, I ran into the narrow-secluded hallway around the corner from the breakfast area and away from the people. I am sorry to maybe have taken a year off Kevin's life that day because of the fear and worry I put on him. Other people saw Kevin rush over trying to save me, but I would have probably been hiding in the bathroom alone if Kevin were not there. Kevin absolutely saved my life.

Need it Or Want it, Give it Away: Chapter Five Opening Poem Liner Notes

Originally I wrote Give it Away as a proprietary reminder to self, to help me see clearly, to help myself operate more as I intend, help myself live honestly, help myself make a difference, not only trying to be my own best bag of bones and skin self, but to help the bigger self, the collective self, you know, all brotherly siblings all. As is same-same with my fraternal hundreds of poetry pieces, I think if it a worthy reminder to me, then quite possibly maybe some of the works feasibly exist as a worthy reminder for us all. Because we are, deny it or not, we are one, all of us singular ones roll up into one collective herd, one collective one, one collective all.

If you or other peering creeper eyes now claim that I preach, assume, judge, or wrongly proclaim with my slingin' of that last sentence, then so be it, I am good with that, I am totally good with that…love you, love you more.

So yeah, Give It Away…my pen first scratched these words in journal to self, years ago now. Under cover of these here flaps back on page 138, I scribe them once more, for you my Birdy & Boyd, and for all of us, for we are, echo, we are one.

The majority of my poetry is one-and-done works, a safe estimate, the pieces completed with zero edits, aka run what you brung. The final Give it Away piece shared here in your book is only slightly modified from the original first run version. This one a little more targeted to the core meaning of its intended all, and barely different from its slightly more-vague parental poem. My pen first recorded this bird brain Give it Away pronouncement as my intent, attempt, and desire to help, to share and to contribute to my family, to my friends whom all are also family, to my community whom all are also family, and to my world whom all are also family. To help us all because of course, like duh, echo-echo…we us are one. There is no them in family and there is no them in us, we are one fucking one, one fucking all, one fucking one team one. To help share and contribute, so we can all learn, grow, and live…live underneath a little more sunshine, and live outside of a few fewer shadows.

From the first sliver of my memory I have found massive meaning and created much-much love-love in sharing, both as giver and recipient. I try to share everything I sense and possess, everything I see or can find, you know, everything I believe that could help someone, help their situation, or help someone close to them. I do not own this here life, fuck that noise, this life is not mine. This here life not mine, it is yours, my life is yours, it is for you Birdy & Boyd. This here life not mine to shine keep and safeguard, no, but rather only exists for me to give away, aka it is for me to share. This here life not mine but this life is meant for everyone, all our sisters, all our brothers, all worldly siblings fucking all. And why is that you may ask? Because we fucking need to help each other. We need to motherfucking share what we have, fricking all of it, aka give it away, so we can all have more. More, more of what dad? Share so we all have more safety, more peace, more comfort, more connection, more love, more strength, more hope, more courage, more initiative, more willingness, more get up and go gumption, and more fricking resolve to face our fucked-up hard and scary shit.

The comprehensive and universally applied 'Give it Away' feature film containing this plot continues to play on looped repeat and the budget has all but dried up to create a new flick on life as we know it, aka we humans suck-ass at sharing our shit.

We could do better with all these things, we should do better with all these things, I think we all want to do better with all these things, I hope we can start small to do better with even one of, these things. Now I am compelled to share the filler material left behind on the thoughts only virtual cutting room floor after writing the Give it Away piece. But dad why? Well, so you my beloved brood do not skip over them there chapter opener poetry-stylized words without hesitating to hear them, taking a timeout to taste them, pausing to ponder them, stopping to see them, and maybe even one day, learning to live some of them out loud yourself, your way. But dad why, so you can brainwash us? Fuck to the no my love birds, but to share something I deem critically important, aka a vital piece of me, trying to shine a big ass light on the thought however the frick I can.

Getting right down to it, the Give it Away piece spawned on the bottom of three rivers merging. Amid the one pager itself, no way could I adequately explain the entirety of inspiration, drive, and emotion behind the final semblance of words. So here now, my attempt to do so.

The first of three founding rivers propagating the Give it Away piece...I was still working for Trek in Waterloo and at-time doing battle with the marketing department. Sadly, a smaller clique of marketing folk put the "I" before team and although the group possessed resources to help the bigger goal, including benefits to the industry, aiding our retailers and improving Trek profitability, the marketeers would not share. Future status and self-advancement associated with the squirreled away tools was sought, hence their hoarding overpowered any interest to release their aid to the world. The non-team-players held back their capitals and instead, cunningly schemed for individual praise and compensation later, although the bicycle retail world desperately needed said tools at the precise moment. No, the rogue marketing power mongers were not willing to sell, license, or share their resources, no, the answer was no.

The second of three founding rivers stemming Give it Away...I spent much-much personal time apart from my Trek responsibilities starting and running DreamBikes. For years I served concurrently as operations manager, executive director, president, and board chair for this gem of a 501c3 nonprofit, an organization to help cyclical probable-in-peril teenage kiddos. I was at the time heavily on the move in several regards...removing bullshit partner barriers and inefficiencies with the Boys and Girls Club of Madison, correcting much of the inactivity and time suck within the DreamBikes board and lastly, I effectively resolved my banging-of-head against the wall of confusion concerning DreamBikes with some Trek management peers. Claiming myself on the move, meaning to say I appropriately paused, backed up, thought freely without restriction, decided a new way, focused intently, pushed hard, and a resulting bigger and more positive difference was occurring at the nonprofit, undoubtedly. Between me and a few of my management crew, we were literally saving young lives, removing unnecessary socioeconomic and racial barriers for our store team family, keeping the kids in school and supporting our high school graduates with thousands of dollars for college. Those scholarship monies were drawn from our own proudful and self-supportive DreamBikes financial operating system.

The third and final poetic river...I was dating at the time, after splitting up with your hot ginger momma, and before I met Nora at East Towne mall. I connected with some women through online dating sites who showered me with more conditional demands than allowable time for quality togethering, or rather to say, therefore squashing, mood killing, or dismantling both current day togethering fun times and possible future state togethering opportunities for us both.

Not so far removed from and same-same as with all my other sometimes stupid shit, there is not only much-much heart-heart and meaning within the brevity of my wannabe poet words, but seriously, this one packs a punch.

I could place the words Give it Away on the cover of its own book and struggle massively to stop writing such the explanative real-world narrative. And why is that? Because this story of us all helping each other, well…this 'help one all' tale is not a story or conversation with an end, no, not in the slightest, there is no end to it. What I mean to say is, we humans are all the same, all, we all need help, all. We humans all deserve the same-same respect and life opportunities as another one, all fucking all. We could offer our love to others openly, freely, fully, and limitlessly, aka give it away. We could help others more all, exercising such efforts alongside abandonment of self. Truthfully then, we would be doing such benefit-others share work for the collective us, and for all of humanity.

I have lived to believe a thing or three, and here are some of my experiences. Not here is scriptured law, not here an attempted universally applied and to be lived-by truth. I think it is that we all want success, happiness, and peace. Yet we seek, we struggle, we pray, we bow, we strive, and we suffer. We may sit in pew or stand in line as hard life rain falls upon our bleeding heads incessantly, waiting for someone to come save us. Cool if we feel this in our hearts, super dooper looper cool, and blessings to those of us in this position. Still, many times we struggle arduously, absurdly so, within varied areas of our lives. Amongst these challenging times, such our suffering seems unfathomable as, 'Is this the right way to do it?' We think it should be easier, we say to selves, and why is life so fucking hard anyway? A strangely positioned juxtaposed happening is resting softly where we are, amid the fight and the flee, accepting that which is present, whatever it is, embracing contently whatever lies in our hands in the here and now, and accepting personal responsibility for everything occurring or not coming together in our personal-sized worlds, amen. Furthermore within Give it Away is surface mention of need and want. Need and want is factually the core of the crafted piece, although hidden. To and for me, here is need and want recited, by my measure.

NEED is fixed and hard, need is oxygen sustaining, needs are objective facts and truths, need is proven self-evidence that we possess determined and required non-negotiables, need is what must be done, aka need is us doing life.

WANT is variable and soft, want is heart, want is desire, want is dreaming, want is hope, want is drive, want is strength, want is meaning, want is purpose, want is love, want is sunshine, want is choice, want is us living life.

Doing life versus living life…need is doing life, and doing life is often disguised as life doing us, aka just shut the fuck up and take it. Want is living life, and living life is the good shit, the variable stuff, the choices we make, or maneuvers we take. Bottom line net-net, I believe we get what we give, hence my notion of need it or want it give it away. Hah, alas if our need or want account is overdrawn, we should not bother going to the bank. We should deposit often, performing frequent little drop off's, keeping our hands out of the cookie jar, building up our available balance and not depleting it. Say what dad, what the hell are you blabbering about? Well my little birdies, check this out…I believe Mother Teresa perfectly nails down my needs and wants deposit concept with her 'small things-great love' mantra. "Don't look for big things, just do small things with great love…the smaller the thing, the greater must be our love." Wow, that's pow-pow-powerful, by my measure.

I believe we should give all we can, helping our sisters and brothers and siblings because when it comes time that we ourselves need assistance, who will be around to aid us? Yes do this, and repeat often as humanly possible.

This here silly poppa bird brain goes straight to the bank with the notion that life can be easier than it is now, aka not so damn hard, if we share.

It can be easier because someone else somewhere must have been through some of this same challenging life exercise already, and they have mostly figured parts of the darn thing out, already. If they already know, will they share? If much of our hardships are similar, why is there not a legacy family owner's manual passing down to generation after generation? Is this concept too simple? Or too much work? Does it in fact contain too much variability and is immediately outdated, like expired fruit?

Although much of the aforementioned shit is somewhat different, such the crap occurring throughout different times, does each and every one of us have to fucking start over and again, developing unique-to-us the individual proprietary solution toolboxes on our own? Perhaps, yet perhaps not. Of course, like duh, we are different, aka sans-robots. We come from different technical and emotional origins. We are traveling our individually unique paths. We journey at different velocities. We need to learn our hard-fought lessons our own ways, well, I suppose. We must learn everything on our own, right? So not to be cynical, combative and distrusting, right? Because we only know what we know, right? Because we don't just buy shit and trust the outlandish claims to be true, right? Therefore we are positioned towards different concluding and determinative harbors, right? Well, but really? Really, for real really? Hum…I don't fucking know, aka IDFK.

Still similarly shared…we all strive, we all push, we all run, we all drag our tired asses, we all cry, we all bleed, we all fall down, we all break, we all get up, we all get up, and we get up until we cannot fucking do it anymore.

We struggle with so much of what was sold to us as good and worth it…sold to us with no critical mention that our train leaves in twelve minutes and are we not already packed and ready to go? To board our one and only train? The train leading to our one and only tunnel? Our one and only tunnel that journeys to our future? Well now, oh wait, look at this, I fictionally found the travel notes stuck under the sole of my shoe:

Dear Citizen, your train trip of life is long. Pack water, a good hat, extra socks, more water, plus one more pair of socks might be wise. Good luck, signed Yours Truly, Life as You'll Learn It.

Hah, needs and wants and all of our get-up and go struggles, what a wild and wacky ride, like a rollercoaster…wacky compared to the brainwashing of the 'sold to us' children's books filled with all those cute bunnies and glimmering rainbows, wacky compared to the shiny-shiny Facebook profiles, just sayin'.

Then there now, me myself while living this here sheltered entitled privileged padded WASPY and streets paved with gold life, I too have struggled, really struggled. Struggled...oh for fuck's sake wait and hold up, wait a fricking second. What the what, struggled? Struggled who, me? Really do I claim that I have struggled? Hah, um yeah and for fucked sake factually, fuck that stupid fucking shit.

I am not homeless. I do not maintain a cemented location south of the fuck you all other white punk ass bitches hold-a-brother-down Jim Crow line. I am not a disease infested ninth child born to a poverty stricken and unemployed single mother in India. I know no true fear, I know no real pain, my belly is never empty, I thirst fucking never.

No, I need the fuck not, not for any of those precious lifeblood grains of rice that others are driven to cut down and slay for. Rather, these here silly bird brain's pockets are overflowing with kings' fricking riches. In my own dumb ass and stupid fucked-up nonsensical way, I try within the Give it Away piece to jump down from atop my gold inlay high horse, smack myself in the fucking head, lifting my precious children from out the gutter and feed them, then going to collect their vital medicine from the free clinic, hence trying to say fuck to the no, I am no better than any woman any man any humanoid, period fucking period. Billions of sisters brothers and siblings around our world suffer hundreds times worse than me yet they complain not, aka I need to shut the fuck up.

Now, I Rant
We are in this thing together, all. We are, One. We are scattered and in many ways disconnected, but we came into this world through One singular fucking door and out from under One singular fricking rock. We, us all one, every singular soul, we bleed the same fucking blood, factually. I am not trying to be cute or make some stupid makes-sense-to-only-me rhyme. Honestly, put your church-going biological STEM thinking caps on for a minute and humor me. Ok, two doors to choose from in this gameshow.

   Door #1: Creation. Here we are, all of us seemingly different people and cultures, as we surpass the 8-billion few of us on this here globe. Ok, map the damn thing backward and follow your theological north star, way back. Way-way back, further, further still...furthest. That documented family photo is of our Adam and Eve with their Father The Creator...She, He, It, An Artist Formerly Known As, the however you would like to say highest-ever power looking over their shoulder. Please do not get snagged in semantics and crucify me here, but give me a short-lived pass so I can struggle and bear my own cross down the hall...if this is your jam, and totally cool to that, then we were birthed from One mother and One father, right? As it is written, so is it also as so? We bought that movie and have it saved as a favorite, some of us. Ok, let's pull the loaf of bread apart into its bits...we have One mother, One father, and we are One small family that began with One Garden of Eden mini-me. Then, our One family-from-the-garden grows and expands and moves away, and keeps growing and keeps traveling. With some sprinkling of Tinker Bell's mystical powder from her back pocket, here we are today all of us, all 8-billion One all of us.

How do we, how do we all have the same blood and yet we claim not to trace our family tree back to the same roots, that One root, and that One tree, all of which came from the same place, from within that One and only garden that will ever matter, amen? Because we yearn for this shit…every virtual global togethering day in November we all go home to that One place from where we all came, so as to share, so as to give thanks, that place with the golden mailbox out front, that one mailbox with the big 'H' on it, aka Humanity. We ALL are sisters, we ALL are brothers, we ALL are siblings all but why do we claim as not, neither to treat each other nor love One another as such? Fucking all One family, all One love, all One team One. I cannot see it another way, alas veritably, I know very little.

Door #2: Evolution. Marty the Monkey is Bob's Your Uncle and all of us silly monkeys are caged up together within the same globe, choked and choking, congested under Mother Nature's wing and not a single Jesus Fish in sight. So hit rewind and run it back to the oldest version of the *Warriors* gang movie ever found in the video store library. If we in fact evolved independently as multi tribes of some whiteys and some dark, from different all over the cannot-get-there-from-here places, how is it that we all kinda are the same and some of us aren't more like giraffes or flamingos? Was there one special sauce in the human cauldron and another recipe built from scratch in another nature's kitchen for fuck's sake? Jeeze Louise and fuck to the no, like are you kidding me or what? What the hell do I know, because I did not learn shit in school after 5th grade, but please humor me if you will.

We all have red blood. If some of us had orange or green blood, I might concede that our points of origination are plausibly different, but least as it seems to this silly bird, we all formed or sprouted at One shared and singularly definitive time, aka the blooming start of us all, then we just kept running from those big bully dinosaurs. If I still did acid I could clearly see through my psychedelic lenses the mystical doorway where the T-Rex's are vacationing right now, and mocking us. Elsewise, I do not need to be tripping to see that we are all of One race, fucking One, the hooman race, fricking all. And no I do not intend cuteness when referencing my worldly kin, legitimately we're all fucking related.

Us evo-hoomans moved away from our home crew, obviously, then gathered in tribes, some of us learning to fish, escaping the I-am-going-to-eat-you polar bears, and live in houses made of snow, while our siblings a world away sought refuge under the only singular shade of a leaf for a thousand miles around, rummaging for bugs in the dirt to eat under the scorching night's sky of the dry tundra. We all the branches of our same One-family tree then adapted to environments, both the snow and the dirt, so as to survive and learn to thrive. But no mistake about it, we are all of One family.

What About it Anyway?
None of us have 100% of our shit together, fucking nobody no one.

From a multiplicity of helpful hands, we could remove the governor, ditch the restrictor, trash the limiter, leave behind the clinging and prized self-promoting bits some of us hold so near. If we dropped all we covet so closely, oh my fucking god, life could be so much better for all of us.

I desire us to do better helping each other. Help to improve the world's conditions for us all and on purpose, not waiting and magically wishing for a more shiny world to appear one spring morning. And oh yes absolutely, optimism matters, most def legit, I hope we have our sunshine and rainbow thinking caps affixed solidly atop our noggins on most gloomy days, so we can achieve more of what we want and seek, instead of legally changing our name to Eeyore and dragging around our own little black raincloud on a string for the rest of our lives. Brown, tan, white, purple, rich, poor, educated, homeless, mental-mood-challenged, who the fuck cares, we are all the same. We all want calm, we all want comfort, we want easy days, and a love that does not leave us. And yet, although wanting the same things others want from us, sadly neither budges, tragically neither gives in.

Someone already has surely crafted the key to this puzzling hardship. Some of us keyholders though, we might triumph in the safety of owning the key. We could garner praise for the hoarded key, perhaps boasting of our enshrined and hidden away precious opener tool, convinced that our superiority is better, and we hold our said nexus tight and hidden. Keep guarded our pass-through tool we might, rather than loaning it or sharing it or giving it away for the benefit of others so for them to live and love more easily. It is OUR key, we reinforce to ourselves, so it is our choice, so it is our right. Here now is one of the great conflicts of life so says me: Retaining and protecting what seems valuable to self, even though others need it more and said guarded thing could reduce much suffering in the world, if we just shared our fucking shit.

Trying to Help, Trying to Try
My eyes see and my heart feels other's pain yet at times, I stand by helplessly, unwilling or unable to support them, and it sucks. Conversely I myself have seen and felt pain while waiting helplessly, hopelessly, me wanting others to lend a hand, me waiting for others who never arrived, and that sucks too. Sure, I might show up, yet the poor souls are not yet ready to receive my hand, but I try to keep trying, I try to remain available regardless. My father tried to help, my teenage therapist tried <u>also</u>. But no, I was too angry, I was too scared. Running and running, I could not even fathom my plausibility to stop, not for a single second. When the devil himself had his wretched wing wrapped tight 'round me, a few outstretched hands zoomed by, but I could not reach them. I screamed and screamed for linked rescue but the only reply was that of my own voice. Seemed the well of wishes had dried up, alas insufficient timing.

Within These Here Hands and Amid Others
Oh sure, there are the big things we offer up, and also there are the small. Our connection time brief, our sharing hands rare yet I try, even when preferring not to, I fucking try because one day, I will need but maybe not desire such offerings. Sometimes easy to say- hard to do, but I try, I truly try hard AF.

Car...Stop the Game
Here now, the end of chapter five, the last topic chapter of this here your second-editioned volume one. Up next are the first two chronological period chapters, aka the dissected crumbs of this bird's tale from the start, game on.

Six

~

Life With(out) Mother

Mirror-Mirror Why Do You Hate Me So?

Birdy and Boyd

Beg your pardon my precious for the variability within this here your chapter six opener. My loves, my darlings, my precious…this a dark chapter for me. This a hard chapter for me. This a hard chapter for me to write. This a hard chapter for me to resuscitate and therefore, to re-live. Even with most of the words written and dumped into the rough draft document beforehand, I spent over six weeks just shuffling the contents around, aligning it in language I can speak, and aligning it all, in truth.

Through truth, there too comes darkness.
With truth, I bear my darkness to you here.
With truth, I also bear my monsters to you here.

There is some coloring-in with word animation in the opening story piece upcoming but fucking trust me, my monsters were real. I was not hammering away at this chapter for all those six weeks, although I did nothing else during that time. Let me explain. During that time, those six weeks…I was walking in the woods with my hood over my eyes, just trying to let go. During that time, those six weeks…I was doing short bike rides wearing my darkest lenses, just trying to let go. During that time, those six weeks…I was taking mid-day naps with the blanket covering my face, just trying to let go.

This a hard chapter to write because I dug up the most painful parts of my life, the painful parts I left behind long ago. And speaking with the pointy end of my tongue razor-sharpened in truth, they were the painful parts I did not want to explore, not at all, because I otherwise wanted to let them lay as they were and lay as they are. But uh yeah, fuck that stupid fucking bullshit, this is a book of truth, and not a book of leave that shit alone and don't even fucking look at it or go near the fucking shit. Fuck to the no, this boy ain't playin'.

So more than explore these long ago buried or left behind painful parts of me and my truth, I hunted them down, exposed them for all they are and all they are not, and I stared the motherfuckers down until they walked off. I looked and examined and dissected the most horribly painful parts of me, until the most painful parts of me became deflated and defeated by my stare, and defeated by my courage to do so, thus defeating the most painful parts of me, by the hand of inquisition within truth itself. My memory and the taste of those painful parts burned me several times as I held them in my hands during those six weeks. I also hit a few emotional barriers and landmines along the way to carefully navigate. This cautionary tale is perhaps my own neurotic protectiveness, or maybe just my drama-queen proprietary old-school Roger Ray pain whiny-whiny bullshit which slides off you like Teflon, but alas, the risk of harm to you both by sharing so much of my recorded painful parts drives my arm high to wave the slow-the-fuck-down-and-be-careful yellow flag.

The uncovering of detail within my painful truths necessitated the deepest of self-questioning into many matters of my life…bad, dark, and scary as fuck matters. Caution because as result of my need to ascertain total truth, the final deliverable here existing perhaps as the most fragile of realities laid out in this entire whole of bird brain work.

I and for myself, never went center-of-earth deep into the truest of true feelings regarding my childhood mental rattling or even more recent, into the breakup of me and your ginger hot momma, but I go there now, some of it here, and some additional sprinkles throughout the larger body of this here bird beak babble. I never journeyed to the center of my emotional earth before because it already hurt enough. Such internal chaos cut me deeper than deep, and I already bled pints from it. Not intending to tear open my long-ago closed emotional scars but no other option exists by my measure to face shit head-on and otherwise, my narrative footprints then given an opportunity to sidestep the truth, and that shit ain't gonna fucking happen. Nor do I care to gamble and tragically expose your precious-precious bullet-riddled hearts, hence the pause and yellow flag gate check.

On some midwestern-nice level, I should not share my truths with you at all, thereby dismissing the benefit or value of such documented detail. But sticking to my right-coast trajectory, being me-myself the unconventional one, playing this hand with all my chips, aka making the biggest bet of my life here, I choose not to filter and I hold nothing back, left-coast judgements be damned. Please proceed with caution, best you can. Please protect your loving heart, best you can.

I try, and forever will I try, to do as I would have done unto me.

I would rather know, I would rather know all of it. I would rather know everything, even too much, than not enough. I am dead fucking serious, and I appreciate very little please and no thank you when others assume what they think I want to hear, what they think I need to hear, or magically-who-the-fuck-knows what they think they should, or rather should not, fucking tell me. Fuck that fucking bullshit…madness on parade. You feel me yet Birdy, you feel me yet Boyd? *Huh, I am not sure and maybe, meaning what dad?* Well, let me try this…explaining the aforementioned concept of others assuming and judging me alongside the notion of too much rather than not enough. Now here a partial definition of done unto me…I try not to be late, so to not disrespect people's time, I know the feeling from the other end and it sucks, so sometimes I go overboard just to be safe. This not far removed from my mantra, I would rather be two hours early than two minutes late, to which Travis the Boyd comments, "Well I'd rather be right on time", *smirk-smirk*.

I cannot effectively operate from a position of not knowing enough truth, never have, nor do I believe I ever will.

As brutally painful as it may be, as brutally hurtful as it may be, and truthfully, as brutally hateful as it may be, I would rather know everything, even if their feelings are nothing but a subjective whirlwind emotional tornado, and even if their thoughts ideas or assumptions are wrong. I would rather know, and I would rather know all of it, right fucking here, and right fucking now pretty-pretty please with jimmies on top. So here I give you my all, and I truly hope none of this backfires for you or for your gorgeous ginger momma bird. If some of this my bird brain ramble splashes back in my face, then so be it.

Yours truly me myself just slamming caution to the wind here…I will humbly and willingly carry the weight of harm upon you because then and only then, am I being truthful within my own heart, and that is from where everything good in the entire world originates. Be careful please, amen.

Exactly like every other single word, implication, and backstory contained within this entire book, cover to cover, here lies truth.

I choose to share truth with you fully, so if you so choose, you can know, but therefore, here you will also find parts of me you may not want to know, least not yet, and parts of me you may not want to see, least not yet.

  I need to caution you here. This may be hard to read.

  If my father wrote his truth to me, bearing his monsters and all, I quite possibly maybe and probably would have burned it instead of read it.

This Here Chapter Six Composition
Following the opener story upcoming, each life period narrative in this chapter six will include a header. There are some neutral-to-good periods in this chapter, those periods containing some sunshine, and I will try to identify them as-so-such, with a sunny description in their period or section header title. If you prefer not to read the periods or sections of shadow in this chapter, least for now, please seek the headers appearing more sunny than dark.

Chapter Six Baptism of Fire: Dark Trilogy
My darlings, my precious, immediately forthcoming, three introductory poems lay waiting to support and help frame the chapter. Within my held-aside future but in-the-works book of poetry titled *Sunshine & Shadows*, the trio of pieces upcoming will also reside inside that one-day publication. There within the flaps of my to-come bright and dark poetic works, these pieces shared here will live farthest and hindmost, deep undercover of the darkest cloud, inside the backside Shadows section. The raw and repressive ring of dark trilogy opening poems transposed here were all written under shadow, and factually the third piece LIGHTLESS was constructed while restrained in terrifying dark-dark-dark fucking darkness. I declare extreme caution here my precious. Please precious beware, and please-please guard-guard your heart-heart.

I give you these pieces of me, so to have, all of me.

I give you all, the pieces of my whole, so to hold, as you choose.

I give you all the pieces of my whole, so to hold, my truth.

Sans intention to hurt, void intention to scare but I may, then I bleed your result.

I share with you now, these additional pieces of me.

Spice

Sometimes I don't show I'm alive

For sometimes for sure

Somedays it's better to surrender

If just for this day and no more

Show-show no life at all so not to get eaten

They await-they await for me to move a slight muscle

I withhold my some shimmy, I inch not a bustle

I rest there not trying to motion

There's not much left in me, no magic potion

I've given up the try to not get eaten

Gobbled up and swallowed, they've won, I'm beaten

My monsters consume me both inside and out

The voice once heard in my ear so gentle now only shouts.

Be It That of Destiny

The pained silence almost deafening

My wandering brain lingers threateningly

Amid my aloneness I try to run, to escape

Can't see why I try, my will now just breaking to break

Am I overly ambitious to wonder where I stand

To contemplate where I've been, to worry where I'll land

Hours tick by, the days roll on through

I want something different but get nothing new

The pains of the past they flood all four walls

My future once open yet the curtain calls

I only feel weight, pushing me down

Once wanting to surface, no wait forget it, just let me drown.

LIGHTLESS

Sadness slithers, noiseless, up from its lair

Fangs drawn and doubtless to devour its prey

The craftiest of devil...lightless

Expertly able to hibernate, consume, and kill at will

A barbarous, cold, and inhuman demon

An apocalyptic eye, ever looming, and imminent

Fuck you, my bastardly monster

I unceremoniously relinquish the notion of victory.

Lightless liner notes found at the end of this here chapter six within the footers section.

Chapter Six, Life With(out) Mother ~

I was freezing. My toes were numb. I could feel my frosted breath flee my face as I stood there in our hallway, shaking horribly and too terrified to move a muscle. It was totally dark, in the middle of the night, and I had to pee.

We never had any lights on upstairs after we went to bed and there were no lights coming from downstairs or no light coming in from the windows of my room or anything. There was no light, and I could not see anything. But just like it is every single night, I could see the dark outline of the doorway to the room at the end of our hallway. The dark outline of the doorway that is just past the bathroom that I had to try to get to, without being grabbed by them.

A weird glow from the room spilled all over the floor and splattered the walls in the hall, like it always does, every single night. The door was open to the room, just like it always is, exactly the same every night when I get up to pee. The same glow was coming from the room, not a light, just a glow. I did not ever know what the glow was, even though I would get so close to it every single night I could almost touch it but then before I could look at the glow, well, it would happen, and then, well, you know, that was always the end of it.

I would see this glow every night for almost two school grades and I also knew who was in the room, just around the corner inside of the door to the room at the end of the hallway and I knew they were about to step into the hallway. I would see them at the end of the hallway every single night and I would see the weird glow every single night, although it happened brand new every time, I could never remember I would have ever seen it before. Every time it was there again…every night. It was always new, and I never remembered it from the night before, and I never knew what was going on except every time, I knew I was in my own house, I knew who and what was waiting for me in that room at the end of the hallway, and I knew I had to pee.

This is our family's big house and we have lived here for as many summertimes as I can ever remember in the whole wide world. We live here together: Me, my mom, my dad, and my two sisters. My big sister Laura was older than I was, not by a whole-whole lot but not by a little bit either and my bestest friend little sister's name is Beth and she is my best friend. This is the first house I ever remember living in ever, and right across the busy street from our house was my dad's church. He was mostly at his church, although he came home for dinner and he was mostly around on Saturdays when we watched cartoons.

My dad's church looked kind of like a scary castle but every time I went over there, my dad and the dark stinky walls of the big kinda castle church actually made me feel better. My dad's church made me feel happier than at home where they made me go to sleep every night. I never asked my dad if it would be ok, but I wanted all of us to sleep in my dad's church forever and ever and never have to sleep in our house ever again. This house always felt bad to me, even though I was still young, and I did not know why it felt bad at all.

At first it was fine and then starting in the basement, the monsters showed up, and they tried to eat me.

I always felt weird inside our house and only when my best friend little sister Beth and I went outside did I feel better. Maybe mom and dad would let me sleep in the garage or in the back yard from now on or something, if my teacher won't let me sleep at school or if dad won't let me sleep in his church. Whenever mom would let us, I would try to always go outside, and Beth would always come with me because we were buddies, we were best friends. Everything was so much better outside once the monsters came and once the glow started at the end of the hallway upstairs at night every single night. I liked it better outside and I never felt like they could find me outside like they did inside every single night.

Outside was better than inside, even when it was raining.

Mostly, Beth and I played in our black crunchy driveway but also sometimes in the backyard. The house felt like it was wobbly or something. Like maybe there was a rock stuck underneath it that has to be pulled out and then it won't be so wobbly all the time. It feels like it sometimes moves back and forth or side to side a little or something, depending on who was inside and where everyone was inside. Maybe the floor was like crooked or something and it made everything else feel wobbly, but I did not like it at all. Maybe the monster cracked the floor in our basement and maybe our house is going to fall into a big hole or something, sometimes that's what it feels like.

Our basement scared me so-so much. I never go down there anymore or anything. Beth and I used to play down there so much and a whole-whole lot, especially when it rained and the basement would fill up with water. Beth and I ran around in our boots, splashing running and laughing as we played with floating pieces of wood from our dad's projects. I never go down there anymore after the monster under the water bit me and tried to pull me under. I was glad the monster only bit me and did not catch Beth in its teeth. Beth never bled from the monster bite like I did that one scary-scary time so she was not as scared as me, but I was her older brother and because her and I always went everywhere together and did the same things, always together, Beth never went into the basement again either at all after the monster bit me. It was so scary the day he bit me.

It hurt me so bad that I have never felt such a horrible pain like that ever before in my whole life ever. My left foot was cut so bad after the monster bit me that I could not even walk or run away fast from the monster or anything. It was so scary. I felt the monster bite me and he grabbed me and I couldn't run away or anything and it hurt so much that I guess I started screaming and crying and stuff and Beth did not at all want to get bit by the monster either so she ran upstairs to get our dad so maybe he could rescue me from the monster and Beth ran so-so fast so speedy fast, fast as she could. Our dad is so brave and he is so fast and he is so strong and our dad came flying down the stairs as speedy fast as he could even run in the whole wide world to save me from the monster who was biting me and trying to pull me under the water and trying to eat me and trying to kill me.

Our dad came speeding fast down the stairs just like an upside-down shooting firecracker or something and our dad was mad at that monster for me and our dad was coming to save me and my whole life and our dad just jumped into the water and he was so brave, no rain boots or anything.

My big strong dad lifted me up so easy as a gallon of milk or something and pulled me away from the monster under the water. I tried to see over at my foot and I thought the monster still had the whole part of my foot in his mouth and I thought the monster had bitten the whole thing off, because it sure felt like he did. It was hard to see my monster bitten foot after the monster bit me because my dad was running up the steps so fast and he was holding me so tight. He was really squeezing me very hard and although it hurt a little bit, I was happy because I wanted him to hold me and not drop me because then the monster might get me again and my dad might not be able to save me. I wanted my dad to squeeze me harder and make sure he did not drop me. I tried to see my foot but my dad was squeezing me so hard but then I saw my left foot as my dad was saving me and it was still there and the monster had not bitten it off, but then there was a horrible problem with my foot.

I didn't really care too-too much at all care about my foot because we were still flying up the steps and I hoped my dad could get me all the way to the kitchen and slam the door closed to the basement so the monster was trapped down there. We finally got away from that monster and my dad saved my whole life but once we stopped in the kitchen upstairs, my mom started screaming.

When my mom saw the same thing that I had seen coming up the steps, when she saw what the monster had done to me…my mom was really, really scared and upset. My dad was trying to save my whole life and he had me in his strong arms so he had not seen the monster bite yet. My dad is so fast and we got away from that monster so speedy fast, fast as we could. My dad set me down on the kitchen floor trying to pay attention to my mom for maybe like a second because my mom was screaming so loud-loud-loud. My dad had to yell at her because my mom was being so-so loud, so my dad shouted louder, WHAT'S WRONG, WHAT'S WRONG? Before my mom could even answer as my dad was still kinda holding onto me I started to fall straight down to the floor and I could not even ever even stand on my left foot or anything, and my dad grabbed me very-very tight to keep me from falling down onto the floor all by myself and then my dad saw my bad-bad monster bite.

He picked me back up off the floor holding me high off the ground and very tight in his arms again like when we were running up the steps and escaping from the monster under the water in our basement that tried to eat me but my dad saved me. My dad is so strong and I do not think he is getting tired or anything because he is holding me so tight because he is so strong. As he was squeezing the tar out of me one of my dad's big strong arms reached down and scooped up both of my legs underneath the back of my knees so he could help me and hold my legs and he was help-help-helping me so much as the blood dripped-dripped-dripped very fast many-many drips out of the bottom of my foot where the monster bit me. My dad grabbed a chair and with me still held tight in his arms, and while he was holding my legs so they were not dangling down all by themselves or anything, my dad sat down on the chair he grabbed, trying to get a closer look at the monster bite.

The monster had bitten my left foot and tried to pull me under the water and he tried to eat me and he wanted to kill me but my dad was so brave and rescued me. My dad saved me from the monster, but when my dad pulled me away from the mouth of the monster, one of the monster's teeth was stuck in my foot and poking out, sticking out from the top of my boot about the same size as one of my fingers. The monster in our basement must be very big because he has very big teeth. I bet that monster must be very mad that one of his teeth broke off in my foot when my dad was saving me. The big fat part of the monster tooth was sticking out of the bottom of my boot and the skinny pointy end of his tooth was now poking out the top of my rainy red rain boot. Oh no, I am so scary-scared. The monster tooth was really stuck in there and neither my mom or my dad knew how to pull out monster teeth or anything.

I could not see the bottom part of the monster tooth but I felt it poking out of the bottom of my foot when my dad put me down on the floor as soon as he saved my whole life and we made it to the kitchen.

How in the world are we going to take my boot off with that monster tooth stuck in my foot?

My mom was still screaming, and I was crying really hard because I was really scared and the monster bite hurt really-really bad. My dad told my mom what he was doing and then my dad jumped up out of the chair, holding me very tight, and we went outside to get in the car and go to the hospital. There was a big puddle of blood on the floor in the kitchen from my monster bite and when my dad got up to take me to the doctors that could help with my monster bite my dad had to walk straight through the puddle of blood and he left blood footprints all the way outside to our car, which he put me in.

I hope they have very special doctors at the hospital who know how to remove monster teeth and I hope they can fix the monster bite and stop the bleeding and keep my foot from falling off. I never want to go down into our basement ever again, never ever never. My foot hurt so bad and I thought the monster's tooth has poison in it so I started to worry that maybe the poison will make my foot fall off. I do not want to even like live my life forever and ever with only one foot ever. I will never be able to walk or ride my bike ever again or play hopscotch or anything ever again with only one foot ever. It was so scary.

It was a long time before the monster bite went away and we did find some very good monster teeth doctors because my foot did not fall off at all or anything. I did not go back to school until after Christmas and for a lot of Saturdays I could never go outside and play because I couldn't even yet walk on my foot that had the monster bite on it no-no not yet. I was very happy my dad saved my whole life and the monster did not eat me or bite my foot off and the monster's mouth poison did not make my foot fall off.

Upstairs from the place where the monster lived was our bright sunny playroom in our house. It was always so warm in the sunny room and we had lots of fun toys in there and it was the very best room we all days loved to play in. We could look out the windows from our sunny playroom and see our dad's church across the street.

The sunny room was my favorite room in the house because I was always looking for my dad through the windows and hoping he would come home soon and because the sunny room was not a good place for monsters. The monster lives in the basement so I knew he could never eat me when I was in the sunny room. My mom and my dad were always so brave and they must be very, very strong to beat the monster because they would go downstairs almost every day and my mom and my dad would always win over that monster and come back up the steps from the basement and not get eaten by the monster or anything.

The safe no-way-monsters-allowed sunny room had two big doors made out of windows that went to different rooms of the house and those doors were never closed so we could always hear our mom when she called us for lunch or something.

I loved those doors made out of windows in the no monsters allowed upstairs sunny room because the window doors helped to let more safe light inside which monsters do not-do not like.

We played in the no-monsters-no-way-allowed sunny room almost every all the time when we were playing inside because I would never, ever, ever go upstairs into my room or where the hallway is upstairs unless it was bedtime and only when my mom and my dad would force me to go up there at bedtime. I never wanted to tell my dad what happened every night upstairs when I would get up to pee in the middle of the night because, well…because.

I only played in the sunny room because I would never ever never go in the basement ever again because the monster lives down there…but then I just wanted to go live in my dad's church or maybe my teacher would let me sleep in school at night or something because then I could not go into the sunny room either at all after the monster found me there in the sunny room. I thought the monster only lived in our basement but maybe he has a friend monster or maybe it was the same monster who either dug out the walls or ate the inside of the walls between the sunny room and the monster place in the basement. I hated our house so-so much because the monster who already tried to eat me in the basement or maybe it was his friend monster, but I got another monster bite in my whole life.

The monster attacked me again, biting me, cutting me very-very badly as I tried to escape from the sunny room where that-again or friend-monster-brand-new bit me there in the sunny room. Just like last time there was a big puddle of blood on the floor in the kitchen from the monster who tried to eat me that day. I hated our house so much. I wanted to live across the street in my dad's church because I really-really wanted to because I did not want to live in this house anymore no way not at all really.

Every single night they are at our house upstairs at the end of the hallway every night, and upstairs in that room, well…well, you know…and besides, monsters live in our basement and in the sunny room. I do not…no not at all know where I could sleep in a place where my mom or dad would say it would be ok but I hope they say it would be ok. I would rather sleep outside in our yard or something and even when it is cold than sleep in this house ever again forever and ever, even when it is raining. This house is so scary now and I hate it so-so much and there is nowhere anywhere at all nowhere inside this house where I can play or sleep or anything, because they are upstairs and, well…and because monsters live here.

It feels safe at my dad's church, not like it does across the street at our house.

This Here Chapter Six

Chapter six is the first period chapter, arranged in chronological order. This here chapter six spans from my birth to fifteen years old, before I dropped out of high school. Intending now to present foundational information, and share with you much of what you do not know about me, here lies my truth, just so you know. Love-love you both-both my precious birdies very-very much-much.

Frightening & Forbidding Florida

During the two years of my mother in, and out, and in and out of mental health facilities, BigBird was trying to bring us back together as a family, best he could. My father tried to get us four kids and our mother out of the house doing stuff, attempting to normalize our out-of-order birdhouse lifehood. We went on several car-camping trips, and each time accompanying us were my father's traveling cookstove, camp pots pans and utensils. The specific outdoors kitchen gear was packed into the back of our big-ass station wagon, correctly arranged inside a large purpose-built contraption that BigBird custom fabricated in his woodshop.

While in first grade and still living in the monster house, before my seventh birthday, I pulled the first legitimate harmful maneuver of my life, stupid, just fucking stupid…something frankly outside my realm of comprehension, still. My mother's already precarious, aka unstable mental health was on full display, and she didn't need any negative influence from me, no not at all but, well, hum, well, anyway, you'll see.

Yes for sure she was at times suicidal, physically enraged and out of this world delusional before our trip to Florida, but I carry a moderate load of guilt for then single-handedly pushing her over the edge. This went down in February 1971, several months before our family would lose the mother bird forever.

The Okefenokee Swamp is a national wildlife refuge, crossing over from southern Georgia into northern Florida, covering 700 square miles. The wild nature of the area is bright and breathtaking while also clouded over and creepy. I know you both are somewhat exposed to the wild nature of Florida and the prowling alligators after visiting your Nonni and Grandpa in the sunshine state. Weirdly associated but during the opener of our Lies Between Us Roger Ray Bird podcast episode number one, my Friendwords SuperStar Coach Sarah mentioned that if someone's car broke down, I would just show up to help. I was choking on my own tongue from the irony after she framed the broken-down car scenario. I struggled pathetically to put any words together in response to Sarah, wiping back a few tears and almost needing to excuse myself for a break before I even began. During the immediate handful of days before Sarah and I recorded episode numero uno, I was writing this chapter six and specifically, working on this here Florida section.

The bizarre kismet association got my goat after Sarah made her innocent example, of my tendency to help others and factually now, ugh, tears parade down my cheeks once more as I clack, clack, clack about it.

The Florida camper park was full, bustling with activity, and by that time we had made friends with some fellow nearby car-camp families. My father's 10-person canvas tent was our overnight shelter when we stayed at the Okefenokee campground and it was after dinner, the sun already down. We were not in our tent yet, but still running around playing with other kids near the flaming fire rings…some of us waving flashlights every which way high and low and side to side. I remember the general loud and chaotic nature of the place, least as I perceived, also I was, consciously frightful of the slithering and biting reptiles lurking about. At six years and eleven months old, it's hard for me to sort out and know for sure how the adults comprehended the scene. We already walked through the Okefenokee visitor center and toured the swamp with our father, so I was well educated on the local crawling and creeping critters.

Us Bird kids generally liked all animals including reptiles, my sisters liking snakes a bit more than I did, especially Beth. Least to me, the entire area was moderately unnerving with the vipers black bears and alligators on the loose. Impossible to assume the adult perspective but generally I myself felt uncomfortable, both physically and emotionally. I recall that my mother was slightly sick during the Florida trip, or now I might more accurately redefine it as sad, depressed or disengaged but my father was definitely in charge, and he single handedly led us around. So, amidst this my perceived hectic environment one night, a neighbor camper got a flat tire on their car and the car was stranded somewhere outside the big camping park. My father was helping the broken-down neighbor who needed a tire jack, which BigBird had. In the dark of the scary night, my father drove off with the guy.

Unfortunately, and I'm sure my father believed the situation harmless enough, but he left us kids back at the campground under care of our mother. BigBird kept a flashlight in the station wagon glovebox and after already gone from the campground, I discovered his handy light left behind, sitting there on our picnic table because us kids were previously playing with it. It was the only light he had and I knew he would need it, so I set off to find my father.

In the dark of the creepy-crawly Okefenokee Swamp, when BigBird was off somewhere and when my mother was not paying attention, I walked away from our campsite.

I used the flashlight to light my path on the side of the road and once outside the campground proper, I determined my father was farther away than I could quickly walk to. I knew BigBird would soon reach for his flashlight, so with great determination, I sped up my gait…then parttime jogging and parttime speed walking off to only God knows where. Not finding any broken-down cars or my father's station wagon with its emergency flashers blinking, I grew nervous my assistance would arrive too late to help. So, trying to hurry things along, I stuck my right thumb out as I walked backwards down the road. A mid-aged solo white man picked me up in his car and I sat next to him on his front bench seat. He asked where to and I guided him, "Just up there a little."

After the road ended at a T, driver man asked me which way I needed to go now. I believe he then suspected my uncertainty. Although I hesitated, the man kept driving after my "I think left, yes please go left" instruction. Before not long, we were driving all around through the dark of night.

I remember driver man being pleasant at first, but then he either grew mad or concerned, maybe because I'm wasting his time or perhaps that he's in sole possession of a lost six-year-old kid at night. The man pulled over, he said he wanted to talk. Flustered Florida person tried to understand as I explained…I was helping my father who needed a flashlight, but I honestly had no idea where he was. By this time we had meandered around long enough that I no longer cared about the darn flashlight, but just really-really wanted to get back to my dad. The man sat there upset and silent for a long fifteen seconds, contemplating my words then indifferently, he restarted our juvenile goose chase.

After some processing and eliminating, the mildly mad man found the correct campground. We drove around the winding blacktop until I finally identified our campsite but, well, I did not recognize our campsite per se. Our family's car was sitting there with its engine running and lights on. Also, easy to recognize were BigBird and my mother, huddled around with several other adults in the road, slightly to the side and behind my father's station wagon. We pulled up and now our headlights were shining directly onto the interested group of adults, them glaring our way and shielding their eyes trying to identify who was inside this strange car. We got out to greet them and my father aggressively lurched forward from where he was standing.

Marching intently towards the driver, BigBird glanced over at me but only briefly. Opening the spirited conversation with his elevated voice, BigBird finally calmed down as the man apologized, explaining he picked me up hitchhiking a couple miles outside of the park. Traditionally around that time when I did something wrong, my mother would threaten me with, "Wait 'til your father gets home", or BigBird would yell, yank me by the arm or spank me with either his hand or implements. That night in Florida, I do not remember my father speaking or acting negatively towards me at all. Actually, I do not remember much of anything after the man who drove me around for almost an hour and let me sit next to him in his front seat, he then left and drove away. I remember my father thanking the man for getting me back safely, and I remember my mother was rather out of sorts, but my memory fades quickly from there…brain shadow, brain shadow.

Later I learned, as my father wrote in his letter, my mother freaked out during that Florida trip and I hold a strong certainty my running off alone into the creepy dark night was her cause. Regardless, we rushed back to Maryland immediately afterwards, my father driving us home non-stop once it was time to go, a 750-mile trip from northern Florida to west Baltimore.

A few months later, we would only and forever need one less chair at the dining room table.

Bye-Bye Mommy

I was born on a springtime Tuesday, inside a downtown university hospital, the second child to a 25-year-old mother and a 26-year-old father. My mother Patricia Lou a former 4th-grade teacher, now a housewife, and already with a three-year-old daughter at home. My father Ray Norman a fulltime minister for a large downtown church on the edge of the worst slums in Cleveland.

Your Grandma Pat proclaimed me a good baby, who sucked my left thumb and loved carrots so much that my skin assumed a slight orange tint. The birth certificate provides no proof of detail, but my mother mentioned me as a 10-pound birth weight baby. Both my parents wore glasses, BigBird with his large lens engineer-style spectacles, and my mother donning her once-stylish cat eye frames. BigBird smoked cigarettes his whole life, a habit that would later kill him, and your grandma Pat smoked until she got locked up. My father was not a fitness-minded big bird, but remained active and moving most days working on projects around the house. I know not any of my mother's recreational cool things, hum, collectively and mostly, well, well…it feels like she was not really my mother, no not at all.

My father Ray hailed from Detroit, oops sorry, that's already well established. Mother Patricia grew up in Zanesville Ohio. My BigBird Ray and my mother Patricia met through a mutual friend on campus at Miami University in Ohio. Your bird grandparents married in Zanesville and quickly moved to Boston where your Grandpa With Ginger was finishing seminary grad school. My big sister Laura Lee was born in Fall River Massachusetts where BigBird pastored a small Protestant church after completing his master's at Andover Newton Theological School. Laura was about a year and a half when the birdie family moved to Cleveland.

My sister Elizabeth Anne, aka Beth, followed me into this world by 14 months while we were still in Ohio. Shortly after my best friend little sister Beth was born, our birds of five moved to the rough and tumble west side of Baltimore City, landing in the Howard Park community and we lived on Hillsdale Road just off Liberty Heights in the monster house, and across the street from my dad's church.

My father was berated in Cleveland and our family fled Ohio after BigBird was labeled a communist.

BigBird was then unable to work at any church in the state of Ohio, after congregation higher-up's opposed my father's campaign for people of color to become full members of the church. BigBird demonstrated for and spoke out in support of racial equality, thus losing his job and almost forfeiting his career. Getting my father into hot water were his demonstrations for civil rights and challenging the governance of the local United Church of Christ organization against impoverishment, BigBird arguing poverty as un-Christian.

Perhaps as my father suggests in his cursive 18-page reveal, the stress of three children under the age of five in addition to several family relocations in rapid succession proved too much for my mother to handle. My mother's amassed anxiety became overblown after the bloody riots in Baltimore following Doctor Martin Luther King Junior's assassination.

On April 4th in 1968 when shadow engulfed our nation's peaceful unity, our sisters and brothers rose up, powered by their uncontrollable emotions after the 1964 Nobel Peace Prize awardee and one of the world's leaders on non-violent equality was savagely murdered by gunshot in Memphis Tennessee.

Six people died in Baltimore after Doctor Martin Luther King Junior was murdered, and a total of 43 people died nationwide as a result of the riots.

Ray Norman grew up the middle child of three, in the same Detroit house where me and my two younger sisters set up residence after your Grandma Pat was initially hospitalized in December 1968. My father fancied photography as his favorite hobby and eventually earned some money from shooting weddings before he was married with children.

Although only learned once I cared for Uncle Ralph in late 2020 and during the first quarter of 2021, my father's parents Thurman and Gladys were devote Baptist church folk. The young future BigBird was mentored by the local Baptist reverend and my father enrolled in a youth seminary program, which I assume led him to pursue a church career. Uncle Ralph did not recall additional detail, but I am blessed to least know as much, otherwise my father's work with the church a complete mystery to me. The open gap of why BigBird committed to a job spreading religion out unto the world escapes me and honestly, my heart hurts a little because of the unknowing.

During his last year of seminary, BigBird gained acceptance to Ohio State University, planning to undertake studies for a Ph.D. in American History. Once learning his wife Patricia was pregnant with my big sister Laura, future academic plans thwarted and instead, my father entered the workforce amongst all them other rats a racing. Perhaps after the church administrative mutiny of his theological career in Ohio, my father felt his options were limited but regardless, he remained committed to the church once later landing in Maryland. Maybe he stuck with the religious paycheck because of much-needed family expenses but as you will read elsewhere, BigBird had plans to leave the church after a fulltime black minister could be hired to replace him, across the street from our monster house.

My youngest sister Christina Grace then joined our family, and I attended both nursery school then kindergarten at a west Baltimore church in the neighborhood of Woodlawn, barely over the city line in Baltimore County. Adjacent to Woodlawn is a large wooded area, Leakin Park-Gwynns Falls Park, owned by Baltimore City. My father's friend Jan Ports was the minister of the Woodlawn church and we also later attended Jan Ports' Bethany church on Sundays because it had a Sunday School program for kids. BigBird's church which was about 10 miles away did not have early morning church school. So, every Sunday, our father drove us to Woodlawn, dropped us off at Bethany, he would go preach at his church, and come back for us later.

Leakin Park-Gwynns Falls in Woodlawn spans over 1,200 acres and you would think the space would be an amazing and vibrant place for recreation and playful family weekends, especially for nearby city residents, but no-no-no to the fucking-hell-no negative.

On some level, if simply viewing Leakin Park for its physical appearance and geography, I suppose it could be considered a beautiful space but one I would never ever never visit, other than speedily passing through. Later in my teens and once learning of the burial ground realities, I never saw anything but darkness there. Leakin Park is clouded by shadow, heavy, heavy, heavy shadow…the most popular place to dump murdered bodies in Baltimore. Baltimore averages over 300 murders a year and 100 bodies have been found in Leakin Park alone. I safely assume the Leakin Park number would be higher if they dug around. Famously in 1968, two weeks after Doctor King was assassinated, the bodies of four murdered and mutilated children were found in Leakin Park, and I am sure it was a detail coming to my mother's attention back in the day. Baltimore's annual per capita murder rate is over 50 murders per 100,000 people, and many years the ratio is closer to 60.

While residing in the west Baltimore monster house, I completed first grade at Howard Park Elementary, only a block away. In 1971 and after returning home from vacationing in Florida, my father finally left his fulltime church career and began work for Mayor William Donald Schaffer within the Baltimore City government. But his religious path did not end so easily and BigBird led one service every Sunday at a small church called Trinity, located in the Hampden community, slightly north of downtown Baltimore. My father's first responsibility working for the mayor's office was to study and propose solutions to combat poverty in the city.

Placing myself in BigBird's shoes and although I am assuming, 'Poverty Fighter' sounds like a dream job to me, long as the Mayor could institute true change.

Mayor Schaffer is legendary, a well loved and respected four-term mayor serving 16 years total until becoming a two-term governor of Maryland. My father sang praises for his boss the mayor, albeit an outspoken and hard-driving white man running a majority black city. Mayor Schaffer famously renovated Baltimore's downtown area, worked like hell to clean up the streets, and attempted to deescalate the somewhat overpowering violence within the city's vibrant drug trade. Baltimore at the time had one of the highest per capita killing rates in the country and hah, still does.

Modern day the Baltimore drug violence continues to run wild, especially sparked by the fucking Perdue Pharma-forced opioid epidemic for fucking fuck's sake, followed by the P2P meth and fentanyl outbreaks. Astonishingly, at the end of 2023, the drug abuse problem in this country is worse than ever, and is also escalating rapidly in the most fucked up direction. Statistically in 2019, Baltimore was ranked number two in the nation for per capita murders, and number one for cities over 500,000 people, well as arguably the number one city in the world per capita, for heroin overdoses. Day by day the chemical mishmash of hyper-deadly drugs evolve, and the literal roulette faced by today's addicts is beyond controllable, or even foreseeable.

Shortly after starting work for the city, my father enrolled in the nearby Johns Hopkins University to pursue an Urban Planning master's degree.

BigBird attended night classes following his day's work for the mayor and my father earned his second graduate degree when I was 12 years old, right around the same time I began abusing drugs. BigBird spills the tale better than I ever could, so you'll read later but echo-when I was four, my mother's poor mental health became a legitimate fucking problem, demanding multiple residential hospitalizations. After two years in and out of mental health treatment centers, my mother's emotional condition crumbled and became an insurmountable challenge. Finally in June 1971 when I was seven, my mother was committed and locked up for good, against her will. Your Grandma Pat was packaged up and transported to the Baltimore area Spring Grove state mental hospital and remained there for years, never returning to our house or family life ever again…bye-bye mommy.

Heart Songs

Why so much the significance of movies in my life? Whyever do I mention them so very often? IDFK why such chatter surfaces on and off and on again. Maybe I'm just making shit up but apparently, least as appears to me, many average middle-class type humans gain much of their influential knowledge from taught school, reading books, and examining different news mediums. Whereupon, I followed none of those…no school, not books, nor news. I follow none of those still, and specifically, books partially defined as fiction books.

Predominantly my lessons learned and gained knowings were delivered to me out on the street through my trials triumphs and traumas, besides gaining emotional insight and instructional guidance from what the cinema screen taunts to teach me.

I echo-echo-do not read fiction, but sure do enjoy a two-hour entranced engagement at the movies. Outside of what I faced straight-up to live and learn myself, what flows through me as visually-sensed knowings, forced-upon felt feelings, and emotional hold-ons were supplied to my head and heart originating from movies. Movies, aka my secondary mind and mecca marrow mediums.

The Cuckoo Collection

When amid my years of late 30s, I first tuned into some emotional health plotted movies, although not always did I realize the association before starting the flick. Accidentally, I found myself oddly entertained by The Shining with Jack Nicholson. I not only discovered a meaningful connection with the scary cinematic smash, but also found some slight humor in it. I believe watching The Shining helped me come to terms with the fact I wasn't singled out and attacked by my monster-mother-monster as an anomaly.

After The Shining, although it took a while, I could better face the conditional reality of poor mental health. In my 40s with determination, I sought out several movies providing additional reassurance that my family's struggles are not so bizarre. The flicks I categorize in this regard represent personal growth perspectives and various life struggles, not only the drama of people losing their marbles. Listed here they are, in order of when I discovered them, starting back when.

1. The Shining, Jack Nicholson
2. Days of Thunder, Tom Cruise and Nicole Kidman
3. 12 Monkeys, Brad Pitt
4. One Flew Over the Cuckoo's Nest, Jack Nicholson
5. Silence of the Lambs, Jodie Foster and Anthony Hopkins
6. A Beautiful Mind, Russell Crowe
7. Peter Pan, Robin Williams
8. Phenomenon, John Travolta
9. The Family Man, Nicolas Cage
10. August Rush, Freddie Highmore and Keri Russell and Robin Williams
11. Silver Linings Playbook, Bradley Cooper
12. It's Kind of a Funny Story, Zach Galifianakis
13. Good Will Hunting, Matt Damon and Robin Williams
14. Girl Interrupted, Winona Rider
15. Seven Pounds, Will Smith
16. A Star Is Born, Lady Gaga and Bradley Cooper
17. Rudderless, Billy Crudup and Anton Yelich and William H Macy
18. Finding Forrester, Rob Brown and Sean Connery

Eight of them hit me the hardest, in their own sort of way.

1. Days of Thunder
2. Phenomenon
3. The Family Man
4. August Rush
5. Good Will Hunting
6. Seven Pounds
7. A Star is Born
8. Rudderless

Days of Thunder hits hard because of the rage concentration, attempting to control emotions, the lasting effects of head trauma, and an addiction to an otherwise safe activity that gets taken too far. Additionally, the dynamic of excessive talent mistimed and misplaced fascinates me greatly, because I have brushed up against some of the same.

The wildly dynamic untapped mind when allowed to work at its potential fascinates me in ways I can barely begin to describe.

I cannot remember when I first watched Phenomenon but same-same as the fifty-plus times I have seen it since, this movie changes me, every fucking time. Perhaps because of from where I came do I associate so profoundly with this flick...someone lounging on a lower rung of life, not someone who others expected anything of, but well, hum, overall I am drawn to this movie because of the love story, the physical trauma, and the demonstration of limitless mind powers.

This one takes my breath away every damn time: The Family Man. Set during Christmas time, immediately there is an inherent holiday mysticism to the movie, never mind the magical switcheroo that gets thrown, twice, both times with heartbreaking awareness. The lack of oxygen in my chest is brought on by the realization of fractional moments, near misses, one particular saying of I love you, a lone I promise, and a handful of I'm sorry's.

Speaking off the cuff here but perhaps my number one life not-to-do is retain regret.

I try to say I love you, and often. I try to say I'm sorry, whenever I have misstepped or hurt someone. I try to say yes, most all times yes when reality appears the thing might actually work out. I attempt the maybe's, because odds are I might make it, and this for the benefit of avoiding that goddamn damaging daemon regret, as expertly acted out in The Family Man…regret.

Where do I even begin trying to explain August Rush, oh man and for fuck's sake. Here the multi-faceted cinematic impact upon me is almost too great to dissect. Hum, well, I suppose it begins with the superhuman driving force of a known but simple hope. The merging awhile billowing musical genius underpinning this movie is about strong as it gets. A sheltered foster kid sets out alone upon the world, guided by perhaps the strongest intrinsic need of all. Along the way, an adventuring August encounters the zany Robin Williams, and an insane string of events kicks off. My connection to this flick includes the value of stepping up to do the right thing, relentless pursuit of a notion no one else around you believes, outstretched hands, and maintaining the dream of a thus-unknown paternal connection. Hum, dang…maybe the zinger for me is, and not realized until now, well, is this true? Yes I think so, it is August's pursuit of his mother, a mother he has never met, but believes she is out there somewhere looking for him too. Not once during the multitude of times watching this movie have I survived without tears shed, fucking never, but tears of humility, appreciation for life, and mission accomplished.

Good Will Hunting resonates with me so very much because of the focus on self-confidence, self-worth, relationship realities, exercising special talents, mental health counseling, emotional healing and re-invention, and of course because it's fucking Robin Williams. Matt Damon masterfully plays a mathematic genius, so I associate his wicked-smart character with you both, both of you wicked-fricking-smart. In addition, I revere Robin Williams because of honoring him in real life, after he defeated his monsters in 2014, and before they defeated him.

Seven Pounds just kills me, aka leaves me absolutely motherfucking breathless, because of the main character doing every single possible little thing he could ever humanly do to right an un-rightable wrong, and because it's fucking Will Smith. Will Smith's character…his absolute commitment to tackling something worldly incomprehensible is downright inspiring, no not the result, but his dedication to the journey and his the 'doing it' parts.

A Star is Born melts me down every damn time, aka oxygen-depriving, because of dysfunctional family dynamics, depression, struggles with self-confidence, alcoholism, and worse. Besides, the singing is amazing and Lady Gaga rocks that fricking shit. I never saw the older versions of this movie, only this one, and I was verifiably jolted awake by the story.

A tragic tear-inducing shock becomes revealed part way through the showing of Rudderless, frankly an occurrence which is unspeakable, aka leaves me gasping for air for Christ's sake. The musical creativity at the foundation of this storyline is outstanding, awhile the dark lurking underlord main figure pops up only from time to time. The residual state I am left in after watching Rudderless is a painful numbness, but the sensations are also a factual reality, like getting hit in the chest with a fucking fifty-pound sledgehammer, so I am thankful for the borderline bipolar range of emotions associated with this deep-deep movie.

Big Bad Monster House

Most of the houses in our new Pimlico neighborhood were three level single family homes, with big porches and decent sized yards. Our corner lot on Whitney Avenue, it being our second Baltimore area residence, was a pretty cool house, no monsters so far, and there was a big tree in the front yard that we climbed and played around in often. Being that we only had the second floor and the reduced space third floor, there was not a lot of room for the five of us. Christy occupied a small space on the third level which wasn't a bedroom at all, more like a dead-end hallway. One night I was rocked awake by screaming and immediately I jumped up crying, my room consumed with thick smoke. I couldn't see anything, our house was on fire. After Christy fell asleep, the lamp next to her bed sans lampshade fell and set ablaze her mattress. We all escaped ok, only then to stand outside in the middle of the night for a couple of hours as the fire department removed the mattress and attempted to clear the smoke.

The fright of the night forever lingered weirdly throughout the house in an associated manner, alongside the memorized scent of the burning bed.

Black Cars with Dark Tinted Windows and the Weird Searchlight Thingies

I was home when they arrived. Beth and I were playing inside the house but not paying attention to what the people were saying. That is, until BigBird shouted and they walked swiftly for the front door, immediately. The entire brief ordeal was extremely bizarre. I never saw or heard my father lose his temper with an adult before, never. I never ever saw or heard him treat another adult with anything but respect and kindness before, ever. Yes my father yelled at us kids a lot but only when no adults were around. When BigBird yelled in the house, I performed a hard pause to make sure I wasn't the one he was shouting at, nope, I'm good, spinning back around with avoidance and just kept playing. I was put on notice that BigBird was pissed again, but thankfully I was not in the line of fire, this time.

As the adults left, BigBird did something really strange, something I don't remember him doing before, fucking ever...he slammed the front door really, really, really hard after them. When he slammed the front door, it also stopped me in my tracks. My father was madder than I ever saw him, ever, ever, fricking ever, and weirdly it was not aimed at any of us.

I remember being totally puzzled what in the world could possibly make him so mad, outside of one of us kids pissing him off for a hundred of reasons. Beth and I stood there, pausing our play and mortified but only for a few seconds, until our dad rushed to his bedroom and closed the door. Which also, like most never happens…the door to our father's bedroom was mostly never closed. The incident frightened me greatly. I had no understanding of the origin for my father's rage, zip-zero none. Although I could not entirely process it at the time, my father just screamed at three very official looking government or undercover police type people and it made me far beyond nervous, well, it seemed wrong, like BigBird broke the law. Since it felt so wrong, like BigBird broke the law, wasn't he going to get in trouble for that? Wouldn't those government people come back and arrest my father or like something? If BigBird got arrested, what would happen to us kids? We were still young, even Laura, too young to take care of ourselves if our father went to jail.

Our mother was already gone like forever, but maybe our dad was going to jail.

The entire episode was unsettling, extremely unsettling. It was like a too-young-to-know-better tornado siren, you know, everything just stopped. After our dad sheltered in his bedroom, I ran to the window and Beth followed me, trying to collect a few clues. I saw the adults standing around talking, next to their two big black police-like cars with the weird searchlight thingies hanging off the driver's door. After about two minutes, both cars drove away. I never saw the undercover-like police cars like ever return.

Immediately following the big black cars with the weird searchlight thingies incident, our lives changed. Several times our father required us to dress up in our good clothes and pretend to do silly things around our own house, like slow-baking cookies and doing the same thing over and over, or sitting together quietly as photographers took our pictures. Other people talked to my father and wrote down what he was saying. We went on several outdoor family photo shoot expeditions too. Soon after, newspapers and magazines arrived inside our house with pictures of our family on the cover or front page. BigBird then became extremely active with single parents organizations and men's groups, well as his churchman duties, continuing to meet with young couples recently engaged and already married husbands and wives experiencing trouble. Multiple nights per week my father would go to meetings or have get togethers at our house with other single parents.

Finally, I read one of the magazine articles featuring my family and basically, BigBird was on a national public relations press campaign fighting for fatherly rights when at the time, such nonsense was not done that way. Evidently my father was told he did not possess the skills or the rights or the legal opportunity to raise four children by himself, because he was a man. BigBird was mouthing off publicly and properly about the absurdity and injustice of fatherly discrimination. The resulting national and local press crusade provided a supportive platform for BigBird to share his single father's right story. A couple of these articles are digitally scanned and saved in my laptop hard drive as pdf's. Also, these scans are in my OneDrive documents cloud which I am sure you can access. Passwords are in my documents firebox at home and FYI, Travis you have memorial permissions to my Facebook page.

Back to Whitney Avenue for two more sentences my preciouses if you pretty please.

There was dead silence after the adults got kicked out of our house, so not wanting to poke the BigBird-bear, we just kept playing. I did not know what that weird and scary experience was about, and because it was fleeting, I mostly dropped it into my mental inbox folder labeled 'Life Misunderstandings'.

The Little Working Man

In my youngest years I served newspapers and hustled other work wherever I could. Verbally I contracted with an older couple in addition to an elderly woman in the neighborhood to cut their grass once a week in the summer. After then gaining my third grass cutting client however, everything fucking changed. Thrilled to have several streams of income before I was ten years old, but when my father picked up on what was happening, I was arguing with BigBird about starting my own lawncare business. At first, I could not understand what he was blah-blah-blah saying to me. I thought he was trying to block me from my industrious money making scheme. Finally I figured it out and oh for fuck's sake like are you kidding me or what, I was properly pissed once grasping his demands. Looking back at the ordeal, I totally get it and actually, my feelings commend my father and I no longer condemn him like before. Now I understand what was up, but not at the time. BigBird forced me to carry my own weight, aka teaching me the lesson of responsibility. Initially though, I hated him for it through and through. Without another option, I begrudgingly did as my father required of me.

I got on my shitty old adult three-speed bike, well, it was technically my father's big boy bike because I did not have a bike of my own yet, and pedaled BigBird's crappy bike to the hardware store. I purchased my own brand new damn gas can with my own damn money. On the way back home, I filled up my red metal can at the gas station, yup you guessed it, with my own goddamn money. Now, stupid-shit step one of my father's three part golden lawnmower rules was complete. BigBird's non-negotiable lawncare business deal enraged me but I pushed hard, driving him even fricking further away from me, and exceeding what I felt was my father's unfair treatment, at the time. Hopefully, so I desired, I could earn enough damn money cutting lawns to buy my own flipping lawnmower.

Of course, duh, BigBird laid out his rules without emotion, sans blaming and rather, he stated matter-of-factly the clear directives, like reading an ironclad contract. I was eight or nine, third or fourth grade when I opened my first business and my father's fricking rules were not only firm as fuck but crystal fricking clear.

1. ONE. I will purchase my own gas to use when I cut other people's lawns.
2. TWO. Since I will use my own gas, I need to first purchase my own gas can.
3. THREE. I will pay a flat-rate rental fee, per use, to operate my father's mower.

BigBird suggested I open a savings account and in short order I agreed, thinking it a good way to track my money in and out of my lawn business.

That very Saturday morning we went to the local bank, and I came home with my own savings account bank registry booklet. Throughout the summer I rode my father's fucking bike to the bank every week and made deposits, trying to hold back enough working cash reserves for the upcoming week's gas can refills, maybe a bit more, and FYI, this time finding me before the drugs. Although I used money for candy and magazines, I tried to minimize my spending on most other things, now proudly excited to grow my bank savings account with laser-focus intent.

Not long after, I bought gardening shears to improve the quality of my work, oh yup, crawling around hands and knees trimming sidewalk and driveway borders with my own damn lawn scissors. At the end of my first flipping full summer enslaved within BigBird's mower rental program, I went to the damn bank and withdrew my damn money, except for two dollars so to keep the account active. I asked my father to drive me to the hardware store and I bought my own damn mower, no more fricking BigBird mower rental bullshit. I only realized the valuable feels of prideful ownership once loading my brand new mower into the car, and it was glorious.

Suddenly then, my angst over BigBird charging me rent was entirely gone and I was extremely grateful for the lesson and self-reliance exercise.

Although, I held my appreciation away from my father and kept it deep inside myself. My resentful punkdom was almost fully developed by this time, at about nine or ten years old, aka I was mostly mad at the motherfucking world but held it inside to boil and bubble. Once in control of my own profitability I needed a new challenge, so I began saving money for a bike. I did not want to ride my father's big stupid ass clunky bike serving newspapers every morning. For the next year and a half I continued to cut lawns but then discontinued my once-prideful summertime business in favor of something else.

Once a year at the end of May, there was a neighborhood event holding an opportunity to make a summer's worth of cash money in one day. The annual Preakness Stakes horse race at Pimlico is a long time tradition, over 100 years old, with big prize purse money and huge crowds. 100,000 spectators flocked into nearby neighborhoods looking for parking, then were challenged to unpuzzle the hauling of their massive party supply loads to the track. We initially used little red wagons to truck the heaps of beer to Pimlico, usually for $10 per run, or more. The family play wagons proved to be insufficient for the multiple cases of beer, never mind the partiers bringing full or partial kegs. The second year of hustling during Preakness and for years afterwards, we walked a couple miles to Greenspring Shopping Center and borrowed full-size shopping carts from the grocery store. Some of the guys would dump the carts into the stream near the firehouse after the profitable once-a-year workday was done, but I was too conscientious for that and returned my cart back to the store within the next few days. Easily we cleared $100 or more, depending on how much we hustled during Preakness Saturday.

Meanwhile, in the winter and whenever Mother Nature blanketed more than three inches of snow on the ground, Mark and Danny and I got up early.

Maybe we would help our fathers shovel our sidewalks or do the job ourselves, but then set off in unison throughout the neighborhood with snow shovels in hand, us treasure searching to dig up a bunch of money. Working as a team, the three of us could clear a sidewalk in mere minutes and those winter days when a decent mid-Atlantic snowstorm dumped on Baltimore, we made darn good money.

Through elementary and into middle school, seven days a week my early morning routine was the same: I'd awake before sunrise, get dressed, grab my bike, and unwrap the bundle in front of my house left by the Baltimore Sun newspaper delivery truck. A large canvas bag was issued for lugging the papers around. Folding the stack of daily periodicals into thirds, a rubber band secured each one or if Mother Nature challenged my day's delivery with rain or snow, a clear plastic bag was utilized, tying the top securely and saving the thrifty rubber bands for nicer weather. With my billowing shoulder bag loaded, I'd set off on my bike to do work, riding about a mile to reach my delivery area. Leaving the house I bombed down the steep Pimlico Road hill in the dark. Coming home I'd ride the longer way around near the fire station and past Luckman Park because I could pedal up that hill, but not the steep upgrade of Pimlico. The bike I finally bought with my own damn profits from cutting grass, the bike I loved so much, was a single speed BMX bike, this being years before the invention of mountainbikes. If running late from my paper route to get home before school, I pushed my bike up Pimlico Road. I dreaded the hurried uphill route but was thankful not to have a full sack over my shoulder for the hike-a-bike home.

Accountability ran 'round the clock for my Baltimore Sun newspaper customers seven days a week, 365 days a year. One task associated with throwing papers on assigned lawns was collecting monthly fees from subscribers, which I disliked, well, factually I hated that shit. Collecting sucked because per mostly, I did not like any fricking adults, aka Fuck the Adults. Certainly, I tried to avoid talking to them often as possible.

Although my clients intentionally subscribed to the printed news service, number two suck factor of collecting arose when many of them were displeased to have me ring their doorbell asking for money owed.

Two critical life lessons quickly emerged during my dreaded paper collection annoyances, teachings I was thankful to learn in life sooner than later.

1. Firstly, when I found myself trapped doing something I disliked, I happily discovered if putting my positive intention into it, I grew better at the activity every day, thus improving the likeability factor, or least decreasing the suck factor. Meaning, if the chore was required, I tried not to fight it and make shit worse for myself, aka founding concepts of MathTest. Initially I grumbled and blamed others but then realized I was only punishing myself, because no one else gave a fuck. For most of my first collection season, I mumbled horribly when speaking to customers. Although some adults did not care about my soft slurred indistinguishable speak, or they teased me about it, several grownups took the time to address the issue.

These kinder older humans gave me guiding advice and exercised role plays with me, opening and closing the door several times as I practiced and improved my debt collector pitch. In short order, I gained some slight self-confidence once able to better communicate with most people, most of the time.

2. Yes, my organizational and record-keeping skills were important, but more than any other technical aspect of the collecting job, one thing hit me hard and remains with me resoundingly to this day. Collecting life lesson number two is a thing I try to do wherever I go, still…bring a pen. One evening I set out collecting with only my payment ticket book and that's it. I engaged with a customer and for some reason I needed a pen. The client claimed not to have a pen and somehow, I either lost money or had to do extra work later, all because I did not bring a pen with me. Critically for me I learned, wherever I go, for any reason, if meeting with someone or not, bring a pen and actually, bring two.

After a year serving papers on my bike amidst any weather, my regional newspaper boss asked if I wanted to ride in the car with him. This guy was a slight creep stranger to me and although I had doubts, I got in his car anyway. Every morning for over a year he picked me up…we served my route plus five or six more, me especially happy to be inside the car when Mother Nature was raining or snowing on the out of doors. Overall it was a sweet deal because I was gone from home the same amount of time, but the guy paid me extra money to help him. I never told BigBird that my stranger boss man drove me around every morning, hah, my father and I were barely speaking to each other by that time. My paper boss was cool and never pulled any funny business, aka he never laid a inappropriate finger on me.

Prior to my official teenage years, when the Baltimore Sun newspaper route had mostly served its purpose and following several satisfied summers of cutting grass with my own damn mower, I finally began real work. Mister Paul Ankers Senior paid me cash weekly at his automotive machine shop, based on an hourly rate and I put most other hustles to rest. I came home from work dirty as a damaged rat dragged through the sewer, but I loved it. My dirty ratness demanded I take a bath or shower every night before bed, hah, but never for years did my hands really get clean.

Summarizing my early life…in general I learned to fucking earn it, never expecting anything to be easy or given to me freely. I learned to do shit the right way, maybe to excess. I cannot reflect to find where I had a supreme level of excellence pushed on me before working for Sonny. Well, perhaps sometimes more than wanting or needing to do stuff the right way, I chose to do shit the hard way, like trimming lawns with my gardening shears. Well why in the hell would I do that? Hum, was I trying to see if I could handle more suffering and pain than I already had, possibly somewhat self-abusively? Well, factually actually, that notion resonates with me, and is a dynamic I never considered before. Perhaps my stout work ethic arose from my NEED to stay away from home, and therefore, not having any better options, I put everything I had into my work.

Letting My Dirty-Ego Drive

Into my early teens, regularly I allocated some drug money to buy gas and pre-mix oil to go dirtbike motorcycle riding, so long as my bike wasn't broken.

Some days when cutting school and not otherwise preoccupied with multiple decent size mid-day drug deals, I went off midweek moto-ing all day. My buddy David Ankers got a dirtbike too and we rode together often as we could. After my confidence mounted but before possessing enough skill, I chose to neighborhood street ride south, meeting David at his house then we zoomed off towards the trails from there, about two miles away. Normally I left my house traveling due east solo on one way and randomly trafficked roads, directly towards Mount Washington, riding slow all the way to the tracks. But this time we took off past Luckman Park on some of the busiest thoroughfares in the area.

David and I successfully blasted through the traffic light at the three-streets spiderweb intersection of Pimlico Road, Cross Country Boulevard and Greenspring Avenue. Such transport was a bold maneuver in city limits aboard our loudly illegal dirtbikes. With no cops in sight, once through the intersection, I took off speedily. My bike was a Yamaha YZ 125C higher powered and purpose-built machine capable of racing motocross while David owned a Kawasaki KD 100 smaller-displacement recreational trail riding bike. Ripping down the road and brimming with excitement, quickly I got in over my head. I accelerated from the intersection fast, partially thrilled to be heading towards the tracks with David, and partially showing off how fast my bike was. The eastbound section of Cross Country Boulevard we were on became very twisty very fast, and upcoming were several big blind corners in quick succession. I was rapidly accelerating when my bike reached its peak performance zone, a range of optimum conditions called the powerband, and the bike lurched forward unexpectedly. Only scarcely was I in control of the bike. Because of the run-away horsepower force and my inexperience, I was unable to effectively slow down before encountering the bends in the road.

All motorcycles are controlled by the right hand twist throttle on the handlebars. A delicate and powerful positioning of control is required for the operator to properly regulate the throttle. When under hard acceleration of the powerband, commonly I try to hang on by gripping the seat with my knees and thighs well as my hands clenching the handlebars. If I slackened my controlled handhold of my right wrist, potentially I could fall off the bike, so I perceived. So once in the powerband, I could not slow down because of my inability to loosen my death grip on the handlebars, a real world phenomenon called whiskey throttle. Whiskey throttle references the theorized experience of being drunk and wildly out of control at the helm of a motorcycle, same-same as I was, at the time.

Firstly, Cross Country Boulevard curved hard right and I drifted wide to the outside of the turn, almost hitting an oncoming car and practically bouncing off the wrong-side curb. Freaking, I yanked the handlebars to the right, trying to get away from the bad lane curb but then, I was cutting back across the road at a horrible angle and still traveling fast. David was behind me watching this crazy runaway horse ride gone wild, and the entire ordeal quickly evolved into a ticking time bomb.

I was on a crash course with the right-side curb, zero doubt about the outcome.

Still in whiskey throttle mode, my front wheel greeted the correct curb at a weird angle, with the bike close to full speed. I was thrown apart from my machine with great force, and the moto flipped end over end. I was lucky for the resulting angle that the bike hit the small but stationary concrete road barrier, because the impact sent the 200-pound machine spinning in the air to my left, instead of barreling towards the back of my head. Meanwhile, my body rag-dolled straightforward into the thick woods. Miraculously I did not hit a tree as I rocketed into the forest at 40 MPH, my frame coming to final rest against the backstop of a tree. Reeling in pain and failing every effort to stand, I attempted a determination of my injuries while trying to gain my orientation. Looking around to find where my bike landed, I heard David quickly approaching. He came to a screeching halt, threw his kickstand down, turned off his engine and was yelling "holy shit-holy shit," while running over to pull my crashed motorcycle out of the street.

I could barely move, awhile had the wind knocked out of me. My left leg was really messed up, I presumed it broken, because it sure felt that way. Immediately my knee swelled up like a balloon. David got my bike upright and wheeled it to the curb not far from me. David asked firmly loud if I was ok, but I was off and apart in the woods somewhere, so he could not see my answer.

The pain flooding my body plus a lack of usable breath did not allow me to speak right away, I was trying to determine what was amiss...I shook my head to answer David a hidden side to side no and pulled the now-fogged goggles from my face.

David crouched down to even locate my position then scrambled into the woods after me. Now both of us were extremely disappointed, we would not be making it to the trails today. My left leg was surely broken, and no way could I walk a single step. David helped me up, acting as my human crutch and dragged me to my bike. Before any cops showed, I wanted to get the hell out of there. Thankfully we acted speedily to get me back and seated on my moto because I was losing mobility by the second. Perhaps I should have remained awaiting medics, but I wanted to avoid the cops regardless of bodily harm. David held my entire person steady as I kickstarted the bike with my operational right leg. Positioning the transmission in second gear, my buddy pushed me off and got me rolling.

With my left leg sticking out in front, I rode home then not giving a shit about cop cars or the mounting pain. My forks were twisted badly but the bike was still rideable. While holding the handlebars straight, the front wheel was positioned about 40 degrees to the left, so in order to ride forward, my handlebars were turned severely to the right. It was extremely awkward. Riding fast as I could in only second gear, David caught up to me quickly then rode ahead looking out for traffic. No way could I stop without falling down again because of unable to use my left leg for support. While my pal was apart from me, I took the opportunity to let a few tears roll down my face. Fearing a long recovery, I also recognized the upcoming added delay to my yearned-for off road racing career, a planned life track that might be the only thing capable of saving me from myself.

The while, I forecasted my father to demand I get rid of the motorized two-wheeler. For a sunny day that began with anticipation, the proverbial clouds rolled in, and gloom began to blanket me.

David was off his bike ready to catch me as I rolled to a stop in my driveway. By this time my leg felt twice as bad as it did only minutes before. David put my moto away in the small storage shed under our side steps and helped me inside. I mostly got out of my dirtbike clothes and prepared for a trip to the hospital. Stretched out on the living room sofa and waiting for my father to come home, I feared more BigBird's reaction to the perceived harm of the motorcycle than the severity of my physical injuries. My father arrived home, but withheld no outward judgements or punishment. I assume he knew my recovery from such an injury will be lesson enough.

Hospital x-rays showed no fractures, they drained my knee of excess fluid, placed a large Velcro brace on my knee and sent me home on crutches, non-weight bearing. Several days later I attended an appointment with an orthopedic specialist and torn ligaments were determined. No surgery was recommended but I was required to spend the next eight weeks in a full-length plaster cast, for most of the summer as it was. Such time simultaneously included our vacation to the Boyne City cabin. I spent two weeks shoving a disassembled coat hanger down into my cast because of the bad itching below. Held captive on the edge of Lake Charlevoix, yours truly navigating crutches in the sand, and not able to go in the water was far more torture than enjoyment. I grew slightly bitter sitting on the beach watching my sisters frolic in the shallows of the lake, then tried to assemble some kind of resulting life lesson from it all.

I have not had problems with my left knee since, other than three or four flare ups of bursitis, twice requiring a doctor to drain my knee. Today, knock on wood, the left knee is strong and I have no internal soft tissue residual problems, save for the disaster zone of my left foot.

I mindlessly let my dirty-ego twist the throttle that day, showing off for David which gained me nothing except two months of mounting bitterness with self. I became much more conscious of such actions in the future.

I would continue to amass injuries because of my intensity and sense of responsibility to perform, but only a few more times would I get hurt because I let my dirty-ego drive.

Chapter Six Footers
Lightless Liner Notes
Lightless is not the most screwed up poem this here my hand ever penned. The chapter precursor piece however is particularly applicable, articulating what lurks within when shining the truth flashlight back upon my most exposed self. This is a first-person-to-self-poem specificating and front face addressing my dastardly monsters. These are my personal monsters and also, some slight creep occurred from outside influences.

I once ran from my monsters. I do not run from my monsters, aka my pains and my fears, anymore. I once hid. I do not hide from what hurts me or threatens me, anymore. I hid from the world, and I hid from myself between the ages of four and 25. During those 20-plus years, I was on the run and tried to hide in darkness during periods when thinking I could escape the shadow. I consider 20-plus years a long time, especially during my formative years, by my measure. In December 2005, although I was not on the run from any big mean bully monsters at the time, I sought cover and sat hiding with the Devil, sharing in his tainted toiled and troubled tea, thus hiding from myself and my depression. After your momma's tryster with a man who was not her husband, well, I let my hurt impact me profoundly.

I launched thyself over mine the emotional edge…then tumbling, then falling.

I landed in mine the deep dark well, filled five feet eleven inches tall of the Devil's Water, with mile high straight up stainless steel slippery sidewalls, walls not at all good for climbing. Under-mine the shadow however, I did not hide from the world because I had jobs to do. I had you two under my wing and over 100 people relying on me to make good on my paycheck. Finally, I arose into she the glorious sunshine when I found and practiced true forgiveness for your mother bird. Alas I remained splashing about in the shallow end of the Devil's pool, two years' time past accepting your ginger hot momma back into my heart.

On the 17th of April in the year 2011, once reaching rock bottom within the Devil's bottle, I broke his dastardly drunk container, stepping then into the sober light. I consider five years drunk off my fatherly ass a horrifically long and tragic, tragic, tragic time in your formative years, by my measure. Yet however, several years later and after three months into the new marriage number two, I got separated from the light once more after wife two's sexy-sexy with a man who was not her husband.

During those thine the most recent emotional dark-dark-dark days, I saw not even this my hand in front of my then spiritless face. Fuck to the no, I did not return to the drugs or drink, but factually an even more vicious adversary arose. Reprehensibly, I covered and cowered within my darkest place, fucking ever. I collected my travel vouchers and was enroute to my permanent vacation with the Prince of Darkness himself, I did not care, I cared for nothing, not a single darn anything.

The Lightless writing was started then paused, and restarted on and off for sixteen months or so, then afterwards the piece remained in a weird state of modified fluctuation for over a year. I was near the bottom of my emotional barrel throughout most of 2017 and finished my Lightless poem to self on October 13th, not long after Lexie killed herself on September 11th that same dark-dark-dark fucking year.

The Fantastical Non-Flying Rodent

How did my youth serve me? Both parental units did as they could, still and all they did as they did. They did all they were capable of and also what they thought was best at the time. As did my grandparents, my teachers and friends. From my earliest days I challenged my ability to do or do not. I endeavored, I tested but then…also I ran. I broke, fell, and cried.

Thereupon then, I rose. I rose, I got up. I woke every day and did what I could. I learned fright and I learned fear beyond all else.

I believe my miss was not stretching the minimal ponder time to linger there longer, aka me not staying a while when being self-inquisitive to better figure more shit out. But no, wait up hum…no way can I even now see how, how an opportunity for me existed to slow, calm, and give inner peace a chance. Absolutely yes I blew by a missed path or three, but I stayed true to all I held inside awhile saw with my own eyes outside of this here bag of bones human contraption, at the time. Hah, alter my past? Shoulda, coulda, woulda, didn't. Collectively, this chapter six is NOT one I would go back and change one milli-micro-nano, fuck to the not even if holding the wizard's magic wand to do so, no frick-or-frack way, it could have been so much worse.

Sadness resides within still, I have no choice.
And yet no longer handicapped, I rise.
I won't grow, until I get up and go.
Life will not be the same, only different.

Youthfully, Beth and I only ventured across Hillsdale for unique events at our father's church. My best friend middle sister and I collected rocks and several times we set up a folding card table on our allowable side of the monster house street, trying to be entrepreneurs and launch our own retail rock shop. We also tried our hands with a lemonade stand or two over time, with little success. One year I received my own film camera as a present, and Beth got one too. For weeks we walked around our Howard Park neighborhood taking photos of all kinds of stupid shit. The highlight was finding a dead squirrel in our neighbor's yard and we both shot almost an entire roll of film featuring the lifeless bushy-tailed rodent.

The hefting bulk of my youth was only pain, nightmares, and daytime frights.

The best of times from when our mother lived with us in the monster house amounted to the celebrated photo shoot with our prestigious model, the dead squirrel.

Seven

~

School's Out, Forever

Truant in this here life. My supreme stupidity at the helm, but thine hare-brained
hoodlum adventures reckoned to be extremely educational all the same.

If existence were a song would I hear what it said

If life were a dream would I push it aside

If love were a riddle could I see it two different ways

If sunset were a clock would I roll it forward so to always be early

If friendship were a prize would I remember where I won it

If pain were a treat could I taste the sweet past the bitterness

If the future were certain, would I even try?

If I do not rise

If I choose to stay fallen

If I do not stand

I will remain, where I do not desire to stay

My heavy cloak of dread is perhaps the suit clinging to me all the while

My shoulders weaken but it is not my arms that make the difference

It's not my need that moves me

It's not my choice that fits me

It's my heart that decides

My legs awaken when I want it bad enough, and willing

If I want to see smiles I need to open my eyes.

Chapter Seven, School's Out, Forever ~

Six seconds after I walked outside, I walked right back in. Figuring a recanted job offer would arise once I spoke up, barely did I know how to start.

Although Sonny didn't see me at first, he approached after noticing my reentry. Holy fuckballs, immediately I understood something brand new, something remarkable, Sonny Davis possesses superhuman powers, legit, super...human...powers.

Now heading my way, Sonny accurately proclaimed my body language. Straight up, he was now behaving whole fucking heartedly out of character. Sonny knew something that no one else could know but me. He now felt what I felt. Sonny absorbed what I held invisibly in my hands. He changed to match my behavior. Sonny completely transformed in an instant...warm, soft, open, and approachable. Within the blink of an eye and with no one saying a word, Sonny knew, he fricking knew.

For the multitude of years as my young punk customer self, and even during the previous quick new-hire chat, Sonny was rather gruff, invariably gruff, it was his way. Sonny was rather abrasive on many levels, although he was doing what he thought was correct, by his measure. Now I am totally judging but through my eyes, Sonny consistently behaved like a big shot.

However still, walking right back into the store after my awkward dismissal, I tried to hide what I needed to say, least until the moment I actually needed to start saying it, I tried, I really tried, but Sonny saw straight through me, aka emotional x-ray vision superhuman powers.

A foreign Sonny walked up close, huddled into my personal space, and didn't say a single goshdarn word, he motionlessly stood there. In proximity I felt genuine warm and caring concern from him, and truth be dialed in tight, concern unlike I had ever experienced before, ever, from fricking anyone, fricking ever. Holy crap, Sonny practically stepped into my shoes, figuratively literally and every other kind of gosh-dang-it worldly way...his body position perfectly mirrored mine. Fucking hell, I could not believe it, Sonny knew, he understood, he fucking knew.

Without even a nano-second hesitation, Sonny did exactly as I did although he was not even looking at me, his eyes were entirely elsewhere, he was not imitating me, Sonny became me...we existed there together, as one.

Sonny sheepishly looked upon the floor as I did, both hands in his pockets as I did, shoulders rolled forward as mine were, hunched over and desolate as I was. Our eyes focused on the exact same spot on the floor.

Addressing our shared mark on the carpet and now in this new-to-me loving tone he asked with a pre and post pause, "…Are you ok?…". I said I think so. He said "Good, that's good, that's what's most important, more than everything else, I'm glad you're ok."

Softly, his left hand reached out of his pocket. His arm came at me slowly, so to make sure it announced itself, out loud. And in plain sight, so to be noticed, so not to be ignored, cautiously inch-worming towards me, and with a quick bounce-poke-jab of my right held away arm, he tagged me, like meaning to say…'you're it'.

He restarted his spoken word, "Now, tell me what just happened…let me help."

I was actively still choking on my own tongue, knowing I would not be able to respond for least thirty seconds…I tried to pull my shit together.

It was, without an iota of doubt, the single most tender moment I've shared with an older-than-me adult in my life, ever, motherfucking ever, still, fucking even still.

I could do nothing but squirm in place with my chin down, wildly unsettled and shaking my head every which way to the no.

Ingloriously, and I was struggling to hold back the other radical feelings almost spilling from my mouth, but, well…I was willing to admit only one singular issue to my brand new like just minutes ago he hired me fulltime boss Sonny, for now.

Hah, I recall soundly this my humble entry into the rat race…after I was done with school, followed by months of downward-bird depressive drug use, I assumed I would begin work at the bike shop, but I was mistaken. This bird lacking the working rudiments and I had to go away and weather my wings a while, aka wait a year. Getting my first fulltime job at Princeton Sports Baltimore seemed like a foregone conclusion, because Sonny told me several times over the course of the previous few years, I had a job if I wanted it. My error was though, I did not know what I did not know. My ears collected no clues of contingencies or prerequisites, so I gathered I could start whenever I was ready. Oops, I showed up and was informed, oh sorry…they don't hire anyone under the age of 17.

I stewed for months afterwards, miffed the critical-to-me details were withheld or least not shared earlier, but maybe it was my own stupidity at work and I was not listening, most likely the latter. Finally on Tuesday March 3rd, my 17th birthday, I borrowed Beth's 10-speed bike and rode to Princeton, expecting to formally accept the previous offer of employment, least I hoped this to be the case. The conversation went fast, not even a meeting, and certainly not an interview. I received two simple instructions and that was it…show up the following day at 9:30 AM but no later, and enter through the side door.

I had questions, I had so many questions, but both Sonny and the bicycle department manager Jim Wayne brushed me off, dismissing my inquiries, saying we can talk tomorrow. I felt gracious to get the job without jumping through additional hoops. I was dreading another let-down…would I be ineligible due to a simplistic assumption, like holding a high school diploma, like having my own car, which I had neither. For several seconds I stood frozen in place dumbfounded, fighting the missing answers in my head.

I was clueless about the job responsibilities and void of various workplace expectations. Put off by their dismissal of me and then my wrangles…you know, the facts I felt necessary to understand before punching-in tomorrow, well, hum, I guess…I guess there was nothing left to discuss.

Sonny and Jim walked away abruptly and once feeling stupid, I assumed it was time for me to leave too. Powerfully I desired to chase after Sonny, desperate for at rock-bottom one or two clarifications but no, I kept my bird beak buckled. Sucking up The Great Subliminal Dismissive, I left the store.

Well, I think, well, well, oh screw it, and I walked right back in.

Willing to only admit one thing to my hopeful to be new boss Sonny, I dropped my chin and stared somewhere near my feet with heartbroken confusion. Then looking down at our community targeted floor mark, and with Sonny already huddled in close, me now almost in tears I said, "Somebody stole my bike".

Bloody hell, I did not know what I wanted to do at first. Maybe call the police. Maybe try to catch the bike robber. Maybe use the phone and call my father for a ride, or oh screw it, just ask these guys to please give me a fricking lift home, fucking shitbird hell and all. Uh…my brain pixilated blindly. I never had anything personal stolen from me before. Yes and oh sure to be certain I got ripped off and mugged numerous times, but not something like this. This innocently functional thing that once now gone, its absence unexplainably disrupted my life. Actually hold up hum, dang it, a higher critical path then presented itself to me…how will I explain to my best friend sister Beth that someone stole her bike, precisely when I was supposed to be caring for it with my 'I Promise' watchful eye?

The feelings of violation flooded me in bizarrely unremarkable ways. The rawness of sheer abuse cut me in the dark, I never saw it coming…someone swooping in and gaining possession of my functional belongings, then off they were, into the poof of pitch hidden hood. Their dastardly lack of remorse, zero consideration for the owner who might have treasured the now-gone thing. This here my now-gone thing was not left out for public collection, not offered openly for their merriment. Although, oh crap wait up a silly second, I am totally talking out of the fake side of my face…I did my fair share of ripping shit off too, this is, hum…presumptively I spy…thieving karma.

Sonny sprang into action, making good on his offered-up wanting to help. Then dragging in his son Paul, who is Alan's younger brother, Paul was instructed by his boss-dad to drive me around and try to find the Son of a B*, them being Sonny's exacting however abbreviated non-swearing words, who stole my sister's bike. Alan and Paul, although appearing as rather preppy upper-class suburban white guys and besides owning healthy bloodline-egos themselves, it appeared obvious AF that neither of them would hesitate one city-second to throw punches if the situation warranted, especially big badass bro Alan. So then anyway there it was…Paul and I zoomed around in his car speedily, one of the Davis family's favorite play-racecar-driver pastimes, but we saw nothing of Beth's brown Schwinn Continental roadbike. Dreading the arrival and admission to my sister, yours truly now defeated, I asked Paul to please just drive me home, so I could get that mess of a reveal over with.

Beth was not happy to have her bike become then nothing but stolen, no not at all.

Although hers was a nice bike, my best friend little sister did not seem to hold a grudge. Nevertheless, I felt horrifically pathetic for leaving home with her bike then returning without it. Moreover, I then dispossessed enough compassion and common sense to ever replace it, aka me the lame-ass brother bird. I sure did learn however and mostly-most def to a T, to lock my shit up after that though.

One more crumb to collect…why for goodness sake was my bird brain convinced of Sonny's job offer recanting after I walked right back in?

With such low grade self-belief vacantly lingering throughout me, I thought Sonny would join my labeling party of Stupid Bird Boy and laughingly wave me off…like if I'm dumb enough to get my bicycle stolen from the bicycle shop in less than ten minutes, then I cannot, should not, probably not be trusted with a real big boy job.

When Sonny hired me, no assumptions on my part needed to then apply for my superpowers boss to know that my life was a mixed-up mess at the time, because he knew me way better, I was a customer of his for over five years prior. Maybe around the time I was 13, Sonny began joking…I should work there and learn how to put my bike back together myself, so I can spend my hard-earned money on wiser things. When arriving the previous year at sixteen, me possessing two handfuls of money grabbing presumption, I thought I was welcome to start anytime I wanted. Although Sonny was maybe teasing me amid those further backup years, I heard his words arrive upon me as a legitimate job offer.

Once finally waltzing in to accept my treasureful first fulltime position though, Sonny popped my pretty balloon of assumption.

I limped home with my still-unemployed tail between my skinny bird legs while honestly, I did not want to get to work like anywhere, and held no ideas of how it all like flowed anyway…the fulltime employment thing because duh, I never held a big-boy job before so what the hell did I know, I knew a whole hell of a lot of nothing. Like what happens when I get hungry, what am I supposed to do, no clue. Will I be allowed to eat lunch? I do not think they can say no to eating. Where do I eat, outside? Must I go off the property? Is there a hidden location somewhere in the store where I might be allowed to eat quickly? Must I bring cold food or am I disallowed to bring any food, hah…sans-bird-clues. So maybe the go home for a year and grow up reality played to my advantage, at the time.

I did not want to grow up, not really at all although sometimes I was indifferent on the entire fricking matter and every fucking other thing too, yeah right exactly…somedays I didn't care to even be breathing. After the false start stop company-policy-imposed-banishment from Sonny's shop for a year, well then, I had to sort out another fricking way to get me some real fricking bucks, toot fucking suite. My addiction had grown god awful stupid expensive and already I ran dead end into most open avenues to finagle cash.

Months flipping long it had compiled…I banked on the fulltime job thing at Princeton and irresponsibly maxed out my fronting deals, aka my dealers giving me drugs in exchange for my future promise to repay them. Then obviously, my fucking financial future far as I could fricking see it, well, such shit just derailed.

The biohazard cleanup from those drug loans gone wrong trainwreck was a noxious fucking mess.

Blackeye

Alan Davis was supremely fucking pissed off, it was obvious, him all up in my face and deep into my personal proximity and shit. What the frick bro, I didn't do anything wrong. My like-always supportive vice-boss Alan, oh crap, he then pulled his shit back in a manner I instantly recognized and what the fucking fuck, Alan cocked into ready-fire position, him preparing to punch me as we stood just inches apart there on the Baltimore shop sales floor.

Although white rich and preppy as fuck, Alan echo-held proper street cred. Alan Davis had seen a thing or three, and it was crystal fucking clear he already utilized his fists out around town before, you could tell. He was mid to late 20's, and I was 17. Hanging around enough of that about to strike shit to know better, I try to keep an eye out for such offensive and threatening body language but hah, I did not expect to see this fucked-up shit at work. Before able to exit blackeye range, mine or his, Alan was barking sternly using a scary but faintly regulated inside snarl volume…"Do you own a suitcase capable of holding twelve days of clothes?" What, say what…initially I could not respond remotely close to the vicinity of comprehensive bird blabber, I was so confused, like totally trapped in a full blown brain-tilt-a-whirl. Immediately I slipped my handy invisible nametag back on…STUPID…I am so stupid, I am so dumb, why am I so fricking lost with what's happening right now? Generally throughout my loser-loser lowlife loser existence then-thus far, I thought to provide no value to the world in any way whatso no fuck way ever, and my self-deflating thoughts amassed quickly in similar situations as this one. Alan's code language, or maybe it was his conflicting word-action movements, but he baffled me entirely.

That is, until he said that *Sonny and I see promise in you, great promise*. Oh shit goddamn it and fuck me down to the ground, my eyes welled up woefully fast. Alan continued that if I owned no such luggage, he would cover it because they are providing me with an all-expense paid scholarship to attend the prestigiously premier Schwinn Bicycle Factory Service School in New Jersey. I was speechless, and rather embarrassed to wipe away the second through tenth tear from my face in front of my fake fighting boss Alan. Fact literal, I could not fricking talk.

Proudly, and quite warmly, Alan immediately softened up and stopped playing mad. He switched gears to the accurate and appropriate position of the sweet and supportive big brother boss, relaxing his shoulders and everything. Schwinn School was a stone-cold legit and intense 10-day training and certification program, teaching us would-be professional bicycle mechanics everything we need to know, every little thing.

Alan spelled it out…Wilbert and Tommy previously attended the factory technician program, both of them graduating Schwinn School successfully, and yes, his sweet old grandmother Lucille also went through the program and earned her own diploma. Damn, she's even more bad ass than I gave her credit for, Grandma Lucille is so fricking cool. Alan startled me somewhat but was forthcoming and helpful to say that no class has achieved a 100% graduation rate because the curriculum moves along at a rapid pace, and the course material is no joke, aka that shit's hard. I stopped short of attaching myself to a preconceived notion of either passing or failing Schwinn School. Rather, I was ridiculously excited to participate and learn everything I could, especially wanting to expertly overhaul them troublesome internally geared three-speed rear hubs, well as create precision wheels from nothing but a stand-alone rim, hub, and pile of spokes.

Once inside the huge Schwinn manufacturing warehouse, I kept up with the rapid curriculum but could not distract for a single second. Quite literally I did not drink water during the day, fearing I would miss critical instruction while running to the factory bathroom. The first day I mistakenly brought a waterbottle to class then sprinted to the urinal, washed and sprinted back, struggling to catch up to missed parts of the lesson plan zipping along without me while off on my bio break.

Comprehensively, I arrived in New Jersey barely knowing but a few among the myriad of required functional complexities. The preciseness of the upcoming final exam requiring exact execution of set-up, troubleshooting and adjustment tasks was daunting. Clearly, not all students were so focused, skilled, or even lucky. Our class size was about 15 and tragically, three attendees were denied graduation, then forced to as it may play out…too bad true sad, try again at a later time. My feelings forlorn for my peer but failed students who went home empty handed, albeit carrying their gained mechanical skills. Briefly I tried to imagine myself amongst them…how would I feel standing here now, not allowed to step on stage, how would I feel going back to Sonny and Alan after flunking Schwinn School? A humble humility flooded me and I felt ridiculously relieved to graduate the intense program. Similar to the prestige and higher earning potential automotive technicians gain today because of training and certification, well, back in the day, same was true for bicycle technicians graduating Schwinn School. Emotionally challenged to form the words within my head more or less clack them out, but I must share the keyboard revelations realized only now, 38 years later.

Sonny The Great Influencer, Sonny The Tyrannical gave me something.

Sonny did something for me that no one ever did for me in my life before, ever.

Sonny gave me something I never deserved before.

Sonny gave me something I never earned before, or could have purchased.

Sonny gave me the only diploma I ever received for anything before, ever.

For the first time in my life I recognized the genuine value of a hard fought graduate diploma.

All I possess for my Schwinn Factory Service School diploma is still the proudest academic accomplishment of my life, and one of my most prized possessions.

Not only did Schwinn School afford me a slight sliver of dignity and validation, but also kickstarted a career and livelihood I might have missed otherwise. I received my framed certificate only weeks after my graduating high school classmates received their own Baltimore City Public School System diplomas.

While the rest of the world conceivably treats these framed high school cutouts like self-evident human operating license handouts, everybody gets one for simply showing up, hah, and to say hey look at me, duh, of course I am not a lowlife loser dummy dropout like are you kidding me or what, a some sort of entitled high-priced receipt for presumptive higher learning…however for me or someone like me, for someone who has never had one, a diploma, my feelings of gratitude for Sonny and Alan Davis, well, my grace and appreciation exists far beyond any possible written word my fingers could clack, ever. I have skirted and navigated this societal presumption for the bulk of my life, high school diploma, sometimes skirting it uncomfortably, while 99.97% of the people around me joke about it. Maybe even, some of my sisters and brothers sling ridicule and blame aimed at the lame-ass losers without one, yes the lame losers precisely like me. At times it appeared more comprehensible for me to lie, telling people I never learned how to read, rather than admit I never finished high school.

Sonny gave me something, something incredibly powerful and unique, something I am sure even he took for granted, but not fucking me.

Within the eyes and faces of my classmates who failed final testing at New Jersey Schwinn School I tasted the tears of their pain, them going home without proof they learned anything at all in the last week and a half. It was neither a foregone finale nor a framed participatory award. While it may be dismissed by some as only a leftover coat check tag from a 10-day circus playdate, hah…trying to show adult grease monkeys how to precisely adjust a plethora of derailleurs and build precision bicycle wheels from scratch, well, mine is the one piece of paper I honestly treasure more than all others. If my house were burning down, and I could save only one piece of paper, while some might grab their birth certificate or favorite photo, I believe I would grab my Schwinn Factory Service School diploma, and I have Sonny and Alan Davis to thank for that.

Intruder. When my coworker Mark Schloschnagle and I first walked into our shared New Jersey hotel room Sunday night before the first day of Schwinn School, I realized someone made a mistake. We misguidedly landed in the wrong place, so I turned around and walked out quickly. Incorrectly and somehow, our key opened somebody else's room. I was embarrassed, then speedily headed down the hall while Mark poked around in the vacant room assigned to: Not us. Heading for the front desk to grab the correct key, I heard shouting behind me, "Roger come back, come back it's for us".

Upon initial entry, I spied a large fancy bottle of sparkling something and a bountiful fruit basket sitting there so I immediately spun around and exited, knowing for fact this was not our room. Disoriented after Mark called me to return, I walked back towards the puzzling scene. Before reaching the rented door, I heard Mark talking loudly.

Who the hell is he talking to...oh, he was reading the gift card, "Dear Roger and Mark, Do a great job at Schwinn School, we know you will. We are very proud of you both. Have fun. Sincerely, Your Princeton Sports family." The generosity and thoughtfulness of the basket bottle and card blew me away. I was shocked because such kindness was so foreign to me, and so unexpected. Never before had I experienced such a caring and surprising gift, fucking never. Clearly, somebody back at Princeton thought more of me than I did myself, and I knew it to be Alan and Sonny.

Besides the multitude of lifelong business lessons learned from Mister Bernard Sonny Davis, the people relationships I gained at Princeton far surpassed the loving caring and supportive family dynamic I experienced anywhere else, ever...still.

A Day Like That

Even on a day like that, a superbly stellar bluebird day, I discarded the fricking weather good or bad, and woke the fuck up. I learned to start living with my eyes more open, trying to establish an escape route wherever I went, trying to expect more of the unexpected, and trying to be more prepared for most any fricking situation. My sister's boyfriend Jimmy had been playing in the water with the other guys and never saw the back-and-forth argument between me and Johnny up on the railroad bridge trestle. Jimmy had no idea what earlier transpired before he and Johnny then dove off the trestle to race over to the stupid fucking floating picnic table bobbing around in Lake Roland. Quite certain I would never blurt out the details to Jimmy unprovoked, but I would abso-fucking-lutely come clean if he ever asked me.

Once showering the somewhat skank lake water off my person, clothes changed, and moderately stoned, I jumped on my bike and rode back to the trestle. The police, rescue, and ambulance teams were all there, best they could because of the remote and hard to reach location, all of them there due to me and my idiotic stupidity. There was a Baltimore County police boat in the water, but a stander-by told me they already recovered the body, a young man who was very dead, and whose skin was very blue. Memorially, like no sirens, another ambulance already took him away, so I was told.

My big sister Laura and Jimmy then broke up not long after Johnny's drowning. I never saw my sister's boyfriend Jimmy again following the beautiful summer day at Lake Roland when I killed his friend Johnny Powell. I can barely imagine the desperate terror knowing I do not possess the capacities to keep myself afloat atop the surface of a large body of water, the desperation like Johnny just went through. I am not a strong swimmer. I was not in the fricking lake during the horror show playout and maybe if I was, my family would have mourned that day too.

In some ways and by my own measure, I tend to care about many things and certainly, I have proven my willingness to throw around my own beating heart to do what I believe is right at the time. I knew my limits and from where I was atop the trestle that day, I could have barely gotten out there before Johnny went under the final time. It was horrific to watch, actually, it was absolutely fucking brutal to watch.

We do, or we do not do, what we think is right at the time, even if it appears as stupid to others.

That day under the warm sun of a Baltimore summer, we tried to save Johnny from drowning, we tried in the ways we each thought was best. I do not think any of us want to witness the end of human life because it forces us to face our own immortality. None of us wanted to lose Johnny Powell that day, none of us fucking no one. We wanted Johnny to walk out of the water, joking, laughing, carrying on, and continue to live in a way he chose.

To go back and do some things over, I believe we would all try to do better and be smarter, to save ourselves and those around us, if possible.

I have never been comfortable in deep water because of the limitations to keep myself afloat. I am not scared of water, but have a sensible respect for it. I still carry a mildly weird responsibility for Johnny's death. I have mostly worked through the immediacy of self-blame, living to learn and accept the factual reality and shrinking guilt of Johnny's drowning, but the journey hard, very-very fucking hard.

Truth be crystal, Johhny Powell would have never gone in the water that day if not for me, absolutely no doubt. Yes I would have continued as a committed drug addict regardless of this and the other senseless fucking death I myself legit-caused a few weeks before, but I think I then asserted a moderate amount of increased self-blame and shame than otherwise. Johnny's drowning not only poked an unrepairable hole in my heart but also opened my eyes more to the fact that life is precariously fucking razor thin precious, even on a beautiful summer day like that, a day that seemed perfect.

I have carried a well-stocked first aid kit in my car since just after Johnny died, and I rely on the medical bag numerous times every year. Come winter, I carry tow straps, hooks, towing hardware along with an avalanche shovel, work gloves, and a junk blanket to help cars get unstuck from the snow. A couple times per winter I utilize the straps, probably saving the citizens thousands of dollars on an otherwise expensive tow truck recovery service call. Twice I have rescued drunk people amidst negative temperatures and in the dead night of winter after their cars slid off Cottage Grove Road and careened into one of the snowy farm fields. Least one or maybe both of those individuals could have perished if I didn't see their half-buried taillights and stopped to help, opposed to the other drivers who passed by before me. Regarding both of those intoxicated incidents, I perhaps acted recklessly to get them out of there quickly before cops arrived, refusing to attempt an extraction of their car from the snow but rather speedily drove their drunk ass's home. One was an older guy I practically carried inside and put him to bed, leaving keys and a note on his kitchen counter about where to find his abandoned car the next day.

Because of my intent to help others, I switch to burly winter snow tires long before the white stuff hits the ground. I carry a medium sized, five pounds net fire extinguisher in my truck and already used it once, probably saving the brother human's vehicle from burning to the ground.

I replaced then also refilled that extinguisher, now keeping the spare in the entryway of my cabin. In my wood stove main living area I have two more five-pound net extinguishers, prominently positioned with signage. In my wood fire heat detached garage I have two fire extinguishers, also with bright red identifying placards. In my pocket most everywhere I go I carry a fresh Narcan apparatus. I am absolutely ready and able with a sanitized CPR mouthpiece inside a zippered pouch, conveniently waiting inside the console of my truck. Even sans-mouthpiece, I would not hesitate to lay my hands and mouth on a stranger to help rescue their life, I absolutely would not fucking hesitate.

When around water, I am hyper alert to the presence or absence of life jackets, a rescue rope, or an emergency call button. About two weeks after Johnny Powell drowned, I made the firm fucking commitment to jump into the motherfucking water next time without hesitation to help save someone, even at the risk of silencing my own thumping heart. One day it might not arise as a surprise if my obituary tells the tale how I drowned trying to help rescue someone, hopefully after I securely saved their life. Maybe I should now learn to swim proper, but alas I choose to do this introspection writing and the other things instead as my higher priorities.

You both and your mom and Stephanie and Nora are all listed in my sans password iPhone with ICE prefixes, so first responders can find and contact you quickly, In Case of Emergency. The purpose-built Road ID bracelet I wear on my right wrist holds critical life and contact information, connecting helpful citizens to you both my dear children my lovelies my precious.

I solidly believe I still owe the world something…I think I owe somebody something for something I did or did not do along my way.

I believe much of what I do now is because of my frantic feelings atop the trestle so long ago. These being the same types of things I frantically fucking searched for unsuccessfully…a reclusive rescue rope or stick, or life preserver when I wanted desperately to save Johnny Powell, just after I pushed him to go into the water. My intention and my aim is to not let another human life slip through my motherfucking fumbling fingers, when I could otherwise possibly help save them. I try to be more prepared than less prepared, because I know how unprepared desperation feels, and I have bled that result.

This Here Chapter Seven, School's Out, Forever
Chapter seven is the second chronological life chapter and the last gathered collection of words in this here your volume numbered one. This now chapter seven period spans the time from dropping out of school at sixteen, up until my mid-twenties near when I finally shook that clinging drug monkey off my back. An amassment of self-discovery and an abundance of reinvention occurred during this time, and numerous life lessons petried-up inside me. Impossible it is for me to cram everything in here, I couldn't even come close to a complete era narration, so if puzzled with questions please let me know, sooner than later. I selectively chose subjects objects and events from this here time period that I think are most relevant to my tale and to your life, by my measure…just so you know.

Grown Up

Pain consumes given the opportunity

Pleasure has a fuse

Love lies prone

Chunks of my heart can no longer speak

Wanting...awhile hiding from it all

The growing up doesn't stop

The closest thing to bliss evolves

Every moment I face something else

I potentially won't say, or lay

I might not fright, nor fight

I may well fall.

Stemmed & Pinned

The guy approached as if he knew me. I guess he kinda did, we had already talked on the phone and arranged this deal. He was rather hip, yet presented as hard. Although he was brimming with a smile a mile wide, I just wanted to get this exchange over with fast and get out of here with my money. His pal was walking up towards me too, but was rather head-down under his hoodie, hands in his front pouch pocket and lingered threateningly about 15 feet behind and to the right of his leader. I rolled up on the sidewalk from the east and they seemed to slink straight out of the darkness, right there on the corner of Northern Parkway and Park Heights.

"You got it?", the main dude asked, and I half-waved the canvas gear bag in my right hand from hanging position up to about my waist as if to say here it is, yeah I got it. It all happened so fast I didn't even see it coming. The guy was being so smiley and engaged that my eyes stayed on him instead of observing his mate who had swiftly swooped in behind me.

A couple days earlier I was in Park Heights-proper buying two grams of cocaine from people I did not know, when the tables got turned and they asked me if I knew where to buy some weed. Startled, I just wanted to leave with my blow and go but they hooked me for an added minute or two. "Yes, how much?", I replied nervously. "A pound" they said and I chuckled out loud slightly with my "No". Saying I could maybe get a quarter pound but it's good stuff and is kind of expensive, I really didn't want to stick around this vibrant characterized drug dealing scene longer than I had to. They said that's great and asked what was my phone number. Hesitating, the guy and another shouldered up close to me as I handed him the $200 while he put two puffy packs of presumed blow into my palm. Just then a gorgeous young lady popped into our huddle, her scent and overall persona was laughingly sexy and I proudly rattled off my father's phone digits to the guy, hoping maybe this gal is the one who later meets up to buy the quarter pound of pot from me. I'd love to know her better. She reminded me greatly of another supermod black girl I went to school with, just darling cute and outgoing. I made some slight chit-chat with the Park Heights dealer girl and as I was leaving she wrapped her left hand around my right bicep strongly and looking up through her batting eyelashes she said thank you. Her spirited brush of hand factually shot an electrifying jolt into me.

Caused by my delinquent dysfunction, I had mostly let the hot chick charge go from my memory when I met the representing guys two nights later. Factually, I don't think the dudes I was standing with on the Park Heights corner and waving the expensive quarter pound at were even the same guys I met previously with gorgeous gal. My show of the big sack of bud was still in motion when THUD- ouch motherfucker, a steel rod got pinned into the stem on the back of my head. Immediately the pungent stinky funk of sweet gunpowder flooded my hair and filled my face. I almost choked from the wave of repulsiveness. Guns were nothing I was attracted to, and this exact scent was one I was emotionally opposed to, because of the frequent threatened presentation of these killing tools in my life.

Smiley guy number one got frighteningly sour immediately, "Hand it over and no smart shit", he pronounced. I did as instructed. Guy one grabbed the bag and spun around as if he had just bought a bag of chips and soda from me the fictitious food cart street vendor, then waltzed away.

Guy two's left hand rushed my body, wrapping around the front side of my waist then back, pushing my arms out of the way and padding down both my side ribs with blazing speed and accuracy, then reached down to also frisk both my ankles. His warm perturbed breath then softly shouted into my left ear, "Stay right the fuck here bitch or I'll fucking cap you".

Keeping my arms out like wings I shook my flustered head side to side slightly because of the rip off and gave him a moderately volumed, "You got it…*asshole*".

He poked the gun barrel harder into the base of my skull and instructed, "Don't be a smartass bitch". All I said from there was a slight '*whatever*' as he pushed off from my neckbone and ran to rejoin his friend. Knowing better, I stayed there motionlessly for about thirty seconds, and I brain-wrangled how the fuck was I going to make up the $600 of fronted weed that was just stolen from me. Then I just slapped my hands down to the sides and walked the fuck back home to Pimlico, enriched with the putrid over-cologne of motherfucking gunsmoke in my hair.

The Half-Baked Notion of Existentialism

Astronomy held tight my sheer wonderment for decades…speechless was I every time looking upon the night's sky, absolutely mesmerized. My desire was to fly amongst the stars, zooming from one edge of the solar system beyond the velocity of light speed, visiting the different planets and oh good, one conveniently only minutes commute to another, like bus stops in the city. Ah to explore space, the place I peer upon every clear night offered me, a world seemingly within reach between the clouds while still that held-away world, far-far from the carbon patch loam I occupy here stomping upon terra firma.

Then also my echo-early when I grow up someday hopes…an oceanographer reminiscent of the floating hours trouncing the seafloor aside my make-believe boss Jacques Cousteau. The collective wonder, adventure, and travel amid the water-breathing creatures grabbed me profoundly and fascinates me still today. This bird thankful to have practiced least a couple shallow underwater explorations, snorkeling trips inside that when-I-grow-up life I long-ago hoped for, location pin drop Bahamas and Jamaica. Funny how the far away and deep places notion grabs my attention so profoundly, being space and the sea floor. But hum, factually actually the list includes two more.

My introspective writing time takes me deep and far away from my objective conscious reality so that's another one, my daybook journals, my many notebooks, and dear clacky. I never realized my connectedness of desire to escape and perhaps stay away from the depthless surface of this here objective earth mass until only now. Never in my youth did I imagine a future grownup mainstream career of fireman, policeman, pro baseball player, or any human role here on land, nope, none. Seems I really wanted to get the heck away…deep undersea or floating amongst the stars, aka far-far away.

The fourth far-away place you ask? Ok, this might be really weird but I've already rattled this shit off several times, the mirror. The mirror…gazing deep, past the surface reflection as I walk on by, past the initial image of me at face value, past the painted piece of glimmering glass on the backside of the pane, past the focused corneas of my blue bird eyeballs, deep-deep within and only after 30 seconds of digging in do I get to where I am going.

Odd these far-off thoughts have not surfaced or caught my attention before…I wonder…I wonder why was I so intent to get away? Was I desiring something so desperately, something I did not currently possess, something so powerful, magnetic and tractor-beam-like drawing me away?

How did my life in the here and now become so unsettled that I desired nothing else but the ultimate ungrounding?

Factually unstitching the issue now under the light of personal truth, although I claim desire to go far away, well, now under dissection, I believe my truth was factually a need, not a desire. Sure, the surface level knee-jerk viewing of my earliest career-quest flee-not-fight beginnings point to the madness of home, but what were the other conditions in play?

While my mother was still at home, although my father's stressful outbursts concerned me, unless he held his belt folded up in his one hand and held me down with the other, I feared BigBird not. After mother Patricia began her downward spiral then check in of the headpiece hospitalizations, my father Ray's unraveling began with gusto. While still in the monster house and before second grade, I was not bullied or troubled in school. No neighborhood boys bothered me and no girls intimidated me too-too much. So by the process of elimination, least as the facts appear to me, I was unsettled in my own skin, within the shoes I occupied and in the location I resided. Impossible to know how much the parental dynamic pushed me away.

Early days as the drugs consumed me, and although unidentifiable at the time, it was a relentless pursuit of something else and away, aiding to shake my otherwise scared stationary self. After ditching the notion of crewing with Captain Cousteau on The Calypso, surely I knew this here bird would be a motorcycle racer.

Alas 'moto racer' was a relatively short-lived dream, stretching to maybe five years total, yet still, never before had I puffed up any life aspirations with such death-defying drive and enthusiasm.

Drowning Thyself

Skinny, not tall, burnout, quiet, not smart, long hair loser and nothing but a pathetic fucking joke is how I physically presented myself to the world, me not fitting in anywhere amongst the smart kids, the jocks, or the other burnouts at school. I also stood defiantly against adults and the judgy authoritarian systems trying to rule me, me as my PABB self: Punk Ass Bitch Bird self.

A year after I dropped out, my height sprang up and almost like Jack's beanstalk in a seeming instant, I was 6'2". My newfound height helped me also walk figuratively a little taller because I was not perceived so much of a weak and scared little kid. I still struggled supremely with self-confidence though, mostly because my future seemed so damn uncertain, and, well, because I felt so alone.

I rode my bicycle around contracting drug deals, and I on and off thought of one day maybe somehow doing some bike racing.

Famously, at Luckman Park barely down the hill from Whitney Avenue and near my friend David Anker's house, there was a sizeable dirt hill, about a 30-foot drop top to bottom. I dreamed up the idea of building a jump at the top of the hill and launching my bike into mid-air. The hill dropped rapidly so riding off this planned jump, I was basically constructing a ramp off a cliff's edge. Looking back, the defying ramp on that drop-away hill was a supremely stupid idea.

There on the cliff's edge of Luckman hill, David Ankers and I stacked two car tires atop each other and arranged another two tires tall next to the first pair. We lugged a full sheet of four-foot by eight-foot plywood from David's house to the park, positioning one of the long ends of the plywood atop the car tires to fabricate our final ramp.

The jump was such a ridiculous setup that David and I rode our bikes home to then return with our hefty motorcycle helmets.

Normally on our bicycles we wore zero safety gear but the new Luckman launch ramp was no normal situation, nope, not even close. By the time we built the ramp, a handful of kids from the park gathered around, and there too was my lovely brother from another Andre aka Dre McDonald. Dre is a dear friend mentioned elsewhere in this here your book. The additional spectator kids wisely were not wanting to do the jump themselves, but they seemed intrigued if we might actually attempt it. By the time David and I had our helmets on, the small group of kids doubled in size. Principally they taunted us…"No way, no way man you gonna jump that, no way". David mouthed-off a little and I said mostly to myself but maybe once out loud…yeah well, just watch.

David wanted to go first so he rode back from the ramp, now a couple hundred feet away and then paused, planning to build up speed before takeoff. Even with a modern day high tech six-inch travel full suspension mountainbike, the jump was slightly hare-brained. Oh no, we were not riding mountainbikes, we were riding our little 20-inch wheeled BMX bikes. David's slightly younger brother Steven was there and he too wanted to jump. I told Steven he should not do it. Once the ramp awaited us, merely the ominous sight of it made me think there was a good chance none of us would take off airborne then make it back safely to earth this day. I did not want to see Steven get hurt. Steven was adamant and then possibly fueled by me telling him no, the junior Ankers boy decided…if we were doing it, then he was for-sure doing it too. David's launch landed him near the flat bottom, normally a really bad outcome, him touching down barely on the downslope of the hill but thankfully didn't crash. David's front wheel slid in the leaves and his tire looked like it almost rolled off the rim, but he made it out alive, thank goodness.

My turn. Unfortunately, much as I thought David was showing off for the other kids who said he wouldn't do it, I was showing off slightly more. Once my front tire hit the ramp and I pulled up slightly, I knew I had too much speed and tried to lean forward, forcing the front of the bike down somewhat. Then realizing I was probably going to land on the flat ground, I tried to level out the bike then held on, wishing for a miracle. I overshot the downward part of the hill, landing on the flat ground, normally some sorta horrific happening but somehow, I didn't wreck.

I reveled in hearing the triumphant screams of health-gambling joy from atop the hill once I landed safely. I rode the access sidewalk back up and around the side of the hill from the bottom, aglow with my gleeful dirty-ego and shit. David said he wanted to go again but Steven got mad, thinking it was now his turn. Against mine and David's better judgment, Steven grabbed his big brother's helmet then pedaled back to get a running start. I was filled with pride and cockiness, and now because of our gleeful spectators, I wanted to go again and show-off some more. After Steven it would be David's turn, but, but then however strangely, I thought I should be done because of the moderate miracle I didn't crash the first time.

Truth be real, I was not so skilled. My first time off the ramp, I closed my eyes once trying to level the bike. Hah, I thought I should be done and not gamble a second time, yes I should be done. Oh shit, oh no...Steven looked unsure of himself while I watched his face approach the ramp. As his velocity appeared to me, the juniorized Ankers did not have enough speed to stay properly mid-air afloat. I almost yelled for Steven to stop, but honestly it happened way too fast.

Realizing I missed my chance to speak up and halt this disaster before it happened, I quickly mumbled to myself, oh well, least he still has his eyes open, he's doing better than me.

Steven landed halfway down the hill, on the safer downslope part and not on the flat ground but then, oh frick, oh shit no, I'm not sure what happened but he crashed pretty bad and we all ran down to help. Although not seriously hurt and able to walk, Steven's leg and arm were both cut up badly. David and I escorted Steven home on foot and momma Sylvia was steaming mad at us for making Steven do it...we caught no breaks from the Ankers house boss on that Snake River Canyon day. David and I disassembled the ramp and moved on to other let's see what kind of shit we can get away with things.

That Evel Knievel-style sky-bound jump at Luckman Park only occurred once and probably a good thing, a good thing for everyone. Already visiting the hospital myself several times, both for various stitches and had broken least one collarbone already, the injuries began to compile but what the hell did I care, I fucking cared none, I was trying to just...keep...moving. A BMX racetrack sat in Hunt Valley, a posh area in Baltimore County and north of the city. For much as I rode bikes, I thought it was about time I try racing. Once holding a valid driver's license, after a while I borrowed BigBird's car and a few friends went with me to the track. As with most other things in my youth, I totally sucked at it. I rode a few practice runs and did solidly fine, but once officially competing in the qualifying races, I performed so horribly that I did not earn a position in the main event. I returned to the track a couple more times but after never once qualifying for a main, I realized BMX racing was not my thing and I gave up, aka I quit that stupid shit as well.

Fuck That Noise

Home life sucked and the precariousness grew daily. My inclination says to blame and hold responsible: Just my own damn doing for the unrest, and quite possibly for fact, maybe so.

Yet, any realizations or self-talk at the time wasn't changing any fricking thing, and the hatred for my family's house kept egging me on. Although my father mostly left me to myself, I became agitated whenever he tried to talk with me or discuss anything about current or future days. The wobbly unhappiness I felt was overwhelming and without even understanding what I was so mad about, I stole BigBird's car.

I do not remember the impetus but while owning no vehicle myself, intermittently using my father's Toyota station wagon for drug deals and such, one day I grabbed the keys and stormed off. Very well the conditions were a sparked conflict launching my family thievery, absurdly it was over nothing except my asinine and adolescent angst. Initially I assumed the orientation of running away. I took with me the only transportable items of monetary value and sold them quickly. My need was rather for life necessities. A small neighborhood record store on Reisterstown Road in Pikesville purchased my beloved vinyl record albums for cash. The entire exchange was moderately gut-wrenching but a higher need pushed its way to the front of the line, food and gas money. My face was entirely perturbed, only gaining pennies on the dollar for my decent recorded music collection, most of the Beach Boys albums ever made plus an array of '70s and '80s favorites. Although previously never thinking to let my music albums go, I needed the damn money, so I took the stinking cash.

I slept at various friend's houses in Pikesville and in the car itself for over a week. I received a message from another friend…if I did not return my father's car by 6pm Sunday night, BigBird was going to report it stolen and let whatever happens happen, aka my father would let them put me in jail and would not be bailing me out this time. Profoundly my reactive thoughts formed, yeah fuck that shit and I fled further, driving three hours east to Ocean City Maryland. After a handful of days down da ocean dere hon, I ran out of money. I signed a promissory note to mail a paltry $2.00 back to the Chesapeake Bay Bridge toll booth authority before letting me travel the 4-mile-long bridge, my only realistic route back to Baltimore. With bare time to spare, I returned the damn car, right at 6pm. I left the keys inside the front screen door then stomped away for another furied fucking two weeks on foot.

The self-shame sacrifice of my record albums is a condition I cannot describe. Perhaps I should give my father credit for not confronting me, because I held so much pent-up frustration at the time. There's no telling what additional stupid shit I might have done if BigBird tangled with me.

The False Start-Stops of Higher Pursuits

After my self-expulsion from high school and struggling to link a few forward momentum footsteps together, several times my father riddled me this…"What's next?". Of course BigBird pushed me not for a plan or even an answer while concurrently, responses to such quizzical speak entirely disinterested me. My brain flip-flopped selecting a comeback to Ray Norman, hah, I usually tossed the jokerman my unenthusiastic off-the-cuff reply, "I don't know", then speed-walked away with the la-la-la-I cannot-hear-you chant buzzing in my ears, arms a swingin' and everything. I detoured those silly for goodness sake time wasters after I dropped out, those life enhancing verbal exchanges, instead steering my bird butt only towards mine the precious pair, my two-foot-tall Tokemaster and my three-inch faux-gold-plated cocaine straw, toot suite.

The general dynamic of being done with school fell upon me strangely. My peer classmates still had almost two years term left of their high school sentence but now, with my pardoning paperwork completed, then erasing the criminal status of my almost daily school breakout, this jailbird was finally free to leave. Literally I felt like reality grabbed me by my shoulders and shook me while laughing in my face, simultaneously mocking me in stereo as I said to myself, I'm done, I'm done, I am really done. Not that I mastered anything, not that I knew jack shit, but for better or worse, I was done with school, done, done, fricking done. No longer did I have to think about school, no longer did I have to stress about school, no longer did I have to lie about school, or fake illnesses, or cut out, or sneak away or shortchange in any form, because I was done. Then the somewhat remarkable opportunity arose, imagining how I desired my life to play…like pick a direction, and fricking go. A heavy layer of vulnerability then should have been shed, a block of angst should have been dropped, a cloak of misery should have fallen from my shoulders to the floor. Alternatively, the notion struck me hard: I'm done but was now dismally disoriented.

With my academic incarceration sentence then served, the entire world laid at my feet anticipating my intentional engagement. Hah, I knew not where when or how to begin…pathetically, I sat.

I did not wonder, I did not wander, I did not chance, I did not leap, I did not ride, I did not roll, I did not journey, I did not scrape together even the scantest adventure. I sat. I could have done something. I could have gone somewhere, perhaps off hot on the heels of Whatever The Hell My Heart Desires, but I sat. I remained, living thereupon as it may have meant to playout, the game of the one and only way it could go…stay, just stay, go nowhere, do nothing. By that time my self-confidence was perhaps chipped away profusely and nearing the shame of the smallest nibby-nub of me, my thinnest margin, my motivation at its most slender, while my drug addiction chugged along building steam by the hour. Most days in the mirror I glared him down, that loser-loser total fucking lowlife loser-boy shining his smart ass smirk back at me.

Shockingly, after some slight time and sparked by a BigBird chirping, I found moderate amusement to off and do something my classmates couldn't…BigBird offered to pay for some college. Although not wanting shit to do with school per se, and not interested to risk quitting something else, still I desired any form of dropout shame-burying. No-no-no and in no way did I entertain the notion of a college education but hah, as my father prompted, just go do it for fun. Echo-echo I despised reading, but funny looking back now, if I was a reader, I could have read my way to learning everything I desired. Or if transposed into modern day, I could gain my PhD in the study of Any Damn Thing by way of YouTube. Strangely, I faded in and out of feeling somewhat tall and adultlike once the college talk began.

I picked two topics interesting me on a worldly wonderment level and signed up at Catonsville Community College, west of Baltimore…oceanic studies and astronomy. The act of going to class was extremely awkward, I wasn't fricking good at it no not at all, I was intimidated, I was embarrassed because I labeled myself as stone cold stupid.

Not meaning to judge blame or deflect, yet still, I think my exacerbated dummy nametag weeded-up while doing battle with my high school assistant principal. Knowing not a solo person at college and making not a single acquaintance, almost out of the gate I found reasons and made excuses not to go. The intimidation driving around the beltway towards the higher-learning campus was overwhelming, and, well, almost crippling. I did not know how to do this college thing, I sucked at this college thing, I did not belong here. Every one of these other people were smart, they knew what they were doing. Visibly, they knew instinctively how this college thing worked, I did no way not. They were here because they embraced the academic experience, they seemed so damn happy and sure of themselves, they surely belonged here, I surely didn't.

After a self-gifted resentful week and a half off, one day I rallied hard and applied myself with vigor…arriving to Catonsville holding not only a packed snack but also a handful of slight time to spare.

I drove around on campus for 15 minutes and not finding a for-Pete's-sake single parking spot, then oh great now late for class, I turned around and that was the end of it…quitter, quitter, quitter, game over. Thereupon fuck it all anyway, I ran straight home to burrow myself deeper into my drugs. Calculating generously, maybe I attended three astronomy classes and perhaps five of the sea life study sessions.

Once restarting college classes over a year later at Towson State University, a location east of and closer to home, a campus sporting a bigger breadth of a spread and the geographical joint definitely more familiar, the, ding-ding…round-two dynamics were more better. I attended with my sister Beth, driving together but attending different courses. I did finish one of the two new signups, Introduction to Business, much I believe because I paid for it myself this time, after earlier mindlessly burning up BigBird's tuition dollars at Catonsville. Also to relieve some slight additional pressure, I selected the pass-fail option because of no need to gain credits. The Pass completion certificate lives today inside my documents safe at home. This being the time before I owned a reliable automobile, so Beth and I, her now a dropout too, we commuted to Towson together in BigBird's Fiat Spider convertible sportscar. Most likely because Beth helped to keep me on task and I actually made it to campus, I stuck with the intro business class, famously making it the first mainstream humanoid thing in my life I did not quit.

No Way Out
Starting around ten years old, I engaged in a competitive but play-filled argument with my pal David Ankers over which one of us would own a hotrod car first. We fantasized out loud more and more how radically hot-rodded-up we would each build our future cars. This game continued for summers after winters, certainly during the time I worked with him at his father's automotive machine shop. Years later when I was working at Princeton Baltimore, an intern bike mechanic guy came to work with us for a few months from another Schwinn Bicycle Store on Maryland's eastern shore, a young dude about the same age as me, and his name was Harry.

Harry drove a kinda-cool-on-the-outside 1968 Chevy Camaro, painted some weird dark purple color, with cheesy mag wheels and featured a manual stick shift three-speed transmission. Harry's car was not hot-rodded-up but almost immediately I lusted after the car, picking it apart in my brain with budgetless lofty rebuild aspirations, and besides, I recognized that car famously from years before. My hotrod build-a-car fantasy game with David Ankers resurfaced in my conscious top-of-mind, and without any effort whatsoever, I envisioned the radical potential deep within Harry's '68 Camaro.

I recognized it famously from years before as the same model and year car driven in my favorite flick Aloha Bobby and Rose, a movie I saw in theatres over five years prior. After some slight back and forth and right before Harry moved home to the eastern shore, he sold me the Camaro for $1,700, aka my first car, aka me-now-in-car-euphoria. Instantaneously I fell into hotrod heaven and solidified a shared car connection with other Baltimore motorheads.

My friend Ricky Pushkin had his super cool blue Ford Mustang Mach1 hot rod fastback, and Ricky admitted openly his plans to do some drag racing one day. Dude pal Jon Balk drove his big fast hot-rodded Oldsmobile station wagon, and no fucking body drove crazier or better than Jon Balk. Another Pikesville friend Richard Berger owned different import cars but they were also Euro-hot-rodded-up and like the rest of us, Richard was a crazy driver, crazy but good. Also in Pikesville but apart from my other crew was ski-pal Michael Greenstein and his nasty high-displacement Chevy Chevelle. My Pimlico auto mechanic and bodywork guru pal Murphy drove his sky-high-bad-ass nasty Pontiac GTO, and Murph's brother-in-law Scott had a sweet Pontiac Le Mans.

The fastest car I've ever been in was Murphy's white Pontiac GTO. One day above 120 MPH and climbing rapidly, I was no longer mesmerized to watch his speedometer go any higher, but rather held on for dear life, with both hands.

Needless to say I slipped into the cool car crowd immediately with my purple Camaro. I drove the car with inflated defiance and in no time flat, my glovebox was collecting tickets for speeding, stop sign indifference, and various other nonsense violations. I never raced for money but we sped around town with moderate haphazard recklessness. East of Baltimore city was an old-time drive-in restaurant and every weekend hundreds of hotrods converged on the place. The drive-in was a thrilling scene and I attended often as I could. Most always on the way home and barely coming out of downtown northbound, a race on the expressway would ensue which sometimes left us running from the cops. The last straw for me and the Camaro occurred less than a mile from my house, a major speeding infraction. I was zooming west on Northern Parkway towards Park Heights, about to enter triple digits, aka 100 MPH-plus, when a pedestrian on the sidewalk jumped around wildly, his arms waving for me to slow down. About to crest a rise in the road, I was blind to what lay waiting for me barely out of sight.

Panicking in controlled fashion, I let off the gas and stomped on the brake, fucking-toot-suite.

Yup, fuck a City uniformed duck, the cop was sitting right there over the hump in the road, certainly waiting for someone exactly like me and my Camaro. Copper-lay-awaiting sat with his radar gun in hand, and nailed me going high 70's in a 45 MPH zone. In short order, I lost my license for a handful of months because of accumulated moving violation points. After the 70 MPH-plus cop gave me a ticket but let me drive away, I laughed out loud and was fact-one thrilled not to get tagged going over 100, which would have been the outcome based on my public streets raceway mindset.

I was already in enough hot water with the law, on probation from some other stupid shit, so if nailed going over 100, I probably would have been arrested and lost my car on the spot, if not reacting with toot-suite-speed to my savior sidewalk jumping bean. Once unceremoniously kicked off the road for a while, aka lost my license, I began rebuilding the Camaro with high hopes, well, factually, I mostly only took shit apart. Riding my bicycle to the local hotrod shop, Douglas Speed Sport near Reisterstown Road Plaza, I purchased cool car parts, then carried them home on my bike. The speed shop guys were gleefully entertained by me. Me buying a fair amount of cool stuff but they never saw the car, ever. Without imagination I presume, those guys at some point probably wondered if I owned a car at all.

Jon Balk was already driving although he was younger than me. Hah, Jon drove before the rest of us, before even he was allowed to drive. Jon was extremely intense when he drove. I am not sure of the responsibility he felt for a car full of kids Jon was in charge of, but seeming, a job taken very seriously. In another life Jon could have been a race car driver for sure because of his combined fearlessness and skill. Amidst tens of simultaneous distractions, Jon remained hyper-alert. Although I know of one time Jon crashed his car, thankfully no one was seriously injured. I was not there that day but I heard the story a multitude of times, and from various people. Jon somehow slowed down right before the car flipped over, but then also somehow, drove away. I believe the roof-crunching incident was Jon's only accident and for a guy who mostly drove non-stop, those are remarkably favorable odds.

One day I flat-out asked him what is going through his mind as he drives, because the Jon Balk safety factor ran in radical common-sense opposition to his high-speed maneuvers, by my measure. The main thing Jon left me with was his notion of always having a way out. I tried to share this insight with Travis once he started driving, like playing Mario in real life…watching everything, everything: What's ahead, who's behind, both mirrors, how is this body feeling, the music, the sun, the light, the sounds inside the car and out…h-y-p-e-r alert. Numerous times flying around town in Jon's car, I fascinated watching the side of his face from the back seat or passenger's perch. Jon's extreme focus and intensity every time I was with him, the scenario impresses me still. When I encounter congested or hectic traffic conditions even today, I clearly envision Jon behind the wheel, him ridiculously intent. I try to do as Jon Balk would do: Hyper engaged, and always maintaining a way out.

Hot Mess - Prom Night - Hot Mess

Driven and necessitated by my drug use, I moved around within many different people groups, simultaneously befriending both the gals and the guys. I grew close with my Pikesville friends and for years I found myself there more often than not. Yes, I went off in all directions but for multiple reasons, Pikesville held me tightest during those later youthful times. Several Pikesville guys possessed true natural swagger. Although I looked up to them, the admired ones also treated me as an equal, aka they did not hold themselves above me. They were more dynamic than average, hence the gravitation and attraction I felt towards them. A multitude of other people shared in my magnetism for these fellas too, not only me. We spent hours and hours atop days and days at Ricky Pushkin's house, awhile intermingling with his dad Barry.

Ricky Pushkin was well-rounded cool, and certainly the music guy, amongst other things. Ricky turned me on to the bands Little Feat and The Grateful Dead. Little Feat soon emerged as my new favorite musical group, displacing The Beach Boys who stood on the top rung of my list years prior. Ricky was also into games, and high-performance stereo systems. Once the heavy-metal nightclub scene began, Ricky was the ringleader there too, at the nucleus of the legit-famous and mega Hammerjacks bar happenings. Ricky was the captaining pilot of his cool blue Mach 1 hotrod when I spent my first all-nighter car cruising the streets and running around, finding slight trouble here and there, all the way until the sun rose the next day, aka my beginnings of grand adventuring, motorhead punkhood style.

Whereas we primarily spent time hanging out in Ricky's house, most of our time with Jon Balk was spent in his car. Jon was the most flamboyantly dynamic and outgoing of the ringleaders, awhile business-successful at the youngest of age. Although Jon got along with his parents ok, as an only child, technically a foster child, Jon certainly wore the pants in the family. Before Jon held a legal license, he was driving his parent's large Oldsmobile station wagon around on his own terms, quickly then assuming the car for himself. Shortly to come, Jon added mag wheels, jacked-up rear air shocks, and a booming stereo to this large and fast American-made station wagon. Perhaps because Jon got a jumpstart on the rest of us by driving before he was of legal age, he gained superior driving skills, or maybe the mastery accumulation because of the many hours spent in his car. The rare moments inside Jon's house were minimal, only as he changed his clothes and before we went out on the town. Jon had a great voice and a good recall of song lyrics, many times properly drowning out the blaring music through the car speakers with his enthused and talented vocals.

Jon was dating a cool girl when him and I first started hanging out, then her and I became good buddies too. One day back when, I encountered Jon's GF in the alternative hangout 'hood of Mount Washington, and she had a friend with her. Her accompanying friend was an extremely attractive gal maintaining long dark hair, a gorgeous skin tone, an ever-present smile, and before you knew it this new goregous girl and I were an item. We remained an item a while, aka my first multi-year wrapped-in-arms love relationship.

The only school function I ever attended was someone else's: this gal's high school senior prom at Pikesville. Like all times in those days, I was high as a kite on drugs during her prom night.

Somehow, I functioned somewhat reasonably, least early in the evening…dressed up in a tuxedo, riding around responsibly in a shared limo with two additional couples, and photos exist to prove it. Perhaps revealing in the photos however, I was deep into my drug needle plunging phase at the time so without requiring sidenotes to explain, I was a damn hot mess on prom night. I plowed through a lot of cocaine that night, somewhere north of an eight ball as I remember.

Despite the grand party before during and after, besides my disorder within and with-out, no one died that night which was certainly a victory, at the time.

Some Sorta Stomp Competition

Even after gaining some competency with my technical work at Princeton Sports Baltimore, I still felt disadvantaged because of Sonny's verbal downgrading. Although I lasted at Princeton a couple of years, the emotional toll fee I paid was great. Collectively, one pick-up gained was to get the experience of a tyrannical boss out of the way sooner than later, so I could better prepare for what laid ahead of me. Hah, and still, now reviewing such my experience of workplace tyranny, I lived to learn the preference of standing alongside a boss who was openly abusive.

I'll take a wide-open asshole any day or night, instead of the passive-aggressive or deep-down dishonest person.

For me, clear visibility is better than a lacky boss faking or hiding a poorly-navigated work ship with me on it. With added time passing since our work divorce, I grew more and more fond of the Sonny experience, both the absolute visibility of his feelings and the capacity to deal with shit up front, instead of playing a deflating game of cat and mouse, trying to decipher what was said versus what was meant.

Walking out of Princeton Baltimore in a huff, I quit my first fulltime job on the spot, partially frustrated from two years of psychological and verbal bullying from Sonny, but mostly because a friend needed my help. My idolized pal Ricky Pushkin's father Barry ran into Princeton one day, telling me his son was involved in a horrific car accident and getting rushed to Shock Trauma right now. Barry did not know Ricky's condition except at the moment it was critical, and the pain in Barry's face is not one I had ever seen, you know, the pure terror of a parent fearing for their child's life. Barry wanted me to please come with him right now to be with Ricky at the hospital. I believed Barry not only wanted to assemble a supportive force to show Ricky he's loved and we want him to fight to stay alive, but also I thought Barry wanted me by his side as an emotional crutch.

I turned to my bicycle department boss Jim and asked if I could leave, factually I pleaded. Please I have to leave and here is why…it seemed like a no-brainer to me, but Jim shrugged his shoulders somewhat indifferently and presented his response to the no-way. There was no way I could leave early. I was extremely puzzled because my good friend is badly hurt, and couldn't Jim see the terror in Barry's eyes?

I begged some more but Jim said no, shaking his head then turning away from me, shuffled some papers around, and tuned me out. Big boss owner Sonny jumped into my emergency time-off request and took over dispute negotiations.

Sonny was a hard driver of people, but also held a mostly hidden tender heart, so my hopes were high that Sonny would put his finger over his mouth in a loving way, like I should shush, then pushes me and Barry out the door with his support, using his once-in-a-while helping hand.

I retold my plea to Sonny as Barry stood there waiting for me. Sonny immediately pulled one of his signature moves and shook his whole body to the negative, then with a ridiculous disapproval tone said, "Ah, no.". Sonny turned his back to me and stomped away in seeming disgust.

Without stopping to breathe, and certainly not needing to fucking think for one single nanosecond more about it, I told Barry to hold on, I just had to grab my toolbox, change out of my car-mechanic-like-generic-uniform with its goofy sewn-on 'Roger' name patch, and I would follow him down to Shock Trauma. I said I was sorry about Ricky and asked if Barry was steady enough to drive himself downtown, Barry said he thinks he's ok.

Crap, my helping switch was already flipped to the full-on step up position, and Barry's 'ok' was not good enough for me. I asked Barry to please hold on and I would drive him there myself, but he said no, he needs to head downtown and see Ricky fast as possible. Ok I agreed and told Barry to go, I would meet him at Shock Trauma in about 30 minutes, or fast as I could drive my shitty blue Subaru station wagon downtown. I asked Barry if there was anything else I could do for him or Ricky right now. He said no and Barry ran back out the door to his car.

Ah yeah, fuck this place, I almost said out loud…my head spun sternly, my lip snarled heavily, and my glaring eyes beamed ravagingly upon Sonny as I did some stomping of my own, straight back to the fricking workshop to gather my shit, punch the fuck out permanently, and go support my friend.

Yeah, Why Not That?

Although collecting some should-be confidence inspiring bicycle mechanic skills and learning to embrace fulltime work because of the generated independence and gained financial maneuvering, once I quit Princeton Baltimore, my available free time actually cast a cursed shadow over me.

After such engaged work responsibilities ceased, my idleness quickly metamorphosized into self-shame, fear, and confusion.

Furtherly disappointed in myself after stumbling backwards in life once more, I seeped into enhanced drug use, and it wasn't long before I met the needle.

Haphazardly gaining additional drug contacts in Park Heights after a couple medium sized deals selling multi-ounce bags of sweet sticky bud to strangers, and with mounting reckless abandonment, I snorted and smoked more coke, snorted and smoked more heroin aka dope, and smoked more crank aka meth, the later however infrequently. Several times I went on multi-day benders in Park Heights and awoke missing memories of multiple hours, and worse. Funny my father never said anything about me not coming home such nights, but as the case may have shown, he knew way better to challenge me on anything around that time, or even mention a single implied word. Possibly I would have exploded on him and moved out if BigBird hassled me about the all-nighters, or fricking anything else. Seemingly his fatherly smartness prevailed, him doing the right thing, leaving me the hell alone.

After it turned out Ricky Pushkin was going to recover from his injuries most likely, and some of his resulting legal troubles began to get sorted, things calmed down. Ricky and his girlfriend collided with another car at an intersection in residential Pikesville and from what I knew at the time, the female driver of the other car was paralyzed after the accident. The woman also had her baby in the car who was unharmed, and Ricky's girlfriend also recovered. Emerging then from the cloud of emotions after Ricky's accident, oops…I realized I was now unemployed. While stomping out on Sonny, I gave zero thought to the consequences of quitting my job and fucking rightfully so, because my friend not only needed my help, but Barry walked in and asked for it. My decision to quit on the spot, aka do the right thing by my measure, was a no-brainer and a maneuver I never regretted, ever.

Maybe somewhat because I was one of the guys in our group who had a real fulltime job and I embraced the challenge of doing more than expected of me, or maybe because Barry now realized what kind of drop-everything-to-do-the-right-thing kind of friend I really was, but Barry asked me to come work with him. Barry Pushkin was a self-employed painter who mostly primped apartments after the old tenant moved out and right before the new renter moved in. He gave the place a new coat of paint, always a value add for a new-to-somebody-else apartment. Barry had contracts with several large rental housing complexes, all in southern Baltimore County. He did some private painting jobs too, but rarely. Previously, I had never painted a wall in my life. Also, I had zero inclinations what the job responsibilities or expectations were, so I followed Barry around like an observant and aim-to-please puppy on a leash. Oh boy, quickly I discovered some of these apartments we had tasked to paint were moderate-or-worse shitholes. Daily, I swiped scurrying cockroaches and lines of marching ants off the walls before otherwise painting over top of them.

A couple of months into the job with Barry, I stopped swiping and just kept rolling…crunch-crunch, right over top of the bugs.

My job tools were a paint roller on an extension handle and a five-gallon bucket of moderately toxic paint. My instructions were brief: Rollout the main rooms and keep moving. Barry gave me direction of what thickness nap size roller to use, how much paint to absorb, how much pressure to apply to the wall and basic technique, which took about two full minutes to explain.

Barry never mentioned the bugs crawling all over the place so I was exercising my grossed-out best judgement, all of it...eventually making the transition from painting to slopping. Barry painted the bathrooms, the closets, and did the fill-in trim work with a paint brush. I never touched a brush or held a small handheld pail of paint, that was definitely Barry's job. Barry never used a roller or five-gallon container of Agent Orange, that was definitely my job. I self-appointed my new responsibilities as kicking around the bug infested rooms spreading the same off-white stupid-ass paint which gave me a fricking headache every day, and wielding my bug-smashing paint roller attached to its dumb-ass four-foot pole. I started to get bored painting cockroaches, then found my mind wandering to the idea of what the hell am I doing? A short while before, I held a good stable job at the bike shop that paid me well and I was advancing every day.

I loved working with my hands, building and repairing a variety of things, especially metal-bound mechanical things and seeing immediately if I performed the work correctly or not. I loved learning, certainly the new discoveries, those things I possessed little or no concept of before. I loved doing a job better than previously presented to me as the standard of expectation. Hum, I thought why don't I try to keep going with that? Hah, I literally asked myself that question out loud, "Yeah, why not that?", just as another cockroach got crunched under the force of my murderous paint roller.

I had learned when working for Sonny to extend my absolute best effort, gaining a thoughtful but critical eye, and leaving my signature on the work.

I did the same with everything I ever touched at Princeton, ever and I loved it, the work parts not the yelling parts, I really loved it. Sonny was direct, which I savored. He told me exactly what to do, with extremely specific detail of how much, how fast, and when he expected me to be done with my assignments. He was gruff with his delivery of workload expectations, but I learned to love it. Soon as Sonny left my workbench, the clock started keeping score...I was in a race to not only go fast, but arrive to the finish line ahead of Sonny's you-better-do-it-like-this-or-else quality minimums. It was thrilling, gratifying, and actually laid the groundwork for a lifetime of focused excellence with everything I do, both at work and out here in the world. Although I was a total punk-ass bird and rather defiant in most ways, working for Sonny allowed me to grab hold of his demands, even when unrealistic, and work like hell to exceed them. Sonny never gave praise directly, but I could kind of tell as I began to not only meet but then exceed his challenges, that Sonny Davis was impressed with me. And even Sonny's subliminal atta-boy praises gave me a lift, a drive, and a purpose I never experienced in all my idiotic years then-thus far.

The positively uplifting but total hidden and personal private shots in the arm from Sonny were actually euphoric, in a punk-ass-bitch-pathetic kind of way.

Reviewing this in my head while inside one of those nasty apartments with Barry, I began to see toxicity-poisoning stars in my eyes, thinking maybe it was time for lunch. But focusing in on the core meaning of the assembled parts, I recognized I was not self-generating any personal pride, challenge, or growth. Nor finding the trademark Sonny-style of push, encouragement, or praise anywhere in my life, not at home or work, hidden or otherwise. My emotions began to sink. I was not getting pride or push at home with my father, and I sure was not getting anything out of primping these cockroaches with my off-white toxic cover-up paint.

Damn, did I really just say that with my inside voice? Well…well, what if…oh man, wait a fricking fog-filled minute. I stopped rolling, feeling the light bulb go off in my head and hoping it wasn't the paint fumes gaining control of me. What if…what if I fabricate-imagined Barry was leaving soon for vacation and we still had lots of apartments to finish? What if I imagined, that right before Barry left for vacation, he found somebody to replace him, and the substitute painter boss would work with me while Barry was on a beach somewhere, where it was always five-o-clock? What if… what if Barry appointed Sonny Davis to stand in and manage me?

Oh shit, I was missing the much bigger point of what the hell am I doing painting cockroaches? Wow, this is huge. I need to figure out how to talk to Barry about this in a sensitive way that would not embarrass him or piss him off. Barry was one of those super-nice-just-roll-with-it kind of guys and although I saw Barry get mad a few times, such negativity was rare fair and short-lived. If not careful with my delivery of thoughts to Barry, I might offend him, probably lose him as a friend, probably lose Ricky as a friend, and because Ricky is a ringleader, I will probably lose most of my other Pikesville friends too. Besides, I would probably also be unemployed, again. My strategizing began…how to best explain to Barry we should do a better job painting these insect-infested rented shitholes. If I could work closer in line with my high excellence standards I learned and embraced with Sonny, well, I would prefer that, and maybe we could make Barry more money at the same time.

Hold up no and wait a darn minute…inspecting my own polished dirty-ego buttons, why should I push my standards upon Barry? Maybe I should not. Why should I care more about Barry's business than he seems to himself? Maybe I should leave this one alone, then again, maybe I should not.

Yes, maybe I should drop my roller into the bucket of Napalm, shut my damn mouth, and walk away from this job too.

Barry could go back to working by himself, maybe Barry likes working by himself, maybe I factually suck at painting, maybe Barry doesn't want any judgmental lip from me. I could go out right now and try to find another bike store job, there are like ten shops a reasonable distance from my father's house. Why not continue the challenging but rewarding career track I already started with. Hum, yes, maybe that. Final gut check…truth be told, there was no way I could leave Barry now, especially as they deal with the physical recovery and legal fallout at home after Ricky's car accident.

Ok, that's it, I decided…I told Barry we need to talk about some stuff. Barry said great, in two days we will talk after work. I went home and prepared my sales speak. I thought through my pitch and tried to focus on my critical points…we could do so much better, we didn't need these shitty pest-infested jobs, we could focus on quality contracts and make more money.

The paint boss meeting time came and I was ready, well, until I wasn't. As I sat down with Barry across from me, when it came time to actually say the words, I had an epiphany and changed gears. Realizing I was entirely flooded with self-absorbing assumptions, I faltered on the fact I held not a single known detail of Barry's work desires or how much money he truthfully made painting the creepy-crawly apartments. I also knew not the type of work conditions Barry wanted to avoid. Before I could say anything, I totally choked.

Realizing I was about to bird blabber my assumptive judgments and play the role of asshole, I pitched a different spiel. After all my mental wrangling, my big bold we need to talk board room meeting opener produced the following factual words, "Do you like the cut-in trim work better than the rolling?". He answered no, brush or roller did not matter, he was fine doing either. I paused and then almost on cue, Barry picked up the speak and revealed he was letting me get accustomed to rolling the walls before he put a paint brush in my hand. He asked if I wanted to learn cut-in trim work and I cautiously said yes, it looks hard to master but I said I would like to give it a try. He said great, we'll start tomorrow. Unsure of what to bring up next inside our big important talk, I said that's all, and we got up to leave. Barry joked, "That was easy". Once inside Barry's truck together and driving home, I casually riddled him if he liked painting the apartments. He said yes, they're easy and he makes more money than higher-end residential jobs. Instantly I realized, oh for shit's sake…I myself was the darn problem, not the damn bugs, not the damn apartments, and not the damn Napalm roller. More precisely, my dirty assumptions judgements and blaming were the fricking problems.

The fricking bird brain problem was me and my judgmental orientation, and my perspective of what I was currently doing or not doing with my life.

Then thinking, hum…how did I for-fact want to spend my breathing time right now? Should I stay with Barry for a while or go do something else? I decided to stay, minimally until learning the coveted trim work brush skills and also see where this job might lead me. Well, I thought in review…Sonny was hard on me and I learned to make a game of his dictatorship, but once my line got crossed, I quit that damn job on the spot without hesitation. The painting job with Barry began to suck but I did not yet understand the subsurface hidden-to-me-conditions, and I did not yet put in my best effort. Before quitting on Barry while half-cocked and shit, I spoke up and realigned myself within reality. Hum, I thought proudly, I just learned something…that's the better way to operate, you know, speak up, instead of assuming stupidly then growing resentful on the clock, finally to either then mouth off and get fired, or quit the damn job, all the while remaining clueless.

First things first the next day, Barry handed me a painting brush, new in package.

Mostly because I never held a brush and secondarily because I was otherwise off to the side grumbling into my pestilence bucket, I never noticed paint brushes in detail before. My precision paint brush training was a humbling experience, more involved and harder than I anticipated. Not even thinking, I began to rip the brush out of its small flimsy plastic case. Immediately Barry jumped in and put his hands over mine, like motioning me to stop…for goodness sake just stop.

He said to preserve the case because we want to protect this brush going forward. Embarrassed by my own ignorant clumsiness, I slowed down and listened. Barry asked me to look at it, feel the shape…notice the weight and balance of the brush. We practiced precisely how to hold the new trim cut-in brush for multiple minutes, similar to my mechanical drawing class at Poly, we spent one entire freshman class period learning how to hold a pencil exactly. The paintbrush felt heavier to me once I noticed it. I was humbled by this newfound art-craft beginning. Not only did I learn to lower my heart rate and stand soundly in my own shoes, use extreme focus and practice a steady hand, but I learned the new skill of gauged perception, pace, paint coverage approximations, and feathering of lines. Such skills as applied to painting a room are perhaps assumed, mistaken or dismissed, but they are ones I am honored and proud to possess, and I have Barry Pushkin to thank for all of it.

Not long after competently guiding my paintbrush around the closets bathrooms and cut-in needs for some weeks, Barry told me the apartment work would slow down soon, I believe that he was hinting I should consider alternative plans. Without thinking too much, I then visited Mount Washington Bike Shop, the closest bicycle service store to my father's house. I met briefly with the owner Geoff Crenson about possible employment opportunities as a mechanic. The gentle bike shop owner was verbally impressed that I completed Schwinn School and was surprised by the number of wheels I had built, the exact kind of person they needed, or so Geoff Crenson claimed. I already knew a couple other people working there, kind of, and Geoff offered me a job.

I did not accept Geoff Crenson's offer right away, but went back to talk to Barry first. Although he claimed I was the best employee he ever had, and he's had a few, Barry excitedly and forcefully said I should leave the painting behind and get back to the bike business. Barry said no problem, he will be fine without me so with that, Barry and I parted ways professionally and I accepted the job of mechanic at Mount Washington.

As Barry and I stood there shaking goodbye hands to our co-work times, it was weird because I knew to see him within a few days, hanging out with him, Ricky, and our extended Pikesville posse. The first time I went back to chillax at Ricky and Barry's place after not working for him anymore, Barry saw me and told me to wait right here while he ran off, coming back and saying, "Sorry I forgot this…", him then handing me the properly cleaned and back-in-package used trim paint brush…it's yours not mine, ex-bossman Barry said.

Barry and I remained dear friends, enjoying a deeper relationship after our painting time together, and, well, frankly a rare post-employment condition I was extremely grateful for, by my measure. Barry was like a stand-in father for me, much because of our shared time together across both work and home settings, but more in a buddy kind of way.

Barry who although did not push me, I learned much while with him, both directly and because of my self-challenging sort-outs. Mostly, I believe it was the accountability and personal validation shaking me awake on the job beside Barry.

Mister Barry Pushkin helped me gain the beginnings of a methodized life arranging process, well as interceded a collection of knowledge which might not have arrived for me any other way than chasing down and crunching those fleeing cockroaches.

Emergency Runaway Truck Ramp

Two miles east of my father's Pimlico house was Mount Washington Bike Shop on Falls Road. Falls Road is a two-lane major north-south thoroughfare, connecting urban downtown Baltimore City and wandering north into suburban then rural Baltimore County, and beyond. Falls Road plays the character as the top horizontal T at the intersection with Kelly Avenue. Kelly Avenue serves the role as the vertical stem of the T. Kelly Avenue ran west from Falls Road towards my father's house, towards my elementary school, my middle school, and then on to Pikesville. The first quarter mile of Kelly Avenue leading away from Falls Road is a four lane bridge up and over both the Jones Falls river and the downtown expressway I-83. The Kelly Avenue bridge as it connects to Falls Road is a decent decline, aka a fair-sized downhill. If driving a big truck down the Kelly Avenue bridge towards Falls Road and you happen to lose your brakes, you might as well aim straight ahead at the target of the bike shop, which is centered at the top of the T.

But oh no too-bad-so-sad and boo-hoo, you would flatten the bike shop with your big runaway demolish-everything-in-its-path truck, along with the unsuspecting store staff inside.

I just showed my hand...me giving that exact runaway truck scenario some moderate consideration a time or three during my years working inside Mount Washington Bike Shop. Especially concerning were the weird noises of loud trucks, skidding car tires and mangled automobiles in motion while me and my work family labored heads-down inside the shop, our backs to the runaway truck ramp.

Most of the route from my father's house to the bike shop was downhill, even before jumping onto the Kelly Avenue bridge. A half-mile-long downhill dumped up against an annoying stop sign at the edge of the bridge, before the merge. Before the bridge and as I would fly down the big hill, most times I ran the stop sign without thought, and truthfully it was only a gentle merge, not a hard cross-street at all. I could see clearly, and gauged easily the nonstop and ever-flowing eastbound traffic before reaching the stop sign, even amidst my high speed, so I squeezed right in, then coasting up and over the bridge, aka almost one mile constant of no pedaling, aka glorious. I rolled the stop sign because I could safely enter traffic and because I was traveling ridiculously fast. If I slowed majorly or stopped for the stop sign, I would have to pedal up the slight rise of the start of the bridge, then finally regain the coveted no-pedal descending status down the bridge to work.

Yeah sure, every once in a while my good judgement forced me to slow and make the merge safely, but I didn't like it. It wrecked my momentum and required a few seconds of bothersome pedaling. I preferred to bomb down the hill, building max speed, blow the stop sign safely, and coast over the bridge without having to pedal at all, yes, I love that speed shit. That precise technique served me well for years, well, until one day, it didn't.

One morning per usual, I executed my safe 40 MPH+ two-wheel no-stop merge onto Kelly Avenue but oops, in short order a Baltimore City cop was in pursuit of me with his sirens blaring his lights ablaze and everything. I was moving faster than traffic and faster than him, so the cop didn't catch up to me until I was off my bike and standing in the bike shop parking lot. I considered hightailing it out of there and rather sure I could have gotten away, but I was in chillax get-along mode and not fuck-the-police mode. Copper dude was supremely pissed, yelling and threatening to not only write me multiple traffic tickets and impound my bike, but also arrest me, if he wants to. Cop dude was being a real prickface by my judgements but I remained cool-headed and extremely respectful.

I was downer-high on heroin at the time, well as holding pot, cocaine, and needles on my person, so most likely my down condition assisted my situation.

Once he calmed, I explained…sometimes it's safer for me to keep going at that wide-open merge onto the bridge instead of stopping, because of the risk getting hit by a car who is blinded by the eastern morning sun, therefore not seeing or paying attention to me. He understood what I was saying, but he didn't like it. Didn't like it and still, hah, he only gave me a warning. Hee-hee, I jokingly laughed to myself afterwards…his work peers cop-shop teasing might be worse than the penalties I would receive, after big bold policeman wrote multiple tickets to a guy on a bicycle.

Because of my pitiful primary commitment to role of junkie during employment at Mount Washington Bike Shop, some days I called in sick.

I lied why I couldn't report to work, I lied why I had to leave early, I stole money out of the cash register and I manipulated every possible condition I could get away with.

All this to maintain sliding needles filled with hundreds of dollars of drugs a day into my arms, while simultaneously trying to keep my job. I never stole a bike or parts from Mount Washington. I assumed a weirdly heightened level of responsibility there compared to Princeton. At Princeton, well, hum, oh fuck it…I do admit stealing bike parts from Princeton, and, well, it was not a crazy amount of stuff. I was not taking inventory to trade for drugs or sell for drug money. Why did I steal shit from Princeton? On some level, I needed parts I couldn't afford so to keep my bike rolling, pieces like tires and chains and stuff for my transporter vehicle, so I could commute to work. Partially because I was an asshole. And finally, because I thought Sonny was some days excessively hard on me or others, I believe I deserved a little I'm sorry compensation from my boss without him knowing about it.

At Mount Washington I attempted not to shoot up at work every-day-all-day but many times the situation was unavoidable. Purposefully I tried to leave my *works* at home, aka my drug fixing equipment, when possible. When sometimes still on a bender, aka a prolonged immersion of shooting up from the night before, I knew better and instead, called in sick. A few other employees were regular drug users too and although I did not believe anyone else was shooting, I smoked many a joints and snorted many a lines of cocaine with coworkers. Many times, well truthfully most times, my intended balance of leaving the needles at home got thrown out of whack and I'd either shoot up in the bathroom, or walk into the woods behind the bike shop to do my dirty deeds.

Beyond Comprehension
It was discovered that a rock was in fact stuck under our third Baltimore area house after all. Hoping this place would remain stable and sound, aka I hoped to forever remain separate from my monsters in this abode, but alas no.

The break-in burglary occurred mid-week daytime. Frightfully, quite often one of us four kids was normally home during school days, for various reasons, but thankfully no one was inside at the time. The balls it takes to burglarize a house in broad daylight is a notion that entirely escapes me. They totally ransacked the place top to bottom, except for the stash compartments inside my two-bedroom ceiling posters that mattered. I factually found major satisfaction and humor that for as much shit as they threw around, they never found what they were looking for. Beyond the terror handed to me by my mother and the deaths I caused and also witnessed, this burglary was one of the more unsettled events I experienced because of the personal violation, aka it was creepy as fuck.

Much of my uneasiness was: Since they got in once, when are they coming back?

This was the Ken Oak house, our only Baltimore family home where I felt no major terror fright or fear from my mother. Hah, but then the house scared all shits out of me. Even ridiculously still, a much-much worse occurrence would come for me here not long afterwards. This house was now violated, ravaged, unlockable, entirely unsafe, poisoned, and, fucking wobbly.

Desperate to get the frick away, trying to figure how to stay the frick away, from this house, from this town, from this needle, from fucking all of it, I just couldn't see a way to separate myself from my own little hell and began a self-inflicted termination countdown. It all then turned stupidly ironic when I then got that phone call from my naughty neighborhood friend Ryan about taking off from Baltimore, least for a while.

I am a Fucking Asshole, No Better Than
My prized possessions these days are your various preserved crayon and watercolor artworks, many paper photographs, my 1985 restored Fisher Competition mountainbike, and the bad ass rebuilt 1968 Camaro hotrod. If my shit all burned down, I would not fret too much, long as I could retrieve the aforementioned items before they went up in flames, well, and of course my Schwinn School diploma.

And then the crux of the matter…BigBird's camera collection equaled and even surpassed the entire grouping of all my prized objects, by my measure. In one fell swoop, my father's beloved items were gone, stolen. I dare to imagine such a sickening development befalling me. This here stomach of mine churns sourly as I cast thoughts back to that time trying to imagine the emptiness, the anguish, and the sorrowfulness burdening BigBird after his cameras disappeared because of me…poof, without a trace.

Tenably as I might imagine, my father's heartache focused on his treasured heritage items and the punk(s) that took them, the punk(s) possibly disregarding their value and discarding the rare vintage box cameras on the side of the road like bad leftovers, these ones which I know my father treasured more than the varied others.

BigBird never mentioned or hinted of the word camera, fucking nothing, never, not to me. He never asked me why or who or anything about the break in, not a single word, never, although he knew it occurred because of me his punk child.

He never said a fucking word about any of it, not a single, fricking, word. From what I could tell, he buried the entire ordeal without a chirp. The cops never followed up with me, not that I would have said anything to them anyway. Honestly I did not know who did the break in and because I feared surpassing retribution, I would not offer a guess to authorities about neither the Mount Washington tough guys pulling the burglary, nor my pissed-off Pikesville fronting dealer and his big gun anyway. I never brought it up to my father. I never asked about his cameras, I never said a word, never. I never gave up any explanation about any of it, except what I had already told Beth. I never mentioned anything resembling sorrow or regret for my role in my father losing his beloved cameras, fucking all of them.

This was one of the few rare times in my life BigBird demanded anything of me, the grounding that came my way immediately after the burglary. I certainly deserved it, and more so says me, man I am such a fucking asshole, no better than. My father never punished me in any way regarding his stolen cameras or our ransacked house. I do not remember the detail but I believe my sisters also lost a few things themselves, taken by the burglar's thieving mitts. I believe BigBird punished me due to the need for something to happen, because of my bedroom stockpiled drug materials inspected by the cops, and otherwise it would be unfair, certainly unfair in the eyes of my sisters.

Upon comprehensive review, I would prefer an altered past here if such forces so existed and could please me…desiring instead the burglar's left my father's camera collection behind, stayed out of my sisters rooms, and rather, found the damn $900 stash of fronted sweet sticky bud hidden in my ceiling posters. I doubt I possessed the cognizance at the time, even if me once properly absorbing the magnitude of BigBird's loss, but using a modern-day virtue compass, I'd much more prefer to allow my wronged dealer to withdraw payment from me physically, even though the toll due at the time could have amounted to my final breath. My precept today with such a matter would say…hey mister fronting dealer, come and collect, I don't care what it costs, yeah, go ahead, take your best fricking shot.

Hopes Gone Wrong

With a history of nothing but balloons of aspiration popping in my fricking face, I wriggled deeper into the nooks of my appointed and slightly uncomfortable $550 Iceland Air seat. I turned away from Ryan, so to pretend I was sleeping as we began our eight-hour flight to western Europe. I tried to settle, but it was hard. Under hyper review, I recounted my list of previously squandered life longings.

1. Oceanographer, undersea explorer. Although the associated Jacques Cousteau notion still appealed to me, I was uncomfortable in water, even fucking more so after I killed Johnny Powell, although my condition not an entirely insurmountable barrier. Believably, if I established a workable link to the undersea world like maybe a starter job as an intern research diver, an entry-level occupation with an underwater recovery service, or as a ship-repair diving welder, I could distance myself from the drugs and maybe make something out of this here shitty fucking life of mine, fuck-maybe. Such sub-surface opportunities must have existed nearby. We lived only minutes from the Chesapeake Bay, a vibrant and large setting for such possibilities, and a slight few-hour drive to the ocean. For what I knew, the draw of working on the sea floor could have captured my passion enough to leave the drug trade. At the time, I believe an underwater role was the only thing that could. After dropping out of high school I understood, or perhaps I wrongly presumed, my oceanic career chances now thwarted, so I abandoned the notion and such opportunities now gone.

2. Motocross racer. My passionate enthusiasm for two-wheeled motorsports had long fallen out of favor, and my motorcycle fallen into a permanent state of disrepair. Two of the four engine mounting brackets were broken from the frame and several other mechanisms lay askew. My disassembled dirtbike was scattered around my father's basement and driveway, exactly similar to the Camaro, ah fuck it. A few unanswered necessary repairs too many and I lacked the resources and interest to rebuild the moto. Perhaps my once boundless love and unbridled desire to become a motocross racer could have overpowered all obstacles, maybe even displacing the drugs. Only if spending least a month futzing around with words to explain the heartbreak of BigBird physically dragging me away and banning me from the motocross track, only then could I ever make written sense of my true feelings on the matter, so short of that, I will not attempt to waste my damn time, or yours. With bitter resentment and borderline hatred for my father after the denied entry into the dirtbike racing sport, I then walked away from the dream of my number one big-ass cool thing and such opportunity now gone.

3. Lacrosse athlete. The notion I could be a successful jock in school was something I scantly entertained with even my inside voice. Inwardly while outwardly, I highly admired the lax guys both on and off the field, ultra highly admired. Sometimes I imagined myself interchanged in their place, these the illusions of entire make believe but resulting sensations of pride and satisfaction flowed through me, wherever those unknown locales might for goodness sake possibly exist, certainly such feelings unconnected and far-away fucking foreign to me, at the time.

Gleefully I played these stardust movie shorts on the theatre screen in my brain but got rocked awake by the factualness: I was a punk, and nobody gave two fucking shits about me like whatever. Nobody fricking cares then fuck-theretofore why the fuck should I? Despite the desired hidden contrivance, in reality I was disinterested in the comprehensive fricking institution and missed too much goddamn school to remain a sustained participant fuck-anyway, me actually then forbidden to play sports because of exorbitant truancy and my resulting athletic ineligibility.

Could someone have emerged from the fog to entice me to engage properly with school sans drugs? I highly fricking doubt it, but dangling the imaginary carrot of becoming a lacrosse athlete, likely an accomplished athlete if I was willing to do the damn work, then the possibility of progressing through high school and even advancing to college on an athletic scholarship, such a domitable chance for me I believe existed, but, well, following my school system self-removal, such an opportunity now gone.

4. Automotive design engineer. Peeling back the factual reveal, aligned with the core passion I possessed for automobiles, I now discover a new realization never seen to this mind's eye before: I became a bicycle mechanic because I passed on the prospect to build cars. Dropping out in 11th grade thus abandoning all hopes of attending the elite STEM college as premeditated, General Motors Engineering and Management Institute in Michigan, aka GMI, my previous lofty life plan was then dismantled.

Although possible pursuit of a simple automotive technician career existed while still in high school, I was forbidden to transfer into the technical curriculum trade program T-Course. The parental directives demanded I remain in the college prep B-Course, zip-zero option. Being transparently honest, I gave up on the dream of car designer when I let drugs take over and if I couldn't run at a high level in the automotive industry, I did not want to fucking play at all. Perhaps this elitist attitude was extremely shortsighted but alas, such my path. For a bit I considered and came close to enrolling in an outside private motorcycle technician school, the premier program located somewhere in Florida I believe. But in the end, if I was not allowed to race dirtbikes, my bitter resentment spilled over and I dirty-ego chose to begrudgingly avoid the moto industry altogether. Once withdrawing from school, I fuck-viewed my big boy chances in life as threateningly slim. Visualizing myself knocking on theoretical employment door after door and getting laughed off the stoop because of my almost non-existent educational standing, well, all my inner and outer ambition then retreated, cowered, and hid.

Eliminating the thought of participating in the automotive industry and shunning the motorcycle business with disgruntled opposition, I found that my hands-on passion and work interests actually encircled complex mechanical things, despite my comprehensive incompetence with such workings.

There on the plane, such painful dead end life realities flooded the frontsides of my head and I began to cry, quietly balling like a little bitty bird baby.

Slowly wiping away the tears, I tried to hide my hurt from Ryan and other peeking creeper eyes packed in their seats around me. Although I should have been overly-excited to shortly be skiing and climbing mountains in Switzerland, I just couldn't see a realistic way through all the grown-up rat-a-racing societal shit that I piled on top of my head. Hell, I had no earthly idea how I would even survive the planned two months away from my drug needles while in western Europe...my tears of patheticism continued their cascading parade down both cheeks.

Keep On Walking

On Monday March 19th 1984 I received the first inked stamp upon my passport pages once successfully moving through customs control at Luxembourg Aeroport, Entrée Controle. The entire process was not so challenging and before I knew it, we were standing on the outside curb, free and clear of the airport, a literal huge relief. Soon upcoming was the unknown-to-me complexities of European train travel but thus far, I was surprised by the relative ease and straightforwardness of international ventures.

  We continued by train and checked into our first hotel, actually the only hotel we would occupy the entire time across multi weeks in Europe. Our single-night lodging occurred amid an almost fairytale setting in Switzerland. Grindelwald is a ridiculously cool ski town, nestled high in the Bernese Alps and at the foot of the world-famous behemoth Eiger mountain. In Grindelwald we were not here to attempt a climb of the Eiger, nor here to climb at all, but mainly to ski. Our climbing expedition will arrive next in Zermatt, whenever we get there, maybe next week. The massively gnarly almost 6,000-feet tall sheer north face of the Eiger, aka The Ogre, practically hit us in the face when we opened our hotel room drapes the next morning.

Specifically, the north face of the Eiger is one of the deadliest mountain faces in the world because of its radically flat and exposed structure, carrying a high fatality rate for the relatively few number of climbers who even attempt to scale such an antagonistic rock monster.

We had rolled into Grindelwald after 11 PM the night before, it being the darling little dead-end railroad track town that it is and dang it, our youth hostel destination was already closed. We instead secured a hotel room for the night although that money spent on one night's luxuriant lodging would have paid for almost two weeks of bedding down at the youth hostel, oh well. The next day we checked in and stashed our packs at the international lodging facilities on the cheap, aka hostel, then spent all daylight hours skiing. Grindelwald is way up in the hills and because of its remoteness, the train tracks do not continue through town. The single rail line goes into the Grindelwald station then stops. Whimsically, the train reversal process requires the cars be detached on a side-track and the front engine driven into a wheelhouse, then turned around on a crazy railway turntable.

  The local language was strong German in this central region of Switzerland and presented as a true challenge, but we used hand gestures to make our way around town.

Maybe the natives were slightly put off by us, and it seemed as such, but our interactions were not so bad. I do not remember a single English word spoken with anyone in Grindelwald, that is except with the youth hostel staff and with Ryan. We exchanged our cash to match local currency and did so the rest of the trip everywhere we went, sometimes switching money multiple times within the same country. Out of country credit cards were not accepted anywhere, not that I owned one of those silly plastic scraper-like things anyway. Ryan had a credit card but he couldn't use it once away from the big main airports. Our paper dollar bills were spent on lift tickets, nightly youth hostel fees, train tickets, postcards, and food.

At the time and for me, Grindelwald was both slightly magical and fantastic, awhile unnerving. The Eiger's north face is such an abominable monstrosity that when not skiing, there was no escaping its looming presence. With disappointment, I was definitively put on notice by the mountain. Quite literally unable to relax, such tension was a blow to my lofty Swiss expectations. I believe the unsettledness of my amassed insecurity in Grindelwald was spawned by the hectic and deadly storyline of Clint Eastwood's movie, The Eiger Sanction. Before our trip I watched the flick, and to my emotional demise, I remained threatened by the in-person peak our entire time in Grindelwald.

Hiking back and forth through town a few times lugging our ridiculously heavy fifty-pound backpacks and constantly repositioning my unsatisfactory grip on the tall, unbalanced and unruly ski bag, the collective struggle in Grindelwald seemed almost fricking relentless. For such a historic and classic European ski town, I should have been able to chill, to rest and relax.

Consciously I attempted to shed previous Alps expectations, to lower my emotional bar, to roll with shit…accepting things for the way they are and downgrade my lofty angelic determinations, but I was not doing a very good job, no not at all.

Strict rules at the youth hostel kept me anxiously on edge and our first night, a large commotion ensued. The hostel doors were locked every night precisely at 10 PM and entry was thoroughly disallowed afterwards, no exceptions. The staff worked diligently by the looks of it to communicate this hard and fast rule. A currently residing hostel guest arrived back from town after the 10 PM cutoff, and even though he prepaid for the night's lodging and his gear already sat inside, he was turned away. Perhaps aligned with the Swiss tradition of timeliness, both the quality of their famous clocks and watches, alongside the tight accuracy of country-wide train schedules, but the youth hostel staff clearly ain't fricking playin'. After one too many of his unruly shouts and pounds on the exterior door, a huge pot of water was dumped on the man from an open window above, in the cold dead night of winter. All was silent after that, and not a peep occurred outside the hostel doors for the remainder of the night. It was a silly little disturbing-the-peace infraction, but an incident adding to my anxiety.

Ski About
Similarly to the Eiger, the Matterhorn was a dominant presence in Zermatt, but the iconic peak sat further from village center.

Zermatt presented itself to me as more of a mountaineering climber's town than Grindelwald, with alpinist gear dangling and clanging from climber's packs as they walked about, like chiming neck bell tolls from high-meadow Swiss cows, and the village-center climbing retail shops brimming with alluring draw.

Our plan…ski here a few days while getting settled and hopefully better acclimated to the thin air, before securing our Swiss government-issue climbing permits. Our first day skiing in Zermatt was spectacular. Miraculously, as I discovered with delirious delight…at the top of the ski hill was also the country's boundary. A small sign cartoonishly directed skiers one way or another…one way to Switzerland, back to Zermatt, and the other way to Italy, down into the town of Cervinia. Our first run in Zermatt was eight miles long and carried us away from traditional snow fields, into neighborhoods and through snow-stacked residential alleys but then confused, we were left searching for the end of the run, the bottom of the resort, and just where the fricking frick is the damn ski lift anyway?

Everything melted together and I felt like a violator, like we were trespassing. We skied for-fact far as we could, the terrain flattened, and there was literally nowhere else to go. Oh shit we were lost. Ryan and I must have gone outside the boundaries of the resort, there were no ski lifts anywhere. We stood there with our skis off, looking around pathetically and totally bewildered. Two elderly men stood nearby talking to each other and carrying on joyfully, before we realized they were laughing at us. They did not speak any English, we didn't speak any German, and the mystery soon became comically clear as they teasingly pointed to the train car right in front of us, while laughing hysterically.

A large brightly-colored Zermatt ski area logo was prominently displayed on the side of the rail car, but neither Ryan nor I saw it at first, we were looking high in the air for the presence of a tall ski lift. Our ride back up the hill was actually the cog railroad car sitting there waiting for us to board, barely 40 feet away from our faces. A dozen or so fellow skiing occupants on the rail car were staring straight at us laughing too, as was the train car conductor, him holding the door open and waving for us to come his way like, come get on the train you silly-silly skiers. Entirely embarrassed, we walked onto the railroad car and appearingly became the highlight of the day for the occupants of the lift, everyone on board laughing at our bewilderment, and we too joined in with the hilarity of our clueless selves.

It was certainly a touching moment of friendly fellowship when the stupid Americans could snicker at themselves in front of the Zermatt locals, and the chuckles continued all the way up the hill.

A storm rolled in late on our first day but we remained hopeful our climb could proceed as planned. The comprehensive climb would take three days once we trekked away from Zermatt, until the time we returned. The first day would be hiking to the Hornli Hut, basecamp at the foot of the mountain.

Chapter SEVEN

Apparently some supplies will be pre-stocked for us as treasured inclusion of our climbing permit fees, and we would spend the night in the small hut. Day two would begin pre-dawn as we set off hiking away from Hornli basecamp, and almost directly onto the pitch of the Matterhorn. Hopefully our expeditious timing gets us to the summit and returns us safely to the hut before nightfall. We will have one small headlamp each which should be more than sufficient if the night's sky is clear. After a restful post-expedition snack n' sleep in the hut, we will hike back to town, returning to the youth hostel in Zermatt. Ryan and I reviewed several key climbing notables and challenged some safety scenarios. Mostly, what to do if one of us plummets while attached to the other: How to properly arrest the fall with our body position, correct ice axe anchoring into the snow, and the precise mechanical equipment grasp on our ropes before we both fatally tumble down the mountain like linked ragdolls. Although I had dropped acid every day since we left the U.S., I thought about maybe facing the climb clean, but then again, maybe not.

The following day skiing in Zermatt was an adventurous challenge…high winds and blinding snow, but fresh powder covered everything so even if bouncing off an undesired obstacle, the hit soft, or least the landing pillow-like. On day two we pretty much did the same runs as we did the day before, except now in almost blizzard conditions. We skied from the memory of yesterday's runs, most times literally blind and disoriented otherwise. The low count of skiers on the hill because of bad weather was a godsend, because once in a while I almost hit another person after speeding up on them, due to lack of adequate visibility. More people on the hill in such weather would have been dangerous in a multitude of ways. Such conditions did not bother me, not the frick at all, I was dressed for it and the wild challenge just added to the arousing adventure. I suppose outside and playing in such a storm could be nerve wracking for some other walkabout humans, but my growing unconcerned mortality allowed me to dangle over most proverbial life ledges with carefree ease. I paid respectful service to the almost zero visibility in honor of continuing the frolic, then switched mental gears to envision the terrain from yesterday's skiing memory, like recounting a well-learned board game. Ryan and I attempted to be like Velcro, glued together because of the almost unseeing on the hill and otherwise, we might not find one another for the rest of the day. Day three was a repeat of day two, Mother Nature pelting us with her same blinding snowstorm.

On the afternoon of day three we entered the Swiss government office to obtain our climbing papers, but regrettably, permits were currently suspended because of bad weather. The officials noted, with their broken English…extreme winds and zero visibility up there, aka death-defying conditions for climbers. Their genuinely concerned comments continued briefly, we seemed like nice young Americans and they did not want to kill us. We all chuckled haha and we thanked them for that but privately, I would have preferred to climb regardless, and take the risk despite a totally pissed off and raging Mother Nature. Still, I honored all that I did not know. Perhaps, I thought…if I were up there climbing for ten hours straight in such conditions, then cold and hungry and tired and imaginably just fricking done, wanting it to be over, I might be liable to slip up and make a deadly mistake for either me or Ryan. Mostly by way of protectiveness for Ryan I did not balk at the rules, I did not grumble, because of not wanting to kill anyone else anytime soon, or motherfucking ever for that matter.

I eyed the northeast ridge of the mighty Matterhorn every chance I had to give it a look, provocatively anxious to meet her up close and personal soon, God willing…bad weather or not.

Thus far and thankfully, in town I did not react negatively to the 5,000 feet elevation thin air. Although the tippy-top of the Matterhorn summit is another 10,000 feet higher, aka a two-mile straight up climb towards the heavens, hopefully a one day roundtrip excursion to the peak and back won't cause me altitude problems, once I am in my harness geared up and climbing. Days four five and six cleared slightly once so often but mostly, the harsh weather remained. Then we journeyed down valley some days to ski at sibling resorts, but returned to the Zermatt hostel each night. We checked in with the climbing permit office every day and the answer was the same: All permits currently suspended because of bad weather. I grew worried our opportunity to climb is in jeopardy.

Ridiculously, the next day on the top of Zermatt, a short distance after we got off the lift, when the snow slowed and the sun was out briefly, now following the same track on the same trail we had skied blindly for a handful of days, I was shockingly drawn aback and had to stop.

I was almost breathless with fright to discover we were measurable inches from falling off a cliff over a hundred feet tall, which would have certainly killed us. Several days before, I grew slightly cocky and began to speed around this very section, totally oblivious to how close I came to sliding off the edge of the world. In a flash I felt small, reduced, and was rattled the rest of the day, desiring some consumable marijuana to help calm my frazzled nerves but no, I had to suck it up.

Ryan and I had a few serious conversations about the shrinking reality of climbing the Matterhorn. Neither of us could imagine this storm to linger much longer but every time we said it out loud, another day passed with storm clouds still a-raging overhead. We discussed maybe going elsewhere and then returning to climb in Zermatt later after the storm clears. Briefly he mentioned the climbing and skiing in Chamonix France, so maybe we should go there. I inquired if he knew a good climbing route in Chamonix but he said no, he had only planned for the Matterhorn.

After a few more days in Zermatt without any change in the weather forecast, we decided to leave. Moderately I was sad not to climb, but I considered two additional things. One, maybe we will come back in a few days once the weather clears and climb the Matterhorn anyway, therefore no net loss. Two, maybe it wasn't meant to be, maybe this is a sign, especially with now so much new unsettled snow high on the mountain, which increases climbing danger dramatically. Regardless, the time was not right and instead of forcing the hand of fate, we left, heading for Chamonix.

Chamonix is home to the tallest mountain in western Europe, Mont Blanc, and its withheld 15,777' elevation summit. On the long train ride from Zermatt to Chamonix, and as we approached the crossing of country borders into France, most people were shuffling around and pulling out their passports in preparation. In short order I figured there will be a passport check of some kind, so I pulled my travel documents as well.

Ryan and I were sitting slightly apart in different rows and the train official walked through inspecting passports. After the train conductor guy checked me out, Ryan came over and asked if I got mine stamped. I had no idea what he meant. Evidently, between each country during passport inspections, if you want a commemorative stamp from each country, such a request has to be made. Yes I wanted the cool stamp but also didn't want to be a hassle, so I let it slide and settled back into sightseeing out the window.

Gazing out the big train pane, I faced the slight-past factuality of almost slipping off the edge of the world atop the ski hill in Zermatt, and I challenged my rather rebellious, actually defiant, stance on my own future existence.

My beliefs held court that my life's course had been on a downward spiral since I was four years old and despite my immediate locale and thrill, I saw no way out for myself. But the cleared sight of the ledge in Zermatt caused pause and a forced reality check…what if, what if I died soon, what would be the result? My eyes welled up with pools of unhappy water…my father would be heartbroken, my sister Beth wrecked, and many of my friends dreadfully distraught, least a while. Now away from the drug needle and afforded some additional clarity, I began to see my life as maybe worth something, least a little, least to somebody.

Chamonix is the epitome of 'mountain town'…the wild terrain, the open access, the plentiful resources, the people fully engaging with each other and utilizing the mountain, both through sport and recreation. Chamonix is bigger than both Zermatt and Grindelwald, feeling almost twice as big as Grindelwald. Also slightly dirty, slightly congested at times, and Chamonix certainly more hectic than the previous remote small villages. Genuine backcountry skiers and climbers existed throughout the area. The French enthusiasts appeared more serious, not so fashion oriented, but more functionally purpose built. Multiple times I observed adventurers dropping down from almost nowhere, them plopping out of trees and back into civilization in the most bizarre places after it appeared they resided in the wilderness for days, or weeks. Seeing such core characters using all possible natural resources was inspiring AF. These mountain people seemed to operate hyper-effectively in nature and go where they please.

Such sights were new to me, another pathway in my get-up-and-go soul opened, another switch got flipped…there's an adventurous part of life I am missing.

The bully bad weather followed us into Chamonix and during only a slight portion of one day did I see a complete view of Mont Blanc. An entire sight of the mammoth-sized mountain then gone in a flash, hidden behind a veil of clouds for the remainder of our time there on the far edge of southeastern France. We skied every day and the terrain vast, but the classically delightful high Alps feel was watered down and mostly gone. Now in the strict French-only zone, the language and culture pressured us more than any other time in Europe so far and mostly, the interactions were conflicting.

Our lodging was again, the youth hostel network and the cheap rate of the Chamonix hostel seemed wrong, like they undercharged us, only two dollars per night including breakfast. Hah, but once we discovered there was no hot water, us then required to take freezing cold showers, I felt like they should be paying us to stay there, not the other way around.

Talking to Ryan about climbing, because of the un-climbable weather except for local icefalls, plus a weirdly deflated disinterest to backtrack to Zermatt, we both then lost the drive to put our harnesses on at all. Strange to say but honestly, the cold showers also played a role in our overall moods. Even though the skiing thrilled me, the dread of icy water soaking me head to toe cast a gloomy shade over each day. Overall our moods fizzled and after the dissolution of climbing plans, it seemed our drive and adventure for more ski days grew closer to its end as well.

We walked into the Chamonix train station the next day to buy tickets back to Germany, planning to leave France tomorrow. We stood in line behind about four other people and in short order, more folks filed in behind us. Once it was our turn we stepped forward, now standing against the edge of the train ticket desk. Without even an attempted bonjour, we simply said hello to the guy working the counter. He did not look up. Rather, the dude replied verbally in rapid French wording. Hum, well, unbothered, we started over, using heightened respect…hello, excuse us, we would like two tickets to Ramstein Germany, please. Still looking down, he let out some sort of frustrated sigh. I didn't want to piss the guy off more, so I waited for him to make the next move. Ryan was equally still and quiet.

Then bro dude looks up, glaring at us with contempt, and his arms start waving wildly in the air…fucking literally he was now yelling at us.

We tried a sort of apology, we're sorry, sorry, please calm down plea but the guy was having none of it. There was no French being spoken from our side of the counter and no English coming at us from the other direction. Helplessly, we tried to be nice, we tried to use hand gestures, we attempted to write down Ramstein but he speedily with force brushed the paper back to us, seemingly insulted. Another ticket guy emerged from the back office and began yelling at us too, this went on for several minutes. I could not understand why the guys were so upset.

A young woman from the line stepped slightly forward and caught my attention. She said the guys know exactly what we are saying. They're not going to help you, she said, you should try again tomorrow. Ryan was still trying to communicate but I pulled him back from the desk, telling him what the lady told me and we thanked her as we left the building. Trying not to react or assume too much, I figured we caught those guys on a bad day so we will try again, maybe the next day. Hah, immediately I thought back to middle school and desired to have paid more attention to what my French teacher was trying to help me learn. Back then, I echo-never-thought I'd ever amount to anything or fricking go anywhere.

Collectively, Chamonix was hard, seemingly harder than it had to be. Everywhere else we could communicate, even when neither party understood what the other was saying. Here the train station guys hated us, or more accurately, they refused to help us.

Dreaming we never left Zermatt and rather stayed long as we could, I also desired we climbed before we left, and shadow followed me back to the Chamonix hostel.

The next day after skiing we went back to the train station and I for one was thrilled to see different staff working the desk. There was no line so we walked straight up to the counter with hopeful intent. We gifted the train ticket worker an especially soft delivery, and also attempted maximum kindness, shit, I didn't realize but desired I could have grown some balls and least attempted a weak bonjour…hah, but it didn't matter, today's staff did not want to help us either and actually shooed us away. Ryan and I stood off to the side, perplexed and talking to each other. A customer guy stepped forward to help translate and as it turned out, we had to go back to the hostel, look at our old train tickets, refer to country train maps, and present a proposed stop-by-stop itinerary request to the Chamonix train station staff another day. And no, as it turned out, not later today, only tomorrow, or later. We were told to detail every exchange and transfer we desired between Chamonix and Ramstein in order to obtain tickets. Instead of simply buying a ticket to our journey's end, we were required to buy a multitude of purchased transfers from one stop to the next in order to reach our final destination. Additional comments from other helpful customers revealed this is not the way things work here, the Chamonix ticket guys were being unfairly hard on us, so we were told.

The night before, Ryan and I briefly discussed possible plans to visit Paris before returning to Germany. I assumed, and assumed incorrectly, Paris might be a worse place than Chamonix to struggle with the language. So with moderate frustration, I was ready to leave France, toot fricking suite. As I learned years later following my first trip to Paris, the capital of France is actually a wondrous melting pot of people from around the world, not a massively bigger city stuffed full of only non-English speaking residents. Ryan and I would have done well to ditch Chamonix and board a train straight to Paris, instead of the rather senseless struggle back to Germany.

On the third day, we walked into the train station once more. Oh great, greeting us smugly was the same sales guy we encountered the first day. With what I perceived as great pride entirely consuming him, he stood behind the counter with hands on hips smirking, as we laid out our entire turn-by-turn rail line itinerary back to Germany.

With an aura of glowing satisfaction he sold us a heap of tickets and miraculously not only understood our words precisely, but spoke English back to us rather well.

Paid up with a stack of German-bound tickets in hand, we left the Chamonix house of conflict and returned to the hostel for final packing. By that time, I was thoroughly ready to leave Europe. With the sour taste of the Chamonix train ticket clash still swirling around in my mouth, I tried to let that shit go, I tried to spit out the negativity, I really tried.

Skanked

Back on home turf, painlessly we had access to bountiful amounts of exotic weed but cocaine was nearly extinct at the time. Driving around with a few friends, I dragged us to visit several vacant depots, before finally deciding to head to the infamous Litchfield in Park Heights.

Although always our last resort, the 24 hours a day / 365 days a year one block long open-air drug market of Litchfield Avenue never disappointed when all other sources failed. I only had to purchase pot here a couple of times prior, this was maybe the fourth or fifth occasion I arrived to buy blow here, mostly I scored heroin here, and never once had I bought meth here.

We had mentally pooled our money together and were growing antsy cruising around for some toot. Pre-committed, we planned to score an eight ball. Besides my associated bucks for the today-blow, I held a few dollars in reserve for food and gas to last me a while but not too long. Otherwise I'd have to cook up some sort of other rip off or deal to gain some supplementary life cash.

We turned onto the vibrant commerce corridor and the place was as busy as I had ever seen it. It was nighttime, maybe 7 PM or so. This had never happened before but one of the sidewalk merchants jumped directly into the backseat of my car, him pushing my couple of friends towards the passenger side of the vehicle. Dude presented as speedily accommodating and friendly. Whatchu want, he inquired in a pleasant tone. Caught slightly off guard, I paused to answer. All other times on Litchfield our transactions occurred through the driver's open window, hence my slight hesitated confusion.

As the driver, I took control and spoke for the group. I looked into the rearview mirror to answer him but he was positioned directly behind me and out of sight. With traffic afront of me and cars filing in behind, I had to keep creeping forward so to keep the drive thru supermarket line moving, thus I did not turn my head around. "An eight ball of coke", I said. Not meaning to now say that the guy was gross or dirty or lacked adequate hygiene practice, but I noticed a strange smell as me and my friends collected our money.

Accompanied by a hefty thud, I immediately realized the stench. "Give me all your fucking money", he said with his gun buried in my hair between the slight pillars of my driver's seat headrest. Oh fucking hell, not again, and I felt shamefully sorry for my friend passengers that were about to be nothing but drugless and robbed broke. Also my arms immediately ached as I tried to figure out how the hell could I now fill my drug needle tonight. Dude guy was using his forceful angry 'don't-fuck-with-me' tone so we did what he demanded, well, mostly. I handed my hundred bucks back with my right hand and kept my left hand on the wheel. I sensed him empty the hands of all my friends then jumped out of the car as I rolled slowly along.

We had to sit a couple more minutes for traffic to clear, which just added to the indignity. An exasperated disappointment was huffed aloud by us all. I started apologizing into the rear view, and felt pathetically responsible for what just went down. Once off drug lane, I gave the remaining $50 of gas and lunch money I had to my frowny friends. One gal pal refused my offering but the others distributed amongst themselves my remaining bucks. My stomach churned, mostly because of the stench of stinky sweet gunsmoke drenching my hair.

Hey Dummy...Who, Oh Wait What, Huh, Oh Yup, Hey Dummy That's Me

Pulling some slight additional bits of my stupid self shit together, I was still radically fearful of an underwhelming future, much because I lacked a high school diploma. Investigating the options, I found an opportunity to possibly test for an equivalency GED certificate from the state board of education. Sadly, I scantly researched the options and knew nothing about a practice course or study guide. As the reality set in, I believed myself fairly stupid academically and now four years past dropping out, my realistic expectations told me I would fail. I did not pay attention to my teachers past 5th grade, if I even showed up to class at all. Maybe because of the enhanced endorphins from mountainbike racing, I can only suppose, but I decided, I fucking decided. I decided to convince myself that the attempt of testing for my high school GED equivalency certificate is a possibility...it is possible.

Possible. What is possible? What if...what if I could muster the courage to try? What if I could try to take the test, just try, just show up and try? I could take the test and after I fail, I could re-take it over and over year after year, and maybe slowly improve over time. Maybe one day I would get it right enough, and hold that fictitious certificate thingy, but hah...me still absolutely oblivious to what such a piece of paper could ever do for me, if anything.

Without any knowledge on the matter, I presumed that, well...maybe after I take the test and fail, they will return my answers and I can use my incorrect results as a basis to study for a retake, least this my reasonable hope. So I decided...it was possible, it was fucking possible. It was possible for me to try, and if I tried, I could learn the testing routine and not be freaked out to try again, and again. If I can try to get started, if I can take the test, the first time will be the hardest but then I will have the hardest part out of the way. I can learn as I go from the returned wrong answers...so, yeah...I should...I should try to do that. So I did, I registered for my GED test.

Time arrived and the large cafeteria-type exam room was filled with about fifty fellow testers. The average age seemed about five years older than me, but I am assuming.

Hum, I wondered the story with each one of these people...what might a diploma ever do for them, and also, what might it ever do for me?

A strict time limit was imposed and it was a long ordeal, almost a day-long affair. The test administrators behaved stern and strict, and I imagined maybe a history of cheating existed. I believe our allocated time was around six hours, with least one break partway through. I got done almost an hour before the time limit, but anxiously feared I missed something so I sat there scared out of my wits to stand up claiming I was finished. The first person was done and out the door, then after a quick scan...yup, that's the extent of what I can do, I think I'm done too, least I completed all I knew or to the best of my guesstimate.

I was the second person out of my seat and tried to ignore the judgy smirks of my peers as I walked on by. Driving home from the test I second guessed myself heavily, fearful I missed a page of questions or something and maybe I did. Collectively I felt stone-cold embarrassed once I stood up, then wanted to get the hell out of there fast as possible.

I felt dumb the minute I picked up my pencil, I hardly knew half the material, but tried to rally some slight pride that I showed up and attempted. Blurting out loud once exiting the building, I mouthed to the birds and butterflies with moderate pissed-offness…"Fuck it, just fuck that stupid fucking shit, least I fucking did fucking something".

I wanted to forget about the entire trainwreck of ordeal and never try the test again but then, in late August, I finally got the damn envelope…an apology letter of failure that I hoped would include all my incorrect answers, but sadly, oh hells bells, it fricking didn't. It was a brief single page message, oh fuck it all anyway, it listing my pathetic suck-ass scores in the five different categories.

Writing Skills	Test Score 53	63% Percentile Rank
Social Studies	Test Score 49	46% Percentile Rank
Science	Test Score 62	89% Percentile Rank
Reading Skills	Test Score 55	70% Percentile Rank
Mathematics	Test Score 52	58% Percentile Rank

Wow that sucks, I really am THAT fucking dumb, I fucking failed. Thereupon what the fuck ever, who the fuck cares. I tried to reorient myself back to the original scheming notion…I knew I would fail but maybe someday my hare-brained slow-as-a-turtle's persistence might win the stupid high school equivalency race. I'll try again next year, but hum maybe I fucking won't. Yet still, I wondered about getting my wrong answers back. I walked towards the trash to throw away the asinine single sheet of paper, me disgruntled and still grumbling defiantly. As I made my way to the garbage, there was a bit of writing below and I guess it's the instructions on how I can request a copy of my failed test.

Or maybe it informs the dummies like me how we can test again, or get a practice test, or a booklet, or fricking something, not that any of that stupid fucking shit could actually help this lame-ass loser bird boy anyway, oh fuck it.

I began to read the stupid-ass fucking smallish writing right before I crumbled it up and slam-dunked it into the garbage can. Now verbatim…"Congratulations on achieving the Maryland Diploma. Opportunities in both business and education are now open to you that were previously unobtainable. Your accomplishment should give you a feeling of satisfaction that is certainly shared by the GED office."

What…say the fuck what…what fucking what is this dumb-ass shit? Fucking what? I was still too pissed off to comprehend, I did not understand. What does it say? Like I said, I'm stupid so I don't understand a lot of shit. What does this mean? What the hell is going on? Does this mean I passed? No fricking way. Mistake, it is a mistake, can't they read their own pathetic numbers for fuck sake, actually my pathetic numbers? How the hell might that have even happened?

There's no way, they obviously, hah, obviously they fucked up…I was so confused. My scores are pathetic, obviously I failed, it was clear, and it was only one stupid piece of paper…what is going on? With my brain spinning, I looked for a way out and I inspected the letter more carefully, flipping it over for maybe more of an explanation. The heavy cardstock paper had my address, the return address and my test scores on it…oh hold up…oh shit, what the fuck?

Oh boy oh crap and there it was…a Maryland High School Diploma, perforated at the bottom, attached to the scores page. The pair of heavy papers was folded in half within the envelope so I did not see the actual diploma. Uh, hold up…what wait what…what just happened? I could not believe what just occurred, like literally…what the fuck just went down? What the fuck Sherlock? Um, well, I guess, I guess I actually passed. Those scores looked so damn pathetic to me…but…I guess a 65.2% percentile rank average is a passing factor for a GED…holy fuckballs I fucking passed.

For the longest time I dismissed the value of this piece of GED paper, assuming it was printed as a semi-joke equivalency certificate. Lately however, oh man weird…I pulled it out to grab these precise score numbers and hum, jeeze, I realized there is no language on the diploma itself to indicate it as anything else other than a true Maryland school board diploma, not a sympathy or short bus certificate. Wow, dang, I got that thing done on my first attempt, uh…these facts befalling me as entirely, *poof*, unbelievable.

Back to 1985 and with the uptick emotional value-add of my school board certificate in hand, my mind raced immediately towards various Colorado and Wyoming and Utah and Northern California ski areas, thinking I can make a run at it, me making a run at living in the mountains and fleeing this fucking place, forever. But oh fuck wait. Wait one fucking fucked-up minute bird boy, what the fuck you fucking idiot? Why do I tease my hopes and dreams of living in the mountains afront of my face? I don't have any fucking money. Why should I believe my residential alpine life goal is achievable? Because of course it is fucking not. I'm not going any fucking where, I'm stuck here, for badder or worse, I have no choice.

Yet, hum…Maryland Department of Education told me that previously unobtainable opportunities are now open to me, so damn it, why don't I try to believe them?

I tried to believe, I tried to imagine believing in myself was possible.

Thinking I was beginning to go somewhere, least in mind, hum…I wonder.

I wonder…is there something more possible for me, out there, somewhere?

If something more is really possible for me, more of what, and where is it?

Hangrier and Hangrier

Past high noon, it was late lunch hour and fricking hell, perhaps a wiser decision than how my dumb-ass reality was playing out had me instead pit-stopping for a sandwich in Denver. I was fleeing Baltimore; I was getting the fuck out of there and running away from all trying to hurt me inside and out.

Also I was starving, but Denver was a big yuck-yuck dirty city, and being so close to the mountains, I could not grasp the motivation to pause in or around the metro area for any fricking thing, not even food. I was so fucking excited to be going, even though I knew not where.

Over Loveland Pass and through the Continental Divide tunnel at 11,158' elevation, the Subaru got a break...the incline of the last couple hours then turned downhill. Ugh, so hangry, I planned to stop after the tunnel in Frisco, also a place I knew after skiing at Breckenridge earlier in the year. The town of Frisco in Summit County is a ridiculous mecca for downhill skiing, home to Breckenridge, Keystone, Copper Mountain, Ski Cooper, Arapahoe Basin and Loveland ski areas, all in the same basic vicinity and hum, maybe this is where I should live. Scenic Lake Dillon sits smack dab in the midst of Summit County ski land, and in plain view of the highway through the rather narrow stretch of valley. For some strange reason, even though fiercely hangry, I passed on stopping in Frisco, it didn't feel homey enough for me, and evidently I wasn't truthfully that hungry to pull over and pit stop. After passing Frisco, I almost hit the brakes and pulled over on the shoulder, half-heartedly wanting to back up and get off the highway. Although I lifted my foot off the accelerator and moved it back and forth, hovering over the brake-accelerator-brake for Frisco, I stomped on the gas and kept going before that approaching car behind me smacked my slow-ass bumper. Humph...weird doubting thoughts flooded my head and my brain began to pound on its sidewalls, like I really did not at all hells to the know where I was going. I frightened...was I zooming right by my perfect place? Oh crap...I might really mess something up here. Well, I thought, if it doesn't feel right it doesn't feel right and if I have to, I'll go all the way to Mammoth Mountain in Northern California and backtrack until I finally land somewhere that pulls me in. Mammoth looked pretty killer too, least in magazine pictures.

Once past Breckenridge, I-70 west goes uphill again to the top of Vail Pass at 10,666' elevation. Perched atop Vail pass is a beautiful looking open rest area...maybe I should stop, soak in the views, and think deeper for a while. Going west down Vail Pass is a real screamer and there is least one runaway truck ramp on that steep high mountain, for damn good reason. I could barely keep the Subaru under control, oh fuck-oh fuck-oh fuck, my empty brake pedal went to the floorboard, oh shit-oh shit-oh shit, I just lost my damn brakes.

My heart either stopped briefly or skipped a few beats or even both in rapid succession, oh fuck, glancing frightfully ahead I aimed for the truck ramp, I death-gripped both hands on the steering wheel at the two and ten o'clock positions, oh fuck...I braced for a 90 MPH-plus entry into three-foot-deep loose ball gravel.

Oh fuck oh good lord yes and praise the heavens...a few desperate pumps of the brake pedal brought the system back to life, cheese-whiz, there must be an air bubble in the hydraulic brake line after I worked on the stopping apparatus last. Entirely rattled by the freefall down Vail Pass, I pressed my right hand against my chest to help calm the cardiovascular thumper drum, and with my gosh-darn stomach demanding food right now or else, I committed to pulling over in Vail at 8,120' elevation.

I needed to take a break and get out of this hellion of a carted rollercoaster, well as check its briefly broken brake system. The Vail Valley is rather narrow, maybe three quarters of a mile wide before steep hills on both sides head toward the clouds, so the housing, retail, and ski lift access is rather compacted. First up was East Vail which was not the hub of town but is home to the Golden Peak ski area of Vail Mountain resort, the high-speed quad chairlift, a large parking lot, and the golf course. Being mid-December, the golf course was deep under the white stuff, the quad chair was full and so was the parking lot. Driving back and forth through Vail on the highway during the previous ski season, I remembered the lay of the land although we did not stop here. Basically, there were three exits for Vail being East Vail, Vail Village town center, and West Vail. When I was a short time earlier on the top of Vail Pass gazing out the windshield, I then knew I blew by Frisco for good reason.

I decided on Telluride as my final destination, but then out of necessity slowed onto the East Vail exit ramp, giving myself room and pumping the brake pedal before the stop sign. Yup, Telluride, I figured a fresh start deserved a fresh adventure, somewhere new and rugged. Minimally, I would keep on truckin' another six hours and give Telluride an honest look. Once seeing the place in person, I was rather certain it would be my new home, based on its magazine pictures.

In East Vail, the whole place was packed and I couldn't see a single square footage of retail presence anywhere, more or less a lunch nook. Seeking a place to park I grew hangrier and hangrier. In front of me now was the expansive East Vail parking lot but there was a mystery gate, no signage, and entry required I gain a ticket from the push-button box cloaked in fiscal mystery. Fearing the rates ran by the ski day, I persuaded myself no, can't park there. My mind began its shut-down sequencing mode because of dangerously low glucose levels and now totally confused, I desired on-the-spot surrender to a fictitious hourly parking valet.

My stomach was growling. I couldn't go any further. I needed to turn this car off and eat. I half-heartedly began to drive, then stopped, then slowly started to roll, not sure what the heck to do. My conscious thinking brain melted and dripped syrup-like down my shoulders. Creeping turtle slow, I attempted a gaze-away focus, far-far away from this parking dilemma mental bottleneck. There was a dude, a cool burly dude, riding a yellow Fisher mountainbike and he had his monster of a golden retriever dog jogging next to him.

This dog was nothing like any golden retriever I ever saw…huge head, massive muscles, and his shoulders almost seemed to poke through his long golden locks, while wearing the coolest mountain dog smirky smile.

As I was about to pass mountain man and his mountain dog going the opposite direction, we both stopped simultaneously. I was looking at his dog and checking out his bike, while he inspected my bikes and skis on the roof. Mountain man spoke first, "Nice bikes, who are you?".

Yowzah, I humphed silently, hey mountain dude, that's a weird thing to say. I said thanks, told him my name, and I'm driving through town from Baltimore. He said, "That's a nice Fisher, are you a racer boy?".

Again, wow dude, you're weird. "Thanks, I love that bike but I broke it and they painted it that orange color because I was in a rush to get it back, it had the team tri-color paint job before but yes, I do a little racing, not much and I'm not very good but hope to get better at it". Bearishly he said, "What are you doing here?". Wow, ok, again weird, and now dude is being rather forward.

"I am looking for some lunch, do you know of a sandwich shop I could walk to?". The dude instantly got nice, helpful, and not so weird. Oh yes...he proceeded to yap with mounting enthusiasm, giving me basic instructions to the Mill Creek Court building and a cool little off-beaten-path sandwich shop, and by the way he made crystal clear to me, they have fresh-baked cookies, all kinds, and they are fantastic, warm out of the oven. Cool, helpful, sounds good I thought. I asked him about parking and he said park here in the ski lot, they only charge by the hour. With a less-weird tone and now acting semi-remotely human, the dude introduced himself as Paul and asked what I did back in Baltimore. I shared with Paul that I was a bike and ski mechanic, and also did some novice ski and bike racing. Paul asked where I was going after lunch and although committed to Telluride, I did not want to offend him or his town so I lied and said, "Maybe Jackson Hole or Telluride, not sure." He nodded his head with barely camouflaged disapproval and said, "Ah, ok, well if you want a job as a mechanic in a small pro shop for the summer, I'll hire you if you can build a good wheel".

Holy fuck. In five minutes I got a job offer in Vail. "Sounds awesome", I said, "Thanks Paul, I might have to come see you about that, where is your store?". Paul rattled back at me as monster dog started to whine, "A twenty-second walk from the cookie shop, you'll see it but I'm closed in the winter, I'll reopen in late February after I get back from salmon fishing in Alaska". Um, damn, maybe I should go get a sandwich and a cookie and give this Vail thing some thought. "What's your last name Paul?" and he told me, hum, this dude is somebody, I've heard his name somewhere before. I almost wanted to be a smart-ass and ask him who are you and what are you doing here but I didn't, he seemed to lack the smirky humor for that kind of shit. Paul's full name sounded familiar to me and besides, his overall aura gave me the impression this guy is the real fricking deal. Tempted to chat a bit and not lose this opportunity to build a better relationship, I almost asked if he was a native or what brought him to Vail, but his goliath dog seemed edgy like, Come on hooman let's go.

I thanked Paul for his time and his help, then forecasted he might see me in February for a wheel-build interview. Not trying to be cocky but I pronounced my certification and recounted my over 200 wheels built so far, to which Paul curmudgeoned, "Huh...well, we'll see *if* you show up, and *if* you can build wheels *my* way". Hah...we'll be fine, I almost said out loud, absolutely confident since I build wheels the right way and cockily I self-proclaimed silently...I do it pretty damn well. I smirked and gave him a quick, "Sounds good Paul, thanks so much".

He began to pedal away and I commented his dog is amazing, what's his name? "Marmot", and the pair of mountain monsters took off, with Marmot prancing away, head up high like a Mister Universe bodybuilder show dog. Oh good lord that's the perfect name I thought...that dog was a beast.

Otherwise, I could only imagine Marmot's name to be Woolly The Mammoth.

Feeling rather good about myself there while then, I parked in the ski lot and locked my equipment to the roof rack with a cable going through the bike frames and the heels of my rotomat ski bindings. Hastily I took off to find that cookie sandwich shop and maybe even do a covert walk-by of Paul's storefront. I feasted on a yum-yum Turkey sandwich with awesome flavor sauce at Paul's cookie shop, sipped a Coca-Cola, pulled out a piece of paper and pencil to scribble some life planning notes to self, and put my head down.

Something so weird, actually bizarre, happened next. I was absolutely rocked, by a voice I knew. A distinct voice, there could be no other, no fucking way, I was sure. No way, that's crazy. I look up, and oh shit yes I was correct.

Standing there in line for a sandwich or a cookie was my buddy Michael Greenstein from Pikesville, the little brother of my elementary school classmate Eddie. I previously fell out of touch with Michael and heard he moved out west, but our chanced meet-up was out-of-this-world freakish. I couldn't believe it and called his name out loud before leaping from my chair. Michael is an animated confident young man, outgoing and bold…I really like the dude…he is, the total opposite of me. Almost simultaneously we both said, "What are you doing here?".

I explained the abbreviated backstory of my current coordinates and Michael proudly shared that he is the chef at Sweet Basil…Vail's finest restaurant he made sure to definitively by the way notate…only a two-minute walk from this cookied sandwich place. Michael wondered out loud, "You staying in the valley?...we're looking for a roommate". Um…well, totally bumbling but it didn't take me long to sort out and I bounced it back, "I was heading to Telluride but if you have room, maybe I'll stay". Michael promised to call roommates Matt and JP to check…but it should be fine. He gave me the kitchen number at Sweet Basil and told me to call him at 3:30 before dinner guests arrive, and he would have called the guys before then. Michael said if it all works out, I can come over tonight. He was anxious to leave with his bagged sandwich already in hand, he had to get to work but I said there's one more thing.

I questioned Michael if he knew where the bike shop is around here…a high-end pro shop I was told…and immediately he replied, "Oh yeah, right there next to The Boot Lab", and gave me quick walk-there-then-there directions. Michael asked why the bike shop, and I told him about my run-in with Paul. Michael said that sounds pretty cool, and he took off to go prep his planned gourmet meals at the restaurant. I sat down, getting back to my sandwich and writing paper. Ok let's do the math…I got a summer job offer…check. Maybe I found a place to live and bonus, with somebody I know…check. Now I need a job for the winter. Dag gone…I might have two of my three immediate new life necessities already figured out in only fifteen minutes.

Although previously heading to Telluride, maybe the aligning stars under the Vail blue skies are too much of a cue to ignore.

Too Good to Become True

I walked away with cookies-to-go, then seeing The Boot Lab, but where's the fricking bike shop? Shit was making no sense…I almost turned around while bailing but instead walked closer, oh, there it is, jeez…are you kidding me? It's not even a store, oh good lord…it's more like just a door. Embarrassingly I walked by, and saw the just a door led to just a hallway, hah…this place looks like…just a joke. Paul immediately called me in to show me around. I enter the joke-like hallway…uh, uh, um and fucking hells bells to the what…say what…are you fricking kidding me…holy fucking shitballs…I never saw such an amazing collection of gear, any kind of gear, in one place before in my life, ever. Paul's workplace was unlike any bike store I ever heard of or saw…exotic frames and parts and European cycle clothing filling every inch of the tiny pro shop. Wow, that was a pathetically assumptive poor book cover reading I pulled, aka lame bird.

The state-of-the-art, industry-standard, high-bar and top pro-level roadbike components and tools then-thus far and for-like-ever before were made by an Italian company called Campagnolo. Tulio Campagnolo invented the derailleur way back when for goodness sake. If you're a great service shop, you have a Campagnolo, aka Campy, toolkit in your store but they cost over $2,000 each. Only the most serious shops performing the highest quality work spend the big money on a Campy tool kit. Princeton Sports did not have a Campy tool kit when I worked there but Mount Washington Bike Shop on Falls Road did. Holy fuckballs, Paul had a stack of six Campy tool kits on his sales floor.

Amidst my I-cannot-fricking-believe-what-I-am-seeing nervous out-loud laughter I asked what the hell are these for?

Paul said, "Oh they're for sale, I already sold a few and I'll sell all of them within a couple of months, mostly to high-end customers or pro team mechanics". The boggling concept absolutely blew my mind. I never saw a Campy tool kit for sale anywhere before and never even heard of such a silly thing for goodness sake. Immediately I knew for fucked-fact if I ended up working here, I would learn more than I might ever learn in my entire life about building pro bikes.

He also carried a few very high-end complete mountainbikes from Fisher and a company called Klein. Most everything in Paul's store I had never seen before and some of it I never knew existed. I was entirely blown away and now I desired to work here so bad that I was afraid of messing it up. I thanked Paul and told him I will either see him in February or I'll call to let him know I landed elsewhere. I walked away excited, excited but crazily nervous…this might be too good to come true.

Checking my brake fluid before starting to drive again, everything looked fine but I should bleed the brakes sooner than later when I can find a reasonable covered workspace. I drove around the Vail Valley, exploring up and down the few roads open in winter, before finding a phone booth to call Michael. I imagined myself hopefully living here and began to fall in love with the place. Right before Michael came to the phone, I grew frantic that I had built up my hopes too high, expecting him to tell me one of the guys already found someone else to move in.

Indeed I did move in with my friend Michael the gourmet chef, aka Michael Greenstein my former Baltimore ski buddy and grumbly hotrod big block Chevy Chevelle owner. As it thankfully turned out, his roommate Matt was a supercool California dirtbike guy and the other roommate JP was a pastry chef, however somewhat semi-salty. The four-bedroom chef's apartment residence was located in Avon, about ten miles west of Vail, not far from the base of Vail's sister ski resort Beaver Creek. It was a five or six-story apartment building, a pretty nice place, with an expansive underground parking garage, and located on the edge of a 45-acre park which includes the smallish Nottingham Lake. The guys were easy going and we seemed to get along ok fine. It was weird though…I never lived away from home so apartment life with roommates was an adjustment for me.

One of my more joyful activities was heading outside at night sitting atop one of the many park picnic tables next door. More often than not, my seated position reclined quickly and I found myself lying atop one of the wooden dining tables. In summer, many times laying out my bird frame flat on the grass was preferred. All this alternative positioning because of the show, the hours of wonderment gazing upon the night's sky at 7,431' elevation. At such elevation and being 100 miles from the lights of the big city, the stars are so big and bright that they seem close enough to simply reach out and touch. Astro-finally, I got to spend bulks of time studying the stars. The first couple times I went out to gaze at constellations, I froze my bird butt off so I learned to bring a blanket because of the multiple hours lounging under the mesmerizing sky. Not a viewing night passed without seeing least one shooting star and some nights, multiple rapidly falling lights in the sky entertained me.

My kinda-cool new pastry chef roommate JP connected me with a friend of his who worked in human resources for Vail Associates, the mother organization that owns both the Vail and Beaver Creek resorts. After enjoying the bewilderment of the mountains in the Vail Valley for about a week, I started my first job in Colorado on Christmas Day when I was 21 years old. I worked behind the grill, flipping burgers, frying fries, and making grilled sandwiches high in the clouds at Spruce Saddle, the mid-mountain restaurant at Beaver Creek.

Uncapturable

Residing a mile and a half high in the Colorado sky and working two miles up in the clouds, my wanted retainment of the grandeur became an exercise in botched undertakes. I attempted to snap up the pure mountain spectacularness through photography but that shit did not work, the splendor was too big and the photo capture was too small. The visual ensnarement far too tiny and underwhelming to even begin to tell the tale of the place. I had forgotten that during my time skiing in Europe, I tried to take photos but none of them turned out, none, so I stopped trying.

In and around Vail, once remembering back to my abandoned camera efforts in the Swiss Alps, I then realized and absorbed the amassed truth of the pitter-patter heart matter. The overwhelming panorama of Mother Nature's exquisition spills far off the edge of the shuttered lens' capturability…oh now I see, the true beauty of nature is uncapturable, by my measure. When I see magnificent photos, I am caught in the stare of amazement. The place almost looks like a painted picture, not a real nor true location. Many of the painted pictures, aka photos, grab me and entice me and drag me to them, going or desiring to visit them face-to-fact.

Strikingly, I am then astounded with the splendor of the in-person come-to-life version, echo-far beyond the still image hooking me from the start. This minuscule breathless photo realization fueled my travel fire tenfold, cementing the legitimacy of my internal expanse fulfillment by way of adventuring.

My life's preexisting appetite of must travel was then defined: The uncapturability.

Well but hold up a minute no, there was something more and I dug deep…why travel? Traveling only to inflate breadth and life into photos in unbelievable ways? *No.* So what's the why…*why travel?* Well…travel does something for me…it fills me up…comforts me…helps me feel safe…holds me tight and *travel loves me*…travel is capable of loving me and does…travel is special. Travel does all those things for me. Yes, true, but there's a level deeper. Ok…hum…I'll try better…*think-think-think.* Ok yes, travel not only does something *for* me, but travel also does something *to* me. So I pondered more…what does travel do to me…what does travel offer me? Pull it together would ya bird boy…what's the purpose here, like a solid formed assemblage that's more objective than this loosey-goosey-rickety-framed subjectiveness? Oh wait…oh fuck…oh holy hell and now I got it…wow, this shatters me still…travel.

> Travel. Only when I travel do I see the real picture.
> Only when seeing for real can I truly feel.
> Only once honestly feeling can I factually absorb.
> Only after absorbing can I retain.
> Only when on location…seeing feeling absorbing and retaining do I know anything.
> Oh good lord, I concluded…travel is my knowing…my learning…my education.
> Travel is my fricking true education.

Travel is the education I missed and the education I thought I passed on but no, I passed on nothing, the teachings are out there for me to see and know…the tutoring is right here for me to feel and learn.

Powered by the silliness of that which I am thankful for, my head swiveled side to side…yes, yes, I am an idiot. I am an idiot and all of this is out there for me, all of this is right here for me and now, right this very moment now. I never saw it, until I did, and the humility of my tears reinforced it as such, my now reversed non-knowing and nonbelief of my unedumacated self. An entire new world then opened to me. I have missed nothing, it's all out there for me, I just have to get up and go get after it.

Dark Goggles At Night
Unsure of what I was possibly getting myself into, I accepted an invitation from Spruce Saddle coworkers to go skiing on Loveland Pass.

A bunch of us are going they said, bring your dark goggles tonight they said, wear your binding leashes they said, bring your avalanche beacon they said, we're leaving at 10 they said. Yes, I said but 10? Yes 10 they said, and don't be late. Asking myself silently…is this really a good idea?

Maybe I should have found out more details before I said yes. They said 'avalanche beacon' for shit's sake.

Distributed throughout three cars, we left our home 'hood of Avon barely after 10 PM, which I still didn't understand…why so late? There were ten of us total heading east, up and over Vail Pass, past Frisco, and we parked at the bottom of Loveland Pass in an empty forest service access parking lot. One guy John from California drove his cool Chevy El Camino, which is like an opened-up station wagon, half car, half pickup truck, a cool but slightly silly vehicle. John only had room for one other person in his somewhat impractical car. In the parking lot at the base of Loveland Pass, about 9,500' elevation, everyone got out and started putting their boots on like this was normal. This did not seem normal or even reasonable to me.

Totally clueless, I followed their lead but this made zero sense. We were in the middle of nowhere, in the middle of the night, there were no ski runs, no lights, there was nowhere to go…we were in a fricking parking lot, and no lifts anywhere. Why are we putting our boots on now, I wondered? More cars started pouring into the parking lot with a bunch of crazy-looking people we did not know. My crew started grabbing their skis…time to go they said, wear your dark goggles they said, switch on your beacon they said, let's go they said. The only thought I had was, fricking go where? We started hiking through the parking lot and our big midnight expedition only carried us twenty five feet, then we stopped. What the fuck guys? We stopped near John's El Camino. The cool but impractical car was running…where the hell is John going…what the hell is going on? One guy put his skis and poles in the back of the El Camino, climbed into the car with John, and closed the door.

Oh wow, I did not see this one coming…we all put our skis and poles into the back of the El Camino too, stacking them neatly into the middle of the open-air back of the truck-like car. We piled in…sitting up on the sides of the bed of the El Camino, with our feet up against the edge of the stacked skis. This shuttle run process was unknown to me but now I get it. John started driving us up the insanely narrow and twisty-turny road to the top of the pass, almost ten miles away. Never have I been on such a death-defying ride, never…and we were going slow. The road had radical hairpin turns and we held on tight. I couldn't believe this was even a road. At the top of the 11,990' elevation Loveland Pass wilderness area, John dropped us off and said…see you at the bottom.

The scene was hectic there in the backcountry as other cars pulled up, dropping off their skiers then driving back down the mountain. We geared up…skis on, boots tight, goggles on…ok let's go they said. Go fricking where? There was nowhere to go, there were no runs, no lifts, no trails, no signage, no ropes, no guardrails and no lights, well…but oh wait, we didn't need any of that shit, we dove into the deep backcountry powder off the top edge of the pass. I paused a few times and asked if we were going the right way but I heard only giggles…keep 'em pointed downhill, they said.

With my darkest goggles on, I could see fine in the middle of the night skiing in the wilderness. At 12,000' elevation under a full moon, to my surprise, I needed my darkest goggles.

Ok, holy fuckballs…these guys were certifiably nuts…this was a new kind of skiing for me. We were leaping off livable cliffs, avoiding the unlivable ones, roaring through trees, jumping over little streams, then I was warned with a scream, "Big jump coming up Roger do NOT hit that fucking thing". Good enough of a heed for me, I saw the monster jump ahead as I came out of the midnight shadows and I skied around the ramp. Stopping slightly below and off to the side of the jump, one guy ripped off a backflip, then another dude, then another. They wore some weird kind of black leather and jean vests with Harley biker-like logos on their backs, *The Ravino's*, or so their gang colors said, aka a bunch of crazy inverted aerial rebel skiers from Vail. I never saw anybody go upside down on skis before, not on purpose, and these guys were oddly out of place on snow with their Hells Angels-type of ski wear. I was pretty sure their aerial stunts were not allowed at the ski resorts so maybe this is the place these guys lived for, aka the no-rules no-limits backcountry. Their backflip jump looked like it took a week to build and although I tried to imagine myself hitting that thing, hah, no way. I was entertained to discover this new radical breed of skiers, a level of extreme ski technique I never saw before and really, one I had no desire to attempt anytime soon. I convinced myself slightly earlier to avoid catastrophes and I believed skiing like The Ravino's would quite possibly maybe lead to a personal catastrophe, by my measure.

We arrived at the bottom after some nutty navigating through the wilderness and a pot smoke break. John was standing there with his ski boots on, waiting outside of his El Camino and anxious to ski with us. Oh my God that run was amazing, entirely invigorating…wildly crazy but thrilling. Someone else drove us up the next time, then someone else another time again, then another. We packed it in slightly before sunrise, because some of us needed to get home and prepare for work.

I skied Loveland Pass under a full moon least six more times across the multiple winters I lived there, each night included only minutes of sleep but so worth it…an incredible and startling adventure for sure. Surprisingly, the backcountry adventures under the moon on Loveland were unknown and remarkable treats made available to me only because I put myself out there, only because I rose up and said yes, only because I stretched my limits, only because I tried.

Staining the Snow Blood Red
I observed myself as the least skilled skier of the crew working at Spruce Saddle, although I didn't totally suck, well, maybe I am being a little hard on myself. Still, I was mostly outclassed and sometimes struggled to keep up. To my benefit though, we skied together regularly and I grew progressively better run after run, following these gals and guys around watching what they did and didn't do. As I saw and heard, over half of our workforce possessed formal ski race instruction or competition experience.

We connected on the snow whenever possible…before work, sometimes during a slight mid-day break, after work, and on mutual days off. Collectively, I skied with least one coworker almost every day the mountain was open.

After daily quitting time and cleaning up our workstations, requiring us to stay at the higher elevation after the lifts close, we waited for each other and would absolutely blast down the vacant ski hill en masse for the last run of the day. Last runs functioned like a wild no-rules speed and aerials contest, with most of the gals and guys launching off jumps and performing in-air show-off maneuvers. The bomber runs grew slightly death-defying at times because of the high velocity risks taken, but *knock-on-wood* rarely did one of us get hurt.

Every time I skied with my talented coworkers I improved…coveting and collecting their slight subliminal cues left to me.

At Beaver Creek, aka *The Beav*, one of the chairlifts began operation early so restaurant staff could upload and prep food before the mountain opened for business. Although the practice was highly discouraged, sometimes my workmates boarded the designated lift extra early, especially on a fresh powder day, to take a run or two before clocking in for work. Such practice jeopardized the employee's ski pass and if caught doing something like this, breaking a major rule, the worker could lose season on-snow privileges. No pass meant no reason to put ski boots on, and the so-sad boo-hoo now non-skier would be unable to work on the hill, aka a horrible circumstance. If I ever lost my employer-assigned mountain identification card allowing free winter access to the ski hill, I could not afford to buy one. After tasting the value and freedom of possessing a pass, I feared losing it or giving it up.

Squirrelly-early on a certain supporting super-fine day, one of my coworkers Rocco from New York and I boarded the reserved chairlift extra early and we headed off to gatecrash some untracked runs, because of duh, the gift from Mother Nature, aka the previous night's powder. Rocco and I planned to only do one run but most likely because of the fresh deep pow-pow, a second rip down the hill will be ordered, prior to going back up again for work. At The Beav, an almost-shielded side face of the mountain called *Birds of Prey* features a handful of legit black diamond runs, almost two miles long, and many times bumped out with moguls. Later, the Birds of Prey area was used for multiple World Cup and World Championship ski events, more specifically the high-speed downhill competitions, because of the Birds' long tails and radically steep pitches. Rocco and I selected an out-of-bounds treeless glade between two Birds of Prey runs. Skiing in the illegal out-of-bounds areas was also cause for losing our passes.

With no one in sight that we could see, Rocco dropped into the steep untracked chute first. Partway down the glade, I observed him lurch to regain his balance and deep snow rhythm, but thankfully he did not fall, then stopped safely before the thick forest below. I sensed my heart almost skip a beat when he got out of whack, because a tumble here looked like it could do real damage. Especially damaged if Rocco resultingly rag-dolled down the steepness and connected with an awaiting tree. Now, oh yes let's do this…my turn. Because Rocco experienced something troublesome during his run, I went slightly to the side and away from his path down the remote and narrow snow field.

The powder was deep and heavy, above my knees but my powder skills were strong enough. In the middle of the glade where I was avoiding Rocco's tracks, I felt something sharp and stationary grab my ski bottoms and before I knew it, I got yanked to a full stop and thrown face-first down the steep glade.

Presumedly landing on a rock that violently greeted my right side, I lay tangled amongst my attached skis and poles in deep powder, struggling to breathe through the under-surface snow stack. My muffled screams of agony I'm sure caused an immediate reaction and Rocco seemed to get there soon as he could. I am certain he experienced a major struggle to run up the almost inaccessible incline to reach me. Eventually Rocco dug down and released my bindings from my boots, then righted me slightly so I had air to breathe. Normally when taking an on-snow tumble, bindings are engineered to safely release, designed to prevent additional injuries to ski boot-wearing hoomans. However, I adjusted the tension release of my bindings to a high level so they mostly never let go. Well why the hell would I do that? Skiing with my work crew, we went so fast and landed off jumps so aggressively that sometimes my skis would pop off at the most un-opportune time, causing me to wreck-slam the snow unnecessarily at a high rate of speed. Also when skiing deep powder and if my skis came off, I might lose my skis in the thick snow if not attached by a long leash to my lower leg. Putting binding powder leashes on and off was a hassle to me and I'd rather not have my skis come off to begin with. I used top-of-the-line Marker brand MRR racing bindings on purpose because of their taller than normal retention scale, and I cranked the release tension of those puppies high, setting number 13, so my skis mostly stayed on no matter the radical forces applied on-snow or mid-air.

Rocco quickly absorbed my agony and current handicap, then took my skis away and shoved them vertically into the snow, minorly uphill and behind me in an 'X' formation.

No one was coming here anytime soon, no one was skiing here, probably not all day, but Rocco was placing my crossed skis in the snow as a signal for emergency rescue.

It was early morning before the mountain opened, we were illegally out of bounds, I was hurt, couldn't move, and I was bleeding from my right upper leg area, bleeding fucking profusely. Rocco scrambled to help but no way could I get up, more or less make my way out of this glade, no fricking way. We started to dig out a snow pit around me, trying to take a look at my leg but once I caught a glimpse, oh fuck…I told Rocco no, leave it, dude just go. Blood soaked through the layers of my clothing and was now staining the snow dark red. I did not want to lose my pass but reluctantly, I convinced Rocco to leave me. He bounded back down the hill, jumped into his skis and took off to find Ski Patrol, the on-mountain medical rescue squad.

I tried to peel back my coat, sweater, work shirt, ski pants and underneath work pants to inspect the wound causing all the blood but no, I was sunk too far into deep powder and lacked the wriggle mobility. Besides worried about losing my pass, I collected a new and bigger problem…I grew light-headed, and my vision became blurry.

Chapter SEVEN

I tried to relax, focusing on long deep breaths. Strangely, weird, I fell asleep lying in the snow. About fifteen minutes or so after Rocco left, I was rocked awake by the shouts of two Ski Patrol guys. Being kind of out of it, I was not sure if they were trying to alert me or were communicating with each other. They came roaring out of the trees and ripped down the glade with their tag-along rescue sled to pull me out of there, and probably pull the bye-bye-go-away-now pass from my neck too…boo-hoo so sad. As expected, there was no sight of Rocco. I only hoped he hightailed it to work and didn't get his pass pulled for admitting he was out-of-bounds, during preoperational hours no less. I thought to myself…oh fuck, if Rocco lost his pass I would hate myself for it. What would I do if that happened? Fuck but meh…no brainer, I'd sell my damn skis and buy him a replacement pass. I had three pairs of downhill skis and although used, I could probably sell all of them which would about cover the price of a pass for Rocco. Because me on the other hand, I will soon be without a pass anyway, probably soon unemployed, and then too broke to buy lift tickets because of this bird brain maneuver. So then what would I need my skis for? The answer would be…nothing.

The rescue guys were total pro, getting me into the sled quickly, even with the extreme challenge of backcountry gradient. Speedily they shoved some gauze down my pants but I don't think they even saw my wound. My skis tucked into the narrow medical sled beside me and they strapped me down tight, arms locked at my sides and now with a thick blanket covering my entire person, uh, *what the?*…the blanket covering even my face. So far, not a word was spoken about being out of bounds nor did they in any way threaten the jeopardy of my pass, so I tried to keep my stupid mouth shut, but then I couldn't help myself…"I think I broke my hip and can you please pull this blanket off my face?", or so I struggled to say…but the heavy wool sheathing muffled my words.

Strangely they both barely but briefly replied, "…uh huh…", and we blasted down the glade. My nose and cheeks were itchy from the blanket and I was extremely uncomfortable. Also, I couldn't see a darn thing. I gasped as we stopped suddenly at the bottom of the glade. How the hell are we going to maneuver between the tight trees? There's no way this sled will fit through there, I was sure of it but with barely a hesitation, we changed directions slightly and hauled the heck through the woods, before I felt the smooth grooved corduroy snow underneath.

They then let off the pizza brakes and our speed intensified over ten times…these guys were not at all fucking around.

Still miffed because of the scratchy-scratchy across my face, I soon understood…oh jeeze, this was by design. One patroller was downhill from me, holding onto the two long sled handles steering this train. The other patroller was uphill, the caboose, holding onto a rope and secondarily controlling from behind. Once we picked up speed, I felt the wind swirl around and sensed the accumulating snow on the outside of the blanket, kicked up from the train engineer's skis. If I didn't have a face covering now, I'd be caked in snow. I tried to relax and drop my misgivings…now understanding these guys know exactly what the hell they're doing.

Well, except, why are we going so damn fast? I was really getting bounced around and it felt wrong. I thought the patrollers were mad at me. Attempting not to let my thoughts run wild, I tried to breathe deep and drop my tension and worry. My ears were now ringing from some kind of wild sickening headache and before I knew it, weird…I fell asleep again. I awoke because of the violent jolt of this runaway rescue train. We practically landed on the bare sidewalk near the base lodge, on the edge of the bus stop curb. Feverishly the patroller guys jumped out of their skis and unstrapped me.

An ambulance crew was waiting and their gurney was already out of their medical bus, lowered, and awaiting me on the sidewalk. I was surprised to see Rocco there too which was weird but…shit, maybe they already pulled his pass and he had nowhere else to go.

The patrollers lacking any mechanical or cosmetic gear concern simultaneously dropped my skis on the sidewalk with a bang, then threw me onto the paramedic's gurney. Also, this was weird…I was cold, but sweating. The paramedics had their hands all over me, straightening me on the gurney and starting to pull my bloody clothes away from my right side. Clearly the ski patrol dudes knew the ambulance guys and they worked quickly in unison, pal-calling each other by first names and everything. The fevered flurry reminded me of an emergency room table, so I tried to remain compliant and floppy loose. Oh fuck…my face went blank as one Ski Patroller shouted at both ambulance guys, who were only inches away, and immediately I shivered violently because of his loud spoken words…them there sounds scaring all entire fucks out of me.

"He might have torn his femoral artery, there's a lot of blood, we got here as fast as we could, he was buried high in the glades".

Oh fucking fuck…my brain did a hard stop. Oh fuck-oh fuck, am I bleeding out? Is that why I can't stay awake? I did not consider that possibility…instantaneously this was a new game for me and I disoriented…my thought process sought feverishly for some sort of slight sensibility…somewhere within my bag of bones and skin there must be something to help me realize what the hell is now happening to me, because, I felt really-really really fricking lost.

The four emergency medical guys lifted me onto the ambulance without even strapping me down first…them acting like there was no time. I couldn't see Rocco right away but desperately wanted to judge his face about what the hell is going on here, maybe gain some reassurance, or even inspect his shirt collar area, but out of the corner of my eye I saw him pick my skis up off the sidewalk. My New York friend shouted at me, because maybe he expected the ambulance to soon zoom off with his broken workermate bird inside. Rocco promised to take my skis and put them back in the employee ski storage building, near the bottom of the mountain. Hah, I thought briefly…maybe they will soon be *his* skis not mine. The ambulance crew aggressively cut my clothes away and lacking room in the back of the broken bird bus, ski patrol backed up and I lifted my head to see them leave. Finally I caught a glimpse, and was relieved to see the pass still around Rocco's neck. Rocco and I smirked at each other as he lifted his pass slightly and wiggled it to show it off to me with glee…oh shit-smash, my head was pushed down flat with disapproval by the ambulance dudes.

A huge relief was breathed by all, myself included…Rocco and several standers-by crept to look into the back of the open medical truck and heard the emergency guys say loudly, "…his main lower-body blood-carrying femoral artery is fine." I had a large gash externally on my hip, and oops…internally, something was wrecked. They said I need stitches and x-rays, something is broken they said, maybe not my hip but something. Time to go they said, and started to strap me down. I refused their plan to take me to the hospital because I did not have insurance, and because I had zero money. I absolutely wanted to get things checked out but ambulance service plus emergency room fees plus stitches plus x-rays plus doctors sounded expensive, so I chose financial lessening over speedy care. Shockingly, they understood entirely, "…this happens all the time with you guys", they said…and quickly they checked vitals and performed some other medical troubleshooting for internal injuries.

Reluctantly, I stuck with my original plan to stay behind and they unloaded me from the back of the ambulance, lifted me off the gurney and sat me on the bus stop bench. One guy quickly returned with safety pins and cinched my pants back together best he could, so my drawers didn't drop to the ground. Rocco called my roommate Matt to pick me up. I was nervous the ambulance crew might make me sign something like a bill of debt, or that Ski Patrol returns to yank our passes. The ambulance left after the guys seemed to feel sorry for my bird brain self, saying they'll cover it and claim they never laid hands on me…benefits of mountain town living I assumed.

Thankfully, they also said if I can haul myself to the hospital's main entrance, a reduced-cost program exists for uninsured idiots like me.

One guy threw some dressing on my hip and gave me instructions for my mild shock. I understood the wound care stuff hunky-dory fine, and the other guy handed me a few extra-large gauze bandages. They checked my breathing and said I probably didn't puncture a lung so other than that, they let me go. I couldn't believe they offloaded me and that Ski Patrol never came back.

I couldn't walk but with assistance I made it into my roommate Matt's car and into our apartment, then to live on the couch for three days. I doctored up the wound myself, cleaning it meticulously and closing the gash with semi-inadequate butterfly bandages overlaid with medical tape. After unable to walk and fearing I had a real problem, I went to the hospital for x-rays. I was able to avoid the emergency service costs and hoped the doctor fees were minimal, which left only the imaging charges. The medical staff was pissed I didn't get stitches because now it was too late. One of the nurses mentioned a previous risk of a ruptured spleen, which would have been hard to diagnose in the field with my other abdomen and hip area injuries. We discovered my hip and lung and spleen were fine, but I had three broken ribs on my right side.

I proceeded to the hospital pharmacy in an appointed wheelchair after the nurse graciously said to look for an x-ray bill in the mail next month, shouldn't be much, she claimed. I bought a used pair of wooden crutches along with the biggest bottle of 800 MG Ibuprofen they had. The doctor wanted to prescribe me narcotic pain pills but I said thanks, but actually no, let's not, I'm an active addict.

Literally I laughed out loud, or tried to but couldn't because of my ribs when pharmacy staff offered me the special deal on crutches instead of $85 for new ones. I was already carrying a high-stack of past-due medical bills from Maryland and although maybe I should have let the ambulance team do what they thought was best, the emotional stress over bills caused me to uncharacteristically refuse care. Still, I was thankful for the used $10 crutches program at the Vail Valley hospital. Over the rest of my lifetime I would never once refuse medical care again.

Yes, Lauren this includes you when you broke your arm, your mother refused to take you to the hospital or let me take you, because of the damn deductible, her claiming you were fine and refusing to waste the money. I argued heavily saying we have to check, I've broken plenty of bones to know better, and money doesn't flipping matter, we have plenty of stupid money…look how badly swollen her arm is…and a huge fight ensued but hah, I never won a fight when tangling with the ginger momma bird. She even incriminated herself months later after returning home from your doctor after a routine visit where your old break turned up on x-rays and Andrea berated herself, "Mother of the Year" she proclaimed disparagingly, admitted she kinda messed up.

For thank goodness sake I neither lost my Vail area pass nor suffered a suspension of skiing privileges. Ski Patrol seemed focused on my well-being instead of punishing me for being out-of-bounds pre-opening. I missed over a week of work and downloaded for several more days, riding the lift both ways on foot because I was in too much pain. My hip wound eventually healed fine and I was not much worse for bird wear. My fault in the Birds of Prey glade was not my skills or technique, my fault was being there to begin with. I did not know what I did not know and I assumed the snow was least partially packed under the powder, believing someone must have already skied there that season. I never skied that glade before and I had no idea what laid waiting under the snow. Besides conditions, I should not have been skiing before work and should not have been out of bounds.

Once back on my feet, to add insult to injury I discovered the underfoot rock left a gash in my ski and ripped out a portion of the metal edge, arguably destroying it. The entire experience was a hard lesson learned and although I would go on to continue my ways of leaping before I look, this one smarted- but thankfully wasn't any worse, that torn femoral artery shit would have been no joke.

Playing with Marmot

True to his word, Paul greeted me for that wheel build interview in February 1986. As I finished up the wheels, Paul asked what was my process for gluing tires. Hesitantly I gulped, now realizing I was slightly out of my league, a situation that frankly surprised me. Almost instantaneously I committed to not lie about anything, and admitted I held no set routine. Not missing a beat, Paul started giving me specific instructions on how he does it, how he glues tires, the right way. In Baltimore I mostly built *clincher* wheels.

80% of the road bike wheels I built were the style accepting separate tires and inner tubes, aka clinchers. Clincher rims feature hooked-bead sidewalls to hold the tires despite high pressure innertubes. Otherwise, a second version of road bike wheels exist, used mostly for racing because they are lighter-weight and the tires are much more expensive, the one-piece sewn-together tube inside of a road tire, aka 'tubulars', that are conversely glued on to the rim.

I finished both of the tubular wheels and called out to Paul, "Ok I'm done", for his inspection. He said with a slight surprised and smirky stern tone, "Really? Already...ok, let's see".

He spun the wheel secure in its truing stand, adjusting the alignment calipers in close, closer, closest against the side of the rim and his mood sunshined. "That's pretty good", he said with joyous enthusiasm. Readjusting the gauges on the stand, he checked for the even more important up and down movement of the rim, "That's great, that's really great", Paul said with elated relief.

My second wheel was as good as the first, and even more so. He said ok, now we are going to get a lesson on gluing tires because I was going to need that. I reeled back slightly, wait what...I think he might have said I got the job. Paul continued with how to glue a tire his way, the right way and wow, dang...I never saw or heard of that technique before but like I said, echo, I did not work on many tubular wheels. He asked where I learned to build wheels like that and I said Schwinn School, to which Paul dismissively rolled his eyes and snarked at, "Well, it's good to see they taught you the right way and I'm surprised you got done so fast". Mostly what he meant was the precision of final alignment and the lacing pattern of the spokes, aka the correct positioning of the spokes relating to the directional geometric forces of the front and back wheels, also specifically to the right and left sides.

I began work for Paul in early 1986, before Vail or The Beav closed for the season and while plenty of snow still sat on the ground. At first I worked parttime whenever I was away from the Spruce Saddle, then fulltime at the bike shop once the ski hills closed. His bike business in Vail Village was extremely small, maybe only 400 square feet total, including the sales floor up front and service shop in the back. Like previously mentioned, the ten-foot-wide by forty-feet deep retail space was a combined bike jewelry store and euro cycle art museum. On my first day, I intently noticed, hah, that's hilarious. only two for-sale Campy tool kits were left and the following week, none remained.

Paul also leased an on-site basement place where overflow inventory, assembled bikes, and repair bikes were stored, although I think he went down there sometimes to intently scream or punch something. Initially, my main responsibilities were performing the bulk of bike repairs, building most wheels for new pro bikes, and stay the heck out of Paul's way, in that order. Repairs were bikes previously sold here or exotic bikes purchased elsewhere. Quickly I learned Paul did things a certain way, and Paul's way was without question, non-negotiable. One day a gleeful man customer dropped off his fancy road bike for repair complaining of a creaking noise somewhere near the pedals, and could we please fix it? Paul immediately asked how much man dude wanted to spend. Customer dude lost much of his glee and was briefly puzzled until Paul explained we charge $60 per hour regardless of the work so if dude wants us to find a noise, it will cost one dollar per minute, so how many minutes is he willing to pay for to fix the noise...could take hours Paul said. Boss Paul and dude customer agreed on an estimate and I stayed within the two-hour quote, tracking down and fixing the noise in barely over one hour.

When doing repairs, I kept a digital watch on my workbench, starting and stopping the timer precisely when working on the bike or stepping away.

As the summer progressed, my responsibilities changed and expanded slightly. Then my responsibilities were: Stay the fuck out of Paul's way, do-not, do-not, do-not talk to him until after lunch, go play with Marmot when Paul gets mad and before he starts throwing shit, perform most bike repairs, build most of the wheels, and start to assemble some new pro bikes, in that order. Paul perhaps woke up slow but I learned to not speak until spoken to, least until he consumed multiple cups of coffee, ate lunch, or started to open up to me first.

The first part of the workday I called pins and needles mornings…I tip-toed around, knowing better than to speak a single word until spoken to.

Multiple times I got yelled at, seemingly for just being there. Marmot arrived to work every day and would hang out in the shop or on the sidewalk out front, aka Marmot the monstrous sweetheart. Many times I used Marmot as an escape, so to help our boss calm down, or to flee the shouting…saying I was going to go play with Marmot as Paul's yelling face grew a more rageful shade of red.

While the while, one day when his make believe twin brother 'Nice Paul' came to work, he asked if I wanted to go riding. Uh, yes, awesome, I'd love to, or so I fragmented and struggled to say, and wondered if some hidden meaning lay waiting, you know, if his words were code for something else. Every morning early, Paul went on a mountainbike ride with Marmot and I was invited to join. Initially I was guarded, but in short order I discovered he wanted to include me, and once understanding the situation, I felt euphorically honored. There was in fact no hidden agenda…him sharing casual conversation as I struggled to keep up. Paul was married to a ravishing darling woman, Joanne, and she would visit us at the shop a few times a week. During our morning rides he shared with me history about himself, Joanne, Marmot, customers, some athletic and nutritional philosophies, his business progression, and the sort. Joanne, Paul and Marmot lived in a rather oddball house in East Vail, a beautiful little rustic log cabin, while surrounded by multi-million-dollar vacation mansions. Slowly I began to realize, Paul is a cool dude but somewhere along the way he seemed to get really pissed off about something and couldn't let it go, but I am assuming and judging. I liked Paul, awhile wrestled with the challenge of getting along with him at work.

I only realized the correlation later after discovering the Seinfeld TV show, and hah, viewing the episode featuring the soup nazi character. Multitudes of times, shoppers came in wanting to buy a new high-end pro road bike, usually carrying with them some expectation or temptation for brand or color of bike frame. We typically had well over 20 different road bike frames on display for shoppers to admire and ogle over. The customer sometimes said, oh I like that one or I like this one and Paul would immediately shush them, saying he will decide what options they have to choose from, but not yet.

Paul performed a detailed intake of customers' body dimensions to determine bike frame options, mainly torso lengths and thigh lengths in relation to overall inseam measurements.

The torso length produces a range of matched top tube distances on the bike frame while the correlation between thigh length and inseam produces a range of frame geometries, specifically the ideal seat tube angle for each rider. Paul would tell them they could choose this frame or this other one. Sometimes, oh boy I heard it coming but tried to back up and stay out of the way…the customer would respond playfully and say well, I actually like that different one. Paul would say sternly no, he would not sell them that one, it was not right for them and weren't they listening? If the customer's comeback was at all challenging, Paul would kick them out of the store without blinking an eye, immediately walking away from them, pointing behind him towards the door, telling them to 'get out, get out, get out'. I observed handfuls of customers get ejected from the shop for various reasons, sometimes because it was too early in the day to be talking their words out loud. Paul however was oddly fair, not discriminating against women or men, both of them equally tossed out of the store in grand yelling fashion, while Marmot raced the shunned customer out the front door, trying to run away from his angry hooman and escape the rage-filled room.

Make no mistake though, everything had to be done exactly the way Paul said because he held the deep experience to know what worked and what didn't…it fucking mattered. Riding bikes at the professional level or even at the recreational entry-point, details matter.

Lack or slack of attention to detail can produce disastrous long-term or even, life-ending results.

Besides, his personal reputation was on the line with every small detail, all of which was fine with me because I like that almost-perfection shit too and clearly, Paul knew shit-tons more than me.

Friends of a New Sort
Several bike shop customers befriended me, all guys, and individually we hung out after work, mostly listening to music, smoking pot, snorting cocaine, or riding bikes.

Soon after starting at the bike shop, a regular customer strolled right past Paul almost indifferently, approaching me with the warmest greeting I have ever experienced from a person I never met before, ever.

Charming and dynamic barely begin to describe this Dave guy. He was genuinely interested in me, wanting to know where I came from, what are my hobbies, and what am I trying to do with my life. Dave Turner was absolutely enchanting and every day carried around some bike part thing he was tinkering with. We formed a friendship and soon enough I was visiting his apartment, enjoying discussions of bikes and life and such. Dave's brain seemed to work overtime and the volume of thoughts in his head could fill a book. Dave grew up in the desert of California riding dirt bikes, he was a great skier, and he raced mountainbikes. Before the spring 1986 snow even melted, Dave and I agreed we would travel to mountainbike races together this summer.

After asking Dave general questions about the Colorado racing scene, he said no one else in Vail races mountainbikes except the two of us, and a healthy schedule of nearby races are upcoming.

Every time Dave visited the shop, his head was filled with in-process bike modifications or inventions. Every time I visited Dave at his apartment, his head was filled with food. Dave was most times cooking or preparing something edible when I popped by, and not once do I remember when black beans weren't soaking in his kitchen. The thought of black beans to me at the time was not at all appealing, but shortly after Dave Turner offered me a specially prepared taste, I was hooked, and not what I assumed the food to be. I highly admired Dave Turner, ultra highly admired. His energy and smarts filled the room wherever he went, and his creativity was not only infectious but also inspiring. In short order I felt outclassed by Dave, the while respected and accepted by him. Dave and I drove to races together in his cool old pickup truck. During those early trips I toyed with the chanced opportunity for this guy to help me believe in myself more than I can on my own. I thought Dave could help me dream, I thought he could help me better myself in a multitude of ways.

The Vail Valley held summertime mid-week road bike races, mostly uphill individual time trials after enough snow melted to open the roads. The ten-mile individual contests, aka continuous suffer fests, taught me a great deal about pre-race prep and pacing. The torture tests also forced me to enjoy the taste of pain: How much high intensity effort could I produce, how much could I sustain, and for how long. One of the real hot shot road bike guys in Vail was a guy named Mike. Dave and Mike were friends and soon enough, Dave introduced me to Mike. Mike found out Dave and I were already racing mountainbikes together throughout the state and Mike Kloser said he wanted to join us. Mike Kloser was wildly talented, rather serious, and an extremely nice guy. Mike was also a successful pro mogul skier and he seemed to be a master athlete in any possible discipline he chose to compete in. Slightly later, Mike joined us to try his hand at this mountainbike racing thing.

Mike was extremely fit, a true powerhouse. Most times at the mid-week local time trials, Mike placed in the top three overall if not winning the darn event outright, aka a legitimate aerobic beast. Near Vail, a looming mountain peak stood on display for the world to see, the 14,011' elevation Mount of the Holy Cross. A deep vertical crack with a corresponding horizontal split on the northeast face of the mountain, alas the 'cross', gives the monster its name. Yes this was a climber's peak, a famous 'fourteener' but also, rather unbelievably, crazy ass athletes would hike up then ski down the snow filled vertical crack of the cross, top to bottom in winter. Hah, crazy ass athletes exactly like Mike Kloser, one of the ultra-talented mountaineers who have hiked up the rock peak and skied down the jagged narrow crack of the cross multiple times, aka bad ass.

I remember the first mountainbike race we did with the three of us, it was at Winter Park, a resort area not too far from Vail. A few real hotshot mountainbike pros were also at that event and I fully anticipated Mike to kick ass in the race, if not win the darn thing outright. What I did not realize is that Mike was not so much of a mountainbike guy, yet. The race started and true to my predictions, Mike was off like a rocket, with Dave on his rear wheel and me in the middle of the pack. After a few miles on the course, the first downhill arrived which always thrills me.

I usually pass more of my fellow competitors on the downhill than anywhere else on the course. Less than halfway down the hill at Winter Park, a guy was pulled over feverishly changing a flat tire. Oh shit, it was Mike and I slowed briefly to make sure he didn't need anything. Mike said he was fine, don't stop, keep going, so I let off the brakes and restarted pedaling.

Less than ten minutes later, dang, Mike came storming by me like I was in reverse. Yup, I thought…this Mike Kloser guy is amazing. There was a long uphill climb and I settled into a good pace, knowing there must be a big downhill on the other side waiting for me. I reached the downhill and straight away I passed three or four guys on the decline. There was a slight hazard in the middle of the downhill because a couple of guys flatted. I was happy to see none of them were Mike. At the bottom of the long downhill though, Mike was stopped on the side of the trail a second time, begging fellow racers for an extra inner tube which he got from a dude two places in front of me. I slowed slightly to ask Mike if he was ok and he reassured me yes, I should keep going, he was ok. There was not enough distance left in the race for Mike to pass me again but I was sure if the finish line was a little further away, Mike would have caught me before the checkers.

I finished in front of Mike at Winter Park, but hah, never again, never ever again.

I was in the presence of greatness with both of these guys Mike and Dave. Mike Kloser went on to become a successful pro on the international World Cup mountainbike circuit and won the European World Championships a few years later. Mike's issue at Winter Park was his tires…he was running skinny 1.75" width tires, a selection too narrow for average racing conditions but he didn't know better at the time. Mike was getting 'snake bite' pinch flats which occur when the wheel impacts an obstacle like a rock and insufficient tire size or too-little air pressure exists to protect the inner tube. When the rim bottoms out on a rock because of low-volume tires or underinflation, the tube gets punctured and the tire deflates almost instantly. The snake bite term describes the impression of the puncture left on the inner tube: Two small slits cut in the tube directly in line with the dimensions of the wheel rim edges, producing two symmetrical bites in the tube, akin to a snake bite.

Mike then showed up at Paul's shop on Monday after Winter Park and we sold him wider 2.125" tires, the perfect selection, the same tires I raced with, and we gave him the full rundown on correct tire pressure. Mike Kloser also went on to become a multi-time champion adventure racer around the world, actually the premier godfather of adventure racing, and nowadays Mike owns a cool backpack and outdoor equipment company called OutThere USA. Mike and Dave's drive and energy as athletes, racers, and humans was unquestionably infectious. Drugs were never involved or discussed, hells to the no, these guys didn't do that shit.

Instead of thinking maybe one day my life could be better, Mike Kloser and Dave Turner afforded me the lens to see the necessary pieces existed within me already.

Instead of hoping and fantasizing, Dave and Mike displayed to me that I already possessed what I needed, I only had to grab hold of it and go.

Spending time with Dave and Mike also helped me realize I did not have to be high all the time, and I began to link together some more days here and there free of drugs, although sporadic.

Mike Kloser drove us around in his gold Toyota mini-van following Winter Park, and he did just fine and dandy racing after that, with wider tires on his bike then properly inflated. Dave and Mike turned pro after the summer of '86, but I was not ready. Although I was beating pros every race, and felt shortchanged with my inner tube prize versus their envelope of cash, I was still snorting and smoking cocaine, doing pills, acid, and smoking a lot of pot. I knew I could not perform my best while continuing to use drugs, and I was not ready to quit...nor did I think the possibility even existed...so I calculated my unpreparedness to turn pro and stayed in the expert class. Dave Turner enjoyed a successful pro racing career himself before transitioning to a race team manager and then helped some of his bike company sponsors develop better bike designs. Famously, Dave went on to start his own bike company and modern day, Turner mountainbikes are some of the finest machines in the world, and it's no wonder because this amazing dude Dave the black bean guy is behind it all.

I raced a lot in Colorado, achieving three first place wins, two in the expert class and one overall with the pros, as well as never finishing worse than fourth place expert. I built lots of confidence, learned a ton, recognized a yet untapped potential within myself and got hurt a little but mostly, I embraced my two high-performance friends Mike Kloser and Dave Turner. Mike and Dave, a couple of the extreme few non-drug-using friends I spent time with during my thus-then lifetime.

The Mile High Miscellaneous Me's

Social, what is social? Accepting my spillover retarded socialness from avoiding school or accordingly and oh well otherwise, huddled around the Devil's lair doing drugs, I thought one channel of a sunnier life included my ability to better interact with the outside world. Yes, in Vail I spent social time with Spruce Saddle coworkers but much of what we did was, duh...bake our brains. My slight time spent with various bike shop customers was primarily the shared revelry of our one Jah love, marijuana. Mike Kloser and Dave Turner were busy in their lives and although we spent hours together traveling to races, we had our own things going on and generally, our social togethering time was little.

Factually, I never settled soundly into my own bag of bones and skin while in Vail, socially. Afforded the opportunity of connecting face-to-face with this conundrum, much the while I avoided the meetups with self or otherwise on the matter and this la-la-la I cannot hear you bird brain stayed busy. Sometimes I pushed myself to attend parties hoping to meet new people, but never stayed long, intimidated to strike up with strangers and running from the open drug scene I was trying to better avoid. So off I went, training on my bike and working my ass off so I can afford to stay in the mountains.

Mutual wintertime days off, and a few Spruce Saddle work pals and I regularly hit the slopes in Vail, where our Beaver Creek ski passes transferred back and forth painlessly...but the apres-ski bar scene rubbed me the wrong way. Firstly, I stood around trying to play human...interacting with new people but resentfully silent spending money I did not have. Forcing myself to hang out like everyone else and not take off for home, I tried to fit in and meet people, I really tried. Second, I disliked all alcohol so the self-resentment when I pissed away precious bucks on booze was deflating and defeating in a major way. Third, if I wasn't working that night, I believed it better for me to train on my bike outside or on my indoor cycle trainer than stand around in a fricking bar.

One night at a big apartment bash, things were cool, I was feeling good and figured out a balanced routine to stay away from the drugs, well...until a guy walked into the party wearing the same shirt as me. His version of who wore it better was perfectly ironed and tucked in while mine was crumpled and unkempt. I felt like a spotlight followed me around as I attempted to stay on the opposite side of the room, until two different people commented on my mental turmoil...ha-ha look at that he's got the same shirt as you, right before I fled the scene.

Dave Turner was throwing a big party and the menu was said to include athletes, cool pretty people, unquestionably a great spread of food, and the featured main course for me was...no drugs. This was the type of place I needed to be in and the type of people I needed to be around, although still intimidated. The first step to my social success was making it in the door which I executed opportunely, arriving first. Assisting Dave with final readiness, my alone time with my pal the host put me at ease to know for fact, I was more than welcome here. I stumbled around and before too long, the place was packed. Expecting not to know much of anyone in this foreign scene, I pre-planned and executed a perfect intro. Walking right up to a group of four total strangers, I said hello and joined their conversation. Feeling eight feet tall and breaking the proper social ice to stick here a while, I planned to move on slightly later and meet more people over there, then more elsewhere. I was on my way to a partially-new me. The first question from the first group of four was where I went to college. With only brief hesitation, I admitted I did not go to college...I came here instead. That's ok, I thought, I am fine...I am ok. The second question was well then, when did I graduate high school? Refusing to lie and embarrassed to be the lone loser lowlife in the land, I pulled some weird food or drink or bathroom excuse to leave the group. Soon as Dave Turner wasn't looking, I fled the building.

Driving home from the party I thought, hah...I should have fricking moved to Alaska not Vail, found a remote job near Mount McKinley, bought a cheap useless sled dog as a companion, and lived in an igloo only me and my dog, then I wouldn't have to worry about ironed shirts or explaining my academic history.

Money-money. My general Colorado financial means scenario was rather bird bleak. Between the expense of rent and food and gas, I also had the cost of the drugs, ski gear which needed upgrading, bike parts which needed upgrading, and the expense of race entry fees and travel.

Mike and Dave helped me and I was not always required to pay Mike for gas. In retrospect, I believe I placed too much importance on being accepted or trying to gain more friends. Maybe I should have attempted to live more simply…tucked away in a shitty house somewhere and focused on my inner-self high-altitude reinvention.

Comprehensively, I lost sight of my two highest priorities: Stay away from the needle, and find peace, instead entwined…trying to fit in.

Shithead cocky, what is shithead cocky? Hum, I guess I got too comfortable working with the large group at Spruce Saddle and one day, my stupid talk-shit rambling mouth got me in trouble. Mother Nature absolutely dumped the night before…two feet of fresh white stuff, aka the next day being a powder day. Powder days, aka pow days, were genuine problems for employers because many ski enthusiast employees called in 'sick' to instead, spend the bulk of waking hours rolling in the deep. I never pulled a pow day at work but one such fine bright-white day, a guy called in sick. We could not replace the dude in our workflow and his absence caused extra stress on our team. Fueled by work burden and jealous that I wasn't outside knee-deep myself I spouted out loud, "I'm sure he's skiing, he should be fired", and I walked off, not thinking much more about my words. The next day, the guy I suggested loses his job over a pow day confronts me, and I learned a zinger of a judge blame and assume precept. Yes he was skiing and although he did not punch me in the mouth…maybe he should have. The resulting public verbal assault was bad enough, and I learned a hard lesson…don't judge blame or assume, hah…and don't talk shit. His words help me orient back to reality.

"Roger are you here in town to primarily work? Because I'm not, I am here primarily to ski and I only work so that I can ski…why are you here?".

I lacked much of a response other than to mumble "…you're right…", then walked away with my tail between my legs.

Romantic, what is romantic? My second ski season in Vail found me back at The Beav working behind the grill at Spruce Saddle. My dedicated role was sandwich maker, no longer having to deal with the fry machines or burger grill. I fixed simple grilled cheese, tomato and cheese, ham and cheese, and tuna melts for the busy ski crowd. I met a customer girl randomly during work and we began dating. She recently graduated from Dartmouth College in New Hampshire and came to Vail for a few months of skiing before facing the real world. We had a good relationship until she moved back east to start her rat race career. The romance relationship helped me settle down a little and not worry as much about fitting in but after she left, I let the blanket of gloom cover my shoulders. Well that's not really true…it wasn't gloom, more like a blanket of blue. After she left, my drug use began to spike again, but still no needles.

Most of the same crew returned to work at the Spruce Saddle and thankfully Shannon returned too, along with her sidekick girlfriend. As we hung out more and more, Shannon's cowboy boyfriend-type of guy wasn't around anymore. I heard a rumor she was single.

Yowzah, I wanted to ask her out but was worried about placing more complications upon myself. I also somewhat flashed back to high school when I finally admitted to Cathy Molfetas I had a crush on her. Cathy asked what I wanted to do about it, but then my tongue froze, and I walked away silently. I did not want to repeat that same sort of uncertain fumbling disaster with Shannon.

Although holding steady so far and avoiding the needle…no heroin and no meth, most of the other drugs began to increase over the winter. Simultaneously I struggled with my emotions over not turning pro on the mountainbike, my short-term girlfriend leaving, I struggled financially, and I felt generally awkward, socially. One night at my apartment, a Spruce Saddle guy friend came over and we were smoking pot, before he mentioned of a connection where to score more pot and even, some cocaine. Although yes, the last thing I needed was expensive cocaine, my mood was slumped and I found myself in slight jeopardy.

We called the drug connection guy and arranged a planned buy of pot. Hum, I believed tonight was the right kind of night to let loose and find some of that legacy drug comfort, it had been a while. It had been a while since a big bender…yes, yes I thought, maybe some cocaine tonight will work nicely. As I was leaving the apartment I twisted the knob and opened, yikes…Shannon and her girlfriend were standing there about to knock on my door. I was utterly shocked and could only muster some sort of dumb-ass words like, "What's up?". She said they 'came to see me'. I almost swallowed my tongue in disbelief. Guy friend and I already set up with dealer dude to buy drugs and now…the great dilemma.

Ridiculously, and yes I know, yes, yes I know, I told Shannon The Stunning I was busy and had to go, but thanks for coming over.

Stunning Shannon's sidekick girlfriend worked in harmony with her leader, handing me a torn piece of scrap paper with Shannon's phone number on it, and Shannon The Stunning told me to call her, whenever I thought we could hang out. My friend and I then left. Oh my God, what did I do, I am an absolute harebrained idiot.

We bought the pot, but mostly out of Shannon shame, I passed on the coke. I was not so romantically impeded after already being involved in a handful of relationships back in Baltimore, then chilling with my short-term Dartmouth girlfriend in Vail, but I was, however, an idiot.

Bad Roomie

I remained roommates with Michael and Matt but we split with JP after moving slightly east from Avon. We landed in Eagle-Vail, a sleepy somewhat creepy little neighborhood, a strip-mall-meets-industrial-park type of residential flea market. Me and the guys stayed there a while then broke up, and I had to find a new place to live. Looking back, I don't recall the specifics of the split but it seems to have occurred during a corresponding low point for me, when my drug use began to build again…funny how one reality possibly aligns with the other. I perhaps was not a great roommate and factually, maybe they kind of kicked me out, I honestly do not remember the detail on that one.

The Spring 1987 ski season was wrapping up and after being booted from Eagle-Vail, I struggled to find a place to live.

I slept in my car for a short while, not that long, like two weeks or thereabouts. The short while inside the Subaru was stressful and, hum, well…slightly embarrassing, but I was only doing what I had to do, not that big of a deal really. A large health club in west Vail charged a daily locker room access fee, so my pay-for showers kept me going. Then I was relieved and excited to move in with my pal Bruce, a customer friend from the bike shop, a cool pot-smoking dude who owned a beautiful orange Eddy Merckx road bike, previously purchased from Paul. Concurrently, I was thrilled to finally be living in Vail proper, after almost a year and a half in or around Avon and Beaver Creek. Bruce lived with a handful of other guys I didn't know in west Vail, in a real crazy place called the mushroom house because it literally looked like a big poofy mushroom. My mushroom house strugglings were real and I could not for gosh darn sake connect favorably with the other roomies. As it turned out, and oh bloody hell dude…Bruce invited me to move in without asking permission from the household.

Once I showed up, standing there with all the stuff in my arms and a smile on my face, the guys were miffed and not only miffed then got over it, but they shunned my burnout-ski-bum-leper-self. When Bruce was away from the big topper house, I assumed the feels of a blind shoeless scavenger walking across a floor of broken beer bottles. When Bruce was home, I hung close to him and we did stuff together so I was mostly ok. I had no place for my gear, rent was expensive and I slept on the sofa but oh well, least I wasn't sleeping in my car.

When not remaining in the objective world and letting my current pains creep into my historical brain, I flashed back to my youth, back to the monster house, and now this mushroom house was feeling frightfully similar, mushroom wobbly. As crappy circumstance would then rise up and punch me in the face, Bruce moved back home to the Midwest, leaving me alone with disgruntled roommates. I had recently broken my collarbone but was expecting a fast recovery. Rather gloriously, after Bruce left, I then had a room of my own.

When home, which was rare by design, I tried to relax by living a life of exclusion…camped quietly in my mushy-room with the door closed.

I carried around Shannon's number in my pocket, a valentine of sorts, although I had the digits memorized. I really need to call her with an update. I held off getting together with Shannon because of first being homeless, then the fact I was stuck in the West Vail mushrooming monster house. Maybe we can hang out at Shannon's place, or least find some sort of neutral ground where to meet. Scared to make a negative first impression with Shannon, I silently faded away and ignored her after the mountain closed for the summer.

One morning I scooted swiftly in and out of the mushy-kitchen getting ready to leave for work at the bike shop. The guys informed me matter-of-factly, they never had room for me to begin with. I was happy they were even talking to me but then refocused that the forecast of the speak was looking bad. Trying to be reasonable and not get evicted, I said softly…but then my room would be vacant. They said they had no space available because an old roomie was moving back in, which he did later that night. I was stunned and immediately thought I had to move out on the spot…relocating back to the car I suppose, but I was assuming.

Chapter SEVEN

They told me well maybe I could stay, they guess, for a while, maybe, but I had to take up familiar residence on the sofa, remove my gear from the bedroom, and still pay the $800 per month rent as before. Ok, well, hum…thanks, I said…I'd like to stay, thank you so much. I had nowhere else to go. Although living disengaged from my mushroom cotenants and not definably happy, I had a roof, the place had heat, the brief occasional showers I took weren't freezing cold, and most mornings and evenings I found an available sink in which to brush my teeth.

My top three priorities for mushy housing shifted…one, don't overreact and make it artificially worse for myself than it already is. Heck, maybe I can forge a decent relationship with the new old guy moving back in…yes, I will try my best try with that one. Two, look for another place to live toot suite. Three, pray for a small miracle, hoping I can start getting along with these guys soon. Hopefully the new-old guy helps to break some of the tension for me, or hah…least I'll try not to get my bird butt kicked out of the big poofy mushroom.

Grand Master Flash Plans

After entering my second season being Paul's right-hand man in summer of 1987, I settled somewhat soundly into a comfortable emotional position and planned to stay a while, physically. Yes, here, right here, stay here and stick with Paul indefinitely, trying to continue with these baby forward steps on my betterment-of-self pilgrimage in the mountains. Working for Paul and Pizza Hut in the summers, working for Otto's Spruce Saddle and Doni Lamson's Boot Lab in the winters felt right, it all felt right to me…safe, secure, known and comfortable.

For the mounting doubt in my head and the sprawl of gloom in my heart, I tried to do inventory of the facts and rally towards the good.

The new-old mushy-roommate and I were so-far connecting neutrally. I was proceeding slowly and thinking some slight progress was on the poofy housing horizon, but minimally, least things were not getting worse. Maybe I could lighten up and call Shannon to continue as good friends, without worrying about anything more for now and see where it goes.

If I emotionlessly shared with her my strained living situations of late, I was rather certain she would understand. Shannon grew up around here so maybe she could help me find a good place to live, with roommates I didn't feel the need to avoid. My 1987 racing season started strong and I was much faster than the year before. Although my broken collarbone sidelined me for a few weeks, I was already riding again and anxious to get back to it. Also rolling around in my head was the entertaining notion of turning pro the following season in 1988, a grand masterful plan indeed, so I believed.

Iceberg of Grumpy

Paul's shortness when I first met him outside the east Vail parking lot was barely the tip of the iceberg. Maybe he held an undernourished caffeine component or it was a blood sugar thing, then perking up once he ate his daily home-brought sandwich. Usually it was a positive interaction with a customer that broke his grumpy ice.

Sometimes out of nowhere, all of the sudden he was joking and laughing and behaving kindly with a shopper, after several hours of morning grumbling. Believing I learned how to mostly avoid true conflict with Paul…I theorized…as I worked better I could gain additional respect and hopefully earn more of his increased patience over time. Other than putting up with his dozens of barking fits, it was not a real problem…until it was. Pathetically, I could not handle Paul's chastising.

His lost assurance of me caused an almost immediate and deep-rooted abandonment of self, a giving up and fleeing that tearfully, I knew all too well.

I suffered a singular small clash with Paul which was an occurrence beyond reasonability for influence or change. The chance to remain at Paul's bike shop was likely already gone, maybe the choice to stay at the bike shop was not mine, and as it may have been, I was unquestionably fired, but I did not challenge the crystal clarity of Paul's unfixable position. Recognizing and fully accepting responsibility for the coexistence of my sense of personal urgency atop my impatience to order a silly little bike part, I knew the likelihood of my wrongdoing but I did it anyway. Believing I had accumulated an extra few feet of plank I could walk without falling into a pit of unemployed crocodiles over the possible infraction, I teased the peril nonetheless and ordered the bike part on my own, a foolhardy move for sure.

I did not, and do not, judge or blame Paul for maybe simply safeguarding what he worked so hard to build, I certainly cannot fault the guy for that. I stepped out of line. Maybe he was just done with me. Maybe I was too weak for his football attitude. Maybe it was something else, or barely a single anything at all. Maybe I should have paused and took a breather instead of blowing out of town, yes I probably should have done that, most definitely. The unfair yelling cut me to the bone, stirring something inside me I couldn't even begin to understand, or recognize. I reacted when I could have breathed, should have thought, and if I slowed, I probably would have calmed down to respond, not react. Shoulda, coulda, woulda, didn't. Mainly I was looking forward to more seasons in the Vail Valley, maybe many more. Many more ski days with my Spruce Saddle crew. Many more races with Dave and Mike. Many more plays with Marmot. Many more 3 PM cookie runs for Paul and me, most every day. Maybe a few more minutes in the presence of Shannon The Stunning, oh crap, that's what I forgot…motherfucker, I didn't call Shannon before I left. I never said goodbye to Dave or Mike, nor my tens of other friends either, and I never resigned from Pizza Hut, or thought of notifying Doni or Otto I won't be returning for the winter, so there was that.

Maybe I should have called Shannon, maybe I should have visited her, maybe she could have helped me figure out what I wanted or needed before I fled, maybe. Laughingly, I was radically indecisive about losing the friendship with Dave Turner and never leveled with him about my turning pro over drug addiction waffling, only then to leave town without a word…stupid bird. I'm sure I'll bump into Dave somewhere out in the world but most likely not in Vail anytime soon, or ever, so absurd…stone-cold stupid bird.

Once chugging up Vail Pass there was no stopping me, my mind stoutly decided.

Bombing down the backside of the pass, and then onto the eastbound flat through Summit County, I shielded the right side of my face when driving past Frisco, I didn't even want to look. A silly $2.95 bike part ended my willingness to put up with an emotional outburst, or so I believed. I threw my hands in the air, and gave up because of my perceived double-layer slathering of shouting and supreme unfairness. Once again, I doubted, I quit, and I ran. I let my emotions rule over my better decisions of true want. I wanted to stay in the Vail Valley, and maybe stay forever. My right-side veiling past Frisco was out of shame, awhile the shirking of temptation to slow or stop or stay in Summit County ski-land.

In Vail I heard the mountains tell me as I bitterly rode away from Marmot…stay, please stay young broken birdman, don't go, don't go, you belong here, we want you to stay with us…cry if you must but please don't go, no not yet, we will help you, we will console you, you are safe with us, we love you and we will love you more-more long mountaintime. Why the frick and how the fuck could I not cool it for a minute and think about some perhaps possible options? Yes I was mad but not mad at Paul, well, and truthfully not so factually mad at myself either. I felt more so like, like…like I was just so damn tired of the struggle: Stale and wasted, so exasperated about shit not working out, overtaxed, and just so damn tired of this here loser lowlife piece-of-shit PAB fucking everything up.

Hum but no, there's more than that surface-sorrow boo-hoo shit, think-think-think, must go deep…well, I was semi-sacrificing myself to forced undesirable change by leaving Vail. Yeah but, why precisely? Because deep down I believed to deserve such harm upon myself, that I merited such hurt, that I earned such negative uprooting. Instead of calming down and sitting objectively with my spilled unfairness cart of emotions, I decided to lift a few life dominoes out of the row and stop the conga line of toppling wants, needs, dreams and just, fricking, leave. Swallowed…swallowed, I swallowed it hard, I sucked up and choked down the biggest chunk of something I had ever put away in my life then-thus far, in about a fricking few seconds flat. Yes, true, the easterly travel tears soaked the front of my shirt, that is until they didn't. Rolling towards Denver, then looking at and thinking on only forward thoughts, I accepted and settled within what I learned and gained in Vail, chalking up the sudden change of eastbound travel to just another wonderful life experience.

Dropping a few pounds of high-anxiety dread, I began to silently answer my own equitably precocious question…now what, now what, now what?

The Motivations of Gambling in Vail

Now I realize something fascinating never seen to this mind's eye before. In Vail, I lacked the conscious empathy to recognize however hard I was running away from, or running towards, the other transplants alongside me were running too. But were they running, or were they frolicking? Were they free and living out loud or were they fearful and cowering away somewhere the world could not find them? I never engaged in that deep conversation of what brought you here with anyone during those two years, but I desired I would have. I only dare comprehend my own experiences, but I know intimately the mass build-up of work truth and sacrifice it took for me to uproot from Baltimore then make my way out west. Many of my peers must have faced harder challenges than me but pathetically, I gave it no never mind. I was self-absorbed in most ways, I was there for only me, awhile also learning to open my eyes, open my mind, open my heart, and let my truth flow.

I missed an amazing opportunity to understand so much more about not only those I befriended, but to learn slews more about the human condition as a whole, while sitting in that high-mountain destination melting pot. My friends acquaintances and coworkers hailed from around the world then landed on the same tiny patch of earth as me, at the precise same time as me. Hum, the concept lands upon me with a thud, all those people there on their own adventure. What drove them to leave everything behind and go? Many of them must have gambled so much, coming from far away unknown to me culture lands, places I'll never see, places and conditions I'll never know. The dynamic concerning the shared self-pilgrimage is mind boggling. I did not recognize the at-time depth and shared magic of what it was, until right this very clacky minute, but I desired I would have.

Shoulda, Coulda, Woulda, Didn't

Should I have gone elsewhere than Vail? From Baltimore years ago, I almost stopped in Breckenridge, although I would have preferred to reside near the more radical Arapahoe Basin ski hill if concluding my westward wing flapping there in Summit County. I almost drove to Vail town center, the next exit, instead of pulling over in East Vail, because of the visible commerce. I almost drove into the east Vail parking lot first without worrying about cost, but then hesitated and bumped into Marmot and Paul. I almost stayed on I-70 west awaiting a fast food joint upcoming in West Vail then pre-planned an immediate highway reentry west to Telluride, aka To Hell You Ride, the place with big gnarly mountains a full 360 view around town. I thought to perhaps keep on truckin' to Jackson Hole or Grand Targhee in Wyoming, but Colorado probably would have retained me in-state regardless, mostly because of the developed mountainbike culture. I almost did many other things but as it turned out, I didn't...I didn't, I did what I did and did not all else. Five seconds here or there would have pushed me elsewhere, and as chance would have held me away, I would have missed Marmot and Paul entirely, then I would have become someone else.

Five seconds, five-for-goodness-sake-seconds...this five second realization is so humbling to me...five seconds, five flipping seconds. Humbled...humbled, humbled am I for the almost magic-here-on-earth nature of everyday life itself, five seconds here or there changes everything. Five seconds changes everything.

Should I have stayed in Vail? Maybe an alternative path was to stick, begging Paul not to fire me, or ducking away locally, going away for a few days, and returning later to apologize my best apology. Maybe then I could have stayed. Maybe a better direction was go talk to Paul's wife Joanne, asking for her advice and her help, trying to convince Paul to take me back. Goodness knows he needed my help with the shop's mountainous workload, at the time. Maybe I could have worked for Doni at The Boot Lab fulltime. Maybe I should have restarted anew somewhere else in town, or in another town. Maybe I should have found a better apartment in Vail or Eagle-Vail or Avon. Maybe I should have stayed there and fully committed to racing, turning pro, and staying creepy close to Mike and Dave. Maybe I should have moved to Telluride after I quit Paul's bike shop.

Chapter SEVEN

Hah, quit? I do not think I quit but was fired, an irrelevant matter none the better.., oh well. Maybe I overreacted to the yelling, maybe I am emotionally too weak to handle that sort of stuff.

Perhaps conversely, I should have ridden my bike over to the cookie store, sat down with a paper and pencil to map out my new re-invention of self, after the $2.95 bearing ended my life at the bike shop. Maybe I should have gone on a day-long bike ride in the mountains that day, taking time to sit on a summit, to breathe, to center, to calm, to release, and behave from an orientation of intention. Maybe I should have done something else there, but as things played out emotionally then physically, I didn't. Should I have turned around and not left my apartment when Shannon The Stunning showed up at my door? Did I make a big mistake there too? Well, here we go...oh fucking hells to the no-no way I should not have stayed, I should have left. I should NOT have stayed. I should have left. If I didn't leave I may have not met your momma. If not meeting your momma and placing orders with the stork, neither of you would have been born, and if you two were never born, if I did not have you both in my world, *that* would have been *the* biggest mistake of my entire life, hands down.

Without even starting to imagine what any of those small shifts could have led to, I honor the choices I made, the choices I didn't, and the adventures along the way...every fricking single one of 'em, both the sunny and the dark.

Back Home Dere Hon

After driving straight home from the mushy-monsteree West Vail, I walked into my father's house in Northwest Baltimore City and was almost eaten alive by Beth's big dog Rocky, literally. Some blood was drawn but only slight, and frankly, it could have been much worse. After being gone so long, I was excited to be home and I ran into the house, shouting for Beth, only to have Rocky maul me. It could have been downright traumatic if it weren't for my solid emotional stature, straight off the road from my highly successful betterment-of-self pilgrimage and topped off by the supreme dog love realization only hours earlier. I wasn't going to let a little old dog attack deflate me, although if Beth weren't there, who knows what could have happened, probably much more blood, and all of it mine. I was a bona fide intruder who walked into the front door uninvited, actually ran in the door, ran in the door of the house Rocky felt was his responsibility to defend. Luckily, Beth was only a few seconds behind to pull Rocky off me and gave me a hug which somewhat reassured her pissed-off guard dog ever so slightly. Eventually, Roughhouse Rocky learned I was not there to cause harm but wow, that dog was clinically whacky. Maybe I don't actually need a dog anytime soon, hah, least until I go live somewhere else, and away from the kooky Mister Rocky.

Mostly because of emotional tension and a hasty drive home, my almost-healed collarbone was some kind of weird achy sore. I should have swallowed some ibuprofen about twenty hours prior, but my mind was racing rapid laps around the inside of the car way too fast to remember to open the medicine bottle.

Weirdly sore in the clavicle region but motivated, with a revised life plan outlined in my head and although anxious to catch up with Beth, I couldn't wait to open up one of my new blank notebooks and scribble down the contemplated inner chatter from the last 26 hours.

Laughingly, then back in the once-wobbly Ken Oak house, runway-walk recalling the life-legacy drug addiction I wore, I chuckled out loud that I didn't smoke weed or pop pills or drop acid the whole way home. That meant I hadn't been fashionably high in days. Stepping cautiously back into my bedroom, I felt ten years older than when I left, hah, not two. A feeling of oddness overwhelmed me once back in my prior drug den.

It was familiar, awhile I was a stranger of sorts...I was different, I had changed.

I planned to sit down and immediately crack open the notebook, transcribing my updated life plan but no, wait, something else hit me...now there was a much more pressing priority. Something else needed to happen here before I began mapping my new life orientation. I went downstairs in the kitchen and pulled out a single Ziploc baggie from the drawer under the silverware, sandwich-sized. Oh yes, I thought, oh yes this is going to be perfect, this is gonna be great, this is exactly what I need, this is exactly what I need but didn't realize, until I got here. Back upstairs, I opened the baggie and began carefully dropping in one by one, the multi-colored pushpins holding up my practically wall-to-ceiling posters, first from the ceiling. I laid the legacy papers out on my bed, and next came down the wall art, almost like the guy who hung these is gone now and what's left is only me, me the new and improved him. Some of these had been in the same place for a decade, but now, no longer. I stacked the three-foot by two-foot papers neatly, making sure I won't hurt any dangling corners hanging out, then rolled them up, the posters in one big ream. A large temporary rubber band held them secure until I found a correct sized box and put them away on the top shelf of my closet. Everything felt so different, so much brighter, so much smaller because I felt so much bigger, and, well, these feelings of change, and these feelings of newness were overwhelmingly powerful, so powerful that, oh no, no wait a sec, stop, just stop. To say any more would be an injustice, so no, I won't, I know not the words so I won't, I will not carelessly ramble.

Hum, I felt strongly out of character inside this room...veritably, the only thing I could think of was mapping out a brand-new life plan on paper, not reaching for my Tokemaster or shiny gold cocaine snorting straw. Deciding to instead use residual high mountain benefits to my advantage, both attitude and altitude, I scribbled down what was on my mind during the drive more than halfway across the country.

1. First: Bike racing comes first, period. Put and keep racing in front of drugs, fucking period.
2. Second: Find a good job I love. Put and keep good work in front of drugs, fucking period.
3. Third: Have fun, do shit, travel, don't sit, and try not to slide backward in body or mood.
4. Fourth: Hold steady on drugs. Eliminate more than I increase. No needles, fucking period.
5. Fifth: Start rebuilding the Camaro when time and money allows.
6. Sixth: Throw the broken motorcycle pieces away, I have more important shit to do.

Back to It

Well, or so I figured, since committed to the notion that racing comes first, it makes best sense for me to land a bike shop job, and a good one at that. Not only can I benefit from the discount on much needed replacement parts, but I imagined my highest current earning potential existed in the bike business. Although I initially figured I would go back to Mount Washington, the store had changed ownership when I was in Colorado. I then hesitated on Mount Washington Bike Shop, trying to stick with my documented plan to find a place I would love, not merely like or tolerate.

It did not require much thinking to imagine where such a great work environment might exist for me.

Choosing to go visit Alan Davis at the newer Princeton Sports location in Columbia before visiting Mount Washington Bike Shop, or so I figured, was a great idea. As expected, Alan was elated to see me, genuinely, and somewhat surprisingly so. Hah, maybe he was happy I wasn't dead, based on the condition I last saw him in. At first, and I should have known better, Alan refused to talk about a job. Alan was almost bouncing up and down in his big fancy office chair with excitement, demanding a full rundown of my time in Vail. What did I do, he wanted to know…what did I like, what did I gain, what didn't go as planned, and what did I, possibly, leave behind out west once I came back east. Alan was especially intrigued with my experiences working for Paul at the bike shop.

Alan was mostly up to speed on my drug addiction I think, but I do not believe he ever knew about the needles. I never came clean with Alan regarding my motivational driver heading west, and it otherwise never came up. Fearing I was sucking up too much of his time, I tried to wind down the Colorado chatter. Always the perceptive one, Alan then speedily offered me a job, a really great job with more money than I ever expected, and once I failed to hesitate, he hired me on the spot. I never entertained a conversation with any other bike store about working elsewhere.

Idol

One of the supercool guys I met when working at Princeton Columbia was a legit Mid-Atlantic hotshot BMX racer guy, Wayne Racine. Wayne was sponsored by the Princeton Sports bicycle motocross team, aka sponsored by Alan Davis. Wayne and I rode mountainbikes together several times and we spent hours talking about bikes and racing culture. At the BMX racetrack I idolized Wayne, he was jovial and flamboyant while humble and he most times won the premier class of the day. On mountainbikes Wayne and I were basically equal, except I held much more trail speed and endurance than Wayne. Jumping, Wayne killed me, he was so talented. While at the BMX track, he was ten levels higher than me, aka I sucked at bicycle motocross. Wayne and I were also cut from the same bolt of extreme cloth, pushing harder than hard on the bike and not afraid to fall down. We did not always fall, only sometimes, a relatively very small percentage of the time factually.

Wayne and I usually won our respective disciplines, him on the track and me in the woods, aka pushing hard.

Wayne and I both had amassed a serious collection of concussions already because of occasionally hitting the dirt, but not knowing any better, we brushed off and kept going, us barely able to see the baby dragon becoming a monster through the brain damage stars in our eyes. Back then, we had no knowledge of the mounting dangers of decades-amassed concussions. I grew more serious about racing and about distancing myself from the drugs than Wayne, although he was still hyper-talented and performed accordingly.

Yes I was still using drugs, but trying to lead myself oppositely than years past.

Wayne and I were well-aligned friends, he inspired and supported me, and it was glorious.

Not Falter Nor Hesitate

The Columbia Maryland community is an affluent area, located closer to suburbs of Washington DC than Baltimore proper. At the time, Columbia was a hotspot for triathletes, featuring an Ironman event and race directed by an awesome Princeton customer of ours, The Big Vig. Every year hundreds of spectating area residents were instantaneously inspired to become triathletes after watching The Big Vig's Columbia Ironman.

Although Princeton Columbia was a large semi generic multisport store, Alan approached me one day asking what I thought was needed to build a high-end pro bike business here, aligned with my accounts of Paul's tiny pro shop in Vail. Huh, and what, say what…Alan's proposition caught me off guard, I almost looked over my shoulder to see if he meant to address someone else, hah…someone else behind this here not-me person.

At all other previous times in my life, I would have waffled and thought myself unqualified to even comment on such a question.

Although I hesitated for a second and almost laughed at him, presuming the financial investment to do such a goshdarn for goodness sake thing outrageous, I also knew Alan Davis was not at all fucking around. Alan Davis is not the joking type, especially when it comes to business. Standing here and partially unsure still today, I ponder the validity of what my Princeton friend boss Alan saw in me back then to initiate his puzzling probe. Notwithstanding my drug use, emotionally I had grown taller, albeit in a slightly askew and dismayed way, after my European and Vail experiences.

Debatably then, and derived from Alan's multi-year canniness watching this here PAB evolve, reasonably he appraised an in-motion betterment of me, but I am assuming.

Returning home from Vail and vocation-wise, I thought myself barely worthy of a role within a small and simple bicycle and ski mechanic trade, nothing more, that's all and fricking forever, me barely affording to survive but who flipping cares.

I gave zero fucks for achieving anything, well…that is, ugh…long as I could continue to successfully stay away from that motherfucker the drug needle.

I possessed no career goals or financial dreams for myself whatsoever, zip-zero none. All I gave notice to was racing and one day maybe moving further from the drugs, aka simple fucking survival. In these ways and several more, I guess when I look back, I began a collection of ideas for a possible sustained future, awhile settling however so plus-a-minus into my factual reality.

Instead of presuming Alan's true willingness or budget to start such a Vail-like pro shop operation in the ho-hum sleepy hollow of Columbia Maryland, although I still wanted to chuckle out loud and dismissively judge him away, I quickly assembled my best thought formations.

This was brand new for me…for the first time in my life, ever, I required a generated presentation to flow from my mouth, a no-prep pitch nonetheless, and right here, right now. I was not sure how I would be heard. I somewhat thought to head-dart, you know, fall flat on my face without the chance to even put my hands out in front of me first, but I swallowed a breath of big-boy oh fuck it courage, and went for it. Went for it. I went for it mostly because of high comfort with my audience Alan, I knew enough of the subject material, strangely I did not doubt myself, and I placed no self-defeating limits of my proposal's acceptance into my thoughts or vision. I presented in a comprehensively professional manner, but I have no idea where this put-together shit came from. My main intention was to not get in my own way of succeeding here, hah…aka this was new for me, aka try not to mess myself up.

1. Well, as I told Alan, and I tried not to laugh or smirk…if we are going to do this, we have to do it right. If we start slow with just a little of this and a little of that, I do not believe the right kind of customer will respect us. We could go further and marginally overboard, but I don't think we should do that either, not yet. Let's jump at the chance to build it up, watching carefully to see what the pro-business does digit by digit and day by day, gauging honestly, and forecast aggressively where it could go from there. We will have to keep critical watch over what's NOT working.
2. We will need to attend the training for the state-of-the-art skeletal measurements system like Paul uses in Vail, the FitKit. The company is located in New Hampshire and they host training seminars, will cost about $5,000 per person.
3. Buy a FitKit along with the necessary adapter plates to do the work for the bike shoe and pedal cleat adjustments, will cost about $3,000.
4. Buy a Campy toolkit, will cost about $2,500.
5. Set up a committed fitting area in the store near the service department. We will need a dedicated stationary bike trainer, extra parts like handlebars and stems and more, a four or five-drawer rolling toolbox, two stools for sitting, signage, etcetera, will cost about $1,000.

6. Establish fit pricing, an appointment process, and promotions. Stock some pro bike frames, components, pre-built triathlon race wheels, well as a bunch of rims and hubs and spokes to build custom wheels ourselves and put somebody in charge of it, will cost about $15,000, or more.
7. So what's that total, hum…*silent internal chuckle*…around $25,000, or more.

Hah, I almost laughed out loud when I verbalized that final number…twenty-five-thousand-dollars, or more. I started walking back to the shop, I had work to do, but Alan barked at me.

"STOP and get back here", he said.

Oh fucking hell, what the? I felt like Paul from Vail or Alan's dad Sonny was now yelling at me. Alan had something to say. The only response I imagined hearing would be…oh, ok, well, let's wait on that for a while, maybe next year, or something like that, so I started walking back to the shop because I had work to do, well, that is before I turned around as directed by Angry Alan.

"Call the place in New Hampshire and register yourself."

" Order all the stuff you think is necessary, all of it, I'll pay for everything."

" Work with Lee and tell him what you need."

" I want you to run it, you ok with that?".

"Uh, yes…", I stumbled slightly and mumbled loudly, "Wow, that sounds awesome…I think, I think we can do something really cool here, thanks Alan, that's amazing". Immediately, and oh motherfucker what the…Alan lunged at me, him aggressively jumping all up in my face and shit, what the fricking hell, I thought he was going to punch me, he was fricking furious, his finger came flying towards my nose and I stepped back straight away because he almost head-butted me.

"NO, we ARE going to do something TOTALLY FUCKING AWESOME HERE and YOU are going to make it happen because YOU ARE fucking amazing."

My friend boss Alan stormed off cockily with pride of his commanded positive enabling. My legs swelled upwards with Jack and The Beanstalk type speed and I was eight feet tall again.

Alan super-strutted back upstairs to his office and soon after, I met with Lee our general manager to set things up.

Slightly later, we became the factual fitting pro shop we planned for, and Alan did not falter nor hesitate to support me in every way, and if anything he exceeded his commitments. One of my first pro bike customers was The Big Vig himself. I built him a beautiful yellow Pinarello road bike from Italy with Campy components and of course, outfitted with my hand-built wheels. Our Princeton Columbia pro bike and fitting business bloomed and was profitable, much by word of mouth from the hands-on relationships I built with my hundreds of customers, aka a fantastic win-win. In his own kind of grumbly way, I think Paul back in Vail would be proud of me.

Good Roomie- Late Roomie- Bad Roomie

On the clock at Princeton Columbia, I was struck by an attractive petite peer gal working in the sales department, Vickie. Almost immediately, Vickie and I were dating. When I was 23, she moved in with me at BigBird's house, alas my first live-in girlfriend. Vickie was about the same age as me, she liked to ski, mountainbike, hang out, listen to music, and also smoke a fuck-ton of pot, so needless to say we were compatible in several specific complementary regards. Not knowing what to do right or avoid doing poorly alongside a live-together GF, our dynamic was not so variable. We stayed busy during waking hours with sports and for the most part, we went everywhere together. If we weren't biking, skiing, walking in the woods holding hands or smoking pot, we were working. Vickie did not have a car and thankfully, her work schedule was adjusted by Alan The Awesome to match mine.

On a good day, the drive from Ken Oak Road to Princeton Columbia took about 40 minutes. On a bad day, busy traffic demanded 60 or more of our commuter minutes. The first big problem in the relationship with Vickie rose its ugly head almost immediately, time. For me to be 'on time' for work, by my measure, I need to walk in the building five minutes early. I knew what time we needed to leave home, I've forever been good at that timing shit. Thinking early communication with Vickie would help, meaning I would let her know what time we needed to leave, well, it didn't matter, she was every-day late. The tension concerning getting out the door in the morning was unfortunately carried with us to work. We fought about it almost every day. Some days by the time we got to work for frick's sake, we weren't even talking to each other. It was fucking awful. It felt awful, it looked awful, and with patheticism, I did not see the compounding problem.

Vickie and I began fighting a lot about other shit too, not only about getting to work by my clock, but money, gear, and much more, although we also made up quickly and aggressively. When it was good it was good but when it was bad it was horrible. In the end, the relationship got the best of us, mainly me. After more than a year of this romance wobbliness, Vickie moved back into her shared place with her sister in Howard County near Columbia, although we did not break up. Well, I didn't think we broke up but looking back, maybe I was being naïve.

Embracingly, I welcomed the reduction of stress and oh wow, surprise, I immediately felt incomprehensibly better.

I felt better individually, better in the relationship with Vickie, better on the bike, and better at work. I could now operate by my measure without judging and blaming her, what a huge relief. Not sure if it was going to work out with Vicki long term, but a churning inside me knew living apart is the only way it could, least long as we were working together. I knew I wasn't going anywhere workwise, and never did I consider asking Vickie to change jobs. Hum, I don't think I would make such a suggestion to someone I was dating, no actually that's a lie, I do know for fact I would not do such a stupid thing for goodness sake, meaning me asking my partner to change jobs because of my desires, uh yeah, fuck that noise.

Taking a cleansing breath shortly thereafter, I attempted a thesis regarding my time living with a girlfriend.

Hum, I thought, what worked there and what didn't? It might be a weird thing to think about but I had no baseline or example of what a successful togethering couple looked like. The ugliness and shadowed time of the live-in relationship with Vickie was something I would prefer to learn from and hopefully avoid other such badness futuristically, if at all possible. I never had, duh, togethering parents as a comparison.

Immediately I saw the problem as Vickie's inability to leave for work on time. *Uh, NO.* The problem was Vickie's inconsideration of me and my schedule. *Uh, fuck NO.* The problem was me and my controlling demands of needing to leave at a certain time regardless of another person. *Duh, like NO.* The problem was me and not accepting the relationship for what it was, then appreciating the added complexity of living with a romantic interest I also worked with. *Oh for frick's sake and hells to the NO.* The problem was me living with someone I worked with, the condition seemed to mess everything else up. *NO, NO, NO.*

Knock-knock...hey dummy. Huh, me, say what? Oh wait, ah, now I get it, those are issues, not really problems. *Correct, what's the real problem mister ding dong?*

The real problem, hum...think-think-think...ah, I got it. As I finally saw clearly, the problem was my mistake of dating anyone I work with. Jeeze, first I incorrectly blamed another person, then I blamed myself but hum, weird, this was more of an objective computation...the numbers didn't work. *Correct, nice recovery.* Uh, thanks, I think...yeah now I get it, maybe I should try to never do that again. Don't date anyone I work with, seems to mess everything up and I cannot see how that would ever work for me, by my measure. *Nice, good thought, yeah, why don't you try to do that from now on?*

A few days after Vickie moved out, she asked for me to please bring over some stuff she left at the house, no huge rush. I stopped by one morning to make the delivery. Pulling into her gravel driveway, and sure she was still sleeping, I planned to lovingly sneak in and surprise her with a good morning smoochie kiss on the forehead. If the door was locked, I would simply leave her things outside and not bother to wake her. I pulled up glancing at the porch, hoping I can get in the house undetected but...wait what? What the fucking hell really, are you kidding me? I disbelieved seeing what I was seeing.

The time of day was early enough, and I presumed no one had been in or out of the house this morning already. Vickie and her sister were not exactly early risers. In plain view there on her porch was a bike, a bike I assumed had been there overnight. I recognized the bike immediately and recognized it very well, although I could not believe it and no, it was not Vickie's bike or her sister's bike. Oh fucking well...I said to myself out loud as I opened the driver's door of my car, the same door I slammed shut behind me. Oh fucking well, and what the fuck ever...I grumbled out loud as I stomped across the gravel.

I left Vickie's stuff on her porch, appropriately, right next to the bike. Yup, check...the bike that I assumed had been there overnight by the looks of it, well, it had untouched morning dew on the seat and everything. No more talking out loud to myself occurred next, or to anyone else for that matter. Quietly, I got back into the Subaru, closed the door did not slam the door, and drove away.

No spinning of tires occurred, I threw no rocks at Vickie's window, I did not drag the bike to the gravel and run it over, nor did I lay on the horn as I left. Not a word was spoken between me and my as-of-that-minute but then ex-girlfriend that day, or the next. Several days later, Vickie quit Princeton by way of a brief business answering machine message on the work phone. Oh well, that issue got resolved, so I figured.

The following week I heard the porch-bike owner was now living with Vickie, porch-bike guy being my BMX racing idol friend Wayne Racine. I didn't blame Wayne, I guess, although I was not happy with him. Vickie was super cute and factually I imagined those two to be super cute together, both of them blondies, but I did not speak to Wayne or Vickie after that, nor did they speak to me either. Oh yeah, back to when I was making the early morning delivery…no thank you very little, I did not check to see if the house door was unlocked.

Little Fucking Dark Fucking Raincloud

Long ago I gave up being feathers-ruffled about the Vickie thing. Years later, Wayne's name popped up and my heart immediately sank, in a sickening way. My brain scanned back over the past three decades and somehow, however supernaturally, I felt factual mental and neurocognitive tingling's, me then tasting some of Wayne's pain across the time of all those thousands of days from then til now. My right lip absorbed a couple of tears, and one soaked in on my left side too.

Well then thereupon motherfucking hell…here they come and theretofore they go, those little dark rainclouds, and this is just how the fuck life works out for some of us sometimes.

I felt guilty that I let go of my old friend because of a girl, and because of a relationship I heard didn't even last long for them. I felt guilty letting go of my friendship with my once-idol Wayne and allowing so much distance to grow between us due to any goddamn reason, well, um, because, because, fucking because it came out that Wayne Racine actually needed the exact fucking opposite of distance.

Wayne needed people to stick by him, not fucking give up on him.

Wayne needed his friends like me to stick by him no matter fucking what.

I think we all need that, human support no matter fucking what.

Wayne's mental health took a tragic nosedive and in August 2020, Wayne Racine took his own life. Wayne ended his beating heart after a multi-year struggle with depression. Although I have not dug around to gain detail, and certainly I am assuming, but I believe these my thoughts have great merit. There is a good probability Wayne struggled with CTE, because of a lifetime of concussions, this being the same assumption I have of myself, me and my presumed partnership with that fucker CTE.

Hot Rod Momma

When I was away for two years in Colorado, my best friend Mark Weinreich dated one of the figure skating pros from Northwest Ice Rink for a while, Shelly. By the time I got back to Baltimore, Mark and Shelly the skating pro had broken up but they still seemed like good friends, although I never really knew the depth of their relationship.

Shelly lived by herself in a north Baltimore suburb, inside the house where she grew up, accompanied by her two hot rod momma badass cars, a flat rear window 1976 Chevy Corvette with its removable t-top roof sections, and her 1965 Ford Mustang, both in the perfect color for such automobiles, red.

Shelly was beautiful, one of those rare humanoids who is almost too much…too cute, too cool, too gentle, too easy-going, too perfect, and too nice. After Vickie and I broke up, I was working for Princeton one night at an off-site consumer ski show downtown Baltimore and basically as friends, Shelly and I drove to the show together. Before I barely knew what was happening, sparks were flying between Shelly and me, and the magnetic attraction from my driver's seat to her passenger perch was extremely powerful and hard to resist.

The next day I checked in with my long-time best friend Mark, he said no problem, he was already dating someone else and gave me his blessing for me to spend time with Shelly. Shelly and I were living together in her house not long after our first date. She no longer worked at the ice rink but was a bartender at a busy and successful beach bar on the Delaware shore, about three hours away. She made good money, mostly cash, and spent most every weekend during the summer in Delaware working. Shelly being away for weekends and seeped deep within a party scene made me worry somewhat, but she never once gave me indication of anything inappropriate happening in Delaware. She rented a room in a large house with multiple coworker roommates, a mixture of guys and girls, most of whom lived there fulltime. On several occasions I visited her down da beach hon and once I got there, I felt absolutely secure nothing inappropriate was happening. I was met with genuine open arms by her workmate-roommates, them saying that my girlfriend brags about me all the time. Still, the general bar scene made me unsteady.

First Child

Beyond working fulltime at Princeton Columbia, I also trained over 10 hours a week on the bike, and raced often as possible. Shelly was still working at the beach on weekends, usually leaving home Thursday and not getting back until Sunday night or Monday. My super sweet girlfriend Shelly did not ride bikes and after I surprised her with a very expensive Fisher mountainbike tandem, a bike built for two, she curtly said um no thanks. We shared our time around the house watching TV and movies, hotrod cruising in Shelly's Corvette many times with the cool car t-tops off, and went skiing together now and then. Our relationship was good and before long, I felt some additional something could like help make our shared homelife even better. I gave the situation some true conscious thought and I finally realized some filler material would work nicely.

I became a father to my first child in March 1989, a rambunctious little blonde-haired boy named Bailey, a darling-versioned Woolly The Mammoth of our own…a long haired yellow lab Newfoundland mix who loved water and snuggling with his momma Shelly and his daddy Roger Ray.

I loved being a doggie daddy. Bailey was hilarious, a legit maniac around water. When I operated from a bucket washing cars, I learned to keep Bailey inside because he would dig and dig in the bucket, not only splashing the contents about but eventually knocking it over entirely. He seemed to not be able to control himself around water, a condition I would find is a bird boy trend with my second son too, the humanoid version T-Bird and his displayed mismanagement of hoses and water soaker guns.

The dynamic of Shelly going to the beach every weekend wasn't horrible because I was off racing anyway. Shelly joined me at the races every once in a while but it was rare, because she most always needed to work. At the end of every weekend, I would come home from races with awards or prized cash and Shelly would come home with a box jam packed full of work money. Most always, the first order of business was to wash and sort Shelley's bartender money. Typical fare bar drinks at the beach accounted to mostly brightly colored sugary concoctions that when spilled left a sticky mess all over everything, even the cash going back and forth across the bar. Shelly made multiple hundreds of dollars and usually thousands every weekend. Our teamwork cleaning and stacking her dollars was some of our best quality time together. I brought Bailey to most races, unless Shelly was home and preferred not to travel with me over the weekend. Shelly and I enjoyed parental play time with Bailey, and we were a good little family, long as it lasted. Shelly was amazing, too amazing for my long-term bitch bird stupid ass. She deserved so much more than what I offered her, then later took away, same thing with Bailey, our future poor darling torn-apart-household woolley boy.

Rocky the Whacky Dog

My best friend middle sister Beth has had dogs most of her life. Her big dog Rocky who tasted my blood when I gleefully returned home from Vail was a great canine and pet in many ways…loyal, a good defender, and a good companion. Beth loved Rocky very much, very-very much actually. As the sad-sad tale then played out, whacky Rocky swallowed a dish towel which became lodged in his intestines and required emergency surgery to remove, a challenging ordeal, especially because Beth could not afford it. But Rocky was her dog, so, duh, of course the emergency surgery proceeded. Thanks all goodness, the chosen operation saved Rocky's life. Beth was making regular installments, yet before she could pay off the vet bill, Rocky bit our niece Brittany in the face, aka Laura's daughter Brittany. Beth made the brutally fucking hard but fact-one-necessary decision to have whacky Rocky put to sleep after he crossed the line and attacked one of his hoomans.

The Enlightenment of Minutes

Over four years' time had passed since I first entered the self-propelled two-wheeled industry, and by then the general practice of billing bike shop service customers by the hour, or a flat-rate version of by the hour sunk into this bird's cranial sponge as standard. By then, the customer shop charges routine rang my bell as commonplace to the point I gave it no never mind, aka habituated bird. When starting work for Paul in Vail, he explained 'his way' service billing as a straight-up hourly rate but still, initially the bejeweled criticalness did not sink into this biddy's brain.

I believe it was the third day…I paused my stopwatch perched upon my workbench to break away and help a customer on the short runway salesfloor, and that's when the idea of minutes hit me, the idea hit me profoundly.

Minutes count…every minute counts.
Every single standalone minute counts, counts greatly.
Every minute has value, great value, great-great value.
Every minute is a choice, what I do and what I do not within those 60 seconds.
Every minute is an opportunity to move in my intended direction, or sit sour and stew.
Every minute is absolutely fucking precious.
Every minute, every minute, every minute…am I mindful of how I spend every minute?

Sparked by the clocking in and out using my inelaborate workbench stopwatch in Vail, I was rewarded to see the wondrous life opportunity lay awaiting me, within every day, every hour, and of course, every minute…oh my word the treasure within the disconceal, the sharp sanctity exposed, the humble honoring of time, yes, the enlightenment of minutes.

Hunter bird overhead eyes prey underfoot

A butterfly flutters muttering 'sum brand new tune

The sun gives up 'n decides to set around noon

If believing drowning tonight

Count right all the words wrong dragging along

Adversaries of the world fought just to fight

Stopping to sit to now sing this song

Momma bird never told me a word

Poppa just let me be

Nowhere else a dream came to dream

All believed lost lives under me

Broken heart-hearts lost at sea

However far gone just I holds the key

Day to day darkness allows me to see

Back to the beginning I begin to be

The feasted pain within the rain

The bought bright past the light

The understanding within the fright

The gain collected beyond all sought sight

Finally, finally I see-see the real seeings of this here glorious me-me.

Why for Fuck?

Everything I have ever desired, forsaken, or feared...my dreams and my hopes, well, it all currently exists within one singular den, that being abottom the dormant cave within me. Meaning to say I possess it all, already. Thereby how effectively I face, work to resolve, and learn to live with these challenges is a self-evident reality beyond any earthly fucking doubt.

I am the judge and jury of me, long as I retain these withheld inner factual truths dear to heart, aka embrace these responsibilities as *my* way, this my proprietary operational self as Roger Ray Incorporated. And then of course, there is my outer, specifically you my brood.

Never could I explain to uncover my love, my care, and my sacrifice-willing for you two my darling dears.

Perhaps you will experience similar sensations one day if becoming parents yourselves. If so, I hope you can treat yourself tenderly enough while remembering we all try our best. We try our best and factually, that's all we fricking got.

Putting to rest this volumed one second edition, simultaneously I work tirelessly to promote the Addict book hence helping to save lives, while continuing excessively on the opus memoir volumes two three and four. Additionally my produced poetry is in full swing, well as a couple more poignant stand-alone life title publications. And why is it that I do these things exactly? This I do, this I do for you. All for you to echo-perhaps find a slight peephole into who I am and why I do what I do, so to help you figure out more of yourself, and help you fly your best flight, aka sharing some of what lies between us.

Ingloriously, duh, these publications will survive me, yet the thrill, the joy, and the completeness I collected while putting every single aspect of my functional life aside so to do this work for you is something I absorbed without sacrifice whatsoever, I just wish I woulda thunk it up sooner.

Paramountly, as I sift through all these here my thoughts, I am sorry for all I have said or done to hurt you. Never in my wildest daymares did I intend to affect you negatively in anyway whatsoever. Factually, my intent was quite the opposite. So, my two darling dears, I am very, very, very sorry.

Nothing But You

And so then, some slight anxieties flood me imagining when my last day will come, me thinking how I'll spend the final token of my life.

I hope to go painlessly and fast, with you both holding one of each my hands, feeling your soft dear kisses planted on my cheeks as I breathe my very last breath.

Hah...perhaps I slip in the shower, then found bound on the floor. Could be I drop softly to the ground as I chop wood or cut grass. Maybe I leave you as I cycle or ski or hike towards the sun. Perchance my heart just stops as I lay out on a scratchy park picnic table beneath a curtain of stars, and full-moon treasured by the night's mesmerizing sky.

Regardless and without question, please be totally fucking certain that however or whenever, wherever and nearby whomever I make my exit, my thoughts will be filled with nothing but you.

Nothing but you both will create charge within me, and my face filled with only the entirety of love for nothing but you my two darling baby birds, for you my preciouses.

Love you, love you more, love you most because of my bigger birdy bigger boyd bigger heart.

All my hugs and kisses for you forever and always.

Always with you, always a part of you, fucking always.

XOXOXO, BigBirdy-BigBoyd.

Lies Between Us INDEX

A Happening of Consciousness, a poem...8

Astronomy...255, 260

Automotive designer dreams...47, 52, 157, 235, 261, 277

Be It That of Destiny, a dark trilogy poem...214

BigBird's love versus busyness...46, 86, 97, 158

BigBird's cigarette smoking ...75, 224

BigBird's workshop...46, 48

Your Birdy and Boyd's inquisitions...67

Cousteau-bestowed audio-video educational society...46, 255, 276

Drug dealing why and how...59, 96, 247, 255, 275, 313

Fam-Fam, a poem...30

First book I ever read...99, 154

Friendship I Measure None, a poem...15

GED...287

Glossary, Roger Ray's bird beak blabber defined...52

Grown Up, a poem...253

Heart Songs, the influence of movies upon me...227

Huminity, a poem...6

Hunter Bird, a poem...331

If Existence Were a Song, a poem...242

I must ask something of you both my precious...41

I was born on a springtime Tuesday...224

Idol...47, 265, 321, 327

Introducing, the bicycle...155

Lacrosse athlete dreams...51, 96, 276

Lightless, a dark trilogy poem... 215

Little Bird, a poem...45

Lives I Led, a poem...78

Many summits high I have climbed...37

MathTest...56, 94, 234

Mechanical beginnings...48, 51, 156, 271

Monster house...223, 225, 230, 240, 256, 315

Motorcycle racer dreams...47, 51, 235, 255, 276, 320

My book reading how-to...166

My Breath, I Breathe, For You, a poem...3

My Saviors...10, 197

My mother the houseless bag lady...38, 179, 225, 256

Lies Between Us INDEX

My precious, to you and for you...3, 36, 44, 67, 74, 92, 98, 142, 210

Need it or Want it, Give it Away, a poem...148

Needs and wants...204, 320

Nonfictional Novella, a poem...80

Not Entirely Original, a poem...153

Not To-Do's, a poem...151

Number One Priority, a poem...82

Only in the shelter of others...14

Opus, aka my rules for living...69, 121

Paul Ankers Senior...156, 235

Raindrop, a poem...60

Roger Ray's ruinous rage...47, 83, 129, 139, 258, 260, 267, 273

School- high school different curriculum courses...277

School- Baltimore Polytechnic Institute high school...12, 50, 86

School- dropout...12, 50, 86, 251, 259, 276, 287

Singular Focus, a poem...68

Sonny Davis possesses super-human powers, legit...243

Ski racer dreams, downhill...32, 47, 280, 289, 298, 311

Spice, a dark trilogy poem...213

Staining the snow blood red...298

That goddamn 200-pound floating picnic table...250

The great water gun incident...142

The Four P's...174

The life of adventuring...37, 49, 154, 255, 278, 296

The Trifecta of Ugly...40, 89, 92, 95, 101, 107, 110, 114, 121, 140, 312, 326

The uncapturability of nature's awe...295

Three pre-adult supreme passions...47

Treasured connection with self...49

Turning pro...128, 172, 184, 198, 311, 315

We Are Not Meant to Walk This Life Alone, a poem...29

Wilbert Wilkens...48, 149, 158, 165, 180, 248

Woolley The Mammoth, aka thy beloved dog Marmot...292, 304, 316, 319

Notes to Self

Notes to Self

Notes to Self

Notes to Self